NIGHTWALKERS

NIGHTWALKERS
PROSTITUTE NARRATIVES
FROM THE EIGHTEENTH CENTURY

EDITED BY

LAURA J. ROSENTHAL

broadview press

Library and Archives Canada Cataloguing in Publication

Nightwalkers : prostitute narratives from the eighteenth century / edited by Laura J. Rosenthal.

Includes bibliographical references.
ISBN 978-1-55111-469-9

1. English prose literature—18th century.   2. Prostitution—Great Britain—History—18th century.   3. Prostitution in literature.   4. Prostitutes—Great Britain—Biography.
I. Rosenthal, Laura J. (Laura Jean), 1960-

HQ115.N44 2008   828'.50803552   C2008-902055-3

Broadview Press is an independent, international publishing house, incorporated in 1985. Broadview believes in shared ownership, both with its employees and with the general public; since the year 2000 Broadview shares have traded publicly on the Toronto Venture Exchange under the symbol BDP.

We welcome comments and suggestions regarding any aspect of our publications-please feel free to contact us at the addresses below or at broadview@broadviewpress.com.

North America
PO Box 1243, Peterborough, Ontario, Canada K9J 7H5
2215 Kenmore Ave., Buffalo, New York, USA 14207
Tel: (705) 743-8990; Fax: (705) 743-8353
email: customerservice@broadviewpress.com

UK, Ireland, and continental Europe
NBN International, Estover Road, Plymouth, UK PL6 7PY
Tel: 44 (0) 1752 202300; Fax: 44 (0) 1752 202330
email: enquiries@nbninternational.com

Australia and New Zealand
UNIREPS, University of New South Wales
Sydney, NSW, Australia 2052
Tel: 61 2 9664 0999; Fax: 61 2 9664 5420
email: info.press@unsw.edu.au

www.broadviewpress.com

This book is printed on paper containing 100% post-consumer fibre.

Typesetting and assembly: True to Type Inc., Claremont, Canada.

PRINTED IN CANADA

Dedicated to the Memory of
J. Douglas Canfield

CONTENTS

ACKNOWLEDGEMENTS

I have accumulated many debts in completing this project. I would first like to thank Jennifer Hobgood, who served as my research assistant during the early stages of this project and provided invaluable assistance above and beyond the call of duty. I am also grateful to research assistants Megan Campbell and Nicole Menton for their timely and meticulous help. In the final stages of this project, I benefited from the insights and sharp eyes of Tita Chico, Lisa Higgins, Joanne Roby, Elizabeth Veisz, and Peter Sinnot. I am indebted to Jane Donawerth, who helped me with French translations, and Judith Hallet, who helped me with the Latin. Jenny Batchelor, Megan Hiatt, and Katherine Binhammer generously shared unpublished work with me, for which I am grateful. This project has also benefited from many conversations and forms of intellectual support from many colleagues, but Alison Conway, Donna Heiland, Ruth Perry, Bob Markley, Helen Burke, Jennifer Hobgood, and Lisa Freeman have been particularly inspiring and motivating. Any mistakes or shortcomings are mine alone.

Finally, I would like to thank Broadview editor Julia Gaunce for her encouragement and patience.

INTRODUCTION

Let us suppose we had pursu'd
That Path, where treads each costive Prude,
Perhaps, with some rough, Country Boor,
And lawful Brats full Half a Score,
We might have dragg'd a starving Life.
For what? For the sweet Name of Wife!

No LODGE, not basely thus confin'd,
We've liv'd for all Mankind,
Drove steady on, nor cast one Look behind.

These lines from *A Genuine Epistle Written some Time since to the late Famous Mother Lodge* (1735) end a mini "autobiography" in verse told by a prostitute to a well-known bawd, Mother Lodge. Left indigent after the deaths of her parents, the speaker first attempts more legitimate vocations (service, her needle), but tires of the poverty they leave her in and turns to prostitution. The poem chronicles her ups and downs in the trade: initial wealth, a husband who strips her of everything, renewed success in the new world, where "No Indian Queen was half so fine!"[1] When her keeper dies and leaves her in poverty once again, she returns to England, becoming "Renown'd thro' all the British Fleet" (11). In spite of numerous hardships, however, she ends her story by embracing her choice of prostitution over marriage.

Representations of prostitution in the eighteenth-century British popular culture, as this poem suggests, offered a wider spectrum of attitudes than one might expect. Narratives of the life or career of a prostitute appear with striking regularity in this period, often with similar kinds of defiance as we find in the poem to Mother Lodge. Such narratives held, perhaps most obviously, an erotic appeal, and could alternatively serve as warnings to young women against giving in to seduction. Their attraction to readers, however, would also have been more complicated than their inevitable exploration of the tensions between virtue and vice: they offered sensual and sentimental journeys, glimpses into high life and low life, and relentless confrontations with the explosive power of money and the vulnerability of those without it.

The narratives in this volume offer a representative cross-section of the genre as a whole. Each tells the story of a single prostitute figure—Sally Salisbury, Kitty Fisher, Emily Markland, Fanny Sidney, and Fanny Davies—with energy, insight, and even admiration; nevertheless, each author has a different relationship to his or her subject and draws different lessons from the predicament of sex work. The Reverend Martin Madan, who tells the story of Fanny Sidney, claims to have known and ministered to his heroine, whose moral awakening and profound repentance open the gates of heaven for her. Captain Charles Walker, who pieces together the story of Sally Salisbury, collected anecdotes about this famous courtesan by advertising in the newspapers. Salisbury's high-profile arrest for stabbing her lover thrust her into the limelight and inspired this and one other biography, as well as numerous poems, songs, and at least one broadside. While characterizing Salisbury as ruthless, the author nevertheless represents her prostitution as a spectacular form of upward mobility. Kitty Fisher's anonymous biographer offers an entertaining and gossipy celebrity scandal narrative, thinly veiled as the story of a Spanish prostitute. Many eminent men patronized Fisher, who set the standards of beauty and fashion in her day. Sir Joshua Reynolds painted four portraits of Fisher; poems honoring her attractions and satirizing her extravagance regularly filled the presses. Unlike the other women whose stories are told in this volume, Emily Markland is an explicitly fictional character, but one who, the author insists, might be understood as a composite sketch of many abandoned women who reluctantly enter the trade. The author of Markland's story sees prostitution as the most desperate fate a woman can endure, but insists that prostitutes deserve sympathy rather than contempt. While Fanny Sidney and Emily Markland despise prostitution, Salisbury, Fisher, and Davies, like the narrator of *A Genuine Epistle*, have no regrets.

The Elusive Prostitute Voice

The narratives in this volume, with their energy, wit, eroticism, insight, and attitude, not only make compelling reading in themselves, but they also provide an important context for and counterbalance to more familiar representations of women in this period. Prostitutes, of course, figure prominently in the literary imagination of the eighteenth century. In Samuel Richardson's *Clarissa*, for example, the heroine spends a considerable portion of the novel held captive in a house of prostitution. In her innocence, Clarissa at first does not recognize the function of the establishment or the profession of the ladies surrounding her. For eighteenth-century readers viewing these scenes through the lens of a popular culture that saw such houses around every corner, however, little mystery would have surrounded the activities in this domicile. The bawd Mrs. Sinclair and her "daughters" play a crucial role in the novel: they emblematize the rakish Lovelace's libertine past, they maneuver Clarissa into relaxing her guard just enough to become vulnerable to rape, and they even seem to participate in the rape itself.[2] After the rape, the prostitutes try to recruit Clarissa into their trade, replacing Lovelace as the primary threat to the heroine.[3] In Richardson's novel, as in many canonical texts from this period, the prostitutes serve (at least in part) as negative versions of the heroine, their lives a haunting alternative to domestic virtue.

In the otherwise exhaustive collection of fictional letters that constitute *Clarissa*, however, we learn very little about what the world might have looked like through the eyes of the prostitutes themselves: they are among the few characters in Richardson's sprawling masterpiece that never set pen to paper. In this novel, then, we read a lot *about* prostitutes, but find little imagined through their eyes.[4] Similarly, literary critics have found great meaning in this period's obsession with female struggles to remain virtuous, exploring the various ways in which authors negotiate this challenge through novels, conduct books, plays, and pamphlets. The traces of the women who made different choices have attracted less scholarly devotion. In this sense, many accounts of eighteenth-century print culture resemble *Clarissa* itself, leaving prostitutes on the periphery. A series of letters from Mrs. Sinclair explaining her motives for keeping a brothel and exploring her feelings about Lovelace and the heroine would radically alter *Clarissa*; similarly, an understanding of the popularity of prostitute narratives, such as those included in this volume, demands that we rethink the way this period's writing represented women, gender, work, and survival.

These narratives, I hasten to add, do not offer the "prostitute's perspective" in any unproblematic way. The possibility of truly reconstructing such a perspective may lie beyond our capacity. Narratives verifiably written by actual eighteenth-century sex workers are difficult to come by, although a handful of them survive. In 1748-49, the courtesan Theresia Constantia Phillips published her memoirs in three volumes, promising in each to exclude stories in the next volume about any client willing to settle his debt.[5] At the end of the century, memoirs apparently written by prostitutes Margaret Leeson and Ann Sheldon appeared in print.[6] None of the narratives included in this volume bear the claim of having been written by a sex worker, so they cannot be imagined to represent the "prostitute's voice" in any literal sense. (The stories of Sheldon and Phillips, though certainly worth reading and worthy of editions, are too long to include in an anthology like this one, which reproduces the full versions of the narratives. A modern edition of Margaret Leeson's memoirs, however, is currently available.)[7] Even if we could verify the authorship of such memoirs, we would still need to hesitate over any claims to a "prostitute's perspective," as individual experiences would have varied tremendously. An elite courtesan like Kitty Fisher would have had very little in common with the impoverished women whom James Boswell encounters under bridges. Women (and men) participated in the sex trade in a variety of ways and from a variety of positions in the period's social hierarchy: then as now, there would never be a single representative "perspective."

Another reason why the "prostitute's perspective" in the eighteenth century might always elude us is that the very meaning of "prostitute" was not entirely stable. Certainly all of the women in this volume engage in prostitution in the modern sense—that is, they exchange sexual labor for money and other forms of compensation. Culturally, as I have argued elsewhere, the definition of prostitution as commodified, alienable, and potentially alienating sexual labor had some force at the time these narratives were written.[8] For centuries in England, however, a woman could be called a "prostitute" or a "whore" to indicate that she had engaged in any form of illicit sexual activity rather than necessarily to imply the exchange of money for sexual service. Humphrey Mill's 1642 poetic treatise against sexual immorality, for example, designates women who pay men for sex as prostitutes.[9] Even in the eighteenth century, the legal status of prostitution remained vague. Suspected prostitutes (and other kinds of offenders) were often sent to Bridewell Prison on the charge of being "disorderly" or arrested for other, related violations rather than for prostitution. In the early part of the century, reformers brought suspected prostitutes before magistrates, but the magistrates did not necessarily have any legal foundation for punishing them. In this volume, Sally Salisbury goes to jail for stabbing her lover and Fanny Davies for theft, but none of the women experience or seem to fear legal repercussions for prostitution itself. Technically, the law did not even identify prostitution by name as an infraction. Most eighteenth-century laws were directed toward those who facilitated prostitution, such as the 1752 Disorderly Houses Act.[10] Both legally and culturally, then, there was considerable ambiguity regarding who prostitutes were and what constituted prostitution.

Nevertheless, to concede that the narratives in this volume do not provide a "prostitute's perspective" and that such a perspective might not even be possible to define in this period does not mean that these narratives hold no interest, that they do not complicate our understanding of the period, that they do not offer insight into the experience of sex work in the eighteenth century, or even that they bear no relationship to historical figures. Sally Salisbury, Kitty Fisher, Fanny Davies, and Fanny Sidney did not write their own life stories, but historical women inspired their "memoirs." Several different women may have inspired the story of Emily Markland. Prostitute narratives may not give us consistently reliable facts about eighteenth-century sex work or offer a "prostitute's perspective" in any unproblematic way; they do, however, describe a kind of female experience that has attracted insufficient scholarly and critical attention. Further, they point to a kind of female public visibility that tends to be omitted from discussions of gendered tensions between the public and the private spheres, except to note in general terms that women who fail successfully to negotiate this difference end up becoming prostitutes or acquiring the reputation of being prostitutes.

Prostitute narratives have received little attention, but there is no shortage of them in the period. In addition to those published in this volume and those already mentioned, a reader might look at *The Crafty Whore* (1668), in which two prostitutes compare notes and strategies; *The Velvet Coffee-Woman* (1728), the story of a successful prostitute ruined by an Irish fortune-hunter; *The Life of Lavinia Beswick* (1728), about a woman who attracted the attentions of wealthy men, gained public acclaim as the first "Polly" in John Gay's *Beggar's Opera*, and eventually married a duke; *Memoirs of the Celebrated Miss Fanny M[urray]* (1759), a gossipy narratives that tells the story of a high society courtesan; *The Life and Adventures of a Reformed Magdalen ... Written by Herself* (1763), which offers wide-ranging picaresque adventures and, as in John Cleland's *Memoirs of a Woman of Pleasure* (1748-49) (easily the most famous example of the genre) a "tail-piece" of morality; or *The History of Emma; Or the Victim of Depravity* (1800), which tells the story of a seduced and abandoned girl who must become a prostitute to support her baby. Prostitute narratives appear in John Dunton's *Night-Walker* (1696); the various editions of *Harris's List of Covent Garden Ladies* include lively descriptions of prostitutes available in London.[11] "Jack Harris," a famous pimp who supplied the information for *Harris's List*, makes an appearance in *Fanny M[urray]* and *The Life and Adventures of a Reformed Magdalen*. The appendix to this volume includes a more comprehensive list of prostitute narratives, although surely many more remain to be identified. Intriguing in themselves, they also explore a broader range of sexual and gendered possibilities than most canonical fiction, although Defoe and Richardson clearly owe much to this genre.

Narrative Form

For readers more accustomed to novels, prostitute narratives may appear not only more ambiguous in their representations of sexual morality, but less linear in their organization. The reader cannot expect to find a single predicable lesson expressed through poetic justice: sometimes the heroine dies from her travails or excessive ambitions, but other times she flourishes—or at least finds security. While domestic novels for the most part move predictably and inevitably toward marriage, prostitute narratives turn to different possibilities. Prostitute narratives often begin with some kind of averted marriage possibility, after which the heroine turns her attention, by inclination or necessity, to financial concerns. Prostitute narratives are commonly episodic, relating each different encounter, adventure, or humiliation. As women not necessarily destined to form families, the heroines of prostitute narratives represent a more radical and often disturbing form of individualism than the individualism represented in the novel. Even Robinson Crusoe, after all, marries and finds spouses for the men left on the island. While exploring extreme isolation, *Robinson Crusoe* nevertheless also weaves together new social relations. Roxana, by contrast, remains essentially alone—except for her companion Amy—for most of Defoe's eponymous novel, in part because she must constantly keep up her deception. Her awareness of her children's lives only highlights her own isolation. Prostitute narratives, then, do not generally move toward the creation of a family or a community, but trace the fate of those abandoned by those institutions to an unfeeling marketplace. While Sally Salisbury stays bawdily irreverent and Fanny Sidney becomes pious, both have only their own labor and their own bodies to rely on.

Writers of domestic fiction, such as Samuel Richardson, Charlotte Lennox, Frances Burney, and Jane Austen explore the complexity of the social world and the heroine's painful and complex efforts to find a place for herself within it. In prostitute narratives, however, we have dropped out of the drawing room and its intricate social relations. Prostitute narratives delve into an underworld that domestic heroines only experience by fleeting glimpses, such as when Evelina finds herself suddenly and frighteningly surrounded by whores in Burney's eponymous novel, when Clarissa languishes in a spunging house (a kind of debtor's prison), or when Arabella from Lennox's *Female Quixote* defends a cross-dressed prostitute. A surprising number of domestic heroines, as Ruth Perry has pointed out, find themselves suddenly trapped in a brothel or momentarily face to face with a prostitute.[12] Unlike domestic novels that at least on a superficial level offer wish-fulfilling fantasies of romantic attachments that transcend economic interest, prostitute narratives expose the fallout of the period's prosperity, mobility, modernity, imperial expansion, and increasing consumerism. Even before the heroine "falls" sexually, she often "falls" economically, from membership in a family to isolation, homelessness, and the necessity of making her own way in the world. Even Kitty Fisher—easily the most successful prostitute in this volume—has moments of desperation brought on by the lack of a supportive network or community: sometimes she appears at the theater in the latest fashion surrounded by admirers; other times she hides out from her creditors. In prostitute narratives, the story commonly opens with the heroine's loss, through ambition, desire, or misfortune, of access to crucial family support; she must make her way entirely on her own, a fate that the narratives represent with various degrees of anxiety, admiration, and pathos.

While domestic novels commonly glimpse the prostitute as domesticity's terrifying alternative, unfortunate fallout, and haunting double, the narratives in this volume position the prostitute herself as the text's point of entry. Certainly some of them disapprove of this "infamous commerce"; nevertheless, they all invite readers to view the world through a whore's perspective, however authentically or inauthentically. The more sentimental narratives fill in the parts of the story that Richardson omits. The stories in this volume of Emily Markland from *The Histories of Some the Penitents* and of Fanny Sidney from *An Account of the Death of F.S.* trace the sentimental journeys of two women, one fictional and one possibly not, who become vulnerable to seduction through economic circumstances, who turn to prostitution out of desperation, and who ultimately reform through recourse to the Magdalen House, a charity set up in 1758. Fanny Sidney's story, told in the third person by Martin Madan, represents prostitution as an act of desperation demanding compassion rather than condemnation. Unlike prostitute figures in the more libertine narratives, Fanny does not seek luxury or sexual pleasure. Though writing as a Christian moralist, Madan portrays even the heroine's first sexual experience in relatively sympathetic terms: Fanny had been accustomed to an elite, sophisticated social circle encompassing both men and women. When she loses her fortune through the death of her father, however, her suitor no longer considers her as a potential wife. The suitor takes advantage of his accustomed intimacy and seduces her. Left with a child to support, Fanny eventually turns to prostitution for support after failing to make enough money in several other vocations. Madan's narrative places less emphasis on female weakness and instead explores the limited opportunities available to women in Fanny's situation. The first story in *The Histories of Some of the Penitents in the Magdalen-House*, an anonymous novel composed of four different narratives, offers a more optimistic but equally sympathetic prostitute history. The author insists that Emily Markland also falls victim to circumstances. When Emily becomes orphaned and thus impoverished, she takes a job as a servant in a wealthy household. Her transition from a humble, middle-class upbringing to servitude in a dissolute elite family leaves her vulnerable to seduction: she has entered a world she does not fully understand. Her father, though a clergyman, had failed to instill sufficient moral instruction. The son in the wealthy family courts Emily, who falls for his charms and his promises. In her retrospective account, Emily blames herself for succumbing to temptation; nevertheless, the narrative also describes several mitigating circumstances that portray her seduction as understandable. As in the story of Fanny Sidney, the refusal to condemn women for turning to prostitution marks the sentimental narrative. Emily and Fanny both willingly engage in sexual activity, although circumstances leave them vulnerable; in other sentimental prostitute narratives (not reproduced in this volume), however, the heroine bears even less responsibility for her sexual activity. In William Dodd's novel *The Sisters* (1754), for example, an unscrupulous relative tricks one of the heroines with a fake marriage to an already married man. In the memoirs of Teresia Constantia Phillips, a suave aristocrat invites the heroine to his room on the pretext of a good view of a parade, drugs her wine, and rapes her. After the initial rape or seduction, economic circumstances and family abandonment force the heroine into prostitution in many sentimental texts. Some heroines in these narratives die miserable deaths, abandoned by all; others reflect on whether or not it would be better to die than walk the streets for a living. Often, however, the narrative adds a mitigating circumstance that renders prostitution the more responsible choice over death: the heroine has a child, a sister, or an aging parent to support. Such circumstances imply that the abandoned woman's life might not be worth living if no one depended on her; nevertheless, they also defuse moral objections to her choice to enter prostitution. The purpose of sentimental prostitute narratives, then, is rarely to condemn women for entering prostitution; instead, these narratives render the prostitute's predicament comprehensible and even sympathetic. Rather than negotiating a complex social world to find her one true partner and thus her place in society, however, the sentimental prostitute seeks only to relieve her own misery and the misery of her children.

Reform Narratives and Libertine Narratives
As should be clear by now, prostitute narratives in the eighteenth century tell many different kinds of stories. In eighteenth-century British culture, there was no forgone conclusion about how a prostitute's life would turn out. Fanny Sidney dies tragically, but Kitty Fisher eventually marries a wealthy man. Certainly many prostitutes in the eighteenth century died from disease, starvation, or violence; they languished in prisons, worked in fields as indentured servants in the American colonies, and unwillingly helped colonize Australia and Sierra Leone. The famous prostitute-turned-bawd Charlotte Hayes, however, retired to considerable wealth (not unlike the fictional Fanny Hill). Other prostitutes married and left the trade, or found other kinds of work.[13] Reformers vigorously encouraged families to reconcile with daughters who had become mistresses or prostitutes, and laboring-class prostitutes do not seem to have been rejected by their communities in the first place, especially in the first half of the century.[14] Many women seem to have moved back and forth between prostitution and other kinds of jobs, or supplemented low-paying work with prostitution.[15]

While prostitute lives and prostitute narratives point to great variety within the general experience of sex work, the narratives at least can be roughly grouped along a spectrum with the more sentimental narratives at one end and the more libertine narratives at the other. In this volume, the stories of Emily Markland and Fanny Sidney fall on the sentimental side, while the stories of Sally Salisbury and Fanny Davies tend toward the libertine. These are overlapping rather than entirely discrete ways of writing about prostitutes: sentimental texts certainly exploit the erotic potential of their subjects and libertine texts can include moral judgment. Libertine heroines, however, might be understood as those who attempt to free themselves from the reigning conventions of gender, class, and traditional morality. Libertine narratives often represent these heroines as dangers to themselves and others; nevertheless, the narratives also glamorize them in certain ways as well. Sentimental narratives, by contrast, represent the prostitute as a victim of circumstances. Significantly, in most sentimental narratives the heroine does not want to be a prostitute; libertine heroines, by contrast, tend to embrace their profession. Sentimental narratives demand that readers sympathize with the prostitute, but that they also consider the circumstances that led to the heroine's predicament as a warning to others. Certainly many texts combine both approaches: George Lillo's play *The London Merchant* (1731), for example, places a libertine heroine in a sentimental drama with interesting results. Lillo's Millwood is ruthlessly ambitious, but the sentimental structure of the play allows the audience, very briefly, to see her as a victim as well. While many texts combine elements of both, then, this inexact distinction can nevertheless help us map out some of the significant differences within the prostitute narrative genre.

In general, sentimental prostitute narratives tell stories of downward mobility. Their heroines often begin in middle-class comfort (though rarely opulence), and then suffer some kind of disaster: the death of parent, for example, brings sudden poverty and increased vulnerability to seduction or rape. Alternatively, a rape or a seduction alienates the heroine from her family, leaving prostitution as one of her few options. As Ruth Perry has recently shown in considerable detail, the eighteenth-century's increasingly capitalist economy cut women off from their traditional economic importance in the family without providing sufficient alternative possibilities in the public sphere. The popularity of sentimental prostitute narratives, Perry suggests, reflects the increasing economic vulnerability of women and mourns the loss of traditional kinship ties that offered both emotional and material security.[16] A dramatic increase in prostitution, documented by historians and attracting considerable comment in the eighteenth century,[17] surely emerged at least in part as a result of these shifting economic conditions. Sentimental prostitute narratives, then, offer an emotional and ideological response to material conditions.

Many of the period's sentimental prostitute narratives were inspired by or published to support the activities of a new reform movement that emerged in the middle of the century. This movement differed significantly from the earlier Societies for the Reformation of Manners: instead of dragging suspected prostitutes before magistrates like the earlier reformers, the new reformers hoped to assist and transform them; they established the Magdalen Hospital in 1758 as a humane alternative to imprisonment.[18] The Magdalen Hospital provided refuge, support, training, and religious instruction for prostitutes who declared that they wanted to reform, and while the limited number of women it could actually serve was too small to make a significant impact on the streetwalking population, the Hospital became a fashionable and popular charity (patronized by both Richardson and Fielding) with a wide-reaching influence. It helped usher in a new era of reform in which moralists positioned themselves as sympathizing with rather than excoriating prostitutes. Rather than blaming prostitution on the lascivious nature of women, the new reformers blamed an increasingly complex commercial culture for the visible rise in sex work.[19] Many prostitute narratives even suggest (as does Richardson's *Clarissa*) that sexual experience in itself does not necessarily destroy a woman's virtue or eligibility for marriage. *The Histories of the Penitents* explicitly advocates this charity in its introduction, although the story of Fanny Sidney might raise questions of its effectiveness.[20]

While sentimental narratives demand sympathy for female vulnerability, libertine narratives, by contrast, tell stories of female empowerment, although not necessarily in celebratory ways. As James Turner has shown, libertine writing at the early end of this period can be saturated with misogyny, representing women as greedy, sexually insatiable, ruthless, and even cruel.[21] Richard Ames's *Female Fire-Ships* (1691), for example, insists that men face even greater danger from prostitutes at home than from colonial ventures abroad:

> Women indeed to outward view they seem,
> But are their Sexes scandal, blot and shame;
> Like Angels they may seem in Dress, and meen,
> But could you view the frightful Fiend within,
> Who whets their lewd desires, and eggs them on,
> To act those Mishiefs they too oft have done;
> Not Midnight Spectres, nor sad Scenes of War,
> Would half so dreadful to you Sense appear;
> Not Canibals upon the Indian Coast,
> Nor Desert Shores to Men by Shipwrack tost
> Can be so dangerous, as are the Wiles,
> The treacherous Kisses, and bewitching Smiles
> Of Mercenary Jilts; whose only Trade,
> Is daily acting Love in Masquerade:
> True Canibals, who can with ease devour,
> A dozen Men while Time shapes out an Hour.
> The Body as gross food they cast away,
> And only on the Blood and Marrow prey;
> With nice fantastick Appetites they burn,
> And nothing but the Spirits serves their turn.[22]

This poem, like many texts in this period, links prostitution with the hazards of global expansion. In the libertine *Female Fire-Ships*, sexual desire becomes a force that levels all women, undermining claims to female authority based on class, education, or accomplishment. The author warns that

> At Tunbridge and at Epsom Wells each year,[23]
> Like People of best Quality appear:
> Blush when they hear a Word they judge obscene,

While thousand lewd Ideas lurk within;
And Artful Wiles they take a Pride to vex,
And bid defiance to the other Sex:
But if at last betraid by Inclination,
Or overcome by your too Foolish Passion;
Or if by Presents most magnetick Charms,
You are at length conducted to her Arms;
Not Fleetstreet Cracks[24] who on young Striplings prey,
Are half so Lewd and Impudent as they.

Some libertine writing, then, purports to demonstrate that even women who appear dignified and respectable are no better than street-walkers under their veneer of self-control. William Wycherley makes a similar point with the Fidget ladies in *The Country Wife* (1675). While these ladies insist on their superiority to "playhouse creatures," they guard their reputations while indulging their sexual desires in private.

Libertine narratives, then, commonly represent the kind of empowerment women might achieve through their sexuality as dangerous, frightening, exotic, and unfeminine. Rarely simply victims of circumstances or economic desperation, prostitutes in libertine narratives are creatures of desire. In the eighteenth century, however, their desire is not necessarily sexual—they sometimes seek erotic pleasure, but tend more immediately to pursue luxury, comfort, prestige, and power. But however much libertine narratives may disapprove of or express disgust for prostitutes, they nevertheless tend to represent them as forces to be reckoned with. These narratives never entirely contain the possibility of admiration for their heroines—albeit a different kind of admiration than found in sentimental narratives. *The Authentick Memoirs of the Life, Intrigues, and Adventures of the Celebrated Sally Salisbury* and *An Authentic Narrative of the Most Remarkable Adventures, and Curious Intrigues, Exhibited in the Life of Miss Fanny Davies, the Celebrated Modern Amazon* both purport to warn their readers against dangerous women such as their heroines, although neither narrative explores the outlaw escapades of its heroine entirely without some degree of admiration. Both Salisbury and Davies come across as powerful and independent women who destabilized the boundaries of class and gender. Both reportedly passed as men on occasion: Fanny Davies adopts male disguise to escape the law, but also to avoid the annoying disapproval of proper ladies. She even at one point makes a profitable assignation with another woman before revealing her true sex. Sally Salisbury reportedly caroused the streets of London disguised as a rake.[25] In the *Authentick Memoirs* reproduced in this volume, Salisbury viciously attacks one client when he tries to trick her with some fake coins, nearly tearing him to pieces. Libertine narratives, as these brief descriptions suggest, do not generally appeal to the sympathies of the reader; instead, they position themselves as warnings against dangerous choices and dangerous people, but at the same time tempt readers with stories of adventure, empowerment, wealth, luxury, and social rebellion.[26] Salisbury and Davies both begin in humble circumstances and work their way up to luxury and prestige through prostitution. Both face ordeals and humiliations along the way, but at the same time earn tremendous amounts of money from wealthy men. While sentimental narratives describe how respectable middle-class girls can sink into poverty through sexual mistakes or victimization, libertine narratives suggest that the commonest of women can rise to wealth and status through beauty, ambition, ruthlessness, and the mastery of elite manners. Both kinds of narratives, then, explore anxieties generated by the increasingly mobile world of eighteenth-century society.

The difference between the libertine and the sentimental prostitute narratives, then, might be mapped out in several ways. First, the libertine narratives tend to find the prostitute's sexuality fascinating in itself; they treat sexuality with frankness and (sometimes misogynistic) humor. Walker's account of Sally Salisbury, for example, opens with an admiring litany of great courtesans from history. Sentimental narratives, by contrast, represent sexuality as at *best* something women go along with because they are in love and at worse a harrowing experience of abject humiliation and degradation. A heroine may sleep with a man she cares about, but sentimental narratives generally represent such moments as the surrender to male pressure or aggression. Second, as mentioned, libertine and sentimental narratives offer opposite economic trajectories, but both explore economic mobility. Libertine heroines often begin in poverty and work their way up to association with the most elite classes, or simply to wealth and luxury (although not necessarily without considerable hardship along the way). Their stories can end with an abrupt plunge in fortune akin to Roxana's "blast from Heaven" in Daniel Defoe's novel or comfortable reform with a "tail-piece of morality," as in John Cleland's *Memoirs of a Woman of Pleasure*. Sentimental narratives, by contrast, tell stories of an economic fall, which can be caused by, but often instead leads to, a sexual fall; these can end in tragic death or happy recovery. The two kinds of narratives also differ in terms of the heroine's power. Sentimental narratives depend on the victimization of the heroine: while the heroine may be guilty of an initial indiscretion, social forces conspire to degrade her into prostitution. In fact, sentimental narratives are, arguably, *about* those social forces— the limited economic opportunities for women, rigid codes of gendered behavior, exacting standards of sexual behavior—as much as they are about individual choices.[27] While critics have rightly pointed out the exploitative aspects of sentimentalism, at least superficially these narratives expose and confront the dark side of this period's changing economic conditions. In both libertine and sentimental narratives, however, prostitution points to emerging forms of social disruption, including global commerce, empire-building, economic mobility, commodification, reliance on waged labor, the market in luxury goods, new forms of gender identity, and changing attitudes toward sexuality.

While the stories of Sally Salisbury and Fanny Davies fall into the libertine genre and the stories of Emily Markland and Fanny Sidney aim for the sentimental, *The Juvenile Adventures of Miss Kitty Fisher* combines these perspectives, producing the most sensual version represented in this collection. Other narratives, including Cleland's *Memoirs of a Woman of Pleasure* and the lesser-known memoirs of Fanny Murray, Margaret Leeson, Ann Sheldon, and Teresia Constantia Phillips, similarly combine elements of each style and similarly produce more sensual narratives. Certainly stories of penitent Magdalens take advantage of the erotic potential of their subjects, deliberately or not: the Magdalen Hospital itself regularly displayed reforming prostitutes for pity and admiration, but left them vulnerable to erotic voyeurism as well. Nevertheless, reform narratives tend to leave the actual work of sex work to the reader's imagination. While the sentimental narratives avoid the explicit or extended exploration of sexual activity to maintain their propriety, the most explicitly libertine narrative often describe sex but lack eroticism, perhaps because their heroines seek wealth, power, and prestige rather than pleasure. Their heroines so fully instrumentalize their bodies that sexual encounters become strategic rather than passionate. The authors of the memoirs of Sally Salisbury and Fanny Davies, in fact, propose their heroines' relative abandonment of feeling as particularly disturbing: Sally keeps her eyes on the financial prize, viciously attacking anyone who stands in her way. Fanny Davies combines prostitution with others kinds of social and gender transgressions. Sentimental prostitute heroines, by contrast, labor under an excess of feeling: unwise attachment to or optimistic trust of unworthy men (or women) often leads them down this hazardous path in the first place.

The Juvenile Adventures of Kitty Fisher, however, combines elements of the libertine and sentimental that produces an eroticism less salient in other kinds of narratives. Like Salisbury and Davies, Kitty Fisher possesses ambition, yet not of a ruthless or even particularly transgressive kind. Like them and certainly unlike most sentimental heroines, she passes at one point as a man. Fisher's male impersonation, however, takes a strikingly different form. Both Salisbury and Davies disguise themselves as hyper-masculine figures: Salisbury reportedly roamed the streets with the "mohocks," a legendary group of rakish young men who committed acts of violence for amusement and as part of an elite arrogant form of rebellion. Davies at one point passes as a "stallion"— an attractive man who takes money for sex with women. When Kitty Fisher cross-dresses, however, she does so only to avoid responsibility for debt and disguises herself as a castrato. Fisher, then, becomes an alluring but castrated young man in this narrative—a seductive, comic, and less threatening version of female masculinity. In general, *The Juvenile Adventures* represents its heroine as a gentle and sensuous girl whose career in prostitution becomes an extension rather than a violation of her feminine gender identity. While Davies and Salisbury want money and power, Fisher seeks luxury and pleasure through the admiration of men.

The Juvenile Adventures works structurally as a libertine narrative: the daughter of a tradesman, Kitty rises rather than falls. She attracts attention for her beauty and manners, experiences the shifting tides of fortune of a prostitute's life, but eventually works her way into the company of the most elite classes. She endures her share of hardships, as do many libertine heroines, yet finds ways to move forward. *The Juvenile Adventures*, however, also borrows techniques from the sentimental narratives. Like Fanny Sidney and Emily Markland, Kitty Fisher embraces a dominant feminine gender identity, although with a different inflection. Virtue does not shape her identity, but her sensuality, enthusiasm for fashion, vanity, and even naïveté place her within certain conventions of acceptable, or at least expected, womanhood, in contrast to the outlaws Sally Salisbury and Fanny Davies. In the mid-eighteenth century, reformers often blamed a girl's upbringing for her fall into prostitution: neither Fanny Sidney nor Emily Markland came from sufficiently religious families, and their parents failed to prepare them for the myriad snares a girl could face. *The Juvenile Adventures* goes a step further, following in considerable comic detail John Fisher's excessive devotion to and pampering of his only child. Many reformers believed that most London prostitutes came not from impoverished, laboring-class rural or urban families—which is what historical research suggests[28]—but rather from middle-class families that overly indulged their daughters, who then in turn aspired to a level of luxury that placed their virtue in danger. The beginning of *The Juvenile Adventures* could have been written by such a reformer, or at least by someone parodying this reformist suspicion. In the early years, Fisher's father, an engraver, turns his workshop into a nursery so he can be with his daughter all day. Later he indulges her with every luxury he can afford—and some that he can't. Through this excess that Kitty's mother constantly warns against, the daughter acquires a taste for luxury that shapes her career. The author represents the father's indulgence as a form of *self* indulgence and even as an incestuous form of desire. At one point, for example, a fine lady admires Kitty as a child, offering to adopt her and thus give her advantages that her father could never afford. The father, however, cannot bear to part with his daughter. Later in the narrative he locks Kitty in the house to defend her against potential suitors, but the neighbors begin to suspect that he wants her all to himself. When Kitty grows up, her father tries to set her up in business with a dress shop, but Kitty, having learned no discipline as a child, ends up appropriating most of her stock for her own use. In her career as a prostitute, she never loses her taste for luxury, but she also never loses her feminine delicacy and sensuality. Though all libertine heroines, then,

Kitty Fisher, Sally Salisbury, and Fanny Davies develop into very different kinds of women.

The Cultural Politics of Prostitute Narratives

We find, then, a wide range of ways of representing prostitution and its significance in this period. In spite of their great variety, however, most prostitute narratives have a few characteristics in common. Whether libertine, reformist, or somewhere in between, most prostitute narratives at some point warn their female readers against whoring and their male readers against falling into the snares of a whore, with varying degrees of sincerity. Yet most eighteenth-century prostitute narratives also present their subjects with some degree of admiration. Captain Charles Walker offers perhaps the harshest portrait here in his memoirs of Sally Salisbury: his heroine endangers everyone she encounters through her greed and caustic wit. At the same time and without denying the frequent misogyny in this narrative, Salisbury's actions carry a radical force as well: she enters high society with no patience whatsoever for aristocratic equivalences between birth and worth. We can see that sexuality becomes a leveling force, giving Sally power over clients, entrance into elite society, and personal wealth that looks no different from anyone else's. The difference between the whore's profits and rent drawn from a family estate disturbingly disappears. Attempts made by elite ladies to humiliate Sally over her class position excruciatingly backfire when Salisbury frankly exposes the sexual preferences or sexual inadequacies of their husbands. Clients can rarely outwit this wily whore, despite many such attempts. Similarly, the author of the story of Fanny Davies explicitly presents his or her outlaw subject with disapproval; nevertheless, it is difficult not to admire her resourcefulness and independence, or to see the injustice of the world through which she moves. Peter Linebaugh has made the case that eighteenth-century crime narratives represent the nascent class war of the eighteenth century: ostensibly written as warnings and lessons, crime narratives can also lionize a hero who rebels again emerging property relations.[29] The stories of Sally Salisbury and Fanny Davies might productively be read in similar terms: both emerge as similar kinds of outlaw rebels with no patience for elite snobbery or bourgeois hypocrisy. In these prostitute narratives, however, the critique of property relations lies not just in violating the boundaries of possessive individualism, but in taking possessive individualism to its disturbing logical conclusion. These women are *very* possessive and dangerously individualistic.

The narratives not only confront the dominant culture's hypocritical attitudes toward female sexuality, but they also confront the economic vulnerability of women. One might even make the case that these narratives explore prostitution more as an economic activity than as a sexual one. Many mid-century reformers optimistically promoted training willing prostitutes for service and for manual labor, and in most narratives the heroine tries various other ways to make a living. When she rejects prostitution, Fanny Sidney, though born into comfort, becomes an agricultural worker and later the assistant to a tradesman. Before turning to prostitution, she tries to earn her living through needlework and acting. Emily Markland attempts to set up a business with her limited resources; she later tries to find another position in service and work with her needle. Even Kitty Fisher, according to the *Juvenile Adventures*, tries to find work as an actress as an alternative to prostitution. Yet for various reasons, none of these alternatives work out for the heroine. Needlework simply doesn't pay enough money to support a single mother, as Fanny Sidney discovers. Emily Markland can't even get minimal employment because, alone in the anonymous city of London, she lacks a character reference. Kitty Fisher finds the stage a more competitive and less lucrative venue than it first appears. These are individual, fictionalized stories about particular circumstances; nevertheless, they suggest to their readers the social problem of limited employment opportunities and limited safety nets for women.[30]

In spite of their considerable complicity with dominant culture, then, prostitute narratives also document resistance. Certainly Viviene Jones is right to challenge critics who celebrate prostitute figures as models of feminism, and to point out that glamorized stories of prostitutes in this period probably bear minimal resemblance to the lives of most women in the period's sex trade.[31] Within certain boundaries, however, these narratives intermittently challenge crucial aspects of eighteenth-century culture. Criminal biographies, in spite of their often explicitly moral arguments, record a kind of folk heroic status granted to the outlaw, as Linebaugh has shown. The parallel to prostitute biographies is not precise. In libertine narratives, however, prostitutes emerge entertainingly as the worst nightmare of bourgeois reformers, and not just for their frank sexuality. In these narratives, prostitutes fully absorb the emerging commercial ethos and embrace the period's flourishing commodity fetishism. Libertine texts sometimes even praise prostitutes for stimulating the market: by their own indulgence in luxurious imported textiles and new ways of wearing them, they set the bar of fashion ever higher. Thus they fully absorb a highly select (and parodically skewed) version of gender and emergent commercial ideology, investing fully in their charms in order to reap the greatest return. Intentionally or not, they satirize the values of the commercialization and commodification by enacting them with disconcerting consistency. Further, while these narratives can be sexually exploitative, certain prostitute-heroines (such as Kitty Fisher, Fanny Murray, Margaret Leeson, and Ann Sheldon) embrace erotic pleasure in ways that defy emerging norms of femininity—and their narratives do not necessarily "punish" them for their enjoyment.[32]

Sentimental reform narratives promote an explicitly conservative message, but at the same time direct their criticism toward society rather than individual women. Certainly they insist that young girls should beware of seducers in all forms, be they handsome young gentlemen or seemingly kind old ladies. At the same time, however, the often-noticed insistence in these narratives that the girl is not truly at "fault," or that her faultiness is minimal, does more than open the door for exploitative sentimental pleasures (although it does that as well). Instead, the relative innocence of the heroine demands that we look to other reasons besides personal inadequacy for her recruitment into prostitution. Reform narratives categorically disapprove of prostitution, but in this disapproval they open up the possibility of a skeptical view of the cultural forces that have left prostitution as the heroine's best or only option. As Jenny Batchelor and Megan Hiatt have argued, the stories in *The Histories of the Penitents* in particular minimize female culpability and explicitly point out the limited choices for survival in eighteenth-century culture.[33] While they rightly point out that in this sense *The Penitents* takes a more critical stance than the reform movement as a whole and while reformers sometimes excoriated prostitutes for their apparent lack of sexual restraint, even this heavily male-dominated, moralistic project brought to the surface critical problems and contradictions in the society at large. Explicitly Christian in their perspective, not even the members of the Societies for the Reformation of Manners in the early part of the century typically blamed prostitution on the inherent sinfulness or weakness of women. The SRM writers, unlike the next generation of reformers, had very little sympathy for abandoned women; they tend, however, to write about prostitution as a social and historical problem rather than a static moral one. Prostitutes embody rebellion in early reformist writing;[34] they represent a refusal to respect hierarchies of class and gender. In the view of early reformers, prostitutes exploit the Mandevillian opportunities of an early commercial society, transforming desire into profit without moral limits. In doing so, they not only drain capital from "legitimate" business, but they incite rebellion and disorder among workers and apprentices. George Lillo captured this anxiety with precision in *The London Merchant*, in which a prostitute leads the apprentice-hero into theft and then murder for her own profit. For reformers and other writers in the first half of the eighteenth century, prostitutes become figures for the (dangerous) refusal to conform to emergent bourgeois norms and values. SRM members saw rampant prostitution as an explicitly modern problem brought on by the expansion of trade, urbanization, and an increasingly commercial culture.

While mid-century reformers aimed to mold proper bourgeois subjects with solid family values, they resisted what they saw as an emergent ideology of femininity based on beauty, fashion, and economic non-productivity. They objected to the modern encouragement to educate daughters in ways that would prepare them to be fashionable wives—and, failing this possibility, fashionable mistresses—rather than productive workers within the home or outside of it. The Magdalen House focused on training women for nonsexual labor—which, implicitly, their families should have done in the first place. Reformers again and again rehearsed the dangers of the eighteenth-century's emergent consumer society, encouraging girls to resist the material desires that would lead them astray. Of course, they discouraged sexual desire as well, but, unlike earlier reformers, tended not to represent it as a central motivating force in prostitution. In the mid-century reformist rhetoric, female desires for clothes, china, furniture, leisure, and coaches seem more often to lead to prostitution than any desire for sexual pleasure.

The reformist critique clearly has its limits, in spite of its intriguing anticipation of modern feminism's emphasis on economic productivity and skepticism toward the "beauty myth." Reformers observed the paradoxes and contradictions of commercial culture, but only wanted to mitigate its fallout rather than rethink the system: they were by no stretch of the imagination revolutionary. Nevertheless, they repeatedly expressed their suspicions that commercial success and imperial expansion had increased female vulnerability. *The Histories of the Penitents* in particular, but other documents as well, explores in considerable detail how limited economic opportunities for women have led to the misery of entire families. The main chance for security seems to be marriage; eligibility for marriage depended on the absorption of emergent gender ideologies emphasizing personal attraction and passivity. Yet those who best absorb this ideology become the most vulnerable to prostitution. Reformers point out, but do not revolt against, this situation. Instead, they suggest (of course) that women remain sexually virtuous, but they also recommend that families prepare their daughters for labor, whether remunerative or domestic, rather than as showpieces of delicate femininity. At least obliquely, then, they acknowledge the antifeminist economic forces behind the ever-expanding problem of prostitution.

Not exactly "true" but not exactly "fiction" either—neither reliable sources for historical fact nor "novels" in the terms we have come to recognize—prostitute narratives thus offer a counterbalance to and complication of the picture of eighteenth-century culture one might draw from reading the more familiar canon of fiction. Certainly many prostitute narratives express a similar sense of sexual propriety and warn against its violation (with varying degrees of sincerity). Nevertheless, the narratives themselves radically complicate the notion of social attitudes toward sexuality that one would derive from reading Richardson or Austen. They also demonstrate the absence of a single inevitable imagined trajectory for a woman who engages in prostitution. Unlike some eighteenth-century novels, these narratives suggest that readers in the eighteenth century did not necessarily assume that such a woman would inevitably become a pariah, would become incapable of maternal tenderness, would have no sense of responsibility to other people, would not eventually be able to marry or find "legitimate" employment; they complicate any assumption that readers would expect a prostitute to end her life in disease and misery. The ideology of domestic novels may have triumphed by the century's end, but this does not mean that eighteenth-century culture did not allow for multiple points of view and various imagined possibilities. In fact, thinking about the advocates of domesticity as embattled rather than triumphant perhaps explains the extremity of some of the arguments.

Unfamiliar to both general readers and specialists in eighteenth-century studies, these narratives, then, offer uncommon perspectives and uncommon adventures. Setting libertine narratives next to reform narratives demonstrates the range of perspectives with which eighteenth-century writers viewed prostitution, pointing to the period's complexity and conflicting views on this subject. While these narratives bear historical significance, they also offer compelling reading experiences that mix the pleasures of adventure tales, bawdy satire, sentimental journeys, and true secret histories. They may not offer direct access to the thoughts and feelings of eighteenth-century sex workers; nevertheless, each in its own way bears the traces of women whom history and literary criticism might otherwise have forgotten.

Notes

1   *A Genuine Epistle Written from the Time since to the late Famous Mother Lodge* (London, 1735), 10. This poem is reproduced in Janine Barchas, ed. and Alexander Pettit, general introduction, *Eighteenth-Century British Erotica II*, Volume 1 (London: Pickering and Chatto, 2004).

2   Judith Wilt, "He Could Go No Farther: A Modest Proposal about Lovelace and Clarissa," *PMLA* 92.1 (1977): 19-32.

3   For a fuller reading of *Clarissa* and prostitution, see my *Infamous Commerce: Prostitution in Eighteenth-Century British Literature and Culture* (Ithaca: Cornell UP, 2006). This introduction overall has benefited from work done in *Infamous Commerce*.

4   Interestingly, in the third edition of *Clarissa*, Richardson adds the stories of how Sally and Polly became prostitutes as part of Belford's "Conclusion" at the end of volume 8. (I owe this observation to Marie McAllister, who generously pointed out to me this difference between the first and third editions.) With these additions, Richardson might have been responding to the increasing mid-century sentimentalization of prostitutes. Neither story is particularly sympathetic; both, however, mostly blame the girl's upbringing and her family's pretensions. The impression that Richardson thus gives of brothels being filled with improperly educated daughters of the middle class is consistent with the analysis of mid-century reformers, although historical evidence does not support this conclusion.

5   Theresia Constantia Phillips [Muilman], *An Apology for the Conduct of Mrs. Teresia Constantia Phillips*, 3 vols. (London: Printed for the Author, 1748-49). On Phillips's life and career, see Kathleen Wilson's excellent discussion in *The Island*

Race: Englishness, Empire and Gender in the Eighteenth Century (London and New York: Routledge, 2003), chapter 4.

6 Margaret Leeson, *The Memoirs of Mrs. Leeson, Madam, 1727-1797*, edited by Mary Lyons (Dublin: Lilliput Press, 1995), Ann Sheldon, *Authentic and Interesting Memoirs of Miss Ann Sheldon*, 4 vols. (London: Printed for the Authoress, 1790).

7 See note 6.

8 *Infamous Commerce*, chapter 1.

9 Humphrey Mill, *A Night's Search, Discovering the Nature and Condition of Night-Walkers with Theire Associats, Digested into a Poem by Humphrey Mill* (London: Printed by Richard Bishop for Laurence Blaicklock, 1640).

10 On prostitution and British law in the eighteenth century, see Tony Henderson, *Disorderly Women in Eighteenth-Century London: Prostitution and Control in the Metropolis, 1730-1830* (London: Longman, 1999), chapter 4.

11 See Hallie Rubenhold, *The Covent Garden Ladies: Pimp General Jack and the Extraordinary Story of Harris's List* (Gloucestershire: Tempus Press, 2005).

12 Ruth Perry, *Novel Relations: The Transformation of Kinship in English Literature and Culture, 1748-1818* (Cambridge: Cambridge UP, 2004), 265-87.

13 On the career of Charlotte Hayes and stories of particular prostitutes who married, see Rubenhold, *The Covent Garden Ladies*.

14 See Randolph Trumbach, *Sex and the Gender Revolution. Volume 1: Heterosexuality and the Third Gender in Enlightenment London*, (Chicago: U of Chicago P, 1998), chapters 4 and 5.

15 Bridget Hill, *Women, Work, and Sexual Politics in Eighteenth-Century England*, (New York: Basil Blackwell, 1989), 173.

16 See Perry, 265-87.

17 Trumbach, 3-22.

18 See H.F.B Compston, *The Magdalen Hospital: The Story of a Great Charity* (London: Society for Promoting Christian Knowledge, 1917) and more recently, Donna T. Andrew, *Philanthropy and the Police: London Charity in the Eighteenth Century* (Princeton: Princeton UP, 1989), 119-26. Andrew shows the significant break between this new reform movement and the earlier, more physically violent ones and their interest in turning prostitutes into "useful" citizens. For an excellent discussion of the relationship between the Magdalen Hospital and "Magdalen literature," see Markman Ellis, *The Politics of Sensibility: Race, Gender, and Commerce in the Sentimental Novel* (Cambridge: Cambridge UP, 1995), chapter 5.

19 In individual cases they also blame, as Ellis points out, nefarious males. For an extended analysis of prostitute reform movement in the eighteenth century from which this brief synopsis is borrowed, see my *Infamous Commerce*, chapter 4.

20 Katherine Binhammer interestingly suggests that Madan's narrative might actually be a deliberate critique of the Magdalen House, which certainly received considerable negative attention at the time from a variety of perspectives. "The Epistemology of Seduction: Women, Knowledge and Seduction Narratives in Britain

1740-1800," unpublished manuscript, chapter 2. I am grateful to Professor Binhammer for sharing her work in progress with me.

21 James Grantham Turner, *Libertines and Radicals in Early Modern London: Sexuality, Politics, and Literary Culture, 1630-1685* (Cambridge: Cambridge UP, 2002).

22 Richard Ames, *The Female Fire-Ships. A Satyr against Whoring. In a Letter to a Friend, Just Come to London* (London: E. Richardson, 1691).

23 Fashionable resorts visited every year by some members of the elite.

24 Common streetwalkers.

25 This rumor appears in *The Genuine History of Mrs. Sarah Prydden, usually called Sally Salisbury, and her gallants,* (London: Andrew Moor, 1723), 33.

26 This sort of double edge has been observed as a key part of the criminal narrative genre. On this point, see for example John J. Richetti, *Popular Fiction before Richardson: Narrative Patterns 1700-1739* (Oxford: Clarendon Press, 1969) and Lincoln Faller, *Crime and Defoe: A New Kind of Writing* (Cambridge: Cambridge UP, 1993). Libertine prostitute narratives overlap considerably with crime narratives; in fact, Salisbury and Davies were, according to these narratives, also criminals.

27 I make this case in *Infamous Commerce,* chapter 4.

28 See Henderson, *Disorderly Women* and Trumbach, *Sex and the Gender Revolution.*

29 Peter Linebaugh, *The London Hanged: Crime and Civil Society in the Eighteenth Century* (Cambridge: Cambridge UP, 1992). See, for example, chapter 2 on Jack Sheppard.

30 For a thorough overview of the shifts in the economic conditions for women in the eighteenth century, see Perry, chapter 1. On early forms of industrial labor, see Maxine Berg, *The Age of Manufactures: Industry, Innovation, and Work in Britain, 1700-1820* (Totowa, NJ: Barnes & Noble, 1985).

31 Vivien Jones, "Eighteenth-Century Prostitution: Feminist Debates and the Writing of Histories," in *Body Matters: Feminism, Textuality, Corporeality,* edited by Avril Horner and Angela Keane (Manchester: Manchester UP, 2000), 127-69.

32 Of this group, perhaps the case could be made that Leeson suffers the most for her prostitution. But as I have argued elsewhere, Leeson only gets into serious trouble when she tries to reform. (*Infamous Commerce,* chapter 4).

33 Introduction to Jennie Batchelor and Megan Hiatt, eds., *The Histories of Some of the Penitents in the Magdalen-House, as Supposed to be related by Themselves* (London: Pickering and Chatto, forthcoming). I am very grateful to Batchelor and Hiatt for being willing to share their work with me before publication.

34 On the political use to which seventeenth-century writers put the prostitute figure, see Melissa M. Mowry, *The Bawdy Politic in Stuart England, 1660-1714: Political Pornography and Prostitution* (Burlington, VT: Ashgate, 2004).

A Note on the Texts

Authentick Memoirs of the Life, Intrigues, and Adventures of the Celebrated Sally Salisbury is based on the first edition (1723). A second edition was published the same year with a key, which I have drawn on for the notes. There are two versions of the memoirs of Kitty Fisher: *The Uncommon Adventures of Miss Kitty F——r* and *The Juvenile Adventures of Miss Kitty F——r*, both published in 1759. They are identical in many places, except that several anecdotes, including the most explicitly erotic ones that appear in *The Juvenile Adventures* do not appear in *The Uncommon Adventures*. *The Uncommon Adventures*, then, is probably an expurgated and shortened version of *The Juvenile Adventures*. I have used the fuller *Juvenile Adventures* in this volume. *The Histories of Some of the Penitents in the Magdalen-House, as Supposed to be Related by Themselves* also appeared in London in 1759 and in Dublin in 1760. I have included one narrative out of four from this text, which was probably written by either Sarah Fielding or Sarah Scott. Lady Barbara Montagu presented the manuscript to Samuel Richardson for publication.[1] An edition under the name of *Spectacles for Young Ladies; Exhibiting the various Arts made Use of for seducing YOUNG WOMEN, and the dreadful Consequences of straying from the Paths of Innocence and Virtue, in a Stile that cannot offend the chastest Ear; and, at the same Time that it amuses with its surprizing Variety, conveys Instruction by the most effectual Method* appeared in Cork in 1767. William Dodd repeated Emily Markland's story in his posthumous narrative *The Magdalen, or history of the first penitent received into that charitable asylum*, which was published in 1783, 1789, and 1800. Martin Madan's *An Account of the Death of F.S. Who Died April 1763, aged Twenty-Six Years. In a LETTER to a FRIEND* went through at least seven editions on both sides of the Atlantic. I have used the first London edition here (1763). Finally, *An Authentic Narrative of the Most Remarkable Adventures, and Curious Intrigues, Exhibited in the Life of Miss Fanny Davies, the Celebrated Modern Amazon* appeared in two different versions: the fuller version that I have included here, and a shorter one by a "Mr. Thomas" that is similar but not exactly the same. Both were published in 1786, and the anonymous fuller version appeared in a Dublin edition as well as a London edition. I have used the London edition.

I have tried to keep any editorial intervention to a minimum. I have, however, modernized the quotation style and sometimes punctuation for clarity and I have silently corrected obvious typos. I have abbreviated citations from the Oxford English Dictionary (online version) as OED; citations from the Oxford Dictionary of National Biography also refer to the online edition. The narratives are filled with topical references and contemporary gossip, not all of which I have been able to identify. Rather than speculate, I have left them unfootnoted.

Note

1 For a very helpful discussion of the authorship and publication history of *The Histories*, see Batchelor and Hiatt, "Introduction."

Authentick Memoirs of the Life, Intrigues, and Adventures of the Celebrated Sally Salisbury. With True Characters of her most Considerable Gallants

CAPTAIN CHARLES WALKER

Sally Salisbury (1690?-1724) was born Sarah Pridden, the eldest of four daughters of Richard Pridden, bricklayer, and his wife Mary. The family moved to London when Sally was three. At nine she was apprenticed to a seamstress but ran away from home, making her living selling fruit in Covent Garden and probably working as a prostitute as well. By age 14, she was working for the brothel-keeper Mother Wisebourne. She later worked for another famous bawd, Mother Needham. From this very humble beginning, Salisbury came to circulate in the highest echelons of society. Her lovers may have included Lord William Bentick, Lord Bolingbroke, George Brudenell, Third Earl of Cardigan, the Duke of Buckingham, and the Prince of Wales.[1] In 1723, however, she stabbed her lover John Finch in a dispute over an opera ticket. Her case went to trial on 24 April 1723. She was sentenced to a year in prison, but, given the horrific conditions of eighteenth-century jails, did not survive.[2] Her trial caused a minor sensation in London, inspiring two different accounts of her life, a broadside, and various other publications. While The Genuine History of Mrs. Sarah Prydden *(1723) makes some attempt to create a morality tale out of the heroine's life, Captain Charles Walker's version offers less judgment. His* Authentick Memoirs *pieces together various anecdotes about Salisbury, some of which may have been submitted to Walker in response to advertisements he took out in newspapers. In Walker's version, Sally Salisbury emerges as a tough, independent young woman with a wicked sense of humor. She happily drains elite men of their cash and has no tolerance for stinginess or condescension (from men or from other women). Walker's heroine emerges as heartless, remorseless, and unsentimental, yet the narrative also provides enough context to explain the heroine's callousness as a reasonable response to the callous world in which she finds herself. In the*

---

1 Barbara White, "Salisbury, Sally (1690x92-1724)," *Oxford Dictionary of National Biography*, Oxford UP, 2004-06.

2 See *The Weekly Journal, or Saturday Post*, February 16, March 2, April 6, April 21, and May 4, 1723; *Select Trials at the Sessions-House in The Old Bailey*, 4 volumes (London: Printed for John Applebee, 1742), 336-43.

picaresque tradition, Salisbury survives through creativity, will, strategic resistance, and a wicked sense of humor.

Authentick Memoirs of the Life, Intrigues, and Adventures of the Celebrated Sally Salisbury. With True Characters of her most Considerable Gallants.

By Capt. Charles Walker.

London: Printed in the Year 1723
(Price 2*s*. 6*d*.)
The Epistle Dedicatory to Mrs.[1] *Sally Salisbury*

MADAM,
NEVER was Poet so much tortured about the Choice of a *Patron*, as I have been for a proper *Advocate* of the following *Memoirs*. For tho' in the *Female Class* of Life, I could have fastened upon Numbers, which bear some Resemblance to *You*, in your general Behaviour, and Actions; and tho' many of our own Sex, would have gloried in the Patronage of these Amorous Adventures: Yet in so vast a Collection, I could not find One equal to the *Singularity* of your Character.

A *Beau* of the first, or second Rank, would have made but insipid Patrons; a *Coquet* would have proved a mischievous One; a *Jilt* a negligent One; a *kept Mistress*, a weak One; or a *common Runner* of the *Town*, a ridiculous One.

I had once determined to fix the terrible Name of some *Man* of *War* in the Front of *your History*, a *perfect Hero*, that should like another QUIXOTE defend your *Reputation* right, or wrong; but upon second Thoughts, I concluded the Task too hazardous for any BESUS[2] of this Age; that he soon would have been obliged to carry his Arm in a Scarf, and your Honour left to shift for it self; and so I dismiss'd that Project.

Then I was hot upon begging the Protection of some *powerful Man* in Your Interest, famed for Wit and Love, but I foresaw what Envy it would create to the Person, placed, in a manner, at the *Head* of Your *Affections* by such a DEDICATION: Besides, I was fearful of giving You a very sensible Disgust, in making *You* seem the *Propriety* of *one Man*, when You know Yourself *ordained* for the Comfort and Refreshment of *Multitudes*.

At last, for the avoiding Offence, and gaining a strong Party, I had almost resolved to Inscribe the following Sheets to ALL Your *Admirers*, that is to most

1   "Mrs." functioned as a form of address for all adult women and did not suggest marital status.
2   *The General, who Assassinated Darius, King of Persia.* [author's note] Darius III (d. 330 BC) was killed by the Bactrian satrap Bessus after he (Darius) had been defeated by Alexander the Great.

of the *Loving Subjects* of *Great-Britain*. But then I considered what endless Quarrels might rise amongst so many Competitors, about the foolish Punctilio of who was Dearest to You, and who had possessed You oftenest, so that I soon went off from these Intentions.

From this Insufficiency in the *Men*, to protect so great a Merit, I cast my Eyes toward the *Female World*, to find one there; but I perceived myself running into equal Improprieties on that Side also.

Had I Dedicated them to some *Leading* BELLE of a Modern *Assemblée*, with what Indignation would she have beheld her Name prefixed to the Life of such a *proclaimed Wanton*, whilst she keeps up an unsuspected Gallantry with Thousands.

Had I Inscribed these MEMOIRS to a PRUDE, what a tacit Reflection would it have been upon her stolen Joys with her Coachman; and how strangely would such a Complement have disordered her Stoical Face, and precise Behaviour.

I had once a *pretty Penitent* in my Eye, who has passed thro' many delightful Stages of Life, whose Wit could have justified most of the gay Excesses of Your Story; but I hear, she is employing all those fine Talents in polishing that little Stock of Reputation, which is left her, and so, less capable of giving a Gloss to Yours: So that,

You see, I was under an invincible Necessity of making *You* the PATRONESS of Your own *Fine Actions*: And to be plain, Who is there in all the Fair Circle of Female Practitioners that has Spirit enough to defend each Article of Your Conversation? What Woman besides Yourself has the Wit to extenuate the most Criminal Parts, or Art to add a Lustre to the beautiful Extravagancies of Your Life.

No, Madam, You are the sole Person, best able to protect Yourself. Thus Naked and Defenceless how Lovely do you appear? How Great in this *State* of *Independency*?

But tho' it is not easy to find a proper *Patron* amongst the *Men*, yet for Your Satisfaction I must tell You, the whole *Species* is at Your *Devotion*, and the seeming Disdain of Your *own Sex*, proceeds not so much from an Unwillingness to Patronize Your Actions, as an Incapacity of Copying so bright an Example.

There is a certain Propriety in Your Character, which is not communicable to any Woman in *Your Way*, and even the nearest Intimation would become preposterous in another Hand. Your polite Deviations from Virtue, and graceful Wantonness, are what Alarm your whole Sex, and from despairing to Imitate, they fall to Railing.

Having such superior Advantages, think not that I will run any mean *Parallels* between *You* and the *modern Ladies* of *Your Profession*, or that I will Honour them even with a DASH.[1]

---

1 Scandal narratives often (thinly) disguised names with dashes.

No, your Sphere of Elevation is much higher, and You move with an Elegance peculiar to Your self.

I am half distracted when I hear a *dissolute Creature*, formed only for *falling backwards*, and such insipid Dalliancies, as Matrimony affords, compare those *barren Pleasures*, to the Picquancy, and Heightenings which You give to that *supreme Joy* of SENSE: Or a *Termagant* born only for Noise and Clamour, justify herself by those gay Rhapsodies, and inspired Rants, with which you engage your Lovers.

As You stand without a *Rival* in *Great Britain* amongst the Professors of *Love's Mysteries*, so it is difficult to match *You* amongst the *Ancients*. The *Grecian* Ladies of Pleasure were delicious in their Way; they had fine Particularities; but were not so universally *attractive* as You are.

PHRYNE of *Beotia*[1] was a *celebrated Toast* in her Day, She had a pouting Lip, and a melting Eye which gained her more Admirers, than the fiercer Beauties of her Time: She was most remarkable for the *Elasticity* of her *Parts*, and a certain *Spring* in her *Motion*, which endangered the *Rider*. But somewhat mercenary in the Abatement of her other amiable Qualities.

LAMIA of *Athens*, tho' engaging beyond Measure, at first Sight, yet was high seasoned with the *Jilt*; she had a peculiar Knack of firing the Imagination with an openness of Behaviour; would shew her pretty Foot, and well turned Leg, and then Drop the Curtain on a sudden, and retire, to the unspeakable Torment of her Lover; a Fault, your Enemies could never reproach you with, since you are generally so Compassionate as to go thro' the *whole Exercise*.

LAIS of *Corinth* was a Lady of High Mettle, Generous and Entertaining; tho' her Demands ran high, when a wealthy Magistrate was to make a *Love-Purchase*; yet, to her Honour be it Recorded, she never let a younger Brother pine to Death for want of a *Favour*; but what gives some Alloy to her Character, is, that She was much *Commoner*, than ever *You* permitted *your Self* to be. But,

THAIS is the Girl, which comes up nearest to your Standard; She had something *Strong* in her *Diversions*, loved to associate chiefly with Rakes, and affected *Masculine Pleasures*. She would make a Party at a *drinking Match*, and Loved a *midnight Revel* at her Soul. And how often have You quitted the *fine Gentleman*, and the *Colonel* to drink half a dozen Bottles of *Burgundy* with an *Illustrious-Debauchee*, with an Eye perhaps to the Example of ARIADNE, who quitted her Lover THESEUS, for the tumultuous Conversation of BACCHUS.

Amongst the *Roman Ladies* of Your Calling, to pass over the CELIA'S, the MANILIA'S, the JULIA'S, and Thousands more of that Stamp, famed for little else than *strong Gustoes* of *Pleasure*. I cannot find even the *Kept-Mistresses* of the *Roman Wits*, reach up near to Your Perfection.

The LYCORIS of GALLUS was an *luscious Bed-fellow*, but then, She used by

---

1 Walker refers to several legendary courtesans in this section.

way of Provocative, to read the *wanton Verses* of her Paramour in the day time; without which helps, *You*, MADAM, are *Tousjours Prest.*[1]

CORINNA the Mistress of OVID, Loved a *Game* at *Romps* in her *Cloaths,* and was so *insatiable* in her *Play,* that there was no holding out the *Game* with her: This Mistake *You* judiciously avoid, by permitting your *Lover* to *rise* with an *Appetite.*

The beloved LELAGE of Horace appears to me in no more agreeable Light, than that of a pretty, laughing, talkative, Hoyden. And,

The LESBIA of CATULLUS was everlastingly Slabbering, and Sucking his Lips. But,

In all this Fine *Groupe* of *Obliging Ladies,* none, singly, could ever furnish out that Variety of Delight which is to be met with in *your Person*: In *You* the happy Man enjoys the different Graces of all Climates. In You are collected the scattered Beauties of Your whole Sex. In short, You are the PINE-APPLE of *Great-Britain,* which includes the several flavours of all the delicious Fruits in the World.

Those Hypocrites who pretend to dis-esteem You upon the Account of Your *Profession,* neither consider the *Antiquity* of it; the *Usefulness* of your *Labours* to the *Publick*; or the *Honours* conferred upon your Loving *Sisterhood* by the Greatest, and wisest *Law-givers, Princes,* and *States* in all Ages. For the *Antiquity*; From,

VENUS Parent of *Gods* and *Men,*

Began the Sportive-Dance.

For the *Usefulness* of it—It will be readily granted. The *Ladies* of your *Universal Character* are of wondrous Service to those who cannot comply with the Insolence, Clamour, Insatiableness, Laziness, Extravagance, or Virtuous Nastiness of a *Wife.*

It must be allowed, that such *Gay Volunteers* as your *Ladyship,* give a *young Fellow* an handsome Prospect of the Town, lead him thro' all the inchanting Mazes, and even surfeit him with Delight; so that by the time he is come out of your Hands, he is grown very Tame, and prepared for the dull Solemnity of *Marriage.* It cannot be likewise denied, but that Recreations of that Delicacy are much more excusable, than the smallest Excesses of any other Kind.

That this *familiar Intercourse* keeps *Mankind* in the *proper Channel* of *Nature.*

That more Distempers are prevented by your *kind Alliances,* than gained; and *critical Fevers* of the *Blood* mitigated, if not cured, by your seasonable Interposition.

From such a kind *Medicine* as You are always capable of *dispensing*; that Pious Father St. AUSTIN, whom the CHURCH with so much Justice Reveres, found great *Relief* in his *Necessities*: He had a *Pair* of clever *Wenches* for his Share: By *one* he had a *Love Child,* whom he called ADEODATUS, that is, the

---

1 Probably "toujours prête" or "always ready."

Gift of God: She teized him and followed him, till She grew *Vexatious*, and the *holy Father* then threw her off with a good deal of Gallantry: The *other* he used to recreate himself with, after he had been solemnly Contracted to his intended Spouse who was in her Nonage, and kept her till his Wife was ripe for Consummation.

But that *Ladies* of Your *Characteristick* are of more important Service to the CHURCH, and the PUBLICK, then most of the *liberal Arts*, is evident from Experience.

At *Rome* every Pleasurable Female pays a JULIO *per* Week to the CHURCH; a *Curate*, whose Income amounts to no more than Thirty-Crowns *per Annum*, having an Assignment out of the Fees of Three Courtesans in the *Publick Stews*, picks up a comfortable Subsistence, and to distinguish such *pious Church-Women*, as your Ladyship, Pope SIXTUS erected a noble *Brothel-House*, with Partitions, for the more commodious Reception of Strangers.

Neither have they been less serviceable to their *Country* then to the CHURCH, as appears by the great Succours they have afforded to the Com-mon-wealth of *Venice* out of their Bodily Industry.

Here I cannot omit the great Genius of *One*, and the extensive Charity of the *Other*.

RHODOPE, at her own Expence, and out of the modest Fees of her private Office built one of the stateliest *Pyramids* of *Egypt*. And FLORA generously left the *Roman-People* her Heirs.

Their *Duty* to *Parents* likewise must not be passed over in Silence. The *Baby-lonian* Virgins used to grant Favours for the Support of their aged *Fathers*.

Neither must the *Industry* of the *Cyprian Girls* want a due Encomium: For they publickly *prostituted* themselves to every Stranger, to make a *Fortune* equal to their *Ambition* before they settled in *Matrimony*.

But here we must not forget the Honours, even the sacred Honours, con-ferred on your Profession by Antiquity. The *Corinthian-Dames*, being the most elegant Mistresses of *Greece*, had it always in Charge, from the *State*, to inter-cede with VENUS in any case of Importance; and when *Xerxes* invaded the *Peloponesus*, they had the Privilege of compiling a publick Form of Prayer for the Safety of their *Country*. SOLON, the *Athenian* Law-giver being sensible of the Strength of their *Party*, built a *Temple* to VENUS out of the Amorous Perquisites of your Tribe, which was devoutly Copied here, in that worthy Col-lection made for a CHAPEL of *Ease* in *Russell-Court, Covent-Garden*, out of the *pious Gains* of the THEATRE.

Thus MADAM you see, you have the whole Current of *Antiquity* on your side, and assure your self, the Party will be ever as victorious in *Great Britain*, tho' we are too Phlegmatic to pay those solemn Honours to your Confedera-cy, as the Ancients.

But what the Laws of our Country forbids us to act in *Publick*, you are satis-fied we make more than a Recompence for in *Private*.

What *Catholic* has ever offered up more Extacies at the Shrine of his *Tutelar Saint*, than has been paid to the simple Brade of your Shoe, a discoloured Top Knot, or perhaps two Spans of unraveled Gartering.

Yet amidst the *good Offices*, you are continually doing to Mankind, I must intreat you not to indulge the Vanity of thinking yourself exempt from the invidious Whispers of a thoughtless Multitude: No, there are a Set of Gossips of both Sexes, who are endeavouring to fix a Blemish on your Bright Character, insinuating that the most blooming Part of your Life was spent amongst the *Royal Japanners*;[1] which at present, for your Comfort is no despicable *Corporation*; whilst others equally detracting, fail not to lessen the Dignity of your Education, in that famous College of *Sherard-Street*, under the celebrated Mrs. N—d—am.[2] But your good Sense is always present with you, to pity their Ignorance, and place such popular Mistakes to a Narrowness of Genius: For what Seminary is there, even at *Chelsea* or *Hackney*, which can boast of half those Improvements, in Five Years, as that School wherein you have been Educated, can furnish out in three Months? There, the young Practitioners are led into a promiscuous Conversation from the Day of their Admittance. There, is soon learned an easy and graceful Behaviour, and a Presence of Mind, which never leaves them in an Extremity. In that Academy there can no Danger accrue to the fair Nymphs, from broken Vows, and neglected Charms: There, the Lover has nothing in View, but a Run of Joy without Teizing, Fears, or

---

1   "Royal Japanners" might refer here to men who spanked prostitutes, either as abuse or erotic practice:

[T] he Jest was a *Charing-Cross* Sir,
Where two Whores were a walking along,
    Stuck out with Tyme and Rue,
    But the Jades look'd very blue,
When their Arses were double japan'd.

Three Shoe Boys came up to these Strumpets,
The one lay flat on his Face,
    The second gave a Push,
    While the Third with a Brush,
Did finely japan her Arse.

And at *Smithfield-bars*, three Soldiers,
Met three Jilts stuck out with Rue;
    Each Man took his Lass,
    And soundly slap'd her Arse,
Which made them look very blue.

Mughouse Diversion: or A Collection of Loyal Prologues, and Song, Spoke and Sung at the Mug-Houses.
London: Printed and sold by S. Popping, 1717.

2   Mrs. Needham, a well-known bawd.

Cautions; and for the Satisfaction of all jealous Parents, there has not been a Fortune stole out of this pious Nursery since its First Erection.

Times and Customs alter; but had your *Lady Abbess* been so fortunate as to have lived in that elegant Period of Time, when *Greece* carried away the Prize of Wit, and Prowess, from all the World, both *She,* and *You* would have been the immediate Care of the Publick.

The famous ASPASIA, was much of Mrs. *N—d—am's* Complexion, and Vertue, and so tender was *Athens* of the Safety, and Commodious Subsistence of that *Lady* and her *Virtuous Nursery,* that PERICLES the famous General, began the *Peloponesian* War in Revenge of the Injuries offered to *Her,* and the young Ladies of Pleasure under her Care, by the People of *Megara.*

These Honours paid to your *Profession* by *Antiquity,* cannot fail of giving you an high opinion of their good Sense, and likewise an Opportunity of bewailing the strange Degeneracy of the Men of the present Age, who concern themselves no farther in your *Cause,* then *You* are contributing to their Pleasures: But I presume you will still persevere in this *Virtuous Course,* in hopes of seeing some Amendment in the Times.

But now MADAM to take my Leave of you fairly, I think you will have this peculiar Advantage over the rest of your Sex by seeing the *worst* of Your *Actions* published in your *Life time,* that You may amend them in the next Impression, or if it be not too much trouble, amend your self: They are most of them Venial, and I assure you I would sooner Embark on your Bottom, than that of many presumptive Hypocrites.

If I have failed in one Point of *Chronology,* and detracted so much from the Vivacity of your Spirit, as not to bring you a *Practical Familiarity* with *Mankind* soon enough for a Lady of Your Capacity: Believe me MADAM, I'll endeavour to correct that Fault, and place You with QUARTILLA, who *scarce remembred when she was confirmed* by Man,

I am,
Madam,

March 8th
1722-3

Your most obliged

Admirer,

CHARLES WALKER

MEMOIRS OF Mrs. *Sarah Priddon*, ALIAS *Sally Salisbury*.

The late Accident, which gives Birth to the ensuing Pages, is an unhappy Instance of what Mr. *Addison* has so judiciously observ'd, *That Women talk*, and *move*, and *smile* with a *Design upon Us*:[1] That though their *Thoughts* are ever turn'd upon appearing *Amiable*, yet every *Feature* of their *Faces* and every *Part* of their *Dress* is fill'd with *Snares* and *Allurements*. There would be no such *Animals* as *Prudes* or *Coquets* in the World, were there not such an *Animal* as *Man*.

As therefore we are indebted to ourselves and to our selves only, for that Extravagance of Power which *They* on all Occasions take the Liberty to exert over *Us*, we cannot, upon the strictest Examination, blame the insolent Arrogance of the *haughty Woman*, when we consider the mean Submissions of the *obsequious yielding Man*.

The mischievous *Animal* now before us, pleads *Passion* as an Excuse for, and Extenuation of, the Action she has committed. It is a very common Expression, That such a one is *very good Natured*, but *very Passionate*. The Expression, indeed, is *very good-natured*, to allow *passionate People* so much *Quarter*; but I think a *passionate Person* deserves the *least Indulgence imaginable*. It is said, *It is soon over*, that is, all the *Mischief* they can do is *quickly dispatch'd*; which I think is no great Recommendation to Favour.—It is certain, That *quick Sensibility* is inseparable from a *ready Understanding*; but why should not that good Understanding call to it self all its Force, on such Occasions, to master that sudden Inclination to Anger. Now to shew how odious this enormous Vice is in both Sexes, if you would see *Passion* in its *Purity*, without *Mixture* of *Reason*, behold it represented in a mad Hero, drawn by a mad Poet. *Nat. Lee* makes his *Alexander* say thus:

Away! Begone, and give a Whirl-wind Room,
Or I will blow you up like Dust! Avaunt:
Madness but meanly represents my Toil,
Eternal Discord!
Fury! Revenge! Disdain and Indignation!
Tear my swol'n Breast, make way for Fire and Tempest,
My Brain is burst; Debate and Reason quench'd;
The Storm is up, and my hot bleeding Heart
Splits with the Rack, while Passions, like the Wind,
Rise up to Heaven, and put out all the Stars![2]

---

1   Vid. *SPECTATOR*, No. 433. [author's note] Thursday, July 17, 1712 by Joseph Addison. Addison makes the case that women constantly strive to appeal to men.
2   Nathaniel Lee, *The Rival Queens* (1677), III.i. 47-56. The lines are actually spoken by Roxana, not Alexander. Walker repeats this error from *The Spectator* 438.

Every *passionate Fellow* in Town talks half the Day with as *little Consistency* and threatens *Things as much out* of his *Power.*[1]

How near an Affinity the *Heroine* of these MEMOIRS bears to the Character above describ'd, I leave to the Determination of all *who know* her.

Having been favour'd with the Correspondence of several Gentlemen, since I declared my Intention of writing her LIFE, I think my self obliged in Justice to transmit every Paper that I have receiv'd, with the same Freedom it has been communicated. The first Letter sent me, was sign'd *RENATO;* a Gentleman, who has within these few Days been pleased to make himself known to me. He is a Person of Birth, Fortune, and singular Worth; One of her earliest Admirers, and by her boundless Extravagance only, has for some time been incapacitated from making that splendid Appearance in the World he formerly did, and deserves still to do. His Letter runs thus, *viz.*

SIR,

MANY are the Reports which are spread Abroad, concerning that celebrated Piece of Contradiction, SALLY SALISBURY. She is said to be the best-humoured Creature existing, and at the same time the most morose Animal breathing; she has a great deal of Wit, but very little Judgment; much immediate Cunning, less future Conduct. She is extremely Agreeable, tho' not perfectly Beautiful. These, and many other seeming Paradoxes, which the judicious Reader may easily reconcile, reign alternately in this charming Compound of bewitching Mischief. In advancing but few out of the many Vicissitudes of Fortune, changes of Manners, Acquaintance, Places of Abode, etc. You, Sir, whose Genius is equal to the nice Task you have happily undertaken, may collect just Notions, and form a better Judgment than I, with my Inferior Capacity, dare attempt, and you will oblige the Publick in the most entertaining Manner, by transmitting her Fame to the Posterity in its proper Colours.

You may depend upon the Veracity of every Fact sent you by
Your humble Servant,
RENATO
Jan. 6. 1722/3

CHAPTER I
Of her Birth, Education, and first setting out in the World

BECAUSE I would have the strictest Regard to Truth and Impartiality in the following MEMOIRS, I will not pretend either to write the Annals, or the Diary, of Mrs. *SALISBURY'S Life*, nor will I be accountable for all her Hours,

---

1 Vid. *SPECTATOR*, No. 438. [author's note] These lines quote from Richard Steele, Wednesday, July 23, 1712.

least by that Means I should lye under the Imputation of having forged the greatest Part of her Adventures, or incur the Censure of being wholly ignorant of any: For I must freely confess, that I have been shrewdly put to it even to fix the time of her Nativity; nor have I been less puzzled about the *Place,* as many laying Claim to it (to her immortal Fame be it spoken) as to *that* of *HOMER.*

Some of the Invidious among her own Sex, in the *Hospitable Hundreds of OLD DRURY,*[1] would fain have handed her down to Posterity for a Native of *Sweet* St. *GILES's,* by confidently affirming that she was born in *PARKER's-LANE,* in that Parish. But as *Rumour* is seldom to be credited, I have had Recourse to more Authentick Vouchers, find her Recorded a *SALOPIAN,* and that the good Town of *SHREWSBURY* boasts the Honour of her Birth.

She is the Eldest Daughter of *RICHARD PRIDDON, Bricklayer,* and *MARGARET,* his Wife, and has Three Sisters now living, *viz. PEGGY, MOLLY* and *JENNY. FAME* is very loud in ecchoing out the Exploits of Three of them, but *JENNY* having had the Misfortune of being deprived of her Sight, by that formidable Enemy of Beauty, the *SMALL-POX,* History says little of Her: But all who know Her, say, that she is perfectly Good-natur'd, very Vertuous, endow'd with no small Portion of Sense, and as remarkable for the *Sweetness of her Voice,* as her Sister *SALLY* is for the *Keenness of her Tongue;* and I am assured, that nothing but Mrs. *SALISBURY's* insuperable Pride, has even prevented her from ravishing the Ears of the Publick upon the Stage in the *OPERA-HOUSE;* she having obstinately rejected the Proposals made to *JENNY* upon that Subject: Tho' in Reality, to do all of them Justice, they have pretty Voices, and sing in a very agreeable easy manner.

But to return to Mrs. *SARAH,* the more immediate Object of our present Concern, we find that an Aunt of hers (who married her Father's Brother, and was lately in an Alms-House at *SHREWSBURY*) affirms her to have been born about the year 1690, or 91.

I will not go about to particularize how far she is indebted to her Parents for their Care of breeding her in her Minority, but to speak according to my own Knowledge, she Reads well, fluently, and with an admirable grace; she Writes tolerably, but Spells very indifferently. Yet it is certain, that had she been bless'd with an Education proportional to her own Natural Genius, she would have been a most accomplish'd Woman; nay, I have actually heard some, make no scruple to say, with an Exclamation, That, *Had SALLY apply'd herself to Learning, she would have been the Prodigy of the Age.* It must be confess'd, that she can be very entertaining Company when she pleases; has a surprising Vivacity, and Redundancy of Thought, a ready Turn of Wit, and is very sprightly at *Repartee;* but her predominant, darling Faculty of inconsiderately using both her Tongue and Hands, makes her Conversation far less agreeable

---

1   London brothel district.

than it would otherwise be, and indeed hardly supportable. This odious Quality seems in her to be innate; I have been assur'd by some, who knew her from her Shell,[1] that the uncontroul'd, Termagant Spirit, which has been since so conspicuously display'd; was visibly perceiv'd in the little Vixen when but in Hanging-Sleeves, she being even at those callow Years, haughty and impatient of Contradiction.

Forced by the Frowns of Fortune, her Father and Mother left *Shrewsbury*, came to *London*, and brought her with them, she being then not above Three Years Old. Her Father, to shield himself from his clamorous Creditors, entered himself in the Foot-Guards, and became an Inhabitant of the Parish of St. *Giles's in the Fields*, where he follow'd his Trade of a Bricklayer; and having formerly been pretty conversant among the *Country-Attornies;* as an Addition to his own Business, set up likewise for a *Sollicitor.*

At about Nine Years of Age, *Sally* was put Apprentice to a Sempstress[2] in *Duke's-Palace*, near *Aldgate*, to learn *Plain-Work, etc.* and the Females of her Acquaintance declare her to be an excellent Needle-Woman. But having the Misfortune to lose a Piece of Lace, of a considerable Value, she ran away from her Mistress, and never more returned.

At the very budding of her *Puberty SALLY* commenc'd *Woman*, and the first Use she made of her *Needle* was at her Mother's Expence; who one Day found her sitting under a Table very busy at Work, in altering a *Petticoat* which she had purloin'd from her, and from which she had cut off above a Quarter of a Yard of its *length*, to make it sizeable for her self. This Fact, as she has often declared to an intimate Friend, was to deck her out for a *Hopping-Ball.*[3] The *Petticoat*, she says, was a *Stuff-Sattinet*, the richest Garment her Mother had ever been Mistress of. Dress and Dancing were the sole Youthful Delights of our *SALLY*, and she never wanted a Gallant, suitable to her Years, to introduce her into every *Hop* of Eminence about the Town; it being her Ambition always to be Fine, in order to attract the Hearts as well as the Eyes of her little Votaries.

But for this heinous Offence, the choleric Old Don her Father, highly incensed to see his Wife's Wardrobe so unmercifully abus'd led her into the Cellar, strip'd her, ty'd her to the Stairs-Foot, and severely Disciplin'd her with a Horse-Whip, and intended to leave her all Night in that Condition, threatning her with a *Second Part* to the *Same-Tune* the next Day. To avoid which, poor little Miss, very vigorously employ'd both Tooth and Nail, and found means, tho' with much difficulty, to get loose, watch'd her Opportunity, made an Elopement, and was not heard of for some time.

---

1   From a very young age (figuratively, before she was "hatched").
2   "A needlewoman whose occupation is plain sewing as distinguished from dress or mantle-making, decorative embroidery, etc." [OED]
3   "A dance; a rural festival of which dancing forms a principal part." [OED]

Her first Place of refuge after this Escape, was with Mr. *P—r G—h* (and *Teddy* his Wife, it seems commonly so call'd) a Hatter in the *Hay-Market;* who hospitably entertain'd, and gave her part of their own Bed, till the inconveniency she put them to, oblig'd her to think of some Method for her own Support, without being troublesome to her Friends; or, as the saying is, *to ride a free Horse to Death.*

Now it was, History relates, that she apply'd her self to the *Coster-Mongers*[1] in *Covent-Garden*, with whom she traded for the *delicious Fruit* of *China*. From the natural Mercurial Briskness of her Temper, a sedentary Life had ever been her Aversion, wherefore she rather chose to follow the Fortunes of a *Wheel-Barrow*, than those of a *Distaff*; daily, charming the Ears of the Publick with the Tuneable and melodious Cry, of, *Come who throws here? Who Ventures for an ORANGE?* But to give this Fact another Turn, Mrs. *Salisbury* of late Years, whenever reproach'd for her haughty Airs, and put in mind of her pristine Vocation, would always evade it, as she did once, in particular, to a Person of Quality, in my hearing; by her Insolence and ill Language, the young Nobleman being justly provok'd to upbraid her with driving that *Vehicle*—She pertly reply'd, *D—n you for a Pimp*— (her usual Phrase) *I never had any thing to do with a Wheel-Barrow, but what you or the best of you all might have done; I only play'd at it, when a Child, for my Diversion.*

Tho' to show her *Love* of *Variety*, even in her *Employments*, many living Witnesses don't stick to say, that at different Seasons of the Year, she shell'd *Beans* and *Pease*, cry'd *Nose-gays* and *News-Papers*, peal'd *Walnuts*, made *Matches*, turn'd *Bunter*,[2] etc., well-knowing that, *a wagging Hand always gets a Penny.*

It was some Time before her Father found her out, but after long Search, and much Inquiry, he at length met with her: At first Sight he loaded her with a Million of Reproaches for stealing and spoiling his Wife's *Holyday-Petticoat*, and at the same Time charg'd her with a Theft of far greater Consequence; alledging, That he had been robb'd of Twenty Pounds in Specie, and that no body could have it but She. This Part of the Accusation (as she still does) *SALLY* very flatly denied; and several, who were no Strangers to the Family's Circumstances at that Juncture aver'd that there was very little probability of Mr. *PRIDDON's* having such a Sum in his Custody.

As I shall have Occasion to mention her Parents hereafter, upon many Accounts, I will not, in this Place, detain the Reader with any farther Domestick Quarrels, or any more of our *SALLY'S* Childish Pranks; but will proceed to the next Stage of her Life, wherein she began to cut something of a Figure and wherein I my self had the Honour of her Acquaintance.

---

1   Fruitsellers.
2   "A cant word for a woman who picks up rags about the street; and used, by way of contempt, for any low vulgar woman." [OED]

CHAPTER II.
How She came to Mother WISEBOURN, and how she went from her.[1]

FORTUNE, the constant Fautress[2] of the *Fair,*
Soon pointed out our *SALLY's lucky Star:*
MUSE stop a while (for thou hast Cause to Mourn)
And shed a Tear o'er *Pious WISEBOURN's* Urn.

Thou Mem'rable *Anchor of Hope,*
To all *Blooming Virgins,*
Light lye the Earth upon Thee.—

Thou BALM of GILEAD to all *Love-sick* Swains,
Permit a Votary to sing thy Praise;
To shield thy Mem'ry from th' Opprobrious Pen
Of Mercenary Impotence, and Vile Detraction.[3]

Within thy *Walls* the RICH were ever pleas'd,
And from thy *Gate* no *LAZAR* went unfed!
South-Sea Directors might have learnt from *Thee*
How to pay Debts, and wear an honest Heart![4]
From *Thee* the *Lawyer* might have learnt strict Justice,
Thy Hand ne'er grasp'd a *CLIENT's Fee* in vain;

And when the Cash *ran low* and Blood *ran high,*
The Man in such a Plight thy Bounty felt!
Thy Darling Girls were offer'd to his view,
And with the Chosen Nymph to Bed he flew.[5]

---

1 A well-know London bawd. See Anodyne Tanner, *The Life of the Celebrated Mrs. Elizabeth Wisebourn* (London, 1721?). Tanner credits Wisebourn with inventing the popular London entertainment of the masquerade.
2 Patroness.
3 *Alluding to an Account of her Life, wherein the Scribler has not inserted one Paragraph of Truth.* [author's note] Possibly a reference to Tanner's biography cited in note 1.
4 This poet refers to the recent collapse of the value of stock in the South Sea Company. Many had eagerly invested in this company, whose stock rose quickly and fell suddenly, causing distress, outrage, and widespread financial ruin. The directors were widely suspected of dishonesty. See John Carswell, *The South Sea Bubble* (Stanford: Stanford University Press, 1960)
5 Walker also inserts a translation of this poem into Latin, which I have omitted.

I think my self oblig'd to beg Pardon for this Soliloquy, but having often been one of the Penny-less Class of Mortals above describ'd, and shar'd her generous Benevolence, I could not forbear offering this Tribute of Gratitude to her Ashes, for which Reason I hope to obtain Forgiveness: And now, like a serviceable Nag upon the Road, after the Refreshment of a good Bait, I promise the Reader to jog merrily on.

Who first gave our *SALLY a Green-Gown* is uncertain,[1] but it is reported by many, and more particularly by one of the most reputable Inhabitants of that Neighbourhood, that upon being admitted an Honorary Member of Mrs. *Wisebourn's* Academy, she was (tho' very indifferently) arrayed in *that Colour,* and by the tatter'd Condition of her Vestments, it was generally believed, that our venerable Matron, of pious and charitable Memory, had redeem'd her (as she had before done a Legion of other distressed Nymphs) from Bondage, into which it was said she had been cast by the Inhumanity of some Narrow-Soul'd, merciless Creditor, whose Age and Avarice had rendered him as insensible to Generosity, as he was to the attractive Charms of *SALLY,* then in the bloom of Fifteen.

But the Hospitable *Dame,* conceiving mighty Hopes from SALLY's promising Air and Mein, soon rigg'd her out fit to adorn the *Side-Box* at an *Opera.* From her own Mouth we learn, that an antiquated Doctor of Physick in *Beaufort-Buildings,* extremely smitten with her Youth and engaging Aspect, was the first who became her ardent Suitor, and for the *Last Favour,* tipp'd her, as Hansel,[2] Two *Shining HALF-CROWNS,* the greatest Sum she declares she had, till then, ever been Mistress of.

FAME says, She could not boast of very many Triumphs, before she fell into the Hands of an *incautious, roving Libertine,* who had like to have made her fall a Victim to the *Tomb* of *Venus:* But the Sons of *Galen* and *Hippocrates*[3] still prov'd her best Friends; for notwithstanding the *Inspection* and *Circumspection* of the vigilant Governess, (whose Care was so great to keep every thing *safe* and *sound,* That she us'd often to say of her Girls, *These* Chitty-Faces *make me undergo more Fatigue than a Vinter's Boy, for I scower their Insides as clean, every Night, as if I made use of Shot and a Bottle-Brush.)* The *Fire alas, broke out!* And Mrs. *WISEBOURN* had immediate Recourse to her Never-failing *Engine* Mr. *W—* an eminent Surgeon in the *Strand.* To use *SALLY's* own Phrase, after having *Spit a little for a Complexion,* she retired to the purifying Air of *KENSINGTON Gravel-Pits,* under the Tuition of Mrs. *L—Y B—T,* a City-Sempstress, where we will leave them a while and relate a short Story as told by her Surgeon.

---

1   That is, took her virginity (by figuratively rolling her in the grass).
2   "A gift or present (expressive of good wishes) at the beginning of a new year, or on entering upon any new condition, situation, or circumstances, the donning of new clothes, etc.; originally, deemed to be auspicious, or to ensure good luck for the new year, etc." [OED]
3   Physicians.

He says, That tho' he had the Care of the whole College, it chanc'd to be so full, at the Time of *SALLY's* Mishap, and so anxious was Mrs. *WISEBOURN* for her Welfare, that she would not, by any means, be perswaded to let her go out of the House, tho' there was so little Room in it, that she was forc'd to go through the whole Operation of a Flux in an old Elbow-Chair which was plac'd just under the *Jack*, in the Kitchin. Yet though this skilful Artist made all the Dispatch which could reasonably be expected in such a case, the Good-natur'd, Compassionate Matron thought it very tedious; and would frequently break out into this Pathetick Exclamation; *Poor Creature! She has pay'd dearly for that unlucky Bout! besides her loss of Time, she was Five Weeks, Two Days, One Hour and a Half doing Pennance, from her first* lying down *till her* going Abroad.

But to return to our *Fair Sufferer:* Expresses daily past to, and from *KENSINGTON;* and in less than a Month News was brought to Mrs. *WISEBOURN,* that as SALLY and Mrs. *B—T* were taking the Air in *HYDE-PARK,* a Man of Quality was struck to the Heart by the bewitching Glances of the scarce recover'd *SALLY,* and instantly avow'd his sudden Flame, which could not be extinguished. For *ORONTUS,* a Person of Superior Distinction, at that Time, possessed the Charmer.[1] Fame reports, that Mrs. *Mary Davis* living near to the *Seven-Dials,* was the Plenipo,[2] who Negotiated this Affair with Mrs. *Wisebourn,* and first made Mrs. *Salisbury* happy in the Embraces of a Peer. But Honour is Sacred, and we must go no farther.

> *The Spring had, now, restor'd her drooping Bloom,*
> *Re-animated her decaying Fires;*
> *And made her shine a-new to bless Mankind.*

In a few Weeks she left *Kensington,* and removed to *Villiers-Street* in *York-Buildings;* where, a Sumptuous Apartment was fitted up for her Reception. Here, *ORONTUS* and the *Fair-One* revelled in Delights, and her Youth made him Vigorous even in his Declension.

There let them rest a while, another Scene just opening to our View. Long had the Gay and Amorous Young-Nobleman, (who was wounded in *Hyde-Park,* as above related) stood in suspence as to his Fate in the Passion he had entertain'd for the Beauteous *SALLY.* Whole Nights and Months he sigh'd in vain, till at length that necessary Implement, an *Exchange-Woman,* wrought the Cure. An Interview was appointed, and the punctual *SALLY* met; the Emotions on both sides, were too great to be express'd, tho' the Pain *CURALIO* felt (for such is his Name) was somewhat alleviated by a genteel Salute, with which the glowings of her Cheek and Heart kept equal Pace. For tho' *ORONTUS* always Descended in a *Golden-Shower,* the Youth and Beauty of *CURALIO,*

---

1 A "key" published with a second edition identifies Orontus as "Lord B—".
2 A slang shortening of "plenipotentiary."

scarcely arriv'd at Manhood, appear'd to her like another *Adonis,* (as she had often declar'd before this Meeting) and was the sole Object of her Wishes.[1]

CURALIO made many Proposals, but she refus'd all Offers except that of a signal for an Assignation; no sooner was the Time and Place appointed, but she appear'd flush'd with Pleasure.

The God of Love sat Basking in her Eyes,
Resolv'd like Venus to obtain the Prize.

Thus looking, thus wishing, each went a different way; *CULALIO* to his restless pillow, and the *Blood-Warm'd-Fair,* to the wither'd *ORONTUS.*

But e'er Three Suns had roll'd, Affairs of State requir'd the Attendance of the *Sage Adviser: ORONTUS* high in the favour of his *Royal Mistress* posted for *Windsor,* where, in *Debate,* we'll leave Him.

Fortune being thus propitious, a Messenger was instantly dispatched to *CURALIO,* with the Joyful News of the Departure of *ORONTUS,* and that He would be at least Ten Days Absent. *CURALIO,* like Lightening, flew to his most *Adorable Fair;* and by her Contrivance (Females being ever most expert in *Love Affairs*) hasted with an appointed Guide to the intended Scene of *Consummation.* Three Days had they been Fortune's Favourites, and on the Fourth, the same Guide, who had been the Conductor of *CURALIO,* brought News of *ORONTUS's* Return. The Messenger was in the greatest Consternation as well as the *Happy Pair,* tho' to their great Satisfaction, they were assured, that *ORONTUS* was dispatched to the *Secretary's-Office,* where the Importance of the Affair he was entrusted with, would detain Him some Hours; by which means the *Lovers* had the Opportunity to make another Assignation, and to part in the most Agreeable manner, *CURALIO* to his own House; and the well-pleased *SALLY* to her Apartment in *York-Buildings.* Every hand was employ'd to put Things in a suitable Decorum, for the Reception of *ORONTUS,* who was every Minute expected, and in a few Hours arrived. Upon the first sight of Him *SALLY* very artfully began to bemoan his Absence, seemed Transported with his Return, and the Peer immediately made *Politicks* give way to the *God of Love,* repeating these Lines of my Lord *Rochester.*

Cupid *and* Bacchus *my* Saints *are,*
May Drink and Love still reign;
With Wine *I wash away my* Care,
And then to Love again.[2]

---

1   The key identifies Curalio as "Lord H—g—k." Zeus descended to Danae in a golden shower, which Walker uses here to suggest the generosity of Orontus.
2   John Wilmot, Earl of Rochester, "Upon his Drinking a Bowl." The original last line reads "And then to cunt again." See David M. Veith, ed., *The Complete Poems of John Wilmot, Earl of Rochester* (New Haven: Yale UP, 1968), 53.

Happy *ORONTUS!* and yet more happy *SALLY!* whose late *Stollen Pleasures* with *CURALIO,* were as *Successful* as they had been delicious, and whose *Joys* as yet, knew no *Interruption.* But *Decency,* for a while, requiring me to withdraw; I will now entertain the Reader, with an Account of *SALLY's Religion,* as communicated to me by *RENATO.*

CHAPTER III.
Of Her RELIGION, and POLITICKS.

SIR,

FEARING lest your other Correspondents should neglect making a Diligent inquiry into the *Principles* of *Religion,* which possess the Mind of our *Modern Heroine,* I conceive it my Duty, out of the Love I bear to Truth, (*Truth* being the most material Thing which ought to be regarded in *History*) to give you the justest Account, that I have been able to collect.

Her Parents educated her according to the Doctrine of the *Church* of *England,* as it is taught in the General, *viz.* to *protest against the Pope and Popery,* which she most Religiously practiced 'till she enter'd the 22d Year of her Age; when an Accident brought her into the Company of a Couple of *Clergymen,* disguised in *Secular Habits,* The one was a Venerable Old Nonjuror,[1] the other, the Reverend Dr...... Dean of — the good Matron who kept the House was perfectly well acquainted with them both, and privately told *SALLY* who they were; her little Breast immediately burnt with a Desire, (as she Phras'd it) of *throwing in a* Bone *for* them *to* pick. She put on a grave Countenance, and with an Air of sincerity told them, she had for some time been perplex'd with a scruple, concerning a Relation of hers, who had lately taken the Oaths for a Benefice in the Country of £75 *per Annum,* after his having refused them for Sixteen or Seventeen Years; The Gentlemen seem'd equally surprised at this unexpected Attack, they cast an Eye at each other for some time, with Looks which discover'd much disorder of Mind, and after about Nine Minutes of Silence, the *Dean* ask'd her, *Why her Relation's having taken the Oaths, to the QUEEN his Lawful Sovereign, should cause scruples to·a rise in her Mind?* The words *Lawful Sovereign,* Cut the Nonjurer to the very Soul, he could no longer conceal his Resentment, but with the usual *heat* of *Party* charged the *Dean:* The *Dean* being of the safest Side, answer'd him as *warmly,* to which the Nonjuror as *briskly* Reply'd: But I think it not to my purpose to give the particulars of their Argument, it is sufficient to let you know that the next Morning *SALLY* declar'd *she was of the* ORTHODOX CHURCH *of* ENGLAND, *as it stood before the* REVOLUTION, nor do I think it needful to Inquire whether her *Conversion,* came from the force of the *Nonjuror's* Argument, the *Strength* of his

---

1 Clergy who refused to take the oath of allegiance to William and Mary after the deposition of James II in the Glorious Revolution of 1688, thus remaining loyal to the Stuarts.

Back, or the *Depth* of his *Purse;* but a *Convert* it seems she was, and for a Month after there was no keeping Mrs. *Malapert* Company in Peace, she was eternally putting forth her Impertinent Interrogatories; such as *Who Murdered the* KING *I pray?*[1] *What right had* Oliver Cromwell *to do as he did?* Nay, sometimes she would bring out a Word something like *Abdication,* in this manner, *Yes, yes,* ABDILLICATION *was of great use to you, etc.*[2] In short by all the Accounts that I have been able to gather, Her Conversion was *sincere,* and her *Sentiments* remain as *firm* as a *Rock:* 'Tis true, there are some that take the Liberty of saying, she has frequently *waver'd,* sometimes, towards *Popery,* at other times towards *Presbytery;* but there are none so hardy as to say positively she has been totally Changed. Therefore I desire, she may be Recorded according to her own Account, *A* Member *of the* Orthodox-Church *of* England, *as it stood before the* REVOLUTION.

I am,

SIR,

Your most obliged Servant

RENATO. Jan. 12. 1722/3

CHAPTER IV.

Containing, The New-Market *Progress; The* Adventure *of Baron F—,etc.*

LETTER I.

IN the Year 1713, the late Earl of *G*—, Memorable for nothing more than his great Love of fine Horses, and Whores, and Aversion to Honest Women, going to the Meeting at *New-Market,* took with him in his chariot *Sally Salisbury,* and another Harlot, named *D*—*y,* upon whose Laps for want of room on the Seat, he rode all they way thither; one of which he called his *Black,* the other his *Fair Cat.* For the Favours of their Company his Lordship promised, and they expected, very bountiful Presents, but losing all his Matches, and the rest of his Money at Play, he could not perform his Promises, which so enraged the *Viragoes,* that one Evening, his Lordship coming home very Drunk, they put him to Bed, but instead of going to him, as they were wont, they ty'd him therein, then beat and scratch'd him unmercifully, and afterwards rifled him of his Gold-Watch, Diamond-Buttons, Gold-Buckles, Sword-Hilt, and all other Valuable Moveables which having done, and lock'd him in, they went a Caterwauling to other Cullies to whom they told (and made a Jest of) the Story: With these they staid till Three a Clock next Morning, when a Stage-Coach going through the Town, they took Places and went to *London,*

---

1   Charles I, executed in 1649.
2   James II, the Catholic brother of Charles II, was forced from the throne in 1688-89 in the "Glorious Revolution," which began the rule of William and Mary. Parliament declared that he abdicated.   /

with what they had got of these Cullies, and by plundering his Lordship, who knew nothing of his Loss 'till the next Morning, though it was before that time the Talk and Jest of the whole Town, and his *Cats* got too far to be over-taken.

To Captain WALKER,
SIR, The above is matter of Fact, and if put in a proper Stile may deserve a place in the Memoirs; for which purpose 'tis Communicated to you by your unknown Friend

J.S.

Jan. 7. 1722/3.

LETTER II.
SIR,
SINCE I saw your last Advertisement, wherein you desired the Continuance of my Correspondence,[1] I have taken the Pains to enquire into a Story, which when told, I believ'd to be Romantick; but finding the material part to be Matter of Fact, I shall, to oblige you, Pen it: 'Tis too long for the spare time I've upon my Hands at present, so shall bring or send it to Mr. *Jones* to Night, or to Morrow, and hope 'twill be acceptable to you, and Diverting to your Readers. I shall endeavour to meet you next Week, but cannot yet appoint the Time,
Who am your humble Servant
J.S.

To Captain Walker, Jan. 15.
1722/3, *Friday* 3 o'Clock

LETTER III.
SIR,
'TWAS not my Design to have troubled you any farther, but you having desir'd I would continue my Correspondence (such as it is, is at your Service.)
   This therefore acquaints you that soon after your Advertisement (wherein you acknowledg'd the receipt of my first Letter) was publish'd, a merry Friend and I meeting accidentally, he thus accosted me, D—n it *Jack*, the Sight of your ill-natur'd Phiz,[2] puts me in mind of an Advertisement I've seen of a Captain's who designs to Oblige the Town with the Memoirs of *Sally Salisbury*, and the Initial Letters of your Name being therein mention'd, I dare venture my Soul to a Dish of Coffee, that the Letter mention'd, which he assures shall be inserted, is the History of her *New-Market Progress*, which you

1 Walker advertised in newspapers to collect anecdotes.
2 Face.

in a fit of the Spleen have pen'd and sent: Could I sit down to write, I could send him a Story of her, which might, if he wanted matter, help to fill up his Memoirs, but as that can't be the Case, and I am too Volatile to sit still a Minute, I'll relate it to you *En passant,* and you may communicate it to the Captain if you think fit. I desir'd him to proceed, which he did *viz.*

Antoine Baron *de F—g,* being a Younger Son of a Noble Family in — was Educated in a College of *Jesuits,* and design'd for an Ecclesiastick; but that Life not agreeing with him, he quitted the College, by which he disoblig'd his Friends, and being reduc'd to great Straits, to raise some Money, he wrote a Book against that *Fraternity,* which had the desir'd Effect; but it so exasperated their Order, that, to avoid their Fury, he found himself oblig'd to quit his Country, and getting into *Spain,* serv'd as a Volunteer under King *CHARLES,* till in an Engagement he receiv'd a Musket-Ball through the Body, but recovering, was rewarded with a Commission, which he held till the Wars were at an end; when not daring to stay in that, or any other neighbouring bigotted Country, he came to *England.* Long he had not been here, before he had a desire to Engage in the Field of Love with an *English* Woman; and by a Servant or Interpreter he hired, had the Damn'd ill Luck to be introduc'd to the Heroine of the History, or Memoirs now going to be publish'd, wonderfully was he pleased with her Person, Carriage, and Embraces, and accordingly rewarded her; but in Five Days he found himself in such a Condition, as gave him occasion to Curse their *Rencontre,* and imploy a Surgeon: Long did he endeavour to meet her again, not to engage her Amorously as before, but to Chastise her, at length he happen'd a *Revoir son Enemi,*[1] (but the Cure being effected, and the plague and thoughts of Physic over) he before he made the Onset, thus (by his Interpreter) began to parley, "You Damn'd Confounded Pocky Whore, I am glad we are met, for now will I give you as many Stripes as I've taken Pills, Bolus's, and other Hellish Slip-slops on your account," then with Cane, uplifted, going to Strike, the Cunning Jilt Clasped him and his Battoon in her Arms, and feigning a Cry, thus spoke, "Dear Sir, hear me, and hear me out, and then I'm sure instead of beating, you'll not only pardon but pity me." Her sham Tears moved the Baron, who then reply'd, "Well, let me go, speak on, I'll hear you;" when both sitting down, she thus proceeded, "You must know, Dear Sir, that I, unhappy Creature, am the unfortunate Offspring of a good Family; but my Father, being an extravagant Man, spent his Estate, dy'd and left me Destitute, Pennyless, and almost distracted, not knowing which way I should be supported; for my Education was such, as had not qualified me any way to get a Living; sometimes I had thoughts to get into Service, out of the sight of those that knew my Birth, and to continue as I then was, Chaste and Honest; but too soon, alas! those Thoughts vanish'd, and I found my Spirit too high for Servitude, at other times (knowing the *Catholicks*

---

1   To meet again his enemy.

were Conspicuous for Charity, especially to Converts) I had Thoughts to turn *Roman*, profess my self inclin'd to a *Religious Life*, and hoped to obtain Letters of Recommendation, and thereby admission into some *Convent* Abroad, but reflecting that that would be a work of Time, and upon serious examination of my self, finding I had not *a bit of* Nun's *Flesh about me*, I laid aside that design; about that time a Man of Quality liking my Person, and believing my Circumstances would make the Conquest easy, laid Siege to me, attack'd me with Gold and Rhetorick, which (I not knowing what else to do) soon made me beat the *Chamade*,[1] and Surrender up *Fort Virgin*, on Condition that he should hold Possession, allowing me an Annual Stipend. He is too enterprising a Warrior that way, and happening not long since to Storm a *Rotten Fort*, I soon suffer'd by his Misfortune, and you (unknown to me then) by mine; thus, Sir, have you heard the Truth, which I hope will move you to Pardon and Pity, which if you grant, to make amends to a Gentleman I adore, and unwittingly injur'd, I (being perfectly recover'd) offer and hope you'll accept the use of my Person now, and whenever you please, *gratis*, which I do assure you, I shall esteem as the greatest happiness." The Credulous Baron thus mollifyed, first kindly embrac'd her, and then instead of a *Wooden*, made use of his *Carnal-Weapon*, which being over, and a Supper providing at his Expence, the Designing Jade (resolving Revenge, for his having put her in bodily fear) thus began a fresh Discourse, "My dearest Baron, I'm so Enamour'd with your Person and Embraces, that (as you are a Foreigner) the fears of your leaving *England*, are to me an uneasiness, and I should account it my greatest Happiness were I assur'd of your stay, that I might oft Enjoy you, were you inclin'd that way: I could, nay would (on Condition, that it might be no hindrance to the having my Joys with you oft very oft reiterated) propose a means to keep you here, if your taking to Wife an *English* Woman of good Extraction, with Beauty and Fortune enough to make you live in Ease and Plenty would do it." "*Speak, Speak on my Charmer,*" says the Baron, in an Extasy (who doubtless wanted,[2] and thereby hoped to mend his Fortune) "*and I'll do as you shall advise, esteem my self infinitely happy, and promise never to leave your Country, nor your dear self.*" "Know then (*says she*) that there is a certain young Lady, who, to avoid being obliged (by the Force or Entreaty of her Father) to Marry a disagreeable Person is fled from him, and is *incog.* where few besides my self have access to her: She is a Virgin about Seventeen, and not suspecting I am otherwise, puts great Confidence in me; she has in her Possession Jewels, etc. to a Considerable Value, and £12000 left her by a Relation, which nobody can hinder her of, at the Age of 21, or Day of Marriage, she is Amorous, and Ambitiously inclin'd, and I am of Opinion, a Man of your Mien and Quality might easily gain her Person and Fortune, in which I will assist you to the

1   "A signal by beat of drum or sound of trumpet inviting to a parley." [OED]
2   Lacked.

utmost, and when you think fit will introduce you to her; as you speak *French*, which she does not at all understand, I will pretend to do so too, and to interpret between you, Let your Gesture be but Amorous enough, and leave the rest to me." This being agreed to be put in Execution next Night, 'tis now proper to inform you, that the sham Fortune was Daughter to a Gardiner, and Apprentice to an Embroiderer, from whose Service *SALLY* had inticed her, and Sold her Maidenhead to my Lord—. The Girl thus debauch'd, and made fit for the Game, got her self Rigg'd handsomely by *SALLY's* Tallyman, but not keeping up to her Weekly-payments, was at that time obliged to abscond, for fear of being Arrested, and in this her Retirement, the unfortunate Baron was introduc'd, and *SALLY* so managed matters, that at the third Visit they were privately marryed, the Wedding Night being over, *SALLY*, to compleat her Revenge, advised the Tallyman to Arrest the Bridegroom, which (as he was going to demand his Wife's Fortune, and before Honey-Moon was over) was done,[1] the Bayliffs kept him in their Custody, whilst his Money and Moveables lasted, then put him into *Newgate*, from whence by Contribution he got removed to the *Fleet*, and there lay in a Starving Condition, till by Virtue of the last *Act of Insolvency* he was discharg'd; he was a perfect Master of the *Greek, Latin, German, French, Italian* and *Spanish* Tongues; and having learnt tollerable *English* in Prison, he became qualified for, and is now an Interpreter about this Town, to any Foreigner that will imploy him, and by this (because for the Reasons above, he dare not go home) *He* gets his Livelihood at *Court*, and the *Baronness* hers in the *Hundreds of Drury*.[2]

I am Sir, Your
Friend and Servant unknown
          J.S.

LETTER IV.

SIR,

IF you think it worth your while, to Insert the following short Tale, in the Life of the Famous Mrs. *Sarah Salisbury*, 'tis at your Service, and *Probatum est.*

A certain Comedian, in his Days of Pleasure, having been acquainted with the aforesaid *Heroine*, found his Amour unfortunately attended by a *Clap*,[3] in return of which, he took an Opportunity, upon the Stage, of saying somewhat, that almost, as bitterly stung her Ladyship, and the Eyes of the whole Audience were immediately fix'd on her; not long after, they met at the Masquerade, where, with great Scorn, she flung from him, and, in the Saucy Tone

---

1 By law, husbands were responsible for the debts of their wives.
2 As a prostitute.
3 Venereal disease.

of a fine Lady, called him *Player!* he reply'd, *our Professions, Madam, are very like one another, any one may see the best we can do for Half a Crown.*[1]

I am, Sir,

Your humble Servant

N.P.

CHAPTER V.
Of her DANCING for a SMOCK at the BATH, & c.

SIR,

IN my first Letter I promis'd you some Facts, relating to (our at present unfortunate) *SALLY,* which happen'd to her in the gayer Seasons of Life, when she revell'd at large among Mankind, and made greater Captives in the wide World, than she her self is now, in the narrow Walls of a Solitary Prison, and I am now going to be as good as my Word.

The Common Town-talk of her Crying *News-Papers,* Selling *Oranges,* and many other Things of the like kind, in the way of *Low-Life,* may be learn'd in every particular Article, from the Mouths of all the Good-Natur'd Females of her standing, within the extensive Liberty of the *Hundreds* of *Drury,* and is quite foreign to my present Purpose; I shall therefore begin with a Relation that made her first talk'd of, with agreeable Pleasure by the better sort, and that is contain'd in the Story of her *Dancing* for a *Smock* at the *Bath.*

Indeed this little Fragment of diverting History is pretty generally known; but it is however very seldom related with that Truth and Justice, which ought to attend such an important part of her Life, as first plac'd her in a distinguish'd point of Sight, at that most remarkable and most remarking Place, which is more publick than any Town or even City in all *England,* (I except not our dear wicked *Metropolis* it self) and therefore I shall lay before you this observable Adventure inside out, exactly as it happen'd.

Proclamation (you must know) was made in very Solemn manner and Form, by beat of Drum and sound of Trumpet, that a *fine Holland Smock,* richly trimm'd at the Bosom and Sleeves, with *Mochlin-Lace,* was to be Danced for in the Town of *Bath,* on such an appointed Day; that there were Constituted a certain Number of Nice[2] and Critical Judges of the activity of the Heels, the Air, the Attitude, the Mien, and Deportment of the whole Body; and, that the Prize was to be borne away by the happy Lass, to whom it was adjudged due by the Majority of Voices, given by the aforesaid Gentlemen so deeply Read, and so profoundly Learned in the great Science of *Podosophy.*[3]

---

1   The key identifies this comedian as "Mr. C—r" or Colley Cibber.
2   Discerning.
3   Pod=foot; sophy=wisdom; thus a word made up to mean something like "the wisdom of the feet."

Many and many Days did the alarming Drum beat, and the shrill Trumpet sound, before the *Female Trophy*, which was supported on the Top of a broken Pike, with a Cross Bar that held out the Ruffled Arms of the *Smock*, adorn'd with Ribbons, by a Man on Horseback. Every maid at every fresh Alarm flew to the Bare, their Bosoms all beat and panted with Emulation, much for the Prize, but still much more for the publick Applause of People of Distinction, that was certain to follow it; Numbers of them having promised to Honour and Felicitate the Entertainment with their Presence. Several of the Lasses could not help humming over the Tunes of the most Celebrated Rigadoons, and Minuets, and shaking their Legs to keep Time with the Musick of their Tongues, as the People pass'd, by way of prelude to a Victory.

At length the wish'd for Day appointed came, the Assembly of Spectators and Judges was Conven'd, and the Stage laid open for every Fair Pretender who had a Mind to venture Theatrically upon this Occasion.

The Scenes being drawn, Three very fine Damsels (if a finer had not unexpectedly appear'd) came to claim the Prize. One of them was very beautiful in the Face, but her Limbs were not of the exactest formation. The Second was of an agreeable make, but her Face not so agreeable, and her Mein affected. The Third had a fine Complexion, a tempting Face, with all the Bloom of Youth upon it; her Body well proportioned, but only that she was rather too Fat, to perform the Exercise she pretended to with so much Dexterity, as might be expected on such an Occasion; each of them however had their Power in this Faculty of *Dancing*, so well known to the Town, that tho' Hundreds before had resolved to try an Experiment for the Prize, yet they all laid aside their design, as soon as they heard that these *Three* Celebrated Lasses had put in for it. In fine, the Judges had named the Dances, the Musick began to Play, and while the *Three* were disputing which of them first should begin, our *SALLY* enter'd, and an universal Clap welcom'd her Approach on the Stage: She appear'd in a *Smock* as white as her Skin, and adorn'd much like that of the *Trophy*, for which she was to contend; Scarlet Ribbons bound up her Sleeves, her Petticoat was a Flower'd Damask, her Stockings Scarlet, her Shoes Laced and ty'd up with a Green String. Her Rivals ey'd their unexpected Rival with a Conscious fear of her excellence, observing that she had the Perfections of each, without having the Imperfections of any one of them. She went up to them with an Assurance of her own Power, and of her future Success, telling them that she would end the Controversy between them, and *begin* the *first* Dance, provided she might *Conclude* with the *last*. The Proposition was Confirm'd by a Second universal Clap from all the Spectators; and her Rivals, Envious as they were, and Jealous of her future Performance, consented to the Proposal.

She Danc'd, and no sooner had she ended her Part, but the *Three* other Competitors quitted the Stage, upon which the Victory was declar'd to be hers, without putting any Second Person to the Tryal, (tho' some present offered it) which was entirely partial, and contrary to the meaning of the Donor, who presented the *Smock* for the Entertainment of the Town. This Incident made her Fame Celebrated, and her Company Coveted, among some Spectators of Quality that were there, and whom she had particularly distinguish'd, for giving her more than ordinary marks of Applause. She likewise very Craftily and Subtilly remark'd those Judges, that were the most for doing her this Favour, and in Gratitude to them, sought their Company that very Night, and thought there was no way of giving them sufficient Thanks, but by granting them the *last favour*. Accordingly *two* of the Partial Judges, with whom I have the honour to be perfectly well acquainted, She, that very Night, and in the self-same Smock, gratify'd to the abundant Satisfaction of them both. To speak a little plainer in the Town Phrase, she lay between them all Night, and proved her self as well vers'd in that part of the Mathematicks, which is necessary for a Lady of Pleasure to know, as if she had studied it all the Days of her Life.

I shall now proceed to another Part of this little History.

Failing in a great measure of the vast Expectations, which she had conceived of picking up some Cully, with a Coat of Arms, and a well Lined Pocket, by means of this publick Applause, she was forced to return at her own Charge to Town, and being exhausted by the Expences of the Journey, as she was complaining of her Ill-Luck to a Fair-fellow Trafficker in Iniquity, she was very happily recommended to that useful Piece of Antiquity Mother *Wisebourn*, a Woman renown'd for her Charitable Disposition; who Commiserating the Unfortunate, took her under her protection.

But the good Matron was soon depriv'd of so inestimable a Treasure; and among Crouds of our *SALLY*'s Admirers, the Eldest Son of a certain Nobleman, slyly found means to give her an Invitation to *Gray's-Inn*, where he had taken Chambers for the Conveniency of the Sport. Thither she went, and after a little Refreshment, flew with unusual transport to his Bed, where, by the Accounts given of her by her Bedfellow, one would imagine, that she only, among her whole Sex, had the *Art of Pleasing*.

The Morning following an *Undertaker* knock'd at the Door and ask'd to speak with the Gentleman, the Servant answer'd, *He was a Sleep, and could not be Disturb'd*, the *Undertaker* told him *he must and would speak with him*. This Dispute awaked the Gentleman, and he knowing the Voice, Cried *D—n you MATT, What a P—x has brought you hither this Morning?* MATT, in a sniviling Tone answer'd, *My Lord, I am come to Condole with your Lordship, for the Loss of your Father; What a P—x* (says the Lord) *is my Father dead at last then?* With that he jump'd out of Bed, took hold of the Bed-Cloaths at the Feet, and roll'd them up to the Head, which discover'd a most beautiful pair of Legs, Thighs, and so upwards, to her very Bubbies, for the Good-natur'd Creature had pull'd her Shift up to her Arm-pits that it might be no obstacle to their Diversion, this sort of Treatment very much ruffled her Temper, she sprung up, her Hair all flowing about her Shoulders, having lost her Head-Dress in the Encounter, and with, a G—d D—n you! *You* a Lord, *You* a Pimp! Says SALLY, *to use me in this manner;* The young Peer gave her good Words, soon pacify'd her, and at length prevail'd upon her to get up, and take a Bottle with him and *MATT*, for says he, *this* MATT *is the honestest Fellow in the World, and by G—d he shall Bury my Father.* MATT continued bowing and cringing, reply'd, *I am greatly oblig'd to your Honour, I am very thankful to your Lordship,* 'till they had guzzled down Three or Four Bottles by way of Whet, the Wine had sufficiently warm'd *SALLY*, and, all of a sudden, she flew at the Poor *Undertaker*, hit him an unmerciful Box on the Ear, *D—n you*, said she, *for a Whining Carrion-hunting Son of a Bitch! What do you come to trouble us with your Cant for, and be D—d to you? Go mind your Insensible Flesh, and leave my Friend and me to enjoy our selves!* MATT immediately took his Leave of the Nobleman, and only stop'd short at the Door, to tell my Lord he would go take Measure of the Corpse, and so march'd off.

There goes another Story of her, and her Footman, 'tis short, and I think it deserves a Place; it is as follows, As a Gentleman was conducting her out of her Lodgings into a Coach, her Garter happen'd to unty, upon which she faced about to her Lackey, who was following her, pull'd up her Petti-coats, and exposing her well-shap'd Leg, etc. to his View, she ty'd on her Garter; when perceiving some uncommon Heavings and Agitations in the Wonder-struck fellow, she said to him, *D—n you for a Rascal! It is SO and SO with you? If it be, take that, and go to a Whore;* and at the same time gave him a Crown.

Our *SALLY* having thus, by the Acquaintance of these Noblemen, enrich'd her self, and being grown a brighter Figure in Life, resolv'd now to visit the *BATH*, in a very different manner from that in which she appear'd there at first: She then courted their Favours, but her Design was now, that they should court hers, etc., in effect the Event answer'd the Intention. A certain GARTER[1] pursued her, and address'd her with all the Fervour with which a Youth in Love would sue the Mistress of his Desires, to become the Wife of his Bosom: He begg'd, he beseech'd, supplicated and implor'd; but all in vain. When he found that no Intreaties could prevail upon her, for she with Whorish-Politicks, was as shy, and kept her self at as great a Distance as if she had been an unspotted Virgin. This unlook'd for Coyness, and Resistance, brought him to Address her in higher Terms, hint-ing to her the Advantages of submitting to the Will of a Person of his Dig-nity; upon which she reply'd: *D—n you, my Lord! Do you think this Yard or two of Ribbon can bind me to you? The very Foundress of your Order*[2] *bore no other Title, than what is my Common Name; 'Twas from a Garter slipping from her Leg, which*

---

1   In this context, a member of the highest order of English knighthood.
2   Joan, *Countess of* Salisbury [author's note].

a Mighty[1] King was proud to snatch up, that you derive the Might Distance you pretend there is between us: If I am less Beautiful than my Name-Sake, Why should you pursue me with so much Ardour? And if my Charms are equal to hers, Why should you talk of Distance; in regard to that Beauty, for which a King instituted the Order, from whence you derive this Honour? His Grace at last convinced by this, that he could not overcome her by any meer verbal Argument, drew out a more powerful one from his Pocket, and throwing it into her Lap (just as *Jove* descended in a Shower of Gold upon *Danae*) made way for himself to a closer Admittance there. In fine, the Nymph receiv'd the Gold, and she receiv'd the Man; and she receiv'd more Gold, and still receiv'd the Man; but when no more Gold was left, she would no more receive the Man. Gall'd and vex'd at this, the Peer said, in Company of some Gentlemen, whom he took to be all men of Honour, *That* SALLY SALISBURY, *being a Woman of an Infamous Character; ought not to be admitted into the Publick-Room among so many Ladies of Quality, Honor and Reputation, and still much less into their Private Assemblée.* One of the Gentlemen in the Company, who had not so much Honour, as the Duke imagin'd, reported to *SALLY* his Grace's Invectives against her.

The Night following the *Star[2]* no sooner appear'd, but *SALLY*, with her accustomed Freedom, paid him the usual Compliments, and assur'd his Grace, *That, if she was not intirely convinced of his Grace's good Intentions towards her; a Story, which had been industriously handed about, would much afflict her, for you are to know, my Lord,* said she, *Here is a set of Evil-minded, Ill-designing People, who would have the World believe, that there is not so good an Understanding between me and your Grace as there really is,* The Duke reply'd, He was confident he never said any thing to her Disadvantage; upon which *SALLY* rejoin'd, *My Lord, I am willing to believe as much, for I always thought you a Person of too much Gratitude to say any thing to the Prejudice of a Woman, from whom you have receiv'd so many Favours.* To this, said the Duke, whispering, *You argue very justly,* SALLY; *I would not, nay, I could not use thee so roughly, whom I have used so tenderly!* But *SALLY* did not answer him in Whispers; She spoke fairly and openly to him, in the Hearing of the whole Assemblée, in the Publick Room, in these Words; *Nay, good my Lord,* (clapping her Hand upon his Shoulder) *I do not insist upon it, That you did not meerly forbear saying so out of Good-Nature, but I know you to be a Man of too much Policy, Policy I say, my Lord; your Lordship perfectly well knowing,*

---

1 Edward the 3rd[author's note]. According to the *OED*, "By the time of Selden (1614) it was traditionally asserted that the garter was that of the Countess of Salisbury, which fell off while she danced with the King, who picked it up and tied it on his own leg, saying to those present *Honi soit qui mal y pense.* The Garter as the badge of the Order is a ribbon of dark-blue velvet, edged and buckled with gold, and bearing the above words embroidered in gold, and is worn below the left knee; garters also form part of the ornament of the collar worn by the Knights."

2 The "star" was, like the garter, a sign of rank and honor.

That you can no way reflect upon my Reputation, without casting an equal Odium upon the Memory of your own Mother: Nay farther, my Lord; If you stand upon Distinction, you know your Father got you a Half-Brother, of equal Dignity every way to your self, by a Woman of as Low Degree, but equal in Beauty with my self. His Grace intreated her to be silent, and clapt a Purse into her Hand, full as weighty as that which he gave for her last favour; thus this Scene concluded, and with it I conclude my Letter.

Yours, & c.
RENATO

LETTER V
SIR,
A Certain *Beau* being one Evening at Mrs. *SALISBURY*'s Lodgings, had not been there long, before a *Halfpay Officer* also came thither; their unlucky Meeting occasioned great Disputes, both insisted on a Right to enjoy her for that Night; the Beau, as first Comer, pleaded, that Priority, Person and good Manners entitled him to the Preference; the Officer insisted, that Honour, Wounds, Scars and former Acquaintance gave it him: *Sally* observing that such Cavilling might deprive her of both the Cullies (and some body at that time knocking at the Door) propos'd the Decision might be left to that Person whoever it was, to whom she would recite the Difference, and they should sit silent: This being agreed to, and the Gentleman introduced, it happened to be a Poet[1] who had mistaken her's for another House; to him she recited their Dispute, which having ended, the Poet called for Pen, Ink and Paper, and hoping to find his Account in giving Preference to the *Beau,* and complimenting the *Belle,* he wrote the following *Epigram,* the Publication of which, in *SALLY*'s Memoirs will oblige

Yours unknown,
PHILO-MUSIS.

B E A U T Y
More Powerful than
W A R

I.
Let Braves who to the Army go,
  Their Courage boast no more,
At Home we greater Danger know,
  From Beauty's fatal Power.

---

1   The key identifies this poet as "Mr. P—r" or Matthew Prior (1664-1721), poet and diplomat. Friend to Pope and Swift, Prior published *Poems on Several Occasions* (1707), *A Second Collection of Poems on Several Occasions* (1716), and other works.

II.

More Deaths fly from fair Sally's *Eyes,*
  Than Conqu'ring Foes can give
In War, but One, of many, dies,
  Here, only One, can live.

LETTER VI.
SIR,

AN amorous Friend of mine, Poetically given, being captivated by the celebrated *Sally Salisbury*, wrote (on her) the following Stanzas, which being read
to me, I found I could not be easy till I had seen the Person on whom they
were so handsome an Encomium. I immediately went about it, and met with
but very little Trouble to get into her Company, and much less to get into her
Carcass; and tho' I soon after found, that the venomous Virago had given me
Reason to curse my Curiosity, yet as I can and do freely forgive her, I know
you can and will be so impartial, as to give these Lines a Place in her Memoirs, and you'll oblige
        Your humble Servant

        Forget and Forgive
  Soon as Phoebus *sheds his Beams,*
  On the Hills and Purling Streams,
  The Stars the feeble Night resign,
  Nor CYNTHIA's *self can longer shine,*
  But does her borrow'd Power resign.
  So to your superior Sway,
  Other Beauties all give way:
  A like Regard to both *we shew,*
  He *rules above and* You *below.*

LETTER VII.
SIR,

IN my Juvenile Years I was captivated by the fatal Charms of (that since celebrated Courtezan) *SALLY SALISBURY:* Our Conversation was of some Continuance, but ended, as that of all her other Admirers will do, with the *Defi-
ciency of the Purse;* tho' I must ingenuously acknowledge the chief Motive of my
leaving her was the Present of a *New-Year's*-Gift she made me;[1] but whether
French or *Neopolitan*, I leave to the Determination of the Sons of *Galen.* Yet
notwithstanding all her Accomplishments, about the Year 1713, a certain
Nobleman, among others, was *snar'd* in the same *Ginn;* and if Fame may be
credited, still continues her Admirer. By the Sheets you have sent me to

---

1 That is, she gave him a venereal disease.

peruse, the Account you have given of her Birth and Parentage is pretty exact, tho' Part of her Education is omitted, which was in *Tothill-Fields-Bridewell,* and the Cause this.

SALLY, tho' now engross'd by those of a superior Rank, is yet as common as any of the Sisterhood, who ply in the Hundreds of *Drury;* tho' some have tax'd her with Ingratitude to Mother *Wisebourn,* I can assure you of the contrary, for she hardly let a Week pass without making the Lady *Abbess* and her Nuns a Visit, to regale with a Cup of burnt Brandy. At one of these Nocturnal Festivals your Humble Servant being one of the Company, was alarm'd by those *Religious Officers,* the *Informing Constables,* who decently conducted the whole Clan to a *Westminster* Justice of the Peace.[1] The Rumour of this, soon reach'd the Ears of her pious Parents (for her Mother has been often heard to say that she would not upon any Score be a partaker of the Wages of Sin, tho' it is well known she has frequently stripp'd her Children of rich Silks, to make them appear humble in mean Stuffs) they soon appear'd in her behalf before the Magistrate; but his Worship, who had still a Colt's-Tooth in his Head, cast an amorous Leer upon *SALLY*; and, notwithstanding her Mother's canting Excuses told her she was an impudent Woman to lay Claim to such a Daughter, for that it was plain by her Appearance, Air and Gesture, she must undoubtedly have sprung from the Loins of some Man of Quality, who had given her a piece of Money for taking Care of her. Let me view her again, *says the Justice,* calling for his Spectacles, and at the same time gave her a gentle Squeeze by the hand: *Sally,* as she told me herself, was in hopes of rivaling his Worship's Female-Clerk, but the Informers strictly insisting upon her Character, and the infamous Place she was taken in, old *Limberham,*[2] sore against his Inclination, was obliged to commit her to *Tothillfields* Bridewell, but sent a private Order, that she should not by any Means undergo the Discipline of the House, he having a Design to correct her himself in private. Encouraged by his Worship's Treatment, *Sally* whenever she was insulted by her Mother, would damn her with an Air, call her old Bitch, and let her know she had Authority to tell her she was no ways related to her. At some lucid Intervals indeed your *Heroine* would seem very Dutiful, Loving and Condescending, but these uncommon Qualities in her, were intirely owing to her interested and mercenary Disposition; for many a Guinea has *Sally* got by the kind Concessions of her Mother, who would readily fetch her from her Lodgings to Mrs. *Wisebourn's* or any where else, to earn that Sum; or even a Crown rather than fail. These important Services as well as her Maternal Tenderness to cause Abortion whenever she found her to be with Child, which sad Mishap always put them both into most terrible Apprehensions of spoiling their

---

1   Probably a member of one of the Societies for the Reformation of Manners, a group of vigilante moral reformers who regularly rounded up suspected prostitutes and brought them before magistrates for punishment.
2   Reference to a foolish old keeper in John Dryden's play, *The Kind Keeper* (1680).

future Market, ought never to be forgot, though the good old Woman's concern for the Breed was so exceedingly affectionate, that she always preserved the *Embrios* in Spirits: Nor was the Father, as far as his Capacity would reach, a whit the less Serviceable, who being, as you have rightly observ'd, a Military *Faggot*,[1] and a Soldier's Coat carrying a sort of a Terror with it, was frequently sent for to Mother *Wisebourn's*, to frighten and bully young timorous Cullies into a Compliance with her exorbitant Demands, and who were not willing to part with their Gold after Favours received: He was likewise a necessary Utensil at quelling Disturbances, which at such Houses would commonly arise among his Daughter's Sparks, contending who should have most Share of her good Graces.

What you hinted to me about robbing her Landlord, when she lodg'd at a Brandy-Shop in *New-Street* near *Covent-Garden,* is true History. For this Fact she was seized, and brought before Justice S—s, who at first refus'd, but at length admitted her to Bail, and this Affair was made up in a Pecuniary-way before the approaching Sessions.

I shall conclude what the present Time permits me to communicate, with the Origin of her Travelling Name of *SALISBURY;* a Tyre-Woman[2] upon cutting her Hair told her (as she relates it) that had she not just before seen the Countess of *SALISBURY* pass by, she should have taken her for her Ladyship; *SALLY* being extreamly well pleased with this Compliment, and recollecting the Words which the amorous old Magistrate had said to her Mother, had the Vanity to fancy, that from that imaginary Resemblance, she was sufficiently intitled to assume the real *NAME.*

> *I am Sir,*
>> *Your unfeigned Friend,*
>> *And humble Servant*
>> POLYDOR.

CHAPTER VI.
The Adventures of the Grave Signor GAMBOLINI,[3]
and the very Merry BELLE CHUCK.

SIR,

IN the Reign of her late Majesty Queen *ANNE,* the Gentleman well known by the name of *Gambolini,* fill'd one of the most considerable Posts under her Administration and stood high in the Favour of his Royal Mistress. Indeed Men and Women of all Ranks had a value for him, but whether the Esteem of

---

1 Stick.

2 "A woman who assists at a lady's toilet; a lady's maid; also, a woman employed in the making or sale of women's clothing; a dressmaker, costumier." [OED]

3 The key identifies Signor Gambolini as Lord B—k—e; that is, Henry St. John, Viscount Bolingbroke.

these was more properly occasioned by the ardent Passion he was reputed to have for the *Fair Sex,* or the Admiration of *those* for the profound Depth of his *Politicks,* I am not able to determine; but this much is generally allow'd on all Hands, that no Minister was ever more *adroit* in dispatching the *Affairs of the Publick,* or made a more amiable Figure in the *Drawing Room.* A late severe Writer[1] tells us, that Signor *Gambolini,* was, "A most profligate Debauchee, and that one Evening he was observ'd to pass secretly from an Apartment in the Palace where his Office was kept, to an House of Infamy; and there with two stale Prostitutes, the Leavings of a Frouzy Jew, he spent the whole Night in Riot and Debauchery; while his abused Wife and Family thought him waking about the Publick Cares, and busied in Affairs of the highest Importance to the State. It happen'd that when he was at this most elegant Retirement, the Envoy of a Neighboring Prince Sent some Dispatches to him, to be immediately communicated to the King. *Gambolini* heard nothing of either the Envoy, or the Dispatches. In vain the Messengers flew about the Town to find out this most indefatigable Minister. The Dispatches were laid by unseal'd, and *Gambolini,* thoroughly tired with the Labour of the Night, was put to Bed to the two Prostitutes, with whom he slept away the next Day; while the Envoy, impatient to see himself thus neglected, publish'd the Contents of the Dispatches to the World; who by this Means, saw them before either *He,* or his *Sovereign.*"

Thus is *Gambolini* drawn as a *Lover;* let us now survey him as a *Wit* and a *Politician* in which last Capacity another Satyrist declares, that *he was the smartest Fellow of his Time;*[2] and, continues he, "*Gambolini* is a lusty young Rogue, pamper'd with four Bottles at Night, and clean Diet, which makes him prone to *Carnality.*—He is of a Mercurial Disposition, and his Wit goes off smart and with a Jerk.—*And after his Death he assures us,* '*That* the Dissection of his *Abdomen* will be of general Entertainment: His Brains will be found situated at the Head of the *Os Pubis:* His Animal Spirits acting more vigorously in that Part, than in the Upper Region. I beg, says he, his Body may not be mangled; but that the Executive Part of it may be consecrated to *Priapus.*' Such a Power had *Gambolini* over the Hearts of the *Fair-Sex,* that the same Author affirms, it was, "Every Day demonstrated by the young Wenches, handing up to him *Billet Doux* in their Gloves and Handkerchiefs."—It is no Wonder then, that he was in Pursuit of all fresh Game that was started. Thus upon the first Notice, he rous'd *SALLY* from the same Form, where *Orontes* had found her lodged, upon which the grave Senator, having private Intelligence, immediately dispatch'd a *Female-Steward,* who paid the Lady Abbess, Mrs. *Wisebourn,*

---

1 See *Court Tales,* pag. 2. *printed 1720.* [author's note] *Court Tales; Or, A History of the Amours of the Present Nobility. To which is added a compleat key* (London, 1717). A second edition was published in 1732.

2 *The High German,* DOCTOR. Vol. I. pag 9, 10. [author's note] *The High-German Doctor, with many Additions and Alterations* was published in London in 1715.

140 Guineas for her Redemption, and sent her under Guard to *Kensington,* as already related.

But it was not long before *Gambolini* obtain'd an Interview with *SALLY,* and for three Nights Lodging, gave her three Fifty-Pound *Bank-Notes,* adding, that *He would Glut the B—h with Money, could he secure her to his Embraces only.* Tho' *SALLY* fairly gave him to understand, that such Sums were but mere Trifles, in her elegant way of Life.

Shortly after, upon more *weighty* Considerations, *Gambolini* carry'd off the Prize to his own House, where, no doubt, he thought himself secure for a Time; but *SALLY,* who could bear no Rival, finding by one of the Servants his Love of Variety, and that he had another Mistress under the same Roof, at Night when he came to pay his Adoration to her, as the only Object of his Vows, she, as the Saying is, *rid very Rusty;* flew from his detested Embraces, and leapt out of a Window in her Smock; this alarm'd the whole Family; and *SALLY,* in making her Escape, meeting *Gambolini's* Lady upon the Stair-Case, related the Story of his Attempt upon her, acquainted her Ladyship, that there was a lewd Woman in the *Signor's* Apartment, and that, unless speedy Care was taken, the *Marriage Bed* was in a fair way of being *defiled.*

The good Lady, out of her Compassionate Tenderness, tho' she had some Suspicion of *SALLY's* Virtue, conducted her to her own Apartment, gave her the best Advice, equipt her for her Departure, sent for her own Chairmen, and order'd them to attend *SALLY's* Pleasure.

This Accident caused a Separation of some Continuance between the *Signor* and *Sally,* but at length falling into a Set of Company, most of 'em Courtiers, at a Tavern near the Royal Palace of St. *James's,* he was told they had a very merry Lady with them, and being ask'd if he would make one at an *Old-Game,* play'd after a *New Manner,* upon consenting, he was introduced. When he enter'd the Room, he found *SALLY* standing upright upon a Bed, but revers'd, her Head being in the Place where her Heels should be, she was honoured with having two PEERS for her *Supporters,* each holding and extending a well shap'd Leg; thus every Admirer pleas'd with the *Sight,* pull'd out his Gold, and with the greatest Alacrity pursued the agreeable Diversion.

Between two Marble-Pillars, *round and Plump,*
With Eye intent, each Sportsman took his Aim;
The merry Chuck-Hole *border'd on the* Rump,
And from this Play Sally *deriv'd a* Name.
Within her tufted Chink, *the Guineas shone,*
And each *that she receiv'd, was* all her own.
With echoing Shouts the vaulted Chamber rung,
Belle Chuck *was now the* TOAST *of ev'ry Tongue.*
Sally *no more her Christian Name could boast,*
And Priddon *too, in that of* Chuck *was lost.*

The Signor *with this* Appellation *pleas'd,*
Returning home, his lab'ring Fancy eas'd,
To Prior, *writes* what's past, *and* what's to come,
Dating the Packet *from his* Chucky's[1] Bum.

LETTER VIII.

SOME SPECIMENS OF HER INGRATITUDE
SIR,

Among the many Actions which go into the Composition of a *Character* so publick and celebrated as that you are treating upon, there are none more worthy our Observation, than those which mark out to us, more immediately, the predominant Inclinations of the *Party;* because they serve to give us a perfect Picture of the *Interior,* and to lay before us, in a clear Light, the Features of the Mind, as discernibly as the *Exterior* Lineaments of the Body appear to the naked Eye.

For this Purpose, I shall throw together some loose Incidents, which will represent her Propensity to Ingratitude, in such lively Colours, that one would be at a stand to guess, whether she took more Delight in receiving Presents of great Value, or in requiting the Donors with Contempt.

There is no expressing the violent Avarice that appear'd in *her* on the one Hand, to get whatever she could out of the Persons, that her Charms had any Power over, and she had, on the other Hand, such a Spirit of Profusion, and took such a Wantonness in *Prodigality,* that *she* seem'd form'd by Nature to make the most exquisite Example of *Consummate Ingratitude.* Hence, in Proportion, as *she* more or less touch'd the Heart of any Admirer, *she* got the Command of his Purse, and then made his *Generosity* the Measure of her *Extravagance.*

About a Year or two ago, a *Man of Quality,* was by her made an exemplary Instance of this Cruelty in her Temper. He had, in the Course of his Pleasures with her, been as Liberal, as a large Fortune and a generous Mind could make him, or even, as her own Request, tho' never so Extravagant, could tempt him to be. If she had granted him a Hundred of her Favours, she had receiv'd Thousands at Times from him, and been as fully requited as any Heart, but hers, could wish.

The Gentleman's Affairs having call'd him into the Country, they had been ·
absent from one another for some time, and their first Meeting afterwards happened to be at *Hampstead-Wells,* where they were both playing at the same *Publick Table.* Fortunes of a very different Complection, at that time, attended

---

1   See, the REPORT of the *Secret Committee* [author's note]. Probably a reference to Robert Walpole's *Report from the Committee of Secrecy* (London, 1715), which describes international negotiations in which Prior (see page 29, note 1) and Bolingbroke played prominent roles.

the Lady and her Gallant, every Throw of *SALLY*'s carried along with it Success, while the Gentleman had such a Run of *Ill-Luck*, that just when *SALLY* had got a vast Heap of Gold before her, he was stript of the last Guinea. Hereupon, with a Smile, he address'd the *Fair-Banker* on the other side of the Table, and desired to be her Debtor for Five Pieces only, that he might try to give a Turn to Fortune, by what he borrow'd from so lucky a Hand, She, with a Smile very different from that with which he address'd her, play'd upon his good Nature with an Air of Haughtiness, and Contempt, saying with a base Sneer, That, *it was not lucky to lend Money at Play, and that as she had a Resolution to get it, she had an equal Resolution to keep it;* then sweeping it off the Table into her Handkerchief, and shaking it, in insolent Triumph, with an extended Hand, gave him a side-Look full of Scorn, and so march'd off. Thus she left him the Object of *Publick Derision,* by way of Requital for his *Private Favours.*

Her frequent Visiting, the same Summer, the *Wells* at *Hampstead,* drew the Eyes of the *Gamesters* upon her; their Way of Living, she well knew, was better suited with her Extravagance of Temper and Appetite, than any other whatsoever. The Expence which attends Gaming, among Persons who play deep, is daily greater than a very large Estate would allow any private Gentleman to spend. They Riot in Plenty and Luxury beyond the Nobles of the Land, they are more Voluptuous, and more Costly in their Pleasures, than Rakes of any other Class, and 'tis the Study of one Hour, how to make the next the most exquisitely Delightful, be the Expence ever so great. It must be one of this sort of Men, if any could ever do it, that could gratify, to the Height, the varying Inclinations of Mrs. *SALISBURY* to Extravagance, and answer every fresh Call which her Fancy was perpetually making after Novelties of Entertainment. She perceiv'd that Numbers of them had fix'd their *Eyes* upon her, and that their *Hearts* followed their *Eyes:* But as the *Heart* of none of them was valuable to her, but only according as the Purse could keep Time with its Affections, the Question was, which of them she should fix *Her Eye* upon and make her Choice. As she was pursuing this Track of Thought, she had such a discerning Faculty, that she soon pitch'd upon the most proper Man for her Purpose. He was Elderly, but the Number of his Baggs exceeded the Number of his Years, yet by Nature Amorous, and his Passion was of that sort, which inclining him to a kind of *Dotage* upon whatever Object he once admired, made him more liable to be perswaded out of any thing, and more flexible to the Commands of a Mistress than a young and vigorous Lover. She as soon found out an Opportunity of having his Company, of feeling his Pulse, and discover'd in him an extreme Vanity of carrying off such a Prize of Beauty as herself, before the many longing and desiring Fellows, who were in the Pride of their Years, the Blossom of their Beauty and the fullness of their Strength. She tickled him in this Vein of Vanity till she brought it to the highest Pitch, and then gratified it in Order to have her own Vanity in another way gratified to as high a Degree.

The *Old-Gamester,* well known by this Description, was happy in *SALLY*'s Beauty, and *SALLY* was as happy in the Command of *his* Money, as he was in the Possession of *her* Charms. Every young Fellow look'd with an envious Eye upon the Gamester's Felicity, and he enjoy'd their Envy, growing every Day more Vain, as he perceived them grown more uneasy; to make his Triumph, as he thought, the greater, his Mistress must be set up to light in the fairest Point of Luster, no Cost was to be spared for any Ornaments that his *SALLY* fancy'd would make an Addition to her Charms, and render the Person, whom he could enjoy, when he pleased, more Aimable to others, and desirable to Thousands in Vain. Hence it came to pass, that if several Rakes of Quality envied the *Old-Gamester,* with no less Envy did many a Harlot of Dignity, that had her gilded Charriot and her Coat of Arms, look upon *SALLY,* who almost every New-Day appeared in a New-Dress, and out-shin'd them all in *Atlasses* and *Brocades.* They were now *both* at the height of their Desires, and such is the Vicissitude of Human-Affairs, that, when there is no going higher, a Fall to the other Extream is too generally the Consequence. The *Old-Gamester* had tired out his Vanity with Habit, and one Extravagance, push'd on another, in *SALLY,* and made her every Day more exorbitant in her Demands, till the Old Man grew weary of his Expences and his Dotage together. An unseasonable Accident join'd, at the same time, to forward their Parting; on a Day when the Dice had had a plaguy ill *Run,* and had sower'd the Old Gentleman's Temper, *SALLY* in great Gaiety of Heart, and knowing nothing of his Losses, presented her self before him unluckily in the peevish Minute. She wonder'd to find that *he,* who never dar'd to put on a *displeasing* Look when it was *her* Will to be *merry,* should return her Smiles with the Frowns of such a low'ring Countenance. She peremptorily bid him explain what he meant by that sullen Air of his; He answer'd her as shortly, and as peevishly as she had spoke angrily, That *He had been a Loser at* Hazard *beyond all Patience, and was not at that time in a Temper to hear* Fooleries. *SALLY* hitherto unacquainted with this kind of Treatment, swell'd with Indignation, and in an elevated Tone of Voice made him this Reply.—*I thought till now, I was to be a Partaker of your Pleasures, and not to be troubled with idle Tales of Losses, I can suppose nothing but that this is some cunning Fetch of yours, to excuse your self from gratifying me in some little and moderate Demand which you think I am going to ask. Your Losses are none of mine, Why therefore am I to be made uneasy at them? I think I ought to have my turn of losing now, therefore without any more Words;* clapping her Hands upon the *Table, Let me see Fifty Guineas in this Place instantly.* Thus far angrily, but dissembling a Smile when she perceiv'd him hesitate upon the Question, she alter'd her Tone of Voice, and said insinuatingly to him, *Come lay them down here I say,* touching the Table more lightly with her Hand, *as you have had* ill Luck, *I may have* good, *and I long to put you out of this fretful Humour. No more Splenatick-Looks,* says she, *but let me see you give it me with the same pleasant Countenance as I receive it.* A Demand of Fifty Pieces just after the Loss of some Hundreds, came a little unseasonably. He was very unwilling to grant, and yet not courageous enough entirely to refuse her. After fumbling some time in his Pocket, and saying not a Word, out came the Purse at last with much ado. When *SALLY* saw the Purse, she was resolv'd to be wholly silent, and watch his Motions, till she saw plainly what he would be at. His Fingers were very slow in opening the Purse-Strings, and when open'd, seemed to grasp the Gold with still more Reluctancy. He very leisurely told over[1] *Ten Pieces,* and ask'd her if those would not do for the present. She said nothing, but shook her Head. He then told down *Twenty,* and put the same Question to her, looking at her very earnestly; she looking more earnestly at him, vouchsafed him no other Answer, but what appeared in a second refusing Nod, and a scowling Forehead. At length, the *Old-Caster,* after many inward Struggles, brought himself to the counting of that difficult Number, *Fifty.* But when he had done this, he first look'd sternly upon her, and then greedily at the Gold, counting it over and over again. At last he ventured it out of his Hands, and told it gently down upon the Table; she was not so slow in acting her Part, but the instant it was down, swept it into her Lap, without giving her self the Trouble of telling it, and so soon as she had it safe, she cry'd, *Aren't you a dilatory Old-Pimp? Now have you been much longer in parting with this trifling Sum, than I shall be in spending of it,* Then whisking out of the Room, and giving this Specimen both of her Ingratitude and this Extravagance, she left him to be sole Auditor of his own Accompts, and to Balance his *Loss* and *Gain,* as well as he could.

I shall give you, Sir, but one Instance more of her *Ingratitude,* and so conclude.

It has been the *Fortune* of Mrs. *Salisbury,* who has charm'd so many Men, to be some times captivated her self. A *young Officer* in the *Foot Guards,* who was naturally form'd to *Please,* happened once to get into her *Company,* and at the same time into her *Heart.* She was as deeply in Love with him, as ever any Man had been with her. In fine, she became for once a Suitor, and explain'd to him her Inclinations sufficiently, to put him upon desiring that Favour, which she desired to grant; this Familiarity once begun, pleased both so well, that it continued between them for some Years: she upon all Occasions shew'd an excess of Fondness for him, and there is one Circumstance particularly, which proves it not to have been at all dissembled, which is, that as expensive as she had been to all Mankind besides, she never was so to him, during the whole Course of their Intrigue. Once indeed, when she was in Danger of being under an Arrest for the Sum of 35 Pounds, she sent for the Captain and inform'd him of her Apprehensions; it was not then in his *Power* to answer such a Sum, but it was so much in his *Will,* that being rather contented to become a Debtor himself, than to let her remain so, he tried his Friends, borrow'd the Money, and made the

---

1   Counted out.

Payment, for which she gave him a Note of her Hand, promising him, that he should be speedily reimburs'd, and that she should always acknowledge the Obligation. One would imagine, that if there was any Person, with whom she would keep her Word, it must have been with this Gentleman. Not to be Grateful to a Man, who was not only her Lover, but of whom she was her self the profess'd Lover, argues her guilty of so Superlative a Degree of Ingratitude, so unthinkingly profuse of her own Money, and so cravingly covetous of other People's, that it cannot be said, that the enchanting Pleasures of Gallantry, Love and Fruition, are her chief Vices; but that a strange Mixture of Avarice and Prodigality, of Inconstancy and Ingratitude meets in her; and that these are the reigning and predominant Passions of her Mind. Loving as she was to this Gentleman, as much as she was beloved by him, and notwithstanding this acknowledged Obligation; she, it seems, was inform'd, but a few Months after, of his being actually under such an Arrest, as she had only been under Apprehensions of. He was willing to be oblig'd to the Person whom before he had so willingly obliged. He disdain'd to put her in mind of her Promisory Note, and would have been better pleased to receive her Assistance as a Favour, where he could have demanded it in Justice. He wanted more to be convinced of her true Affection in the Manner of doing it, than even to have the thing it self done. He accordingly sent her Word, that he was in Custody, and could not, easily, deliver himself from thence, without being indebted to her Help. This he signified to her, in a Letter sent by a Porter, and as he strenuously insisted on an Answer, she returned this very grateful and modest Reply by him by Word of Mouth: "Look ye, Fellow, if you have Sense enough to carry a short Message, give the sorry Wretch you come from, (tossing her Head with an Air of disdain) this Answer in plain *English,* That I own the Pimp did once lay down Thirty Five Pounds for me, but that if he was to pay me but one Farthing for every one of the greater Favours he has had of me, it would amount to more than the Sum; and that, as he got into Jeopardy, he may get out again, as he can, for *Sally.*

I think these Three Instances sufficient to give you a Taste of her Temper, and how fit she is, with all her Charms, to be treated, by any Gentleman, as a Friend, a Mistress, or indeed, a Companion even of his loosest Hours.

I send this Account the more willingly to you, because my Friend *Polydor,* long after he had left her on account of the Wrongs she had done him, felt, at some Intervals, a Regret to think that after so many tender Obligations, she could find in her Soul to prove false to him, and the reading of this, may hereafter, in all Probability, alleviate the Sense of his Loss, when he considers, he only lost a Woman, in whose Nature it never was, nor ever can be, to be true to any one Man upon the Face of the Earth.

> *I am Sir,*
> *Your humble Servant,*
> M CASTALIO

Whitehall, Jan. 27. 172/3

LETTER IX.

FROM *POLYDOR* to *CASTALIO*. UPON His having communicated to Him the Foregoing.

SIR,

THE Letter which you communicated to me, and in some Measure which concerns my self, speaks the Wickedness of the *Woman* in so lively a Manner, representing my own former Frailty, of being too easy in believing what I lik'd so justly, and demonstrates your own Abhorrence of her Ingratitude and Concern for the Alteration of my Temper, so kindly, that I cannot requite it any way so well as by sending you an Answer, which will shew you how much I am now likewise convinced of her Ingratitude and Inconstancy to others, to whom she has had almost equal Obligations, by which I shall free you from the Uneasiness you express for a real Friend, for fear of his lying still under an Uneasiness for a false Mistress.

To shew you therefore, *Dear Sir,* that I no longer regret her having prov'd *false* to me, and that I am thoroughly convinc'd of what you very sprightly express, that it is not in *her Nature* to be true to any Man upon the Face of this Earth. Whether she *does* judiciously, *feignedly,* or *does even really love him,* I send you the following *Relation* of the same Kind as the *Three Instances* you have given of her, which when you have perus'd, you may, if you please, communicate to Captain *Walker* as from

Your Humble servant
POLYDOR

Feb. 18 1722/3

NEWS was brought to *SALLY,* that a particular Friend of hers, to whom she ought to have been a Friend, if Obligations could have made her so, lay under the unhappy Circumstance of an Arrest: A Circumstance, which he had frequently prevented from happening to her, not only with unusual Bounty, but with an unusual Manner of bestowing it. It highly delighted her to think that it now lay in her Power to Triumph, with Severity, over a Person who could never have been subject to her Insolence, but by his kind Condescensions to her. She hugg'd herself with the Conceit of fondling a *New Lover* with the ill Treatment of an *Old One.* For being then in Company with Baron *Leonardo,* and having the Distresses of a Female Acquaintance, and who was a Partner in her Pleasure, laid before her, she resolv'd to make her Tenderness known, in regard to a *Harlot,* in order the more Triumphantly, to shew the Hardships, that she put upon a generous and genteel Rake, whom she had, by study'd Insinuations, brought to these Hardships. According to the Fire of her Temper, the Baron was ask'd peremptorily, whether he would go and visit poor Lady *Betty,* a well known Damsel, in Distress, who made her self, by her good Nature, too Cheap; and added, that a Man ought never to hope for the

Condescension of a Woman to his Pleasures, in the flow of her Fortunes, that would not help a Beauty in the ebb of hers.

The Baron, whose Soul was naturally bent to Women, by the Habit of his bodily Inclinations that way, and whose Mind was form'd for Pity to the Indigent, had Generosity to all whom he thought proper Objects of it, instantly struck in with the Proposal, and was more ardent after the Declaration was made to him, than the successful *SALLY* had been in declaring it, to see the *Fair Captive.*

To make the Story as short as I can, they met; and as soon as they arriv'd, Lady *Betty* had scarce drop'd a Tear, and *SALLY* began to second with the seldom failing Rhetoric of a Harlot, but the Baron with a Smile that manifested his Good-Nature, and squeezing *SALLY* by the Hand to signify that he desired her Silence, as not needing her Insinuations to allure him to that Intent, prevented Lady *Betty's* disturbing herself any farther with her Sorrow, desired to know the Sum which occasion'd it, and assur'd her it was ready in his Pocket to relieve her.

Lady *Betty* considering that the Sum was a little of the largest, was too modest to express it, without some Hesitation. *D—n you*, says SALLY; *I told you that Modesty undid this Wench, and now you perceive it to be true. Look ye, my Lord, 'tis but for the Trifle of an Hundred Guineas—and I know your good Nature to the Fair Cause,*—then she hung fawningly about his Neck; and kiss'd him. The Baron knew the Hardship to himself of paying so large a Sum; but his Facility of Temper prevail'd, upon two Considerations; first, that he should relieve the Distress'd, which he heartily lov'd to do, out of a Propensity to Virtue; and secondly, because he was to relieve a *pretty Girl,* that he had a greater Propensity to relieve out of a stronger and more vigorous Appetite, which he had to the Vices of the Flesh.

The Debt being paid and the Ceremonies of the Officers being satisfied, more according to the Purse of the Honourable Friend, than the Circumstance of the *Fair Captive,* they adjourn'd to a Tavern.

In their Discourse there, the reliev'd Lady *Betty,* mention'd, with some Concern, a Gentleman that was Companion of her Sorrows. *Ay,* says my Lord, very readily, being still desirous of doing more Good, *I think SALLY you told me of one who was formerly an Acquaintance of yours, and who had done very handsomely for you, in the greatest Distress, which ought certainly to be remember'd with the utmost Gratitude, is so unhappy as to be confined in that very Place, which I think my self happy in having relieved this* Lady *from* (making, at the same, time a Compliment with his Hand to Lady *Betty) and what is still worse, I think you told me he had not the least Hopes of Redemption; nay,* continued the Baron, *you, my Dear* SALLY, *have own'd your self* (turning to her in the most affectionate Manner) *that he was a Man for whom you once had a particular Kindness, and that his Temper, his Years, his Air, his every Action were so agreeable, that, had he not been guilty of that one foolish Thing* of spending his Money, as you call it (but I can never think it so in regard of so fine a Woman, *whose Lips are better worth Sealing, as CONGREVE SAYS, THAN a bond for a Million*)[1] *you could have continued him in your Favour, with the utmost Tenderness, to this very Day.* SALLY heard with Patience the Lover whom she was still to deceive, but the Impatience she had of hearing the Lover defended whom she had already deceiv'd, reply'd, as she thought, with a discreet, but really an indiscreet sort of Temper (tho' her daily Indiscretions encouraged her still to New ones, as Acts of Discretion) by reason of the Prevalence of her Charms which took Place as well in this as in other Points, and relying thereupon, she thus reply'd; True, *says* SALLY, *D— n him for a Pimp! His Generosity to me, as I told you, is very true, but that is the only Thing I hate him for: I look upon him with Contempt to see what a miserable Ass he has made of himself,* (and then altering her Voice to a softer tone, and hugging the Baron, as she had done the distress'd Gentleman when in good Circumstances) *My Lord, my dear Lord, if ever you expect a kind Look from me, leave this Discourse, and abandon a Wretch that is already abandoned.*

The Baron deep in Apprehension of offending on the one Hand, the Woman he so tenderly lov'd, and yet very willing by his natural Humanity to relieve the unhappy Gentleman, still urged that he understood by her own Narration of the Fact, *that most of those Debts were contracted on her Account,* and begg'd, as if he was supplicating a Favour to himself, that she would give him leave to find out some way of satisfying the Creditors, and disentangling the Gentleman from the Misery in which he was involv'd. He farther signified to her, that if she had a Mind to be the *Mediatrix,* those Sums for which he was arrested, should be Trifles in her pocket, and that afterwards he himself would take care, for her sake, to put him into a Post which would enable him to retrieve what was pass'd. This Opportunity one would think, of giving a Man a Redemption out of Misery, not at her own, but another's Expence, must certainly have been sufficient (when not only so generously, but so handsomely proffer'd by a Gentleman, nay, even urg'd by him) to excite her to do it, if she had not taken a greater kind of Wantonness in *Ingratitude,* than even in the acts of Wantonness themselves.

SALLY was so far from being mov'd with this kind Speech of her *New Companion* to a Compassion for her *Old-One,* that she flew rather into a Fit of Fury against her *New Admirer,* in the midst of Opulence and Wealth, sooner than she would not shew her Ill-nature to a Friend in Calamity, who had shewn her the utmost good Nature when Fortune smil'd upon him.

Fury took so much the greater hold of her, that throwing a Glass of Wine in the Baron's Face, she solemnly swore, that if ever he mentioned *the Scrub or Subject any more, his own* Blood *not* Claret, *should next stain his Shirt,* and that if she once gave Ear to the Cries of her *undone Fellows,* as she call'd them,

---

1   William Congreve, *Love for Love* (1695), Act 1, Scene 5.

there would be no end; for, says she, *There is scarce a Jayl in Town, but what I have made a Present of a Member or two, nor a quarter of the World, but where I have sent some Stripp'd Lover a Grazing.*

I hope by this Time, my Dear *CASTALIO*, I have convinc'd you how much I my self am convinc'd of *SALLY's* Ingratitude, and I should think my self not less ungrateful to you, if I did not relieve you from the *Inquietude* you was under for me by shewing you thus, that I am under no *Inquietude* for her; and to end my Letter as I began, you may, as a publick Testimony of my Temper upon this Occasion, communicate this to the Publick by Capt. *Walker.*

　　I am,

Your most Affectionate and Faithful humble Servant,
POLYDOR

Feb. 18 1722/3
LETTER X
Brother Officer,
WHEN I saw the several Advertisements in the News Papers about your being concern'd in publishing some *MEMOIRS* (which you say are *Authentick*) of the Life of our famously infamous, and mischievously bewitching *SALLY SALISBURY,* I could not for some time prevail with my self to have any other Opinion of the Undertaking or Performance, than that it must be some *Grub-Street* Stuff[1] (you'll pardon my Frankness) like what I have seen before in that Heap of Absurdity and Lies father'd upon the never-to-be-forgotten Mother *WISEBOURN,* at whose *UNIVERSITY*[2] I had been too assiduous a Student, not to know how partially, and basely, she has been treated in that vile Pamphlet.—But t'other Day a certain Friend of mine, one of your Correspondents, to whom you have been pleased to communicate some of the printed Sheets, assured me, That it was his Opinion that the Work was far from being of the Class I suspected, but was done with great Candor and Impartiality; So, Sir, if the following short Passage, of which, I assure you, I was both an Eye and Ear Witness, may be worthy a Place in your *MEMOIRS,* 'tis heartily at your Service.

Your unknown humble Servant
W. RIDER
Greenwich, Feb. 24. 1722/3

BEING a few Years ago, with another Gentleman, in a Noted House of Entertainment, not far from the *Hay-Market,* we heard some Company in the next Room (which was only parted from ours by a thin Wainscot) saying to one another very often, Where is this immortal Bitch S*ally,* that she does not

---

1   Trashy publication for quick profit.
2   Brothel.

come? and such like Appellations. We knowing several of the Voices, and partly guessing at the Person they were so impatient for, it moved our Curiosity to
look out at the Window in Expectation of her coming, to be satisfied if our
Guess was Right. We had not waited a quarter of an Hour, before we saw a
Chair pretty near the Door, and a very grave, genteely-dress'd, somber-look-
ing Matron, we presum'd might be turn'd of Forty, had stopp'd short, seeming to look mighty earnestly into the Chair till it had pass'd her, and then she
follow'd it in a more precipitate Pace, than by the Gravity of her Aspect,
might be supposed she usually went, saying in our Hearing, as she
approach'd the Door, That's a sweet young Lady! A delicious Creature! Blessings light on her, and the Mother that bore her! The Chairmen had now stop-
p'd just under our Window, and out starts your *Heroine* (for she her own self
it prov'd to be) dress'd like a little Princess, in Crimson Velvet, with abundance of Jewels about her: The Matron, desirous of having a fuller View, and
some little Parley with that agreeable engaging Object of her Admiration,
came up full to her, and accosting her with a very low, respectful Court'sy,
said; "God in Heaven preserve your sweet Ladyship! I han't seen so pretty a
Lady in a great while; I beg you let me look at you a little: Your Mien, Person,
and Dress perfectly Charm me!" *SALLY,* who, to give her her Due, can behave
her self as well as any Lady in *England,* when she thinks fit, very civilly
returned the Gentlewoman's Compliment, and, as she never wants a Quickness of Thought, and being in one of her waggish Airs, as appears by the
Sequel, resolved to banter the poor Gentlewoman for her Inquisitiveness and
Curiosity, and after some few Words of Course, she began this memorable
Dialogue with her, which is still *Verbatim,* fresh in my Memory. "*Madam,*" said
SALLY, "you seem to have forgot me! Pray when did you see Mrs. *Brown?* How
does that good Gentlewoman do?" "Your Ladyship surprises me," *reply'd the
other,* "I can't remember that I am acquainted with any Lady of that Name."
"No!" *says SALLY,* "that's very strange indeed, I am certain that you and she
are prodigiously intimate, and I myself have had the Honour of being
extreamly merry in the Company of both of you." "How, Madam," *answered the
wondering Matron,* "I am confident I am intimate with no one Person in the
World that ever went by the Name of *Brown;* neither can I possibly recollect
that ever I saw your Ladyship before, much less, that I have had the Honour
of being in your Company: You are infallibly mistaken, Madam; but who is
this Mrs. *Brown* you mean?" "Mean?" *said the wanton, gamesome Devil,* "Who is
she? Why who should it be or whom do you think I mean? Why 'tis your own
Brown —— —— I mean, pray is not she of your intimate Acquaintance, and
han't I been very merry in your Company?" Then away she trip'd up the Stairs
laughing at her Frolick, and bouncing into the Room where her Company
was, she told them the whole Story, who, I doubt not, were as much diverted
at the Recital, as I and my Friend had been before, tho' we had the Advantage of beholding the whole Scene, and likewise the Behaviour of the poor

deceived Gentlewoman afterwards; who look'd wistfully after the arch Harlot as far as she could see her, and then with Signs of the greatest Confusion and Astonishment, lifting up her Eyes, and extending her Hands, she broke out into these Exclamations: "Sweet *Jesus* have Mercy upon me! As I live she is a vile Whore in all this Finery! Who could have thought it? She looks as much like a Woman of Reputation, as any I ever saw in my Life! But the more's the Pity, she is a Devil in the Form of a Cheribum!"—Thus she ran on, and after having Blessed herself for some Time, she went away muttering. Notwithstanding *SALLY*, upon this Occasion, spoke out her Words very plain, yet, taking her Character in a true Light, she is very far from being the most vulgar Lady, of her Profession, we have in Town, and is seldom guilty of talking obscenely, as any I know.

A Propos. Now my Hand is in, I'll give you an Instance or two more of the *Nature of the Beast.* There is a noted Female in the *Hundreds of Drury*, of her own Vocation, at whose Lodgings, as my aforementioned Friend and I were, some Years since, taking a Flask, Mrs. *Salisbury*, then in very good Keeping, chanc'd to go by in some Body's Chariot, and very fine she was, and mighty pretty she look'd, or, at least, I and my Companion thought so: But our Landlady, either, not liking the Encomiums we made upon Madam (for you know People of the same Trade seldom agree) or prepossess'd with some particular Pique against her, said thus; "That proud *Minx* you seem to have such a Liking to, and who is now so very *Brilliant*, is little better, by Extraction, than any of our *Two Penny Thrums;*[1] and I would have you to know, that the first lac'd Smock she had upon her Skin was mine, and I lent it her to go a Bitching in." This, in a Day or two after we told *SALLY*, who, with a good round Curse, made answer; "She lies like a Bitch! she never lent me a Smock in her Days.—Yes, Rot her, now I recollect, I believe she did once lend me a Flannel one to be *Flux'd* in."[2]—I shall conclude with a Saying of hers, which she very frequently us'd to have in her Mouth;—*It was always my Ambition to be a First-Rate Whore, and I think, I may say, without Vanity, That I am the greatest, and make the most considerable Figure of any in the Three Kingdoms.* And to give you my own private Sentiments of her, she is the most conspicuous *Punk*,[3] that has shin'd in a *Side Box*, or empty'd the *Privy Purse of a PEER*, for this last Century.

LETTER XI.

SIR,

SOME Years since I was (to my great Misfortune) Fool enough to trifle away my Time and Money upon that Trifle *SALLY SALISBURY*. At our first Acquaintance, I did not find, (or at least not think) it very expensive, and to

---

1   A "thrum" was literally the waste end of yarn after weaving, but could be applied disparagingly to anyone raggedly dressed [OED].
2   Purged.
3   Prostitute.

say the Truth, she for some time, afforded me lascivious Love enough for my Money, but when, by paying her too frequent Visits, she perceived I was grown Fond of her, and observ'd that I usually carry'd a well-lin'd green Purse about me, then the cunning Jilt began to make a Property of me, and I verily believe, that had I kept an Account of the ready Money, Expence of Treats, and prime Cost of Cloaths and other Presents, she wheedl'd or (to my Shame be it spoken) bully'd me out of, I should find, that every Solace (after our first Three Months Dealings) stood me in 50 Pounds, and to her may I ascribe my being what (instead of my name) I shall subscribe to this Letter, which, before I conclude, give me Leave to acquaint you, that being in her Company one Evening (and had presented her with a Piece of the richest Silk I could get) her Maid came and told me, that Mr.*Brown* (well known to be Proveditor-General[1] in the Hundreds of *Drury*) was at the Door and wanted to speak with her herself, upon which she ordered her Maid to bid the *Cock-Bawd* come in, which she did, and delivered her a Letter in these Terms

Fair Angel,

WITH the utmost Satisfaction I embrace this Opportunity of paying my epistolary Devoirs to the bright *Astrea*, whose matchless Perfections have captivated my Heart. I am conscious 'twould be a Presumption in me to desire so great a Favour as a few Minutes Converse (to convince her of the Fulness and Ardency of my Affection) did not the Idea of a Goodness, inseparable to so many Charms, present itself, and thereby raise my Hope, and justify my Expectations; by all that Goodness then you are Mistress of, I conjure you, charming *Fair-One*, to believe and Pity the languishing *Licydas*, when he declares he never will (or rather that he never can) cease to adore you. Let this, I beseech you, extract from your fair Hands, or Ruby-Lips, the Favour of an Assignation (which if you kindly vouchsafe, by trusty *Brown* the Bearer) then shall *Licydas* hope to be happy, otherwise he must remain inexpressibly miserable; for the greatest Blessing he covets in this World, is only in the Divine *Astrea's* Power to grant. From her Passionate Admirer

LICYDAS

P.S. Some Circumstances requiring my making use of Romantick Names, I hope you'll forgive the Freedom, since I have endeavoured to call you by that Name which most resembles you, tho' I must beg Pardon and acknowledge the greatest Encomium I can give you is to describe you by your self.

When she had read this, she ask'd him what Anonymous Son of a Bitch sent it, for, till she knew, she would give no Answer to it; *Brown* seem'd unwilling to discover that before me, which she observing, call'd him Pimp, and bid him

---

1 Caterer; that is, pimp.

be free, for that I was a Friend whom she trusted with all her Secrets: Upon this he said; To tell the Truth he is no better nor no worse, than an Eminent *Non-Con*[1] *Parson,* Lusty and Lustful, who oft leaves his Flock in the Country, to regale himself in Masquerade with Persons of your Sex and Function in these Parts. I am his *Jackall,* and generally used to provide him low-Priz'd Ware, but he having seen you (or at least heard of your Fame) no one but your self at this time will content him. Having thus ended his Harangue, she thus reply'd, "Go tell the canting, fulsome, fanatical Pimp, that (though I hate his Sect, and much more to be Priest-Ridden) if he has 10 Pieces in his Pocket to fool away, that I have given you Leave to shew him the Way to my Lodging, where he may gratify his Appetite and Ambition." Her Freedom you may be sure put me upon the Fret, which she observing, placed herself upon my Knee, chuck'd me under the Chin, Buss'd, and then said, My Dear, you seem to be uneasy, I hope you do not grudge me the Noble Present you have brought me, if you do I shall never wear it with Pleasure. I told her No, that was not the Case, but her sending for another Gallant before my Face: Upon which she very pertly reply'd, She had done that not with a Design to affront but to convince me of the Value she had for my Present; for that if the *Pedantick Blockhead* should come, he should only have a little bit of *Old-Hat* to stay his Stomach, till he got to some Harlot of his own Puritanical Flock, for his Money, which she would apply, with what she already had by her, to buy a rich Trimming in order to make up the Silk I had given her into a Gown and Coat, which she could not in Conscience ask of me, who had so generously given her the Silk itself. This Dialogue had continued longer, had not the *Non-Con* conscious Lover at that time come according to the conscious *SALLY*'s Invitation, and being conducted into another Room, *SALLY* left me for above 2 Hours, all which time I was Fool enough patiently to wait; then the Parson being gone, and the Money got, she return'd to me, and I was Sot enough to stay and be content that whole Night with a *Butter'd-Bunn,* and her dissembling Cant, and was so infatuated afterwards, notwithstanding this, and many other Instances of ill Usage, to continue her Humble Servant, untill I was

A Broken Merchant.

Feb 16, 1722/3

LETTER XII.

SIR,

THO' to your Person a Stranger, yet permit me as a Friend to tell you, that I fear, in diverting the Town with Cholerick *SALLY*'s MEMOIRS, you will endanger your self. I mean not the Risque of your Person, for that, as a Cap-

---

1 Nonconformist

tain, I suppose you do not value, but another which ought (if you be needy as common Fame reports most Authors are) to be more dreadful to you, *viz.* The danger of being cited in the *Commons*, having your Pockets empty'd by *Spiritual Court* Proctors, and doing *Penance* in a Place, where, in tracing *SALLY*'s Life, I believe you will hardly find she has ever been since her Baptism; for as in writing of her Life I believe it will be impossible for you to avoid giving her a *Title* which more justly belongs to her, than the Name she assumes, so I also believe 'twill be as impossible (considering what a Termagant you have to deal with) to escape the Danger premis'd. To convince you my Suspicions are not groundless, and to put you upon your Guard, take the following Story, of which may be said, as a Predecessor of yours has said on another Occasion,

Tis true, 'tis Pity;
And
Pity 'tis, 'tis True.

Not long since, a pretty Novice in the *Family of Love*, hearing that *SALLY* had the Art to *Please* and *get Money* more than any of the Sisterhood, had an Ambition to get into her Company, hoping to learn and profit thereby: But as Two of a Trade can seldom agree, so it happen'd with them. In the Quarrel, the Younker[1] called *SALLY* WHORE ; and tho' at the same time light-finger'd *SALLY* beat her heartily, and demolish'd a new Suit of Cloaths just procur'd upon Tick;[2] yet not content with that, she commenc'd a Process at *Civil Law:* And tho' upon it her Antagonist escaped the *White-Sheet*,[3] by Mr. *Clogg* the merry *Proctor*'s taking an Advantage of some Flaw or Delay in the Proceedings of his Brother of the *Civil-Band*, whom *SALLY* had employ'd; yet the Expence so drain'd her Pocket, that being behind-hand in her Weekly Payments to Mr. *Whore-Eater* the *Tallyman*, he employ'd Mr. *Cannibal* to arrest and put her into *Hell* upon *Earth*, alias the *Marshalsea*, to do *Penance* there.

---

1 Youngster.
2 On credit.
3 Offenders, particularly accused prostitutes, were sometimes required to do public penance wearing a white sheet, as in the following poem:

Verses pin'd to a Sheet, in which a Lady *stood to do* Pennance *in the Church.*
   Here stand I, for Whores as great
To cast a scornful Eye on:
   Should each Whore here be doom'd a Sheet,
You'd soon want *One* to lie on.

The Agreeable Companion; Or, an Universal Medley of Wit and Good Humour.
London, Printed for W. Bickerton, 1745.

When the *Civil-Suit* was quash'd, Mr. *Clogg* was observ'd Jocosely to say no one ought to give the Title of *Whore* how true soever to any one, unless they could fully prove, that in *Lawless-Love*, they had *catch'd*, viz. *seen* or *felt REM* in *RE*:[1] That this Saying of the facetious Mr. *Clogg's* may be a Caution to you, is the Intent of this, from

SIR, Yours, and all that,
>   TIM. TIMEROUS

LETTER XIII.

SIR,

BY the Note you left for me at the Coffee-House, you are pleased to compliment, or rather flatter me, by expressing an undeserved Acknowledgement for the few Instances I sent you of some of Mrs. *SALISBURY's* merry Pranks. You likewise intimate, that you would take it as an additional Favour, if I could procure any more MEMOIRS upon the same Subject. I have, to oblige you, pick'd up the following Notices, which, if worth your Acceptance, you may depend upon as matter of Fact.

When *SALLY* (who seems to have been created for no other Purpose but to do Mischief, and to bully Mankind) was a Member of Mrs. *WISEBOURNE's* celebrated College, there was a certain very remarkable *Muscovite* Nobleman introduc'd into her Company by one of our true-bred *London* Rakes, well vers'd in the Experimental Philosophy of these Academies. This Noble Foreigner[2] was in his most vigorous Youth; and the cold frozen Air of the Northern Climate, from whence he came, had not congeal'd his Blood to such a Degree, but that the piercing Beams of *SALLY's* sprightly Eyes, with a few home-shot Glances, found a Passage to his very Heart, which taking Fire, set the whole Mass upon the Thaw, and made it run as warm in his Veins, as that of a *Portuguese* in the *East-Indies*. But what cannot Almighty Love perform, when darted from two beautiful Eyes? And such, indeed, *SALLY's* most prejudic'd Enemies, and even Envy itself, must acknowledge hers to be. Why then should we wonder at our Traveller's being captivated with her alluring

---

1 Rem=slang for remanded; re=referring to. Thus the expression seems to mean that only those would be remanded themselves in reference to the illicit act—that is, the partner—could make an accusation.

2 The "key" identifies the "Muscovite Nobleman" as Count Apraxin, "Son of the Czar of Muscovy's Admiral, then in England." A close friend of Peter the Great, Count Fyodor Matveyevich Apraksin (1661-1728) was the "virtual creator of the Russian Navy," according to *Who's Who in Military History*, by John Keegan and Andrew Wheatcroft (New York: Routledge, 1996), 11. The key suggests that the great admiral's son was Sally's lover.

Looks, when we have so many deplorable Instances of the pernicious Glances of those fatal bewitching Stars at Home? And why should not *Russia* produce an amorous Complexion'd Gallant, as well as other Countries. But to have done with Morals and Reflections, and return to *SALLY*'s Count, whose Eyes were incessantly gazing upon her, and every now and then would approach her, his Joints trembling, and squeezing her fair Hand with an Exstacy, would break out in rapturous Exclamations, in very indifferent *English,* calling her *his Angel; his Venus! his Earthly Goddess!* and what not? giving his Introducer to understand, *in French,* to which Language *SALLY* is an entire Stranger, That the Brightness of that inchanting Nymph's Eyes had quite charm'd his Soul; and that, unless he enjoy'd her, 'twas wholly impossible for him to live; looking at the same time he spoke, with an Air so languishing, as if, in Reality, he was melting away and just expiring. His Companion, who, as I hinted above, was a true Champion of *Venus,* and had liv'd, as we say, *pretty fast,* had a great Veneration for *SALLY*'s engaging Person himself; but having, like many more of our unbridled Youth, out-run his Allowance in pursuit of Pleasure, his Purse could not always keep Time to the Motions of his Heart, and *SALLY* was too much what she is and ever will be, to grant him Love Gratis, or *upon Tick;* so that, to ingratiate himself with her, he had been forc'd to promise to bring her some Rich Cull, whom she might *Milk* to good Advantage; and as a Gratification for that Piece of Service she engaged herself to bless him now and then a *Spare Night's* Revelling in her delicious Embraces. The intended Milch-Cow he had in his View, was our amorous *Russian;* how he came first to insinuate himself into his Acquaintance, I am not well able to inform you, but bring him he actually did, and in the Manner I have told you. By the enamour'd Count's ecstatic Behaviour, the designing Harlot fancy'd herself Cock-sure of her Game, and look'd very pleasantly upon his Companion; who soon after, making some Pretence to quit the Room, she beckon'd him to follow her, which in a few Minutes, he took an Opportunity to do. They met in another Part of the House, when the first Questions our *Female-Mohock*[1] put to the *He One,* were; *Do you think the Pimp will come down? Will he bleed plentifully? Is he flush of Gold?* To all which the salacious young Libertine, his Eyes glowing with Expectation and Desire, made answer; *Make you any Doubt of my Sincerity, Madam? Can you imagine I would deceive or impose upon you? No! my dearest, my adorable* SALLY! *He is all you can wish for in an easy, obsequious, condescending, out-landish, wealthy amorous*

---

1   The "Mohocks" were a legendary group of young rakes who wandered through the streets of London at night making trouble. Salisbury was rumored to have caroused with them dressed as a man: "Sally they say, learn'd her bullying Way, by going o-Nights among the Mohocks, drest like a beautiful Youth: And this is most certain, because she was once taken by two Constables, and would have been punished, had they not rifled her Breeches and discover'd her Sex; but this Termagant she-Hero still laughs at a Story." *The Genuine History of Mrs. Sarah Prydden,* 33.

Coxcomb. Make your best of him, I brought him to that Intent; and have made him believe, that you are the darling Object of a Potent Statesman's Views, and that nothing but the Honour I have of being nearly related to you, could have induced you to leave your own fine Lodgings, or have obtain'd this Interview. This the Gudgeon swallows; and to tell you the Truth, he has been smitten with your Beauty, ever since he saw you in the Stage-Box *about ten Days ago, when He and I were together in the Pit. And now, my Dear* SALLY, continued he, *I hope I am as good as my Promise;* when giving her a gentle squeeze he was for grasping her in his Arms, and so forth. But it was *SALLY,* the inimitable *SALLY,* he had to deal withal, who knows better things than ever to buy a Pig in a Poke, or to distribute her Favours upon Uncertainties. She disengaged herself, very adroitly, from this libidinous moneyless Incroacher upon her Properties and Prerogatives, and, with a half Frown, push'd him away, and kept him at Arm's length; nor would the Politick Termagant *Virago,* at that Juncture, give him a more effectual *Cast of her Office,* for fear of spoiling the Design, from which she began to conceive such mighty Hopes; when, but for that Consideration, 'twas Ten to One, the Looking-Glass, which stood brim full, had not flew about his Ears for his Presumption, in offering his Familiarities to one of her Character, without paying for them. But as Affairs stood, she only said; *I'll assure you, Sir! Certainly, you are in great Haste methinks; can't you have a little Patience 'till I have done with the Count? If the Pimp bleeds well, I'll glut you, I give you my Word I will;* and so, with a sort of a Smile, she left him, to his great Regret, without one Bit to stay his Stomach, when he could almost have sworn he was just going to partake of a luscious Repast. He returned to the Count, and while he was making his Excuse for leaving him alone, *SALLY* (who before was only in a Night-Dress, tho' a very neat one) made all possible Expedition to rig herself out to the best Advantage, and was not very long before she made her Appearance in a Habit fitter for a *Drawing-Room,* than a *Brothel.* The Emotions of the Count's Heart, at her Approach, were visible in his Eyes; he rose up, and accosting her with a languishing Air, took one of her Hands, and fixing it for some Moments to his Mouth, imprinted ardent Kisses upon that fair, but mischievous Limb and then conducted her to her Seat. To have only the empty Satisfaction of soothing his Love-sick Mind with the discoursing of the Beauties and Perfections of that Charmer of his Soul, had already cost him many a Tavern Bill in feasting her pretended cousin, since the happy Minute in which he first beheld her; and could he do less now, when he enjoys that dear Enchantress her own self so near him, than treat her, and that obliging Cousin, who had interceeded so strenuously in his Behalf, and had been at so much Pains to bring them together? Certainly No. The good Lady Abbess is call'd for, and order'd to send up the very best of every Thing her House affords: The Orders are punctually obey'd in a Trice; full Flasks of generous Wines came pouring into the Chamber, and Brimmers of *Citron-Water, Ratafia,* and the like, were handed about like Hail, to the whole Company, at the liberal Count's Request; nor had the good Lady the Tenement[1] forgot to introduce herself, and three or four of her neatest Girls, to be Partakers of his Liberality. The Mixture of so many different Sorts of inebriating Liquids, and the repeated Bumpers had been drank round and round again, began to be visible in every Face, and to set their Tongues a running like mad: The Mother was chearful, and her Children all very merry, and frolicksome. *SALLY,* whose Eyes never want their own native Lustre, being somewhat exhilarated with those elevating Liquors, those beauteous Twin-Stars of hers began to twinkle like Brilliant Diamonds; and laying aside the constrain'd Demureness she had at first affected to assume, she, with an Air of Freedom, began to bestow some very gracious Looks upon her amorous Foreigner, and to prattle very agreeably with him; nay, and to permit him to approach nearer, and to use some Familiarities;

> *As she, insensibly, grew less reserv'd,*
> *Her youthful Paramour grew more assur'd:*
> *He boldly tastes her pouting Ruby Lips,*
> *Kisses her sparking Eyes and snowy Neck,*
> *Presses her yielding Breast, and luscious Palm,*
> *Forerunners of Ten Thousand Joys to come!*

He fancy'd himself actually wrapt up into *Mahomet's Fool's-Paradise;* and, as we may imagine, these Freedoms did but still increase his longing Desire for the Consummation of his Happiness. The Person from whom I had this whole Adventure, assur'd me, that *SALLY* was never seen to look so well in her Life, and that what the late ingenious Earl of *Rochester* said of his *Chloris,*

---

1   Possibly a reference to the popular song "A Tenement to Let":

I have a Tenement to Let,
  I hope will please you all;
And if you'd know the Name of it,
  'Tis called *Cunny Hall.*

It's seated in a pleasant Vale,
  Beneath a riding Hill;
This Tenement is to be Let,
  To whose'er I will.

For Years, for Month, for Weeks or Days,
  I'll Let this famous Bow'r;
Nay rather than a Tennant want,
  I'd Let it for an Hour . . .

Wit and Mirth: or Pills to Purge Melancholy. 6 vols. (London: Printed for W. Pearson, 1720), 6: 355.

might very properly be apply'd to her, when upon this Occasion she put on some of her feigned languishing Glances;

Her Eyes appear'd like humid Light,
Such as divide the Day and Night:
Or falling Stars, whose Fires decay.[1]

It would be endless to recite all the Fooleries and Harlotries that were transacted, nor do I make any Doubt but that you have seen several such Scenes and Pageantries, which are daily practised in those Places of Infamy: So to make short of my Narrative, the impatient Count was extremely eager to be satisfied upon what Conditions he might purchase the Nymph's Favours, or in a Word, What he was to give her for a Night's Lodging? And, in effect, propos'd that Question to his Introducer, and who was also his Interpreter. Upon this the two Cousins, and the Mother, some intelligible Winks having inter-pass'd among them, retir'd to hold a Consultation; and after some Debates (in which *SALLY*'s Cousin fail'd not to make a good Bargain for himself, and to oblige the Old Lady to witness it, that, for his Share of the Prize, he was to have a plentiful Portion of the young One's Love) they return'd, and the Count was given to understand, by his Friend, *That with much ado he had prevail'd with the Lady to yield to his Importunities, and that he was welcome to solace himself, and to take his Fill of Love in her Arms that very Night; and as for the Present he was to make her, it was above her to name any such Thing, but he could not offer her less than a very handsome Purse full of Guineas, and take that as a mighty Favour too, she having refused very considerable Offers of that Kind from the best of the Nobility in the Kingdom.* The Count, who by some Passages he had observ'd in the Behaviour of the whole Family, plainly perceiv'd the Company he was got into, yet *SALLY*'s Charms had so great an Influence over him, that enjoy her he must; for nothing but Fruition was capable of extinguishing the Fire she had kindled in his Breast, and tho' he was far from thinking her a *Vestal,* yet he could not help thinking her a most agreeable, but very mercenary Strumpet. He asks, therefore, of this Bargain-maker, *What he meant by a Purse full of Guineas, and how many of those golden Pieces he reckon'd to a Purse? Oh, nothing under Fifty,* my Lord, says t'other: *It would be the grossest Affront in the World to a Lady of her nice Speculation, to think of any Present less than that; nor am I sure she'll accept it; and if she does, it will be entirely owing to my Mediation, I assure your Lordship.*—But the *Largeness* of a *Whore's Conscience,* you know, is even grown to a Proverb; and *SALLY* here shew'd the Extent of hers; for, otherwise,

---

1   These lines are from Aphra Behn's poem "The Disappointment," a seduction poem that ends with the lover's impotence. The earlier lines resemble Behn's poem as well. "The Disappointment" first appeared in a collection of Rochester's poems, which probably accounts for the author's attribution. See Lawrence Lipking, ed., *The Norton Anthology of English Literature, Volume 1C* (New York: W.W.Norton, 2000), 2167, n.1.

how could she exact upon this Stranger so unreasonable a Sum for those very Wares she had, to my certain Knowledge, sold over and over again, Hundreds of times, to very despicable Chapmen,[1] for much less than the hundredth Part of what she then demanded; and would then have leap'd at Half a Piece, tho' since, to make another Proverb or two good, *She had better Luck than honester Folks* ; and again, *Whore's Luck is the best Luck.* So much for Proverbs. Well but the Count? the Purse? and the Punk? Why, the Punk insists upon having the full Purse, without the least Abatement; the Count is fir'd, and must extinguish his Flame, but without the Purse he might as well go whistle; therefore he finds it an incumbent Duty on him, for his own Ease, to go and fill it, for he had scare sufficient Quantity of Gold about him to discharge the Reckoning, which, by this time, was pretty large. He pays it, and takes his Leave, promising to return again towards the Evening. He was observ'd, as he went out, to bite his Lips, and to appear in a perfect Fume, and was heard to say these Words; *O la Vilaine Magicienne! Une Bourse tout pleine d'Or! Cinquante Guineas! Ventre bleu! Je la donneray, tres voluntiers, au tous les Diables pour beaucoup moins de la Moitie de cette somme la! Cinquante Guineas! Morbleau!* Which in *English* runs thus: *O the vile Sorceress! A whole Purse full of Gold! Fifty Guineas! Z—ds! I would most willingly sacrifice her to all the Devils in Hell for much less than half that Sums' Death!*—The Count, notwithstanding this angry Soliloquy, could not, it seems, forget this Sorceress, this Enchantress, but returns, according to his Promise, bringing a Purse full of *Shiners,* as he had been enjoyn'd. He sat down close by his Sorceress; she look'd upon him, and he gaz'd upon her; she smil'd upon him, and he repay'd her gracious Smiles with fervent Kisses, and close Embraces. They are merry for about an Hour, and then the Count begins to make broad Signs, that he would be glad to be a-Bed. This the officious obliging Mother observes, and *knowing his Meaning, by his Gaping,* sends one of her Nuns to fetch a Night-Gown, Slippers and Cap, while the Maid gets the Bed ready. He undresses himself, and a fresh Flask is call'd for by the Lady, who, seeing no Purse appear, begins to look a little sowre and gloomy. Her Cousin observes it, and winks at the Count, who being quick of Comprehension, draws it out, and sometimes tosses it in his Hand, and sometimes dangles it on his Fingers. The melody of that *chinking* Sound attracts the Eyes of the Fair Jilt, who, 'till she heard it, had been looking another way; but

—*Quid non mortalia pectora cogir
Auri sacra Fames?*[2]

---

1   Customers.
2   Virgil, *The Aeneid,* Book 3, line 56. "To what does thou not drive the hearts of men, O accursed hunger for gold!" Translation from H. Rushton Fairclough, *Virgil,* 2 volumes (Cambridge: Harvard UP, 1928), 1: 353.

The bright Pieces, peeping prettily through the little Holes of the green Purse, danc'd merrily in their Lord's Hand, and *SALLY*'s Eyes kept Time, and danc'd as merrily to the Musick they made. The Count inquires of his Interpreter, *If it was not convenient he should be left alone with the Lady, whose Caresses he was to purchase at so exorbitant a Price?* The Answer to this was, *That he intended to see his Cousin in a Humour good enough to suffer herself to be put to Bed, and then to* throw the Stocking, *drink their Healths, and bid them Good-night.* The Purse is now cramm'd into *SALLY*'s Bosom, a low Bow made her, and a gentle Squeeze by the Hand, all which she answer'd with a Smile.

Now 'tis high time you should know the whole Contents of the Purse; before *SALLY* looks into it. The Count thought Five Guineas, instead of Fifty, was a Sum intirely sufficient to pay for one Night's Embraces with any Strumpet he should find in a Common *Brothel,* and therefore had closely cramm'd Forty five gilded Counters into his Purse, and had laid Five Guineas on the Top. SALLY, willing to see her Purchase, unty'd the Strings, and when she had got in her Hand the Five real Gold-Coins, which bore the Effigies of our Monarchs upon them, she went to proceed further in her Inspection, and the more was her Curiosity incited, because she found the others so very closely stow'd and wedg'd in: She made shift to get out a Couple, and seeing what they were, ask'd him, *What are these, my Lord? Oh Madame,* says the Conscious Bite, *Dey be de ver fine Gold; dey be de best fine Gold in de Varld; dat be de* MOMPOEZ *Gold, Begar, Madame.* MOMPO! MOMPOS! Says she, *The Devil confound you and your* Mumpish *Money too, you* Mumping *Son of a* Mumping *Bitch; you shall be damn'd before you shall* Mump *me so, you lousy Pimp you!* [1] And taking up the Flask, threw it full in his Face; which breaking, made him in a sad Pickle; and seconding her Blow with an empty Bottle, she actually knock'd him down, and then flew like a Dragon at her Cousin, with the Poker, with a *Damn your Blood, you Villain! Is this your Contrivance?* And had he not nimbly avoided the Stroke, 'tis very probably she had split his Skull. While the poor Count lay sprawling upon the Floor, the dangerous *Hell-Cat* had secur'd the five Pieces, and what else she could pick up that was to her liking; for she was not so much blinded with Fury, but that she could discern a convenient Moveable. At last, by the Interposition, and Assistance of the charitable *Mother of the Maids,* and some of her Nymphs, the disabl'd Warrior was disengaged from the Paws of that inhumane Tigress, who, by her good Will, would have fall'n foul of him again, or, at least, have turned him out naked into the Street, but that she was prevented by the better-inclined Mrs. *Wisebourne,* who, in Truth, would never suffer such Disorders and Outrages to be committed under her Roof; so she got him all his scatter'd Garments, help'd him to put them on, begg'd his Pardon, and very civilly conducted him to the Door, and away he went alone (his Conductor having wisely march'd off the Ground) with an

---

1 To "mump" is to cheat.

aching Head, and very little Stomach to embark in another Love-Adventure with so dangerous an *Edge-Tool*, such a *Diablesse* (as he always after call'd her) as that pernicious Nuisance *Sally Salisbury*; of whom it may truly be said, *'Twas Pity she was ever born, except she had been better*; or that, *if she must needs be a Whore, 'twas Pity she had not been less inclin'd to Mischief*; and it is still a greater Pity to see our Nobility and Gentry, most of whom are Persons of Worth, Learning, and Good-Sense, how they degenerately debase themselves from the Glory of their Ancestors, by encouraging such Cattle in their insufferable Insolence.

A Person of the first Rank making a great BALL at his House some time ago, Mrs. *Sally Salisbury* was very desirous to be at it, and prevail'd with one of her Gallants to procure her a Ticket. He did, and being finely rig'd out in a noble Suit of Black Velvet, and a considerable quantity of rich Jewels, she took [a] Chair and went thither, and indeed cut a very good Figure. At her Entrance into the spacious Apartment, where abundance of fine Ladies were already seated, many of them were extremely inquisitive to be inform'd who that *New-Comer* was, and one Lady, in particular, sent her Servant to ask the Porter, and to see what Equipage was waiting for her; but the Porter being ordered by her not to tell her Name to any one whatsoever, the Servant return'd to his Lady, pleading *Ignoramus*. He was sent a second Time, with Orders to get it out of him at any Rate, which with much ado, and a piece of Money, he did at last, and brought the Answer to his curious Lady. Now this Lady's *Curiosity*, you must know, was not altogether Groundless; for tho' she was not certain, yet she shrewdly suspected, as it were by *Sympathy*, that this was the individual *naughty* Woman, who was the Object of her *naughty* Lord's tenderest Desires; the injurious Sharer of what she thought so much her own *Due*; the presumptuous Defiler of her Marriage Sheets; and, in fine, her unworthy Rival in her dear Lord's Love; so that she was not only mov'd by mere Curiosity to be so very inquisitive, who she was, but by a large Tincture of that cruel Disturber of the Mind, Jealousy, Tyrannick Jealousy; tho' hers was purely, as I said before, Sympathetick, as some people swoon away if a *Cat* comes into the Room where they are; or, as a very honest Gentleman of my Acquaintance certainly does, but if the least Bone of a *Breast of Mutton* happens to be where he is, tho' lock'd up in a Cupboard, or otherwise out of his Sight, yet has no Antipathy to any other Joint of Mutton; and of this Nature I take the injur'd Lady's Case to be. Well, the Curiosity of the Lady was not satisfy'd with the bear Sight of her Rival, who appear'd in her Eyes as Ugly as a *Succubus*; No, she must make a farther Inquiry, and must needs know some of her Qualifications, and first of all wanted to see if she could Dance well, intending afterwards to hear how she could Talk. She shall soon be satisfy'd, and both see her Dancing, and hear her Talk presently. She rises up in order to obtain that Satisfaction, and presents her Hand to SALLY to lead her out to Dance, and call'd to the Musick for the last new *Minuet*. SALLY, who knew her full well, as she did most in the Assembly, readily consented to the Lady's

Request, and gave her Hand. Though she Dances well enough in a *Country-Dance*, her Talent does not lie in the *French-Dances* ; and whether it was that her fine new Shoes pinch'd her, or whatever else was the Matter, it is very certain, that she then danc'd consumedly ill, and with an awkward *graceless Grace*, hobbling worse than a *Welsh* Milk-Wench, newly come out of *Glamorganshire*. When the Dance was ended, her Partner, who had danced incomparably well, reconducted her to her Seat, and with an Air of *Irony* and Banter, complimented her upon her fine Mien and Performance, asking her who was her *Dancing-Master*, and then sat down by her.

Our SALLY who is much better at *Repartee*, and Quickness of Comprehension than at Dancing new *Minuets*, immediately understood her jealous Rival's Drift, and reply'd; *I perceive your Ladyship does not approve of my Manner of Dancing: But I can assure you, Madam, my Lord*—(naming her own Husband) *admires my Dancing above all Things, and has often told me, that he had much rather Dance, or*—(speaking mighty plain *English*) *with me than with your Ladyship at any time.*—This dry Answer, as may be suppos'd, stung the good Lady to the Quick: Her Cheeks glow'd like Gills of an angry *Turkey-Cock*, and quite confounded, she sat mute, as one Thunder-struck. After some little Space, the Lady who sat next her on the other side, fearing, I presume, lest her Vixenship should fall upon her too, and to ingratiate herself into her Favour, began to commend her Dress, and in particular said; *These Jewels are extraordinary fine, Madam! They had need be finer than yours*, my Lady, *says* SALLY; *you have but one Lord to keep you, and to buy you Jewels, but I have at least half a Score, of which Number*, Madam, your Ladyship's *good Lord is not the most inconsiderable. Nay*, my Lady,—cries another, *You had much better let Mrs.* Salisbury *alone, for she'll lay Claim to all our Husbands else, by and by. Not much to yours, indeed*, Madam, replies SALLY with her usual Smartness; *I try'd him once, and but once, and am resolv'd I'll never try him again; for I was forc'd to kick him out of Bed, because his— e'en good for nothing at all*, my Lady.—These home Rubs stop'd all the Ladies Mouths at once, and not one would venture upon her again; which the Nobleman who gave the *Ball* observing said ; *Indeed*, Ladies, *I would advise you not to concern your selves with* SALLY; *for she'll be too hard for you all, I see that.*

No Dancing going forward, nor any thing being to be heard in the Room but Whispers, a certain Commander in the Royal Navy, who had been pretty great with SALLY, and had had many a Glass of Claret thrown in his Face by her, thought now or never to dash her out of Countenance at once, and came up to her, accosting her with a *How do you do, sweet Madam? Why that Smock wears exceeding well! That's the Smock you danc'd for at the Bath, is it not?* This very String he had been several times a harping upon in other Places, and had been call'd a Thousand *Pimps* and *Sons of Whores* for so doing; but now the well-bred Mrs. *Salisbury* knew better than to use such gross *Epithets* among so noble an Assembly, and so only said, very deliberately; *No truly, Sir, this is not the Shift you mean; I sent that, with the rest of my Linen to your Mother to be wash'd last Week, and she has not brought it home: If it would not be too great a Trouble to you, Sir, I would beg the Favour of you to tell her to bring that and all the rest, as soon as possible: Excuse the Freedom I take, Sir.* This unexpected *Repartee* was like a Dagger stuck in the very Heart of the Gentleman, as appeared visible in his Looks; for as few or none in the whole Company but what knew his Mother was Laundress to the —— of—; the Eyes of all, that before were fix'd upon *Sally* and her three Rivals, were now intirely turn'd upon the Captain, and a loud Laughter of Applause ensued from every side of the Room; insomuch, that not able to stand it (though he never refused to stand an Enemy's Broad-side) he left the Company, and went away (begging his Pardon for the Comparison) like a Dog when he is asham'd, with his Tail between his Legs; nor did *Sally* stay long after, but took her leave before the *Ball* broke up.

This brings to my Memory something like it, of a certain honest Fellow, a Bookseller of my Acquaintance, not a Mile from *Temple-Bar*, who had an extraordinary Curiosity to be introduced into your *She-Devil's* Company. He made his Application to a Friend of his, a noble Colonel, who, at the time, was a mighty Favourite of hers. The Expedient concerted between them, as the most plausible they could think of to facilitate this Interview, was, That Neighbor *Tim*, should equip himself out like a Shoemaker, and come to inquire for the Colonel at such a Tavern, on such a Day, where he should not fail to be with the Lady. At the prefix'd Time *Timothy* accordingly came, and was introduced as the Colonel's Shoemaker, who brought him his Bill; by his Appointment. He is desired to sit down; and to drink part of a Flask of Wine both by the Colonel and the Lady; who being inform'd of his Occupation, order'd him to take her Measure for a Couple of Pair of Shoes. *Timothy*, glad of this Opportunity to have a Sight of as much of her Leg as he could, draws out his—his—What d'ye call it, his Thing they take Measure with, and began to handle it, tho' somewhat awkwardly, as being a much better Judge if a Book is printed in a good Letter, or well bound, than of a Shoemaker's Method in taking Measure of Ladies Feet, and (but that I'm apt to think the Arch Rogue did designedly) drew up all to her Gartering, which made poor *Sally* say, *Master don't you go a little too high?* But she happened to be in one of her good Humours, nor had her Gallant said or done any thing to ruffle her Temper, which was very lucky on *Tim's* side, he might else have dearly paid for his Over-niceness and Curiosity: But all fell out as he could have wish'd, and he got a View of one of the prettiest Legs in *England*, and indeed her Limbs and the whole Contexture of her Body are formed with admirable Symmetry, and most exactly proportion'd: So that I cannot altogether condemn that frequent Expression of a most persevering Admirer of hers, who will say, in a perfect Rapture; *The Mould in which that dear Creature was cast, is broke!* Tho' if [I] am not grossly misinform'd, Old Mrs. *Priddon* is still living, and I believe very sound, and Cants, Prays, and Plunders her Daughters of what they have *Earn'd* with the *Sweat of their Brows*, as much as ever, notwithstanding her exclaiming against the *Partakers of the Wages of Sin*. But to return from this Digression to our *Timothy*, who was mighty happy, as he thought himself, and fiddled about the Leg as long as SALLY's Patience would admit of, and then promised her Shoes should be very neatly made and brought home to her the next Week, without fail, and so took Leave for that Time. — He is a very merry Fellow, and SALLY's handsome Leg ran so in his Mind, that he learn'd the song of

She's a Leg and a Foot,
Would invite a Man to't, & c.

Which he would be singing in all Companies, and toasting her Health.

The Colonel afterwards disabus'd her, and told the whole Truth of the counterfeit Shoemaker, at which she laugh'd and took no farther Notice, till going by his House, about a Month after, in a Coach, at a Time when several Gentlemen of the Cassock and Band, as well as of the Sword, were in his Shop, she bad the Coachman stop close by the Door, and call out the Master Bookseller. *Tim*, little dreaming of who was come to repay him his Visit, came instantly, Cap in Hand, and ask'd the Lady's Pleasure. *Are not you a sorry Rascal*, said she very loud, *for not bringing home the Shoes I bespoke of you above a Month ago. Don't you deserve to have your Ears cut off?* A grave Clergyman made Answer; *I believe you are under a Mistake, Madam, this is Mr.—, the Bookseller, and no Shoemaker, I can assure you Madam. I am certain I am not mistaken, Sir,* reply'd she, and turning towards *Tim*, again said; *What you lousy Pimp? are you asham'd to own your Trade?* Poor *Tim*, quite besides himself to be expos'd so grossly and banter'd in the Hearing of so many of his best Customers, answered her in a very peevish Tone; *Now you talk so much of Trades, Madam, pray what Trade are you of?* Why don't you know, says she, don't you know my Trade? *I am a* Stone-Cutter *you pimping Son of a Bitch, a* Stone-Cutter, *you Cuckoldy Knave you. Drive on Coachman.* Leaving poor *Tim* utterly confounded.

Now, Brother Captain, I think I have told you Stories enough of your fair *Sorceress*, and being very much tired, I'll conclude, after I have subscribed my self,
SIR,
Your most humble Servant,
W. RIDER
Greenwich, TAFFY's Day[1] 1722/3

LETTER XIV.
SIR,
LOOKING over the Publick Occurrences in the News-Papers, I find your Resolutions of handing down to Posterity the Life and Actions of a Person I was

---

1 St. David's Day, March 1.

formerly bewitchingly involv'd with; and it was (if possible) by the mere strength of Imagination; for at that time I never had seen your *Devil*, who in Fourteen Months time reduc'd my Estate (that was not the most inconsiderable in the County) from Four hundred to Forty Pounds *per Annum* ; and my Self, from a Strong-back'd Lusty Fellow, that after the Repast of Old *Cheshire-Cheese*, Toast and Strong Ale, could leap a Ditch or Hedge with any of our Fox-Hunters, to a Poor, Sickly, Puny Wretch, fitter for an Hospital than a Mistress, as you'll find by the Sequel.

During the Recess of P—t,[1] I often took a Bottle with our M—rs[2] in the Country, and nothing but Charming *Sally Salisbury* took up the Discourse; the Shouts they continually made at Toasting her Health rended the very Skies, and the handsome Encomiums they so liberally bestow'd upon her Beauty, made me not a little inquisitive about her; and upon Inquiry I found she was so far from being, as I at first imagin'd, the darling Daughter of some Wealthy *Londoner*, a fit Match for one of our Young Squires, and far above my Reach, that I found her descended, in a direct Line, from the Loins of *Venus*, and within my Compass, at the Expense of selling a few Oaks, and a *London* Journey. Thus equip'd, with my *Sancho*, to Town I came, mounted on a Milk-white Virgin Palfrey,[3] chose out of the best Stands, as an Emblem of my being undefil'd, and of my Innocence: My Guide informing me we were arriv'd at our desir'd Haven, I order'd my Equipage to approach Madam's Door with Reverence, and a gentle Knock. I dismounted, believing I should not be deny'd Entrance, having in my Breeches what would facilitate Success: Nothing I could say or do would gain me Admittance, but *del Toboso*,[4] from the Window, in such violent *London* Airs, I was no ways acquainted with, ask'd, What Country Put[5] is that? What Gentleman did he come from? What his Business was? This first Repulse greatly shock'd me, but recovering my self in as good Manner as I could, and got together what Rhetorick I was Master of, I told her my Errand. She wonder'd, she said, at my uncommon Impudence, to use one of her Appearance and Quality as I did, and order'd her Servant to bid the Rustick be gone to some Inn, and refresh himself, which was much more proper for him than what he desir'd, after such a Journey.

I protest I know not what Face the Moon bore at the time, but I am sure I appear'd like one Planet-struck, and retir'd, more fit indeed for a Grave than a Mistress.

---

1   Parliament.
2   Members.
3   "A horse for ordinary riding (as distinct from a warhorse); *esp.* a small saddle horse for a woman." [OED]
4   The writer is extending his comic self-image as Don Quixote (earlier calling his companion "Sancho") by referring to Sally as "*del Toboso*" (the object of Don Quixote's affections, Dulcinea, hailed from Toboso).
5   Bumpkin.

In a few Days, rallying my Forces, I took Courage, and by the Assistance of a Female, I, in the Interim, had made my Friend, procur'd an Interview, and we soon struck the Bargain. Never did any Creature appear more beautiful and innocent than she, at that time, did to me, nor were the Ideas I had entertain'd of her in the Country one Jot less than what she really deserv'd: In short, I thought my whole Estate too small a Recompense for her Merit, which she *too too* soon found out, and prov'd her Merit too large for my Estate. The plain Country Gentleman I now laid aside, turn'd Beau, set up a real Equipage, and launch'd out into all the ridiculous Extravagancies of the Town: If I deny'd her a Trifle (as she call'd it) of an Hundred or Two of Pieces, I was sure to have a handsome Peruke of a considerable Price made a Sacrifice to the Flames, as well as a Suit of Cloaths of no small value render'd unfit for Service, with a *Damn you for a Son of a Bitch! Shall you wear such Things, and I want Pin-Money?* I have often wonder'd how she could go through all the Exercises of the Day with so many different Customers I found she had, considering what Pleasure she took in Nocturnal Rambles, as turning *Mohock* and Rake. The Genteel Way of breaking Windows, with whole Handfuls of Half-pence, she was very expert at, alleviating the Crime by her leaving Money behind to pay for them: 'Twould swell a Volume to rehearse the Outrages, Riots, Tumults, and other *out-of-the-way* Ways of spending Money, during my Love-sick Fit, she was guilty of; but as my Acres decreas'd, her Company I had but seldom, and whenever I had it, a good Part of it was taken up with her Advice to me to leave the Town, and go and settle in the Country, and there marry; and as for her part, she had sworn Chastity, and only wanted an Opportunity to retire into a Nunnery, and there to spend the Remainder of her Days; After which, whilst I stay'd in Town, she had order'd her Sister *Peggy* to attend me, and to officiate in her Place; thinking that the small Matter I had left, tho' not worth her while, would however serve her Sister to glean upon. Now the Embers which had glow'd some time began to break out into a Flame, and I had just Reason to believe my Constitution very much impair'd by the *French-Disease*, and I found *SALLY's* Pretence of Retirement was only to refit and clean for a future Market. I can't tell what Favour she met with from *Aesculapius's* Skill, but, with Sorrow I must confess, that Part she was so kind to bestow upon me, to be beyond the Art of any of the ingenious Sons of *Galen* to master. When she was patch'd up she made me a Visit, *Damn'd me for a Son of a Bitch for giving her such an odious Distemper; assur'd me of a Jail if I did not immediately discharge a pretty large Debt contracted chiefly by her self, during our Correspondence;* and tho' she was well acquainted with my present Incapacity, she perswaded the Creditors to send Two Bailiffs, who carried me to a *Spunging-House*[1] in a very weak Condition, and she herself went and rifl'd my Lodgings of all my

---

1   Debtor's prison.

Wearing-Apparel, and therewith rigg'd out[1] her Father, who, by the Help of some Botcher,[2] cut no small Figure in 'em. I charg'd *SALLY* with this Piece of Barbarity, particularly of stripping my Lodgings when I was in the utmost Distress, which so little affected her, that she Damn'd me for a Pimp, and told me my Landlord had seiz'd my Cloaths for Rent, and that her Father, as well as any Body else, had the Liberty of buying 'em: But, *SALLY* said I, *There were several Things not fit for your Father's Wear, as long Perukes,* &c. *You Lye, you Pimp,* answer'd she, *My Father is as good a Gentleman as you are, and as well, if not better, qualify'd for such a Dress: 'Tis true you had some few Months ago a small Estate, but that is pretty well gone: My Father is a Gentleman by Profession, a Cadet in the First Regiment of Foot Guards, and before I dye I hope to see him a Colonel, if Money can make him one: Remember, Sirrah, there are more rise by the* Scabbard *than by the* Blade; and away she flew, leaving me to condole my Loss, by reflecting on the Miserable Condition Fourteen Months of her Acquaintance had brought me to,

Your Unknown Friend and Servant,

Caleb Afterwit.

Shropshire, Feb. 27 1722/3

THAT I can aver I have, for some time past, been as sedate and grave as a Person of my Function ought to be, is to me a very great Satisfaction, but the more especially so, when I reflect that, for some Years, I was one of the greatest Debauchees in Town. At my first Admission, as a Student in this Place, I took more Pleasure to be in the Apartment of a *Female of the Game* than in my own Chambers; and by accustoming my self thereto, I became so harden'd, as not to be asham'd, when I went upon the Rake, to leave Word, or a Note in my Door, to let any Body know at what Bawd's or Whore's Lodgings I might be found. I was then, possess'd of a very good Estate, and should not have had occasion to Study, had not my squandring it away idly forc'd me to it, in order to qualify me to wear the Gown, to get my Livelihood. As your *SALLY* was the Goddess I at the time ador'd, and oft, too often, visited, to Her Extravagance may I ascribe my whole Misfortune, and to Her Ill-usage my Good-fortune of being, from an unthinking Indolent, became a Man of Thought, and a Counsel in good Esteem.

I can't but suppose, that from your many Correspondents, you have receiv'd Instances of her Ill Treatment to her Gallants sufficient to illustrate your History, and perpetuate her Memory: But as her Intrigues have been chiefly with Persons of higher Rank than Country-Farmers, the Story and Occasion of her beating One of that Class may have escap'd your Knowledge; I shall therefore give it you; and tho' by so doing, I, in some Measure, expose my self, yet you may Publish or Conceal it at your Pleasure.

---

1   Dressed.
2   Tailor who does repairs.

Having one Day left a Note in my Door, that I was at *SALLY*'s House, a Farmer, directed thereby, came to pay me Thirty Five Pounds for Half a Year's Rent of his Farm, which by the by was hardly the Eighth part of the Estate which the keeping her company had oblig'd me some time before to Mortgage, and soon after to Sell outright. When I had told over the Money, and left it in Five-Pound Parcels on the Table, till I had written him an Acquittance, in order to dismiss him: *SALLY* was then busy at her Glass adjusting her Hair, and humming over a piece of an old Song, *viz.*

> *Those Eyes are made so Killing,*
> *That all who look must Dye,* &c.[1]

which she so often repeated, that my Tenant took Notice thereof, and looking stedfastly upon her, thus bluntly said; "You may think what you please of those Eyes, but I can tell you, Forsooth, that a Black Heifer I have at Home, has a better Pair by half." This grating Speech so anger'd Mrs. *Termagant*, that, flying to the Table, she catch'd up the Money, Handful after Handful, and threw it at the poor Fellow, with such Vehemence, that she not only broke his Head in several places, but her Looking-Glass and Tea-Equipage, the total demolishing of which so increas'd her Passion, that after all she seiz'd him by the Throat, heartily Cuff'd him, and then sat down and Cry'd bitterly. The poor Bumpkin was so surpriz'd, that he could not speak a Word at first, but recovering, and being got out into the Entry ready to go away, with the Door half open in his Hand for his Security, he popt his Head into the Room, and thus said, "Had your Minxship been a Man, my Landlord's Presence should not have hinder'd my repaying your Assault with Interest: What a Plague made you so angry at the Truth? Did it gall the poor Thing, did it so? If it did, I won't say so any more, that I won't; but this I must say, that I am certain, there's more Danger in your Hands and your Tongue, and I believe in your Tail too, than in your *Killing Eyes*, as you call 'em, and so Good-buy, Forsooth." Then he pull'd the Door after him and departed. *SALLY* thus sensibly touch'd a second time, Rav'd, Storm'd and Cry'd most abundantly, and 'twas as much as ever I could do, with all the Money I had received, and all the Rhetorick I was Master of, to pacify and bring her to herself.

Having thus gone thro' that Story, to every Particular whereof I was an Eye-witness, give me Leave to add another short, but true one, *viz.*

A certain Nobleman, with the Design of bantering a Dignify'd Fortune-hunting Clergyman, and to divert himself, propos'd to help him to a Wife, and the better to carry on the Jest, he first appris'd *SALLY*, and then introduc'd the Doctor to her. The *Levite* was smitten at first Sight, as he profess'd, and at several Visits he made her, took all Opportunities, in fine Oratory and

---

1   From Giovanni Bononcini's opera *Camilla*.

Rhetorick, to express the great Liking he had to her Person, and often to praise her Elegance of Speech, and pretty Manner of Living. She as often acted the Plain-Dealer with him, and fairly told him, That notwithstanding she liv'd so genteely as she did, yet she could not boast, nor would she have him think she had a large Estate; for that, in Truth, she had nothing but a very *Small Spot* to which she had any *Hereditary Right*.[1] To which he reply'd, That she might talk of her Estate as diminutively as she pleas'd, but that he was morally certain, she must have a very considerable Number of Acres to defray the Expences of so handsome a Manner of Living, and to be rever'd by so many fine People as he observ'd she was. *SALLY,* who began to be tir'd with her Canonis'd Suitor, drew up the Curtain, *alias* her Hoop-Petticoat, &c. and clapping her Hand upon *Madge,* said, *Ecce Signum,* Doctor. This is my only Support, and I hope will continue so to my Life's End. The Doctor, in very great Amaze, very abruptly left his Mistress, and hasten'd to the aforesaid Lord with the Account of what had pass'd. His Lordship laugh'd heartily, and at the same time advis'd him not to let the Story go any farther "For, Doctor," said he, "I had only a Mind to crack a Jest, and the Young Lady you have address'd has every Qualification but Virtue, and is well known by the Name of *Sally Salisbury,* and nothing that she either says or does causes any Admiration in those who know her." To which the Doctor reply'd, his Lordship might be assur'd he should not divulge his own Folly, but fear'd his Lordship, for his farther Diversion, might relate the Adventure, which, if he should, he intreated his Lordship would be so kind as to conceal the Name of a Person his Lordship's Recommendation had made credulous, and whom Love had blinded. To conclude my long Epistle, give me leave to observe, that as setting Matters in a true Light is the Business of my Profession, and as Matter of Fact is what I always delight to have in my Power to plead, so I hope the above Stories, tho' ludicrous, being true, will be allow'd not to contradict what has been herein averr'd by,

  SIR,

    Your Humble Servant
     A. TEMPLER.

March 2, 1722/3

---

1 Perhaps a comic reference to Mr. Spectator's claim to have been born "to a small Hereditary Estate." *The Spectator,* Thursday, March 11, 1711.

A CONSOLATORY EPISTLE, from the Distressed Females in *Bridewell*, to *SALLY SALISBURY*, in *Newgate*

Solamen miseris socios habuisse doloris[1]

Ovid.

Purputeos spargam flores animamque

(Puellae)

His saltem accumulem donis—

Virgil[2]

While *Britain's* Sons thy Doom impatient wait,
Each envious Tongue foretelling *SALLY'S* Fate;
While lost to all the Pleasures Man could give,
Alone the solitary Night you grieve:
Think, dearest Heroine, think what racking Pain,
Our Sympathetick Souls with Thine sustain;
Torn from th'Embraces of the Men we lov'd,
Alike from Liberty and Light remov'd.
And yet we do but half our Tale unfold
The Secrets of our Prison still untold.[3]
But half our Fate has reach'd your tender Mind,
The worst and most severe are still behind.
Think then thou see'st us here, a numerous Band,
Of tender Minds, with high uplifted Hand,
The *Hemp,* yet uninform'd, laborious beat,
Contriving *Means of Death* and *making Fate.*
So the pale Sisters (or the Poets Lye)
Spin the frail Thread of those they mean shall dye.
Perhaps (but Oh! avert the horrid Sign
Kind Gods, that look on Innocence like Thine)

---

1   This line also appears in Christopher Marlowe's *Dr. Faustus.* Roma Gill notes Chaucer's similar line in *Troilus and Criseyde:* "Men seyn, 'to wrecche is consolacious To have another felawe in his peyne'" (i. 708-9). In other words, misery loves company. See Roma Gill, ed., *The Complete Works of Christopher Marlowe,* 5 vols. (Oxford: Clarendon Press, 1990), 2: 70-71.

2   "Let me scatter purple flowers; let me heap o'er [my offspring's] shade at least these gifts and fulfil an availing service." Virgil, *Aeneid,* 6.884-5. Translation from H. Rushton Fairclough, *Virgil,* vols, (Cambridge: Harvard UP), 1:569. Walker has substituted "nepotis" with "puellae," suggesting that the ladies in Bridewell honor Salisbury with this solemn greeting. My gratitude to Judith Hallet for identifying this passage.

3   *Vid. Hamlet* [author's note]. "I am forbid / To tell the secrets of my prison house." Spoken by the ghost of Hamlet's father, I.v. 13-14. *The Tragedy of Hamlet Prince of Denmark,* ed. Edward Hubler. *The Signet Classic Shakespeare* (New York: Penguin, 1987), 58.

And now to form thy Destiny we come,
Discording Hammers shake the vaulted Room,
And unharmonious Peals pronounce thy Doom
Was it for this your Beauty early shone,
And to each Sex your fatal Charms were known,
Worship'd by Men and envy'd by your own?
For this did *Captive Noblemen* adore,
And *Garter'd Peers* acknowledge *SALLY*'s Pow'r,
Countries remote, and distant Shires can tell.
By your Bright Eyes *what mighty Numbers Fell;*[1]
Those *Eyes* alas no Triumphs more shall boast,
Faint is their Lustre, and their Radiance lost.
Alas! dear Maid, your *surer Hand* supplies,
Those Deaths, which one flash'd only from your *Eyes,*
So the rash Heroes, who of old repaid,
With Scorn the sighing *Amazonian-Maid,*
Soon felt the Fury of her Love betray'd.
With Rage she view'd her Charms neglected prove,
And *stabb'd the Wretch* that dar'd refuse her Love.
Now, now the Triumph of that glorious Night,
Now the great Scene seems opening to our Sight.
The *haughty Lover* to our Sight appears,
And *Lesbia* Object of your diff'rent Cares.
Methinks we hear the proud *Triumphant Fair*
With scornful Looks, and supercilious Air,
Owning the *fatal Prize*[2] his Bounty gave,
Condemn the Lover whom she meant to save,
Now, now the gen'rous Fury takes its Place,
Darts from your Eyes, and reddens in your Face.
With *Female Rage,* and more than *Woman's Skill,*
In his false Breast you plunge the driving Steel.
Still to your self his swimming Eyes he moves,
Pleas'd in his Pains, and as he Dies he Loves.
But Oh! how transient is the happy Hour,
How faint the Sun-shine, and how near the Show'r.
Much for your self but more for *Him* you fear
Triumph Grim Death attends, and *Conquest* fell Despair.
And Oh! (for sure our Fears Divine aright,
Would we could wrap them in Eternal Night)

1 *See the* Dispensary [author's note]. Sir Samuel Garth, *The Dispensary,* Canto IV, line 57. First published in 1699.
2 *An Opera Ticket* [author's note]. Salisbury reportedly stabbed her lover in a conflict over an opera ticket that he gave to another woman.

Soon, very soon, all pale and Dead with Fear,
At that *Tremendous Bar* you must appear;
Where *angry Justice* keeps its *awful Seat*,[1]
And *Monthly Sessions* ministers to *Fate.*
Then (but the Tryal shall too late be made)
You'll call up all the Woman to your Aid.
Exert those Charms which never fail'd to move,
And faintly touch'd the Stubborn'st Soul with Love.
Alas in vain! the Judge's sterner Heart
Defies Love's Arrows, and repels the Dart,
For ever lost to Beauty's happy Pow'rs
He views indiff'rent what the World adores.
Revenge at ev'ry Sound he seems to breathe,
Each Word speaks Justice, and each Accent Death.
Yet fairest Heroine, yet victorious Maid,
When thy pale Beauties shall in Death be laid,
Think not that ever Man to man shall tell
Tho' unreveng'd, you unlamented fell.
Oft as that sad, that melancholy Day:
Breaks forth with fatal inauspicious Ray,
The pensive *Druriads*[2] to your Urn shall come,
Weep o'er your Ashes, and lament your Doom,
Then with fresh Garlands scatter all the Tomb.
Poets to come shall sing of *SALLY's* Name,
And place you the highest in the Lists of Fame.
Where *BELUS, Grecian-King's* great Offspring *stand*
Each glorious Nymph *a Poniard* in *her Hand.*
In vain the dying Husbands curse their Fate,
Useless their Rage, and impotent their Hate:
So fearless for a while the *Hydra* stood,
In vain *Alcides* saw her stream of Blood.
With hasty Force he still persues his Blow,
And still he saw another *Hydra* grow.
At length the many-headed Monster fell,
His Instant Sword unable to repel.
In vain the Venom Flies, each mangled head
Chatter'd its feeble Teeth, and Lips indignant fed.

---

1   *See the Dispensary, ut Supra* [author's note]. Canto IV, line 194.
2   Inhabitants of Drury Lane; that is, prostitutes.

CONCLUSION
To Mrs. *Sally Salisbury*
Madam,

I HAVE heard many *flying Reports,* to the *Truth* of which, as I give very *little* Credit, I take this Opportunity of assuring you, That if they are *True,* I value them still less.

It seems your humble Servant, is not only to have the *Severity* of the *Law* inflicted upon him, but is likewise threaten'd with a more *severe Correction* from some *who are to fight very Manfully* under your *Banner.*

As to the *One,* I shall be at all times ready to defend your *Virtue* in every *Court* of *Justice,* not excluding even *Doctors-Commons* itself. And as to the other, no Gentleman shall find it difficult to meet with me, for I shall upon all Occasions with the utmost Resignation acquiesce in that *Lot* which is determined for me by *Fate.*

I have nothing farther to add, but letting you know that my *own Share* of this Work is the least part of it, and as I declared at the beginning, *That I would communicate every Letter sent me in the Words of the Writer,* I here solemnly aver, that I have not only done so, but have, as I thought my self obliged to do, submitted the Printed Sheets to the View and Correction of each Correspondent.

The Impatience of the Publick, has obliged me to divide your Life into *Two Parts,* the *Second* shall follow *This* with all convenient Expedition, for herein you'll soon perceive many of your notable Achievements are omitted, particularly the Sequel of *CURALIO's* History, the *Pranks* you *play'd* a Gentleman with whom you were once very intimately acquainted even before you chang'd your Name, and the *Surprising Passages* between you and another Gentleman for nothing more remarkable, than for his unexampled *Condescension* and profound *Humility.*

I have likewise a faithful Register of many Feats performed by you at a certain Tavern near *Covent-Garden* and in several other Places, too Numerous here to Recount.[1]

I am, Madam,
    Impartially Yours,
        CHA. WALKER.
Kensington,
March 3, 1722/3
F I N I S.

---

1   While other accounts of Salisbury were published, Walker's own sequel seems not to have materialized.

CHAPTER TWO

The Juvenile Adventures of Miss Kitty F[ishe]r
(1759)

ANONYMOUS

Catherine Maria Fisher, know as Kitty Fisher but later Catherine Norris when she married, was born on June 1, 1741 to John Henry Fisher and Ann Fisher. Born into a poor family and reportedly a milliner at the beginning of her career, she attracted public attention as an elite courtesan and great beauty in the late 1750s. Her lovers may have included Sir Thomas Medlycott, George, Baron Anson of Soberton, Thomas Bromley, second Baron Montfort, and John Montague, fourth Earl of Sandwich. John, second Earl Poulett and Henry Herbert, tenth Earl of Pembroke apparently considered marrying her. She inspired many verses of both praise and derision, becoming a celebrity in almost the modern sense of the term. After a spectacular career, Fisher married John Norris on October 25, 1766. Norris (1760-1811) was "the MP for Rye from 1762 to 1774, captain or governor of Deal Castle from 1766 to 1774, and son of John Norris, former MP and landowner, or Hemsted, Beneden, Kent."[1] Fisher/Norris died on March 10, 1767, "apparently from consumption, although lead poisoning from the use of cosmetics and smallpox were also blamed."[2] The anonymous author of these Juvenile Adventures *claims to have translated the narrative from Spanish, but the reader will quickly realize that this was not the case, given the comically thin veil of deception. The author might have been trying to avoid charges of libel, as many eminent people make appearances in this gossip-filled story, while at the same time wittily signaling the reader that they both know where this all truly (and scandalously) has taken place. One of the more sensual prostitute narratives of the period,* The Juvenile Adventures *offers us its heroine not with Richardsonian moral judgment but with Fielding-esque comic appreciation—perhaps a female (sometimes cross-dressed, sometimes sapphic) version of Tom Jones, filled with appetite and trying to survive in a world driven by commerce.*

---

1   Cindy McCreery, "Fisher [married name Norris], Katherine Maria [known as Kitty Fisher] (1741?-1767), courtesan, *Oxford Dictionary of National Biography* (Oxford UP, 2004-06).
2   McCreery.

★ ★ ★

The Juvenile Adventures of Miss Kitty F[ishe]r (1759)
Volume 1
Advertisement

That I may not be convicted of any flagrant plagiarism, as many of my cotemporaries are, I shall frankly acknowledge I am greatly indebted for the following romance to a Spanish novel, of which, indeed, this is little more than a translation. The original is anonymous, though I have heard it attributed to Cervantes: but this I do not credit.

I have endeavoured to adapt it, as far as I was able, to English manners; and have with that view altered some of the names of places, &c. The reader need not, therefore, be surprised to find a tavern like the Shakespear, or a bagnio like Haddock's at Madrid. Some of the best writers have authorized such licences, and I have ventured to imitate them.

I am inclined to believe there should be a key to this piece, as the names appear to me, at present, entirely fictitious; but as I found none in the original, I have not attempted to give any, as I might have mistaken the meaning of the author.

The TRANSLATOR

Chapter I
Her birth, and training in her younger years, with the conduct of her parents.

In the capital of Spain, the good city of Madrid, there is a quarter which is best rendered in English by the word Soholio. Here lived an honest man called John F[ishe]r, a silver chaser[1] by trade, and his wife Kate was jolly, good natured, and housewifely. They married for the sake of mutual convenience, and had lived together upwards of a twelvemonth without quarrelling. John was a German by birth and of course now and then uttered a volley of oaths but he meant no harm, and Kate was tacit; so that we may conclude they might have fairly claimed the flitch of bacon,[2] had they been in England.

John began to question his abilities, and his neighbours jeered him, for his wife was not yet pregnant. "All in good time," he would say; "we had better have too few than too many." This was only the copy of his countenance, for never did galley slave tug harder at the oar. He grew very thin, and at length his wife grew prominent. His countenance cleared up, and he in turn

---

1   Engraver.
2   In a traditional Essex ritual, the couple that can prove themselves most happily married over the course of a year wins a flitch of bacon (about 50-60 pounds).

laughed at his neighbours. "See there," he would cry, as his wife passed along, "she is not without her stowage—let a German alone for being a workman— I told you I'd do it."

Kate approached her time with all the favourable symptoms of pregnancy; she had the best advice Madrid afforded, and was safely delivered at the end of nine months to an hour, according to John's reckoning. He got drunk that night, and remained so the whole week. This is the manner of expressing our joy in England, and so it is in other northern climes; but in Spain they are quite unacquainted with this demonstration of felicity. His neighbours thought him mad. "Poor man," they cried, "his success has turned his brain." Had he remained intoxicated another day, he would have been confined for life in a Bedlam.[1]

At the end of this time his money was all gone, and his liquor exhausted; his neighbours thinking him *non compos*,[2] would not trust him for more, so that he was obliged to be sober, in spite of inclination.

The first thing he saw, when he emerged from intoxication, was little Kitty—he flew at her in such raptures, and so bespattered her with kisses and fondness, that had not the nurse and a caudle-gossip[3] interfered, the child would certainly have died under the operation.

When all the ceremony of lying-in was over, John again applied himself to work, but was so fond of his young daughter that he could not be without her, and as his work-shop was too cold for the infant, he converted the nursery into one. When young Kitty was inclined to sleep, all business was at a stand, because she must not be disturbed; his own hammer, and that of his 'prentice and two journeymen were all laid down together, as soon as the signal was given for sleep. By these frequent interruptions he commonly paid his work-men at the week's end more than he, his 'prentice, and they had all earned; so that we need not be surprized to find, that by the time Kitty was three months old, John was upon the brink of going to a jail.[4]

He played at hide and seek with the bailiffs, and if a female relation of his wife had not, out of compassion for his circumstances, taken the child from him and sent it to nurse, he would have perished with Kitty for want, through mere fondness of her.

As soon as his daughter was removed he resumed his work with his usual assiduity, and in a few weeks recovered himself and his affairs. Trade went merrily on, and Kate was buxom. Thus they lived, seeing their daughter once a week, till she could go alone; when John would no longer let her remain at nurse, but brought her home.

She soon began to prattle and John thought her a prodigy. He already dis-

---

1   That is, he would have been confined in an insane asylum such as Bedlam.
2   Incompetent.
3   Midwife. The "caudle" was a drink prepared for the mother and her attendants.
4   Those with unpaid debts could be taken to debtors' prisons in the eighteenth century.

covered more sense and reason in her than in a grown person, and swore it should be improved. The child, it must be owned, was sprightly, and chattered now and then to the purpose; she was agreeable in her person, and had a great feature-resemblance of her father. Her birth-day was kept with as many demonstrations of joy as if she had been an infanta of Spain,[1] when his table bended with Germanic hospitality.

Such was the conduct of her parents in the early part of her life, which bespoke her a spoiled child. As soon as she was big enough to go without lead-strings[2] she was dressed like the child of a nobleman, which could not fail making her be taken notice of, as she was frequently carried in public by a maid, who was kept on purpose to wait upon her. Donna L—, who had no children of her own, was greatly taken with the child, as she was walking in a public garden near Madrid, which pretty nearly resembles our park. The lady inquired of her maid whose child she was, and being informed, she could not help testifying her surpize at the extravagance of her dress.

She took down the directions, and sent for honest John to chase her a pair of candlesticks and enquired concerning his daughter. He replied, she was the darling of his heart, and if she was to die, he believed he should not long survive her. The lady then asked him, if he should like to see her shine in a more elevated sphere than that of a mechanic's daughter? To which he replied, he should. She told him, she would take her and bring her up as her own daughter. He seemed at first to be highly pleased with the proposal, but when the lady came next day to take Kitty in her coach, according to agreement, poor John sobbed, and cried he could not part with her, for that if he did not see her every hour, he was the most miserable man alive. The lady pitied his weakness, and all Kitty's prospects of grandeur disappeared with the lady.

This advantageous offer in favour of Kitty, gave John a greater opinion than ever of his daughter's merit; he became still more lavish in ornamenting her person. Industrious Kate was all this while highly provoked at her husband's folly, and frankly prognosticated he would be the cause of his own and his daughter's ruin. She would fain have had him accept the lady's offer, and was preparing to carry the child to her, when an unexpected blow on the side of Kate's temple brought her to the ground, and prevented her journey.

This was the first act of hostility that had yet been committed since the treaty of their marriage; but when war is once declared it seldom ends without some bloody noses; so John and Kate frequently had a bout, to the no small uproar of the neighbourhood, or diversion of their neighbours. One evening they were somewhat more turbulent than usual: John struck Kate with very little provocation—Kate seized the poker that was heated red in the

---

1   A royal princess.
2   "Lead-strings" were strings attached to the child to keep him or her from wandering off.

fire, and pursued her antagonist; he flew to the street, and she after him; Miss screamed; John cried, murder! watch! watch! They came; he charged his wife; but they would not take her. The poker being cooled, and with it her courage, they returned quietly home. John was now afraid of his wife's mettle, and he dealt his blows more sparingly.

Kitty now approached her fifth year, and her father imagined it was time to think of her learning and accomplishments. As he would not venture her out of his sight, he had a master to teach her to read, and afterwards to write, another for dancing, and proposed a third for music, as soon as he could raise money enough to purchase a harpsichord.

Female vanity could not fail being nourished by this early culture. Miss began already to study her glass; she could ogle, dimple her cheeks, and frown at pleasure; she was a very coquet in miniature. She was so much taken up with these female accomplishments, that she made very little progress in reading and writing.—She had a greater disposition for dancing.—She was as great a proficient in the drop curtsy as Miss A—, and did the minuet step very prettily.

Thus we find Kitty in the high road to being a girl of spirit, so early as her sixth year, when she occasionally wore a patch,[1] to give grace to a side leer, and began to enquire how they made use of rouge.

Chapter II
Kitty is sent to the boarding school, where she cements an acquaintance with the celebrated Miss Kitty ——, with some account of her school fellows, and their practices; her discovery, and its consequences.

John, who grew every day more enamoured with his child, thought of nothing but rendering her an accomplished woman; she had received the first tincture of her education under his own eyes, and he was thoroughly satisfied with her genius; but he had always entertained a notion, that a woman could not be politely educated, without being sent to the boarding school. He accordingly enquired for one of the genteelest near Madrid, at a place which may be translated in English "Hammersmito."[2]

Hither Kitty was sent in her seventh year. She found a mistress, who at first behaved to her extremely polite, praised her curtseying and dancing, assuring her she would soon make one of Monsieur D—'s best scholars.

The first day she was taken out to dance, her little heart fluttered at exhibiting before so numerous an assembly. There were twenty boarders, besides herself, her mistress, the French teacher, her dancing master, and usher, all

---

1 "A small piece of black silk cut into a decorative shape and worn on the face, either for adornment or to conceal a blemish." [OED]
2 Hammersmith, a district of London.

spectators. In the confusion, she trod upon her hanging sleeve coat, and tript herself up, when she displayed as high as her garter. Her school-fellows tittered and her master, in taking her up, blushed.—Poor Kitty was all over scarlet, and could not recall courage enough to go on with the minuet. Her mistress solaced her, by telling her such an accident might happen to any young lady, and not to let that discourage her. Miss G—, who was much about her age, and had had such an accident happen to her a few days before, could not refrain from tears on the occasion. This won our heroine's heart, and from this moment a strict intimacy was begun between the two Kitties.

The beauteous Miss Tonzeno,[1] who has since been the admiration of all Madrid, was now in her thirteenth year,—all her charms budding in the spring of nature. She was at this boarding school already courted by a variety of lovers. Her billet-doux were more numerous than the dispatches of a secretary of state. She never went out without making a conquest, and her triumphs she published to her schoolfellows. Their little hearts, quite unacquainted with the tender passion, began to sigh for they knew not what. She taught them what was love, as well as its effects: those of maturer years, she instructed how to gratify their passions, without any other risque, than that of ruining their constitutions.

When Kitty approached her twelfth year, she was initiated into the abominable mystery. Rochester's poems, and the *Memoirs of a Woman of Pleasure*[2] (translated into Spanish) were privately read by every girl before she was thirteen. The scenes and thoughts in these performances, completed what Miss Tonzeno had begun; and every girl was as much debauched in sentiment, at the boarding school, as if she had been at a brothel in Covent Garden.

In this first seminary of prostitution, Kitty remained upwards of six years, in which time she acquired as many accomplishments as are esteemed requisite for a young lady, such as musick, dancing, French, Italian; with the different kinds of needle-work, for which the women have so many names.

She would have still remained there, if Don Frazeno, a young cavalier of good fortune and family, whose sister was a boarder in the same school, had not formed the project of debauching her. Staying late in the evening at the school, whither he went to visit his sister, the mistress desired him to pass the night there, as it was too late to return to Madrid, and he laid in the next room to the two Kitties. They were unacquainted with their neighbourhood;[3] and they had scarce got into the room, before Miss G— pulled out

---

1 All the stories of sexual escapades at this boarding school are missing in the other version of Fisher's memoirs, *The Uncommon Adventures* (1759).

2 John Wilmot, Earl of Rochester (1647-1680), whose poems were notable for their sexual explicitness. The girls are also reading *Memoirs of a Woman of Pleasure* (1749), an erotic novel in the form of a prostitute narrative, written by John Cleland (1710-1789). Cleland's notorious novel has clearly influenced the author of the *Juvenile Adventures*.

3 That is, with Don Frazeno being in the next room.

Rochester, and began to read a most lascivious passage, in a voice loud enough to be heard in the next room. The young Cavalier heard it very distinctly, and his curiosity was thereby excited to know who they were: he accordingly made a hole in the wainscot with his penknife, through which he perceived very distinctly the two Kitties.

When they had worked up their passions to the highest pitch by reading, they flew at one another, calling out, my dear Cavalier, how I love thee!— They then exhibited a scene, which cannot be related without shocking decency.[1]

Don Frazeno was all this while in the utmost rage, to see so poor an implement substituted in his stead, and had much difficulty to refrain bursting into their chamber, and naturalizing their passionate indulgence. Nothing but the place he was in, and the regard he bore his sister, prevented it. He readily imagined that girls who devoted themselves so fervently to the resemblance would not be displeased with the reality. He accordingly bethought himself of a scheme to possess Kitty F——r, whose revealed charms had set his young blood on fire, and made invention prolifick.

Chapter III

Don Frazeno's scheme for possessing Kitty.—He in part executes it, with a curious dialogue at the inn—and her confession, and resolution of penitence.

The young Cavalier got no sleep that night; his whole thoughts were employed in obtaining Kitty, whose disposition he concluded was already an advocate in his favour. The scene that had just been exhibited to his sight, made him confident of success, if he could procure a favourable opportunity for attempting her virtue. As a last resource, he resolved to upbraid her with what he had been a spectator of, which he imagined would immediately force her to relinquish all pretensions to chastity.

He had come for his sister to pass the Whitsum-holydays,[2] with her father in town, and they were to set out that day for the capital. He was provided with a chaise, and his servant had a horse; he found that Kitty was also to return to Madrid, to enjoy the vacation with her relations, and he prevailed upon his sister to invite Kitty to partake of the chaise, as he would ride. Kitty readily consented, in complimenting Miss Frazeno for her politeness.

After breakfast they set out, and about half way to the capital they alighted to refresh themselves and their horses. The Cavalier had pre-engaged a man to come there, as from the school mistress to his sister, desiring her to return immediately, as she had something of moment to say to her. Miss immediate-

---

1   This scene echoes a well-known moment in *Memoirs of a Woman of Pleasure* in which Fanny Hill spies on two men engaged in homosexual activity. See John Cleland *Memoirs of a Woman of Pleasure*, ed. Peter Sabor (Oxford: Oxford UP, 1985), 157-59.
2   A Christian holiday that falls a week after Easter and a day after Pentecost.

ly got into the chaise in order to return to school, and Kitty waited at the inn for her with her brother.

As soon as the chaise disappeared, he addressed himself to Kitty in these words:—"My dear Miss, I have but a short time to declare my passion to you, and to hope a return. You are the most divine creature I ever saw (embracing her) and I beg you will not lose time, but let us make ourselves as happy as so favourable an opportunity will permit."

Kitty replied, "Sir, I am greatly surprized at such an uncommon declaration, and actually don't understand your meaning. So short an acquaintance as I have with you, Sir, methinks required something of a formal introduction of the most honourable passion."

The Cavalier construed this into an approbation on her part, and taking her round the neck, he kissed her with the greatest rapture. She disengaged herself, telling him she did not expect such behaviour from Miss Franzeno's brother, but that she should take care it should be resented in a proper manner.

"Madam," said he, "with respect to resentment it is indifferent to me, of what kind soever it may be. I would rather have you consent to let me be the happiest man in the world; but if you still refuse, I have it in my power to force you to a compliance."

"How Sir," said she, "force me to a compliance! You very much mistake your abilities.—I can soon alarm the house, if you take any farther liberties.—I should be sorry to expose Miss Franzeno in her insolent brother, but if you come to extremities, I know my remedy."

"Madam," replied he, "can you have the confidence to refuse me anything, after what I was a spectator to last night?"

She blushed in saying—"Sir, I do not know what you mean!"

"Mean, Madam! I mean that you and Miss G— exhibited such a scene of unnatural lewdness, as shocks all modesty to describe.——Such a scene as prostitution is continence compared to, and fornication virtue."

She could not refrain from crying at this discovery,——whilst he still continued to upbraid her.—"For heaven's sake, Sir," said she, "do not reproach me any longer with my girlish follies that I unthinkingly gave into, but which I never before saw in this abominable, but true light."

"Well, Madam," he replied, "if you acknowledge your guilt, I shall no longer try you for it, but beg that you will indulge me in a much more innocent and natural gratification."

"Sir," she said, "is the conviction of my guilt any reason for my adding one crime to another, which may be attended with much more fatal circumstances to my reputation? If a sincere repentance of my past follies, and a fervent resolution never to repeat them again, will be any atonement, such I am resolved upon making. But you may assure yourself, I cannot be so weak as to imagine I expiate one crime, by the commission of another."

So ingenuous a conduct, with her visible contrition, excited Don Frazeno's pity to surmount his lust, and just as he had resolved to make no further attempts upon Kitty, the sister returned. She discovered that Kitty had been crying, and would fain have known the cause, but she was not able to worm the secret out of her all the rest of the journey.

The Cavalier easily prevailed upon his father not to let his sister return to this nursery of vice; and he wrote a letter to honest John, to inform him of his discovery, and counsel him against letting his daughter resume her boarding school education. John having taxed his daughter with the reality of the charge, which she readily owned, he paid her mistress's arrears, and kept her at home.

Though Kitty was greatly mortified at the detection, she had the satisfaction of having the thing painted to her in its true light, which gave her a thorough disgust of having any farther conversation with herself that way: In this respect it was very lucky, for by this abominable practice, she was reduced to almost a skeleton.—Her natural blooming complexion was changed to a livid white, and all her appearance pronounced her disordered,—and this was attributed to the green sickness.[1] But from this time she recovered her health and complexion, the green sickness was cured, and she soon became *embon point*.[2]

Chapter IV
Kitty's conduct at home, upon her return from boarding school; continues her acquaintance with Miss—; Don Harrisino's scheme, with the attempts made to debauch her by a grandee of Spain.

Kitty was now come to that age, when all the seeds of coquettry were in full blossom; her father still supporting her in all the extravagance of dress, and she resorting to every public place; whither she frequently accompanied Miss—.

This, with her elegant figure, so well recovered from her late emaciated state, rendered her the object of all the men's curiosity.—"Who is that girl?—She is a new face.—Is she upon the town?[3]—No.—What, a girl of fortune?—No.—Where does she live?—With her father.—Oh then we shall soon have her,"—were the only questions, answers, and remarks with which every public assembly re-echoed.

---

1 Women with unfulfilled sexual desires were understood to suffer from "green sickness." Apparently, homoerotic stimulation and/or masturbation only increased Kitty's desire for sex with a man, making her ill. She recovered when she ended these activities.
2 She soon filled out again.
3 "Upon the town" means available as a prostitute.

In the city of Madrid there was a famous pimp general named Harrisino,[1] who from an obscure birth and low parentage, had, by debauching of girls, gained an elegant competence. He was not handsome, some say very ugly, and that if Heidigger (who some years since managed the Italian opera in England[2]) had lived in Madrid in his time, they would have been great competitors for anti-beauty.

Don Harrisino (for so he was called) was employed to debauch Kitty. A man of considerable fortune who had seen her in public, and was greatly struck with her youthful charms, had promised this man a hundred pistoles,[3] if he obtained Kitty for him.

Don Harrisino accordingly set himself to work, in order to accomplish his design. He got acquainted with Kitty's father, whom he made drunk, and John therefore thought him an honest fellow. In his cups he told him he had heard John was blessed with a very beautiful daughter, and that he believed he could recommend him a very good match for her,—a man of strict honour and great fortune. John was greatly pleased at this invitation, telling the Don, he should be ever greatly obligated to him, if he could promote such a match for her,—for this was a wicked world we lived in, and there were a great number of snares always abroad to entrap young girls—that though he believed she was one of the most virtuous of her sex, yet opportunity and importunity, with pecuniary temptations, few women were proof against.— That he had given her a complete gentlewoman's education; she could dance, play upon the harpsichord, speak Italian and French, as well as any donna whatever in Madrid.

John, who had got upon the most pleasing subject in the world to himself, would have run on till midnight upon Kitty's accomplishments and perfections, if Don Harrisino, who had no time to lose, had not interrupted him, to know which would be the best way of bringing them acquainted. John told him as he was a gentleman that had seen the world more than him, he should

---

1   "Don Harrisino" is Jack Harris (whose real name was John Harrison), perhaps the most famous high-class pimp of the mid-eighteenth-century. He became known as the author of the extremely popular and frequently updated *Harris's List of Covent Garden Ladies*, a guide to prostitutes with brief descriptions of each. The true author of the lists, however, was Samuel Derrick, who partnered with Harris and took advantage of the famous pimp's copious notes and intimate knowledge of London prostitutes. The memoirs of Fanny Murray include an inset narrative about Jack Harris. See Hallie Rubenhold, *The Covent Garden Ladies: Pimp General Jack and The Extraordinary Story of Harris's List* (Gloucestershire: Tempus Press, 2005).

2   Johann Jakob Heidegger, (1666–1749). Heidegger participated in the introduction of Italian opera to the London stage. He was also reputed to be notoriously ugly. See Judith Milhous, 'Heidegger, Johann Jakob (1666–1749),' *Oxford Dictionary of National Biography*, Oxford UP, 2004-06.

3   Gold coins.

leave that to him. "Well," resumed Don Harrisino, "what think you if I appoint Don Armigino to pass the evening at my house, and your daughter seemingly accidentally call in to see my wife?"

"Very well imagined indeed, Don Harrisino," replied John. "It shall be done, and the sooner the better, for as I told you before, this is a wicked world, and one cannot too soon get a girl well married."

This was accordingly agreed upon, and Kitty was persuaded to wait upon Don Harrisino the appointed night. The fore part of the evening passed very chearfully, though Don Armigino uttered a few sighs, which Kitty took for a tender of a real passion. At length the lady whispered to Kitty they would leave her alone with the gentleman, that he might have an opportunity of declaring himself. She was not averse to this as she had no mistrust of the plot against her, and accordingly Harrisino and his supposed wife (who was in reality a common strumpet) dropt out one after the other, and left Don Amigino and Kitty alone.

As soon as they were retired, he approached her with all the eagerness of a libidinous rake, rushing to possess a consenting harlot. She started at his rudeness, and enquired upon what foundation he took such liberties.—He replied, "Upon that of love, no longer able to refrain from possessing the most beauteous object that ever eyes beheld." She told him that however beauteous or deformed that object might be, it was not to be possessed upon those terms. "Madam," said he, "any terms that you will propose are yours." In saying this he pulled out his purse, in which were at least fifty pistoles, and endeavoured to force it into her hand, but she persisting in her refusal, he put it into her pocket: at the same time he endeavoured with his other hand to encroach upon the purlieus of her vestal zone.

She now called out, "Help! Help!"—No one attending to her cries, she was upon the very point of submitting to his carnal desires; when, with more than usual strength she rushed from him, and having thrown up the window, aloud called "Murder!"

This soon gathered a mob about the door, which induced her ravisher to make no more attempts upon her virginity. Don Harrisino entered, and appeared greatly surprized at what had passed, seeming to chide his guest for taking such liberties in his house. This, however, had no effect upon Kitty, who with all Harrisino's pretended wife's intreaties could not be induced to sojourn the rest of the evening.

She returned home, and acquainted her father with the attempt that had been made upon her, with the fortunate escape she had. He flew into the utmost rage, and vowed immediate revenge upon all the parties concerned; but when she felt in her pocket, and found the purse which had been forced upon her, John's anger subsided, and he soon became of opinion, that since they had not executed their design, and as no harm had happened, it was as well to let it drop, for fear they should want their money back.

Chapter V

The great caution used by her father to prevent any further attempts upon her chastity. A curious love epistle, with its effects upon John; his resolves in consequence.—A blockade of ten days without the approach of the enemy.

All John's happiness, hope, joy, fear, concern, and attention, abstracted from his cups, were centered in Kitty. The late attack made upon her virtue had so terrified him, that he was apprehensive every man who looked at her, had formed the like design. He was resolved that she should never be out of his sight, and therefore conducted her wherever she went, either in public or private. If she went but to purchase a ribbon, a lace, or a few pins, he attended her; and when in company, it was with the utmost reluctance he let her retire alone upon the most urgent occasions.

In this manner he kept her entirely under his eye. When with her, if they were followed the length of a street or two, by a man dressed a little better than common, he would turn round upon him and ask if he was a Don Harrisino or his employer, saying, his daughter was not for his turn, therefore he had better walk about his business. This question and remonstrance he would frequently make to a person who had taken no notice of either him or his daughter, and he was often upon the point of having his head broke for his impertinence.

They were, however, one day dogged home by a chairman, employed by a gentleman to know where Kitty lived, and the next day the following billet was brought her, which her father intercepted.

Lovely Charmer,

If there be a higher bliss in heaven than that of love, it must be the enjoyment of the object one adores,—or at least a mutual animation of sentiments.—Convert this sublunary sphere into a celestial paradise,—turn your kind thoughts to the tender passion, and transform a very wretch far beyond the greatest emperor, or even Jove himself. All this is in your power,—a smile from you, is the purchase of myriads of worlds.

But why do I rave, and pester you with my incoherent thoughts, when you know me not?—Some Bedlamite, you will say, has penned this scrawl, and fancies you as mad as himself to attend to it,—impute it all to love.— Though a stranger to yourself, I cannot be so to your charms, which have render'd miserable, 'till your decree is known, the unhappy
Altimont[1]

P.S. I know, sweet maid, you are under the wing of a rigid father, but if you can cast a charitable tender thought towards the miserable, let not bolts,

---

1 The author might be naming the suitor after the loyal husband in Nicholas Rowe's popular play, *The Fair Penitent* (1703).

chains, or doors deter you.—I am prepared against them; rope-ladders and all the apparatus of escape are prepared. If possible, let me know the most convenient hour for hearing pronounced from thy dear lips my doom.

John read this letter over and over, and the more he read, the more he was terrified; he saw Don Harrisino in every line,—and a rape in every sentence. He was fearful of acquainting Kitty with it, as she might, through curiosity, be induced to know further concerning the writer: and how to secure her again so daring an enterprize, as seemed designed against her, was what much puzzled him. He, at length, took his deary Kate aside, and told her he had one of the most outrageous, barbarous letters that ever was wrote, to shew her. Kate could not read, but she listened. At every line, a deep groan issued from the very bottom of his heart and Kate could not refrain from tears at such a cruel and unhuman lover.

"You see," said John, when he had finished reading, "bolts, chains, and doors signify nothing.—He is already prepared against them.—He is furnished with rope-ladders, and everything necessary for running away with her,—what can be done, Kate?"

"Done," replies Kate still sobbing, "oh! that I'd never seen the day I brought her forth,—that it should ever come to this!—but this is your dressing her in your gew-gaws and finery,—or else they would never have thought of a ravishment."

"Well, well, Kate," resumes John," it signifies nothing now, telling me of this, and that, and t'other, the matter is, how we shall prevent her being stole away, and ravished in spite of our teeth."

"Why, ay," says Kate, "that is the matter.—Why supposed we iron-bar the back garret window—have four strong locks upon the door—and seven bolts,—with two Spanish padlocks for herself and then chain her leg to the bed."

"Do you think that will be enough?" resumed John. "Suppose we were to fix a blunderbuss at the window, and another at the door, to go off at the treading upon a string, which no stranger should be acquainted with."

These resolutions were immediately agreed to, and workmen as instantaneously employed to put them into execution. Kitty saw these preparations, but could not divine the cause.—John's neighbours thought he was going to turn bailiff, and his landlord gave him warning, because he would not have his house converted into a spunging one.

Nevertheless John pursued his design, and next day the room was prepared, when Kitty was informed it was destined for her security. She startled at this information, and begged to know the cause; John was much disinclined to acquaint her with it, but at length shewed her the threatening letter. She read it with great composure, and could find nothing in it, but a little romantic declamation, which all love-letters were crammed with. This representation had no effect upon John, who had Don Harrisino, with a rope-ladder scaling the wall, strongly painted in his imagination.

When Kitty found all reasonable argument could have no effect, she fell upon her knees and begged of him, by all the parental love he had for her, not to force her into that dungeon, which none but a criminal or malefactor could be sentenced to; and now a duet of sobbing ensued, which lasted some minutes. At length he gained power to utter, with the tears still trickling down his cheeks, "If you have any regard for my peace of mind, do not, dear Kitty, oppose my will, but submit to this small confinement for your present securi-ty and future happiness,—and to shew how necessary I look upon it, I will stay ·with you all the while."

Kitty finding her father's resolves irrevocable, she submitted, and all the chains, bolts, bars, and locks, (the Spanish pad-locks not excepted) were accordingly disposed of, for the preservation of her virginity; and when John having armed himself cap-a-peé,[1] with a sword and a brace of pistols, entered the fortress with our heroine, where they remained ten days strongly barrica-doed, receiving their nutriment through a small hole made in the door, which was immediately after shut.

During this blockade, scouts were every half hour dispatched, to enquire concerning the assaults of the enemy, but they could gain no intelligence of them; and John began to entertain some hopes they would force them to raise the siege in a few days.

Chapter VI
*A successful sally is made, and the siege at length raised, to the great consolation of
Kitty.—The rash judgment pronounced upon John revoked by Kate's evidence.—
Kitty's re-appearance in public, with some account of her new acquaintance. A real
lover, and an honest love-letter set at nought, by Kitty's pride, and her father's folly.*

After Kitty and her father had remained nine days in this confinement, he muster'd resolution sufficient to make a sally, when he found no enemy any where to oppose him. Many scouts were again dispatched, to bring intelli-gence, if Don Harrisino had not appeared, with scaling-ladders, crows, &c. &c. to storm the fortress, and Kitty's chastity both at once; but still no advice could be gained of him, wherefore the siege was declared raised, and Kitty and her father, for the first time, descended.

This ridiculous conduct of well-meaning John had soon spread through the neighbourhood, and various were the conjectures of the world, concern-ing his design. Some were so censorious as to pretend, he himself was the only adversary of his daughter's virtue, and that he had formed this pretence, to lock himself in with her, in order to have a better opportunity of seducing

---

1 Head to toe.

her inclinations. This reached John's ears, and an assembly of all his female neighbours was convened, before whom Kate was subpoened, and she gave evidence, that she herself had fixed the Spanish padlocks upon her daughter, and kept the keys all the while of her confinement.

This evidence was sufficient, and John's virtue was embellished, at the price of his intellects, which were once more pronounced not sound.

When Kitty re-appeared in public, she had more admirers than ever. The story of her confinement was in every one's mouth, and they congratulated her upon having obtained her liberty. The late slur thrown upon John's conduct had induced him, greatly against his inclination, to desist always accompanying her in public; and she being no longer under the eye of so fearful a governor, was not unpolite to the beaus and pretty fellows, who found means to get introduced to her.

She now had a train of danglers, who escorted her to every public place about the metropolis; she had frequent opportunities of shewing her superior skill in dancing, and so the young ladies began to look upon her as a very formidable rival.

Ever since Don Harrisino's matrimonial proposal to John, Kitty entertained a great inclination for being made a wife. The attacks already made upon her chastity, and her late severe confinement had caused her to seriously reflect upon the ill consequences of being an easy prey to love.

Amongst all her professed lovers, whose purses were profusely opened to entertain her wherever she went, there was not one who had ever mentioned the word matrimony, but in ridicule. This made her suspect the uprightness of their designs, and they frequently professed how happy they should be in the enjoyment of so fine a creature.

But though in all the circle of her polite acquaintance she was not likely to gain a husband, she had made a conquest not unworthy of her, had she prudently considered her birth and fortune. A wealthy tradesman's son, a pewterer in her own neighbourhood, had long entertained a real and honest passion for her, and only sought the opportunity to declare himself; but the volatile gay Kitty, ever flew from him, when he began to sigh, and ask her if she could love, in replying, "not to sigh with so dull a swain."

Thus she trifled and ridiculed a man who would have made her happy. All her coquettry served but to fan his flame, and finding her flighty disposition would never give him time to seriously propose himself in marriage, he wrote her the following honest letter.

Dear Kitty,

I have often endeavoured to inform you of my intentions, but you have either turned the discourse, in such a manner as to prevent my making a declaration, or abruptly left me to talk to myself. I impute this to your youth, and the gaiety of your disposition, which I do not look upon as a fault in you as it may be easily corrected.

I am, however, reduced to the necessity of putting pen to paper (a thing I am very little accustomed to) in order to acquaint you with my love, and am willing to marry you, as soon as you can obtain the consent of your and my relations.

You see, I am frank and ingenuous,—perhaps it may disgust, but cannot deceive you. I expect you will be as honest in your answer, which I hope you will favour me with, as soon as you have had time seriously to consider these contents. I am dear Kitty, with great love and esteem,

Your devoted servant,

———————

This was the first letter of the kind Kitty ever received, and though her pride was somewhat mortified in thinking of a tradesman as a husband, she was not displeased at the openness of the declaration, and having it in her power to be a wife if she chose it.

She thought that an affair of such importance required the advice of some other person, and she could think of none so proper as her father.

He startled when he first read the letter, and could not be convinced for some time but that it was another design upon her virtue, and that there was still Don Harrisino at the bottom. But when Kitty informed him she knew the person that wrote it and acquainted him who he was, his apprehensions were somewhat appeased; he could, nevertheless, no way relish the proposal,—"What," said he, "have I given you a gentlewoman's education, taught you Italian, French, music, and dancing, to be the wife of a pewterer?—No, such qualifications, and such a figure as yours, may very claim the first grandee of Spain."[1]

These sentiments so entirely chimed in with Kitty's notions, that she did not attempt to contradict him, but was glad to find she had the authority of her father to plead for her excuse. She accordingly answered the young pewterer's love-epistle, in apologizing for her not yet entering into the holy state he did her the honour to propose, by reason of her youth and inexperience; and that moreover the authority of a parent had put it out of her power to dispose of her hand to him.

The youth was inconsolable at this answer; she had so entirely rivetted his affections. His relations took him home, and tried every means to divert his melancholy—but all to no purpose.—Doctors, in vain, prescribed for his disorder, which a kind word from Kitty would have easily cured.

———————

1 A nobleman of the highest rank.

Chapter VII

The operation of vanity upon our heroine,—gives herself greater airs than ever,—
assumes the girl of spirit at fourteen.—Is upon the very point of being ruined.

The different attacks upon, and proposals made to Kitty, with the great regard her father paid to her superior merit, flushed the girl with an opinion that she should never give her hand to less than an earl. This, with her late success upon the unhappy pewterer, made her give herself such insupportable airs, that none of her former acquaintance dared to keep her company.

The first malignant symptoms of her dangerous vanity appeared in a gold watch, which she perswaded her father, who could very ill afford it, to purchase her; from this time she thought the fresh air would be fatal to her disorder, and a sedan chair was called (by her father) upon every occasion, to transport her wherever she proposed going.

Heretofore she thought herself very happy, when she could see a play in the gallery or the pit; but she now found out that it was very fatiguing to go at five o'clock, and wait a whole hour before the curtain drew up; that to pop into the boxes precisely at six, was elegant and agreeable. From these considerations, she rejected all gallery and pit parties, and was so immoderate as to pique herself upon being a girl of spirit.

A girl of spirit, is one who will assist in a riot at a play-house,—ride a race for a hundred—drive her own phaeton,[1] if she has got one,—walk arm in arm with a couple of young fellows in public,—talk loud at church, and put the parson out of countenance,—have no objection to a tête à tête party at a tavern—and do any thing but one, to indulge or gratify her attendant.

Kitty was by this time, though but fourteen, thoroughly disposed for all this, and in order to compleat the character, as far as she was able, seduced her father to purchase her a riding habit, which was white with a silver binding, and with it she wore a point d'espagne[2] hat, with a white feather. A young gentleman, who professed himself her admirer, furnished her with a horse, and they frequently took an airing together.

This was sufficient for the world to pronounce her kept; nor had her lover, perhaps, so good an intent, after enjoyment.

He accompanied her one evening to the play in the upper boxes, and afterwards begged of her to eat a bit of something at an adjacent tavern, as the entertainment had been long, and she must certainly have lost her supper at home. Few arguments prevailed upon Kitty to accept the invitation. An elegant entertainment was ordered, and the wine briskly circulated.

After the repast, her lover began to open his mind to her, and sealed every.

---

1   "A species of four-wheeled open carriage, of light construction; usually drawn by a
    pair of horses, and with one or (now generally) two seats facing forward." [OED]
2   A kind of lace.

declaration with an amorous kiss.—Kitty, as yet, shewed no dislike to his approaches, and she thought she had sufficient fortitude to withstand his utmost attacks, when they became critical. He began to grow familiar with her person; and from a thorough acquaintance with her lips, he introduced himself to her hidden charms, and the whiteness of her bosom was exposed. She had not yet chid him in earnest, as she reconciled the innocence of these familiarities to herself; but when he praised the neatness of her leg, and was inquisitive with his hand to know how high she gartered, she took the alarm, and sprung from him with great agility, at the same time protesting against any further rudeness. He at first took great pains to sooth her into compliance, exhausting all his logic and argumentation, to prove the rectitude of fornication; but when he found she was resolutely bent upon not consenting, he took the hint from her, and became seriously resolved upon making her. He fastened the door, in telling her it was in vain for her to think to escape him, for that all the noise she could make would signify nothing in that house; that when a woman once consented to come with a man alone to a tavern, it was the same thing as if she consented to all he proposed; that the waiters, and people of the place, would not come to her assistance, and that therefore she might as well comply as oblige him to force her inclinations.

Finding herself in this situation, she fell upon her knees, and with tears supplicated his forbearance. But still her prayers were fruitless, and he remained inexorable.

She now struggled to defend herself, and for some time opposed his greatest efforts; but at length his superior force made her weakness succumb. She screamed and bawled as her last recourse, but as he had pre-informed her, no attention was made to her outcries.

There was now no obstacle to possession, and she was necessitated to submit; when he relinquished his prize, at the discovery he made. He cursed his ill-fated stars for giving him so fair an opportunity, at so critical a time, and permitted her to depart with her virginity, upon condition of making an appointment for three days after.

Chapter VIII
A bawd is employed to seduce Kitty.—Her father resolves to send her into a nunnery.—Sets out for France, with some account of her fellow travellers.

This last narrow escape had so clearly pointed out to our heroine the danger of keeping up the character of a girl of spirit that she firmly resolved to give up all pretensions to it. But she had gone too far, and Don Mensario, who had been so familiar with her at the tavern, plagued her with repeated messages, to fulfill her engagement. She gave a deaf ear to all his solicitations; this produced from him a threatening letter, wherein he menaced to divulge what lengths he had gone with her, and blast her reputation in every coffee-house in Madrid.

This renewed all Kitty's apprehensions, and she began to think she was as much ruined, as if she had agreed to his intreaties. He, at the same time, employed a procuress to get acquainted with her, which she easily did, by being frequently at the milliner's where Kitty made her purchase. An invitation early ensued to drink a dish of tea, and after the first or second visit, the old lady made no scruple to tell Kitty her thoughts. "My dear," said she, "I am surprised so fine a creature as you, who is the adoration of all Madrid, should shut yourself up with two old surly parents, when you might shine with the greatest splendor of the first grandee's lady in Spain."

Kitty naturally enquired how this was to be performed, and the other as readily answered. "There are fifty men, to my knowledge, who would throw all the riches of the new world at your feet, if they were in possession of them, for nothing but what you wish to be rid of, though you are too shy to ask the favour of any man."

Our heroine soon took the hint, and replied, she could not think of prostituting herself for hire, to be the empress of the globe.

"You mistake the thing," resumed the beldam, "it is no prostitution to admit the embraces of a man that you like; but if your father should, as in all likelihood he may, force you to marry the man you detest, then you certainly prostitute yourself, to satisfy the capriciousness of a headstrong parent."

Kitty returned that the authority of her father, however great, should not compel her to marry the man she should not be happy with. "The surest way, then," says grey-hairs, "to avoid it, is to dispose of yourself beforehand."

These words were scarce out of the old lady's mouth, before Don Mensario entered, and listing his forces under the banner of incontinence. Kitty was forced to agree to capitulate the next day.

John, who was anxious as ever after Kitty's welfare, had got intelligence of her new acquaintance, with the dangerous tendency of it. This information rendered him dumb and motionless for some time. At length regaining the use of his faculties, he flew to a neighbouring peace officer, and told him, that a bawd had seduced his dear child, his only daughter, and that if he did not go with him that instant, he should be inevitably ruined. The constable (for such we shall call him) taking his staff of authority, repaired with John to the house of the old lady, where having knocked, and gained admittance into the entry, they broke open the parlour door (which was not locked) to get Kitty. The old lady and Don Mensario imagined that thieves had broke in to rob them, which induced him to draw his sword in their defence; but Kitty informing them it was her father, their astonishment was still greater. As soon as the cavalier had sheathed his sword, the constable produced his token of power, and forced Kitty into a hackney coach, notwithstanding all the remonstrances of her lover, and the beldame, whom he threatened with indictments for keeping a brothel.

Kitty was no sooner returned home, than all her cloaths were packed up, and she was informed that she was to set out that very night for France, in order to be put into a convent. She was a first greatly mortified at her destination, and made use of some entreaties to prevail upon her father to defer her journey; but all her remonstrances were in vain, he telling her he saw it was impossible for her to remain another night in Madrid, without being debauched. .

She accordingly took leave of her father and mother, and set out for Amiens. Her journey[1] upon the road, furnished nothing extraordinary, till her arrival in France, when she was shuffled in a coach, with five other passengers, two of whom were mendicant friars, a bourgeois going to Paris, a young lady going to take the vows in the same nunnery where Kitty was destined, and her mamma, who accompanied her. There was room for two more, according to the coachman's calculation, though in fact not one could have rode with any kind of commodiousness.

For the first two or three stages they were but indifferent company, and little more was uttered but the priest's prayers and singing; but by the time they began to be better acquainted, their conversation was familiar, and a party of quadrille ensued between the mendicants, and bourgeois, and miss's mamma.

Kitty's heart was yet too full to be diverted. Such an estrangement from all her relations and acquaintance, to be shut up in a convent, for she knew not how long, was sufficient cause of melancholy to a girl of her spirit and sensations. It is true, she was not to take the vows, for her father was a Lutheran by profession; and she was promised to return in two years, when she should be forgot at Madrid, to those inveiglers of youth and innocence, whom John was so much afraid of; but she looked upon herself now as a woman, and thought every thing that debarred her of a husband, was an obstacle to her happiness. Two years certain to live without one, was an age of celibacy to a girl of so warm a constitution as Kitty, who thought she had lost as much time as had elapsed from the age of thirteen, by being a spinster.

The other lady, who in fact was in a more melancholy situation than Kitty, was under no small depression of spirits, at the great, though voluntary sacrifice, she was going to make. They sympathized in one another's distresses, and their mutual sighs seemed to form an interrogatory and responsial dialogue of reciprocal melancholy.

---

1 In the original it is "voyage," which induces us to believe she went partly by sea. [author's note]

Chapter IX

The great abstemiousness of a mendicant friar, with a discovery that was afterwards made. Kitty's arrival, and introduction at the convent.

Just as father P— the mendicant had a sansprendre,[1] the coach arrived at the inn door, where the passengers were to alight, which they were all immediately going accordingly to do, but he insisted upon their not stirring, till he had played out that hand of cards, which, with some reluctance, the party consented to; and after father P— had called all his winnings, he gave the word for descending.

Dinner, as usual, was ready upon the table for the passengers. The other mendicant ate very heartily of some salt-fish, but could not perswade father P—, who pretended to more sanctity than him, to eat it, as it was Wednesday. The bourgeois paid no attention to the days, but thought his appetite was to be satisfied every day it required it, and victuals were to be had. The elderly lady chose to set a good example to the two destined nuns, whose appetites were already sufficed with reflexion.

As father P— ate nothing but a crust of bread and an apple, he did not sit down to table, and was guilty of no breach of manners in retiring sooner than the rest. When the coach was ready at the door for the passengers to resume their journey, Father P— could not be found.—His fellow-travellers had already been in upwards of twenty minutes, when there were still no tidings of the mendicant. At length the coachman, who was in a violent passion at being retarded so long, was upon the point of going without him, but the ladies prevailed upon him to make another search after him, which he at length complied with, when he found the reverend father in the stable, close locked in Manon the chambermaid's embraces.

The coachman, who was greatly irritated, cursed him for a fornicating priest, whilst the father was endeavouring to pacify him, and prevail upon him to keep the secret; but the bourgeois, who had occasion to discharge some of the copious bumpers he had drank at dinner, was a spectator of the discovery, and he made haste to inform the rest of the company of father P—'s hypocrisy, in abstaining from fish, when he had actually got at flesh.

This accident put all the company into good humour, but the two priests; both the destined nuns tittered, mamma smiled, and the honest bourgeois could not refrain from a horse laugh. Monsieur de Lammon was his name; and he appeared to entertain but an indifferent opinion of priests in general, and was highly pleased at this opportunity of roasting them with impunity. Upon father P—'s resuming the coach, he told him, "the coachman was an impudent

---

1   "Sansprendre" means to "play without Discarding, or taking any in." Richard Seymour, Esq., *The Complete Gamester: in Three Parts* (London: Printed for J. Hodges, 1754), 71. Only certain hands allow you to do this, however, and Father P has clearly been lucky and received a good hand.

rascal, to disturb his reverence before he could say grace; that if the varlet had been in Spain, he would have been put in the inquisition for such an outrage." P— was upon the point of making an apology for his having made the company wait, when Lammon made him this address, which rendered the priest's confusion so great, that he attempted nothing in his defence, and both the mendicants were very bad company all the rest of the way.

Upon Kitty and Miss L—'s arrival at the convent, they were met at the door by three or four of the sisterhood, who congratulated them upon their arrival, and introduced them to the lady abbess, which was not, however, performed without some ceremony.

They found the lady abbess in a magnificent apartment, without the religious robe, dressed in an elegant suit of cloaths, seated in a crimson damask sopha, ornamented with gold fringe, surrounded by a group of nuns, waiting every nod to anticipate her commands.

Upon the approach of the novices, she raised herself something from her seat, and told them, she was glad to find two such amiable young ladies had resolved to quit the world, with all its follies and extravagances, for that holy retreat.—A silent return of compliments on the part of the young ladies, seemed to acquiesce in what the lady abbess had said; but Miss L—'s mamma informed her, she believed her daughter only of the two was come to take the vows; but she hoped such an example would prevail upon Kitty to follow it.

Though our heroine had already, for a girl of her age, seen a good deal of life, and was never at a stand for repartee, she was so tennis-ball-like tossed from one to the other, that she had no opportunity of saying anything for herself.

The lady abbess perceiving her confusion, thought that would be a most opportune occasion to force a compliance from her to take the vows, and continued addressing with her, "Well, my dear, I see you cannot find in your heart to oppose so holy a request; and your modesty, that great ornament of your sex, will not let you declare openly your resolves: suppose I take upon me to say, you have already resolved, and your novicate is only a prelude to taking the veil."

Kitty found herself now under the disagreeable necessity of agreeing to what she said, or opposing it, and therefore plucked up courage enough to answer, "Madam, my father has sent me here, contrary to my will, but not with a view of depositing me for life. If I were intended even for that, I should not pretend to declare my resolves before the end of my noviciate."

This pertinent answer silenced her antagonist, and Miss L—'s mamma was greatly afraid that such good sense would prevail upon her daughter to not decide too precipitately upon taking the veil.

Chapter X

Character of the sisterhood, with their intrigues and cabals. The history of
Madmoiselle de Melioret; an account of her family. The Marquis de L—pays his
addresses to her, with whom she is enamoured—upon the point of marrying him;
and the match laid aside upon a frivolous discovery.—Her grief thereat,
and a tender scene between the two lovers.

Nunneries were, perhaps, originally meant as asylums for a number of
young girls, who chose to retire from the world, and devote themselves entirely to religious concerns. All their provision then arose from their own manual productions; and their edifying lives induced many pious persons to make
them considerable donations. But this, far from having the intended effect,
of exciting them to a more holy life, by taking them off from the labour which
was necessary for their support, introduced luxury, and all refined vice.
Henceforward they were considered in quite a different light from their original institution. Parents looked upon them as useful retreats, where they
might discharge themselves of the burthensome part of their children, in
order to put the others in a state of ease and affluence. Religion had now very
little share in peopling these sanctuaries, which were for the most part filled
with victims sacrificed to the cruelty of relations. These unfortunate girls
thought to compensate in some measure the loss of pleasures they were compelled to abandon, by making them the common subjects of their conversation. The parlour is more frequented than the choir, and the worldings they
can no longer imitate are the objects of their satire. To compleat their misfortunes, these unhappy victims are under the dominion of a lady abbess,
who, being of a good family, thinks herself entitled to appropriate a despotic
power; and being mistress of the revenues of the house, every nun zealously
endeavours to obtain her good graces, in order to participate in her elegant
living, her pastimes, recreations, and dissipations. Hence arises that base adulation which is paid to her, the jealousies that reign, and intrigues carried on,
which produce the greatest ill will and enmity between the (intended) holy
sisterhood.

This picture, which soon presented itself to Kitty, of a convent, made her
entertain a very contemptible opinion of her fraternity; and the means which
were continually used to make her take the vows, made her resolve upon quitting the place the first opportunity that conveniently offered.

She in the mean while cemented a strict intimacy with a young lady, whose
name was Mademoiselle de Milioret, and whose great grief and affliction had
at first attracted Kitty's observation. After they had been some time acquainted, Kitty testified a desire to know the cause of her misfortunes, and Mademoiselle de Milioret very readily gave her the following narration:

"My dear Miss," said she, "as your enquiry does not seem to be to gratify an
idle curiosity, but sympathising in my misfortunes, you appear willing to be

informed of their source, that you may endeavour to alleviate my distress, or share its burthen, I shall make no scruple of laying the inmost recesses of my heart open to you, and divulging such secrets as hitherto have remained impenetrable to the most inquisitive searcher after them.

"My father was of a noble family in Languedoc, and had revenues to the amount of ten thousand livres a year, besides the produce of his places under the government. I had two brothers, both older than myself, officers in the army. Ere I was fourteen, I had several advantageous parties proposed to me, but amongst them all, there was none who had any share in my affections, but the young Marquis de P—, who was not only agreeable in his person, but in his conversation and behaviour. Were I to paint him to you such as he appeared, my dear miss, I am afraid I should raise some emotions in your young heart that would ill suit with the devotion of this cloister. Let it suffice to say, he was a man every way formed to please, and that even those who were not, like me, blinded with love, acknowledge him worthy any woman's affections. He had paid his addresses to me in form for upwards of a twelve-month, and all parties were agreed that he was to be my husband. All the writings were drawn, the necessary consent obtained, and the very day appointed for the ceremony of our nuptials. Happy for me had it taken place: unhappy for me that ridiculous punctilios, and an over-refinement of what is called honor, discovered that he had not been noble but for two generations on his mother's side, and that his great grand-mother's aunt had been married to a Bourgeois. This single discovery made by my father, or some ill-natured envious person for him, set the whole match aside; and when I thought myself on the very eve of being the happiest of my sex, all matrimonial preparations were countermanded, and notice sent the young marquis, that for certain family reasons the marriage was postponed.

"What his grief was at this intelligence, I can best judge by my own. All the arguments used to solace me, served but to increase my melancholy. The frivolousness of the reasons urged for breaking off the match, were so many fresh wounds give to a dying martyr,—a martyr to false honour, and ridiculous prejudice.

"I shut myself in my chamber, and entirely devoted myself to grief for several successive days.—All the arts of my relations could not prevail upon me to touch a morsel of any kind of nutriment. They themselves began now to be sincerely afflicted with my situation, and, as a last resource, they sent for the marquis to prevail upon me to quit my room, and take some nourishment.

"A small summons was sufficient for him, who flew upon the wings of love to my relief. He rapped at my chamber door, and by a kind of sympathetic knowledge, my heart panted, and bid me fly to admit the visitor. What was my transport at beholding the marquis, or what was his joy at seeing me, can be better imagined than attempted to be expressed.—'My dear wife,' (those were his words) 'how happy I am in having this opportunity of visiting you after so cruel a sentence, and inhuman an exile!—In saying this he ran to embrace me, and I, with as much ardour, flew into his arms. Tears and kisses formed all our discourse, but so communicative and intelligible, that all language was a faint description of ideas, compared to them.

"We remained immoveable for some minutes; when at length recollecting my situation, I blushing retired from so close an embrace, and he seemed neither reluctant to let me withdraw, or less confused than myself at our former situation.

"He soon prevailed upon me to quit my chamber, and believe there were still sufficient means to make ourselves happy, even though my relations would not consent to my marriage.

Chapter XI
Continuing of the affecting history of Mademoiselle de Millioret.—Her secret marriage.—Is pestered again with admirers.—A match fixed upon.—Is discovered to be with child,—the terrible effects of her brother's resentment.—He kills her husband.—She escapes in men's cloaths,—travels to Nieuport,—embarks for England,—taken by a French privateer and carried into Dunkirk.—Discovers herself to avoid a dungeon,—is forced to appear against her brother, who is executed.— The treachery of the friar who married her,—takes refuge in a convent.

"As soon as I had been prevailed upon to resume the company of the world, and had broke my resolution of starving, the marquis was again forbidden the house, and I for some days was as disconsolate as ever. At the end of that time, I received the following billet from him:

My lovely spouse (for so I must call you) as there is nothing prevents our being happy, but your resolving to throw yourself into my arms, and for ever be united with me as one flesh and blood, I have prevailed upon father de Calliot (my confessor) to join our hands in holy matrimony. Let me know the hour that will most securely baffle the attention of your relations.
All epithets are too languid to express how much
I am yours,
De P—

"This letter, which it might be imagined would have re-animated my drooping spirits, terrified me more than all the apprehensions of being for ever separated from the marquis. It instantly drew such a picture of all my future misfortunes, that had I not been quite ignorant of mundane perspective, I must have perceived every shade of my unhappy life. But this scene was so transitory in my young mind, and the aromatic gale of love wafted me so easily to Cytherea's isle, that Cupid soon blinded me to all distant views. Nothing but matrimonial joys with my dear marquis occupied my thoughts, and I made an appointment the next morning for the ceremony.

"You behold me now a wife, the Marquise de P—, though still known by no other name than Mademoiselle de Millioret—my father and all my relations, ignorant of what had happened. I now resumed my former gaiety, and was congratulated upon my great philosophy in surmounting a passion, which being indulged, would have so greatly dishonoured my family. Little did the complimenters know my imaginary fortitude was purchased at the price of stolen gratification. My father now thought of procuring me another match, and all the groupe of my former admirers, with many additional ones in the list, presented themselves as lovers.

"Knowing my situation, I was obliged to practice all the female art of coquettry to make everyone believe he would be the happy man some time or other,—they were satisfied in the expectation, whilst the marquis affluently possessed what they were promised. Though my lovers were so easily baffled, my father, who only sought for my being well settled in the world, told me it was high time to think of choosing a husband: that he would not constrain my inclinations, if they did not clash with the honour of my family, but recommended the Count de St.— as a man every way fit to make me a good husband, and be an ornament to his house.

"After my father had made this overture, which prudence dictated to me not to oppose, the count addressed me upon the footing of an only suitor. He was handsome in his person, sensible and vivacious. If there had been no such person as the Marquis de P—, perhaps I should have admired him.

"He was every day more intimate in the family, and every one thought the match was settled,—when of a sudden I was complimented upon growing fat.—I had for some time discovered I was with child, but I was in hopes to conceal it, as the marquis assured me it was not perceptible. However, my relations had already taken the alarm, and all my visits were strictly watched, when they discovered my rendezvous with my husband.

"My brother had by bribery introduced himself into the chamber where we met, and just as we were going to repeat our joys, he rushed from a closet, and in saying, 'Villian, have I detected you in the very act!' he stabbed the marquis with his sword.—I fell upon my knees, and begged him to put an end to a life which he had now rendered insupportable, by destroying its better half.—'Madam,' said he, 'justice demands it, but I find nature more powerful.—Live a monument of thy own shameful lust.' In saying this he flew out of the room to make his escape, 'till such time as he could obtain his pardon. The house was already alarmed, and a multitude were presently in the chambers, spectators of this melancholy scene.

"My husband died in my arms in less than half an hour, and his relations were strictly bent upon having my brother's life for his. An aunt of mine, who had more compassion than the rest of my relations, came to me, and in advising me to make my escape, furnished me with the means of doing it. I could have wept for ever over the corpse of my husband, but maternal amity, and a regard for my own honour, induced me to take her counsel. I found if I remained, I should be witness against my brother, and the means of his losing his life,—and that my father was so irritated, he would endeavour to have the greatest severities exercised against me as a prostitute.

"These considerations induced me to make my escape by night in men's cloaths. I was advised to go over to England, as London is the most convenient place for lying-in privately; but as this was the latter end of the last war, and all communication between the two kingdoms was stopt, I was obliged to travel through Austrian Flanders. This occasioned me much embarrassment upon the frontiers, and I was upon the very point of being sent to prison as a spy, for not giving a satisfactory account of myself, when having discovered my sex and condition to the governor of Lisle, he dismissed me, saying it was an affair of gallantry.

"I embarked on board an English vessel at Nieuport, for England; but before we had been out of port eight hours, we were attacked by a French privateer, and after little opposition on our side, were taken and carried into Dunkirk.

"The horrors of a dungeon so terrified me that I wrote to the governor, informing him who I was, and he gave orders for my being immediately released. There was at that time a cousin of mine, an officer, in the town raising recruits, who was introduced to me. He told me he was acquainted with my misfortunes; and that he had wrote to my relations, and other friends of his in Languedoc, informing them of my being there, and to intercede for my father's forgiveness. I told him his kindness would be the ruin of my brother and myself, which it soon proved; for I was immediately sent for to appear, and forced to give a circumstantial account of the death of my husband; whereupon my brother was broke upon the wheel. All my endeavours to evince my chastity and innocence were of no avail; the father confessor who married us, to save his own reputation, denied that he ever joined our hands, and being looked upon as the outcast of this world, I sought this refuge (which, the bounty of my aunt procured) 'till I shall be called to the next.

Chapter XII
The effect of this history upon Kitty.—The favourable expectations of the sisterhood.—Their dissipations and inclinations delineated.—Kitty takes leave of Mademoiselle de Millioret, and sets out upon her return to her father, who recalls her from the nunnery.

This moving relation of Mademoiselle de Millioret greatly affected Kitty; and the more so, as it was accompanied by frequent sighs and involuntary tears. Our heroine began to think she had escaped a sea of troubles in so secure an asylum, and that it was by miracle her bark, after so short yet tempestuous a voyage, had been conducted into that safe port.

These reflexions naturally induced her to case some thoughts towards taking the vows and the veil, and the arguments of the sisterhood in their favour began to be less disrelished by her than before. Mademoiselle de C—, who had taken some pains to make a proselyte of Kitty, run with great joy to the lady abbess, to inform her she believed the work was done, and our heroine would consecrate her life to the salvation of her soul.

Mademoiselle was recompensed with trinkets for the commission she had so well executed. All the artifices of a nunnery were practiced to exhibit to Kitty the allurements and agreeableness of a cloyster; but these means had a contrary effect to their intent: pastimes and amusements effaced the melancholy images of Mademoiselle de Millioret's misfortunes, and with them all serious reflections upon being a nun.

This will not be amazing, when it is considered that the recreations of a nunnery, among the favourite sisters, are pretty near upon a par with the amusements of a boarding-school. Three fourths of those who take the veil are seduced when too young to form a proper judgment of it for themselves, or are forced by their parents in a more advanced age. These retain all their natural and mundane passions, and converse as freely upon them, as in the gayest private assemblies. Those who really and sincerely devote themselves to a holy life, never associate with the bonnes-vivantes.

When the joyeuses get together, they talk of the intrigues of the world, of the men they most like, of such a handsome fellow whom they wished to have a kiss of, and appeared that day at their grate. One evening a snug party of the most spirited nuns, among whom Kitty was admitted, had got together diverting themselves at questions and commands, and a general question was started, "what they most wished for?" All reserve being thrown off, every one wished to be out of the nunnery, but that being looked upon of course, it was not admitted as an answer.—Mademoiselle de P—, wished for Madame de Pompadour's height, another for her power, and a third for her situation.—Mademoiselle de M— wished for a handsome husband.—Mademoiselle de V—, for a coach and six, as then she would be sure of getting one, and Mademoiselle de R— said she owned she wished for nothing so much as twenty thousand pounds, as then she might command every thing. When it came to a brunette's turn to be questioned what she most wished for, she answered to be a frog; and being asked the reason, she replied, "Because it is forty days in a single act of coition."—This occasioned a general laugh; after which she was commanded to turn Turk in expectation of Mahomet's paradise, where the same performance continued six hundred thousand years, without intermission

This lascivious lady, who was so ill suited for a cloister, made her escape the next evening over the garden wall, where her father's valet de chambre waited to receive her, and carry her to Holland.

The time of Kitty's quitting the convent approached, and her father wrote to her, he believed she might venture to return to Madrid, without being in such danger as she was at her departure.

It was now the lady abbess herself took the greatest pains to persuade her to give up all worldly gratifications for the sake of her soul, and not to emerge from that sanctuary of innocence and religion, into the center of vice and temptation. These exhortations were repeated every morning by the old lady, and they were the chorus of the day by the young ones.

Kitty had sense and discernment enough to perceive she might live in the midst of society, and partake of all the innocent diversions of the world, without committing such crimes as were practiced in a convent; where, under the cloak of hypocrisy, scandal, intrigue, defamation, envy, lust, and unnatural gratifications are all hidden.

The day of Kitty's departure was fixed upon, to the great mortification of the old lady and her nymphs. As Mademoiselle de Millioret was the only one whom she thought worthy of her friendship, she waited upon her alone to take her leave. She found her at prayers, bathed in tears, and wrapt in real devotion; when she had finished, Kitty told her, if all the sisterhood were as sincerely pious, and as amiable in their characters, as herself, she should think it a happiness to pass her whole life amongst them; but as they were of a quite different stamp, and as she found it almost impossible to live in friendship a day with them, so numerous were their cabals, and great their jealousy, and as her father had called her to Madrid, she came to take her leave of the only person she esteemed in that house. That she should reckon amongst her most agreeable hours, those which had passed in conversation between them; that she hoped a separation of their persons, would be no cause of a discontinuance of their friendship, and that she would take the liberty of writing to her from time to time, and hoped she would keep up the correspondence.

"Go, my lovely girl," said Madamoiselle de Millioret, "and shine in a sphere, that your person and accomplishments prove nature has allotted you for.— Bless some happy man with your love, and a numerous progeny. Let me hear of your success and good fortune, which will give me the greatest pleasure of any sublunary intelligence."

At this reply Kitty melted into tears, and it was with some difficulty she could have resolution to retire. Nothing but an information that the coach was upon the point of setting out, could have prevailed upon her to have quitted her dear unfortunate Mademoiselle de Millioret.

Chapter XIII
Kitty's return to Madrid: her reflections upon the road. The meeting between her and her father, and the extravagance of his fondness for her; his distressed circumstances, and her commencing milliner. The force of example in her two celebrated courteszans. Kitty's soliloquy, and consequential resolution.

A fixed melancholy occupied the mind of our heroine all the way upon the road, and she was no way attentive to the discourse that passed between her fellow travellers, who had frequent disputes upon political and religious subjects, and appealed to her for the decision; which, without being acquainted with the merits of the controversies, she always made so equitably, that they found themselves, as they most frequently were, both in the wrong.

Kitty saw herself emerging from a state of solitude into the business and troubles of the world; which the more she knew, the more she feared. Her former experience of the deceit and allurements of the men, made her tremble at the thoughts of conversing with one alone; and the treachery and lust of gain of her own sex, made her almost resolve upon never more having any intimacy with them. It was now for the first time she began to reflect upon the folly of her father's conduct toward her;—how ridiculous it was for him to have given her an education so much superior to her station in life; that his fondness had prevented her being provided for suitable to her appearance, and that the only reasonable offer that ever had been made her, she had through inexperience and his instigation refused; that she was now arrived at her fifteenth year, and had never been accustomed to any kind of work that could procure her a maintenance, and in case her father's circumstances failed, she had no dependence whatever.

These true, but disagreeable reflexions, occupied the mind of Kitty almost all her journey; so that she arrived at Madrid full fraught with meditation in a very philosophical mood.

As soon as her father heard of her arrival, he flew to the inn; and after having embraced her with all the fondness of the most tender parent, he was upon the point of carrying her home upon his back, so great was his extasy; but reflecting that her baggage still remained there, he had the patience to wait till a coach was called.

He was greatly surprised at her melancholy, and was fearful some accident had happened to her, but he could not prevail upon her to inform him what it was; a physician was sent for to feel her pulse, who pronounced her very feverish, and she was ordered to keep her room a fortnight, though nothing ailed her.

Kitty's reflexions upon her return to Madrid, did but forerun the disagreeable consequences she had presaged. Her father found himself greatly involved in debt, which with the new edict that had imposed an additional tax upon silver plate, and stagnated his trade, occasioned his breaking.

Honest John's greatest concern was still for his daughter, whom he was now no longer able to support. He worked as a journeyman, but trade being very dead, he could not always find employ, and his full wages would not have been sufficient for their maintenance. He therefore made a collection amongst his friends for a sum sufficient to set Kitty up in a milliner's shop, which, though she was quite unacquainted with, she agreed to enter upon.

We now view our heroine behind the counter, in her father's house, measuring out ribband, and adjusting commodes.[1] She was for some time extreamly assiduous, and by means of renewing her ancient acquaintance with some of her former school-fellows, she gained a sum sufficient to live upon: but her natural dispositions for gaiety always predominating, she soon relaxed from her severe application, and frequented public places.

So agreeable a figure behind a counter had attracted the attention of all the young fellows who passed that way, who generally dropt in to purchase a ribbon or a pair of gloves, and these easily prevailed upon her, after the first or second visit, to accept of a ticket for the play, so that her diversions were little or no expence to her, except that they took up her time, and prevented her minding her business.

At the same time there were two women in Madrid who made a great noise, and attracted the attention of the whole metropolis: their names were Miss Murrio and Miss Cupero.[2] The first was handsome without being genteel, and the last genteel without being handsome. They had passed through a series of prostituted adventures from low extraction, and had arrived at the point of keeping their equipages, and being the general toasts of the gay and polite. Miss Murrio had at this time no certain support, but laid all Madrid under contributions; whilst Miss Cupero was kept by an old knight, who doated upon her and all her extravagancies. The success of these two women operated upon the minds of most of the girls of an ambitious turn in Madrid; those who were handsome saw every time they looked in the glass all the conquest and grandeur that attended Miss Murrio; and those who were ordinary, had they a tolerable shape, or a smartness of repartee, solaced themselves with Miss Cupero's glory. The example of these two women were greater incentives to prostitution than all the arts of men, or the force of inclination.

Kitty was one night at the play in the gallery, when these two heroines sat in the opposite boxes to each other; and tho' all the rest of them were quite empty, these two were filled with the finest cavaliers of Madrid. This excited Kitty's curiosity to know who they were, and being informed, vanity and envy led up all the troop of insatiable passions. "Have I not charms far beyond either of them!—Am not I young, beautiful and genteel—sensible and polite!—and shall these reign sole tyrants of the hearts of Madrid, whilst I move in the humble sphere of a milliner? Not to be borne." In repeating this soliloquy to herself, she took a full resolution of trying all the arts of woman to get a genteel husband, or at least a rich keeper.

---

1   "A tall head-dress fashionable with women in the last third of the 17th and first third of the 18th centuries, consisting of a wire frame-work variously covered with silk or lace; sometimes with streaming lappets which hung over the shoulders." [OED]

2   Miss Murrio is probably Fanny Murray. *Memoirs of the Celebrated Miss Fanny M[urray]* appeared in 1759. "Miss Cupero" is probably Lucy Cooper. On Lucy Cooper, see *Nocturnal Revels*, 2 volumes, (London, 1779) 1: 16-32.

Chapter XIV

Kitty's opinion of fortunetellers. Goes to an astrologer to know her fate: he casts her nativity, with his behaviour thereupon; sums up her good fortune, with which she is fully satisfied.

Our heroine was not so entirely divested of credulity, as to disbelieve all sorcery was fraud and imposition. Several of her acquaintance had had their fortunes told, and the very things had happened that were predicted. One, who was upon the point of marrying a young grocer, went with him to a conjuror's to have her fortune told, and she was informed she would certainly be married to the person who accompanied her the next day, and the thing came to pass. It is true, the lover had a conference with the old gentleman first, but we must not conclude from thence, that he gave him any insight into the affair. Another, who had lost her favourite dog, went to the cunning man to know where she should find it, and he told her it would be brought home the next day, upon condition she paid two guineas as a gratuity. She had her dog. Some say the sorcerer passed by her door the very day it was lost, and it was seen by some to follow him; but this must have been an idle report, except one can imagine that so great and learned a man as an astrologer would turn dog-stealer.

However, these and many more equally extraordinary prognostications prevailed upon Kitty to believe that these cunning men were cunning men indeed; and she resolved to have her fortune told.

The conjuror to whom she proposed applying to, lived near the place where the criminals are tried (not unlike our Old Bailey). Thither she went with a female acquaintance, who being still more eager than Kitty to know her destiny, would retire with the old gentleman first, and she came out of the closet fully satisfied with killing half a dozen husbands before she was thirty.

The French happily call fortune tellers, *Diseurs de bonne avantures,* for they never tell you anything to displease you for your money. If indeed an accident or misfortune is to happen, it is quite transitory; but they most frequently nip it in the bud, and, like lovers in a comedy, or a novel, you are married and happy at last.

Kitty being introduced into the astrologer's closet, he enquired the year, day, and hour of her birth; which she told him as near as she could remember and was informed; he then examined the lines of her hands and those of her face, and asked what particular moles she had? She answered, she had none in sight, but had a very large one under her left breast; he told her he must see it, but she would not consent to so indecent an inspection. He said it would be in vain for him to attempt telling her fortune without seeing it; that the prognostics hitherto were very favourable; he had already cast her nativity, and found she was born under Jupiter, whereby it was plain she would be blest with pleasure and riches; but that this mole alone would decide the extent of her power, for that though this planet was of very benign influence with respect to authority, it was generally considered as relating to the policy of states.

Such a world of learning, pleasure, and riches, intoxicated poor Kitty, and she thought she should spoil her fortune for ever if she did not shew him her mole; she therefore unlaced her stays without any fear or hesitation. As soon as her snowy bosom was disclosed, the old gentleman put on his spectacles with great eagerness, and examined her mole, whilst he with some transport handled her pouting hemispheres, crying at the same time, "Amazingly great! Surprising power! Wonderful domination!" Kitty was so attentive to the harmony of the words, that she paid no regard to the indecency of his action, though he continued near a quarter of an hour with one hand upon her bosom, and the other under his night gown, which seemed to vibrate with uncommon elasticity; he at length slobbered her bosom with kisses, which he pretended was only to felicitate that fortunate mole, which was the certain testimony of her future power over the hearts of men.

She now perceived what he was at, and began to be under great apprehensions he would go to still more indecent lengths; but whether he had vented the fever of his love, or had surmounted it, we will not pretend to decide; but he was so far master of his art as to impute all his conduct to the inquest of her stars.

He then resumed his pen, ink and paper, and having made various figures and calculations, he read over to her their neat produce, the sum total of which amounted to this:

That she would be the reigning toast of the first nobility in Spain; at once the only object of the women's envy, and the men's adoration. That all the present triumphant beauties would be talked of no more. Miss Rocia, Miss Murrio, or Miss Cupero's name no longer mentioned; but she alone would engross the whole conversation of the beau monde of Madrid, whilst she rolled in the most magnificent equipage, and lived in the sumptuous splendor of the first duchess of Spain.

Such a lot could not fail putting a girl of Kitty's disposition into good spirits; and though she suspected the wise man's continence and he would have been very well satisfied without any pecuniary recompence, she gave him a guinea, though his usual fee was but half a crown.

As soon as the two nymphs had retired from the conjuror, they began to compare notes, and though Kitty's companion had at first thought six dead husbands a very comfortable dower, she began to think the cunning man had not dealt so well by her as Kitty, whom he had given so many living lovers; and she had a great mind to go back to him to have it a little altered, as she imagined he had forgot to tell her the man she should be happy with: but Kitty persisting in not returning, lest he might recant some part of her future glory, she was prevailed upon to defer the visit 'till the next day, when she was

resolved to go with another young lady of her acquaintance, and give it him
for not telling her as good a fortune as he had Kitty.

Chapter XV

The consequence of having her fortune told.—Her uncommon extravagance
and dissipations.—Is chid and threatened by her father.—Her resolves thereupon.
Her acquaintance with Don Cupidino.—Her notion of predestination.—Consents
to his proposals,—lives with him as his wife.—He is ordered abroad.—
Their grief at parting.—His long absence, and her after reflexions.

The flattering hopes which the fortune-teller had inspired her with, gave
her an entire disrelish to attending her shop and her business; and she relied
so much upon his favourable prognostications, that she made up most of her
goods in her shop for her own wear, and though she had a very decent
wardrobe of cloaths for a milliner, she purchased two or three new suits. She
then frequented public places more than ever.

Her father had by this time in some measure recovered his circumstances;
his creditors having found he was honest, though indigent, were as favorable
as possible to him, so that he was in a short time enabled to work for himself.
He still lived in the same house, the shop of which was occupied by his daughter; and though his tenderness for Kitty made him overlook great numbers of
her foibles and extravagancies, yet he was so thoroughly convinced now of
her inconsiderateness, by turning almost her whole stock in trade to her own
use in dress, that he could not refrain remonstrating to her hereupon.

This nettled Kitty, who had no great opinion of her father's intellects; and
as he was ignorant of her high-flown scheme of grandeur, she pitied his weakness in returning him silent answers. He saw every day her band boxes grow
emptier, without her purse filling;—he fretted to his very soul—chid her, and
at last threatened to turn her in the street. His heart wept when he uttered
this severe sentence; but Kitty, who was greatly piqued at such an advertisement, resolved to throw off the parental yoke the very first opportunity that
offered, and put it out of his power to repeat his menaces.

With these revolting resolutions in her mind, she went to the play, and sat
next to the gay, the handsome Don Cupidino. He praised her beauty and commended her wit; she approved his person, and was not displeased with his compliments. He waited upon her home, and made a party for the next day. He was
charmed with the beautiful innocence of her person, and she was pleased with
finding a lover in an officer, and a man of his appearance and fortune.

Every compliment he paid her charms, renewed in her imagination the
whole chain of successes, which the conjuror had predicted to her. This,
added to the effect she began to find this handsome cavalier had upon her
heart, rendered her a compleat predestinarian, and she was thoroughly convinced her stars had thrown him in her way to make her happy.

With so favorable an opinion of her guardian angel, we need not be surprised to find she gave him greater liberties than she had ever done any man before. He was now convinced she was his own, and in order to arrive at possession he told her, he was sorry to see her charms and merit misplaced, that they were destined to shine in a much superior sphere, and begged that she would permit him to take a genteel lodging, and make her the offer of his purse, 'till such time as she could do better.

She was so entirely wrapt up in the opinion that there was no avoiding her fate, that she with very little ceremony consented, and he took her a lodging not many streets from her father's.

John was at first inconsolable at her loss, but finding the thing could not be prevented, he endeavoured to palliate it, and gave out that Kitty was married. Don Cupidino's behaviour in some measure countenanced this, as, being very fond of her, he never slept a night from her for a considerable time.

Thus, like man and wife, they lived supremely happy for upwards of eight months; at the end of which time he receiving orders to join his regiment and go abroad, and they were obliged to separate. Never was there a more affecting scene than this.—Eight months enjoyment had not cloyed the lover; he still adored her, and she tenfold repaid all his tender sentiments. She fain would have accompanied him, nay, proposed putting on men's cloaths, and serving as a volunteer in his company; but he had too great a regard for her, and knew that the delicacy of her constitution would not allow of such an exploit.

He did not leave her without money for her support, protesting the utmost constancy to her 'till his return. She lived in the greatest retirement for some time, seeing no company, and conversing with little else but books. The expected time of Don Cupidino's return was already elapsed, contrary winds and fresh orders had been the occasion of it, and her money was nearly exhausted.—

How extravagant did her conduct now appear to herself! "What," (said she), "am I the dupe to the ridiculous predictions of a lascivious conjuror, who, to screen his guilt, has told me idle stories of grandeur and power? And have I upon so slight a foundation given up my virtue to a man, whom it is true is very amiable, but who perhaps may never more return, or at least not to my arms? I go by his name, which I ever will to the day of my death, but who believes me his wife? Alas! I have bartered every thing that is dear to me, for nonsense and fortune-telling chimeras. Banished from my father—exiled from my relations and friends—estranged from the honest part of my sex, I must live a monument of consummate folly, unpardonable vanity, and ridiculous ambition.—Oh! that I were again cloistered in a convent, or shut from the eyes of the world—to be no longer a disgrace to myself and my parents!"

These were such thoughts as occupied poor Kitty for near two months—in which time she had no connection with the world, but was considering the most probable means of extricating herself from her present dilemma.

Chapter XVI

Kitty's distress, and application to the register office for a place.—This difficulties and obstacles to getting one.—Her desperate resolution, and fortunate meeting with a lady, who takes her home, and makes Kitty her companion. Who the lady proves to be. Don Allenzo's declaration of his passion, and its menacing consequences.

She had yet no news from her much beloved Don Cupidino; the money he had left her was entirely exhausted, and she had already began to trespass upon her cloaths for a support; it was now high time to think of a further resource. She looked upon the conjuror's prognostications ere now in their true light, and resolved no longer to expect miracles.

Her father she imagined inexorable and her pride would not let her submit to supplicate any of her former friends. She had frequently heard of register-offices for servants, who often obtained thereby good places; she accordingly went to the most eminent one in the capital, and registered her name and qualifications for an upper-maid's place in a genteel family. A few days afterwards she got intelligence of a lady who wanted an upper servant, and she applied to be hired.

The lady enquired what place she had lived in last? To which Kitty answered, she had never been in any yet.—"Who then is it to give you a character?"[1] "My landlady," answered our heroine. "That will not do," replied the lady, and in so saying, left her to console herself. This same obstacle, the want of a character, still remained wherever she applied.—So hard is the fate of a young girl, who has once gone astray, and who, though willing, cannot regain the path of virtue, for want of some kind of real protection. Her talents and learning were also frequent objections to a place, as it could not be imagined that a person who had been so finely brought up, would condescend to do the work that would be allotted her.

Kitty began now to despair of ever getting a place. She found her cloaths diminish gradually, and that she still remained a burthen to herself, without any prospect of change for the better.—She had still virtue enough to refrain from prostitution, but had not philosophy sufficient to surmount the difficulties of this life. She had resolved upon drowning herself, and rose one morning earlier than usual to put her design in execution. In walking along a park near the metropolis, which conducts to a famous pond for desperate lovers, she met a lady who accosted her, and enquired of her, whither she was going in such a hurry? Kitty replied, she did not know. Whether the lady suspected by her looks her errand, or retained some knowledge of her face, is

---

1 A personal recommendation.

not certain; but her first curiosity being still more excited by this answer, she begged of Kitty to tell her who she was. She replied, she was an unhappy girl, without either friends or money, who had come thither in order to destroy herself.

The lady counselled her against such rash resolves, and persuaded her to go home and breakfast with her. She then begged of her to give her some insight into her history, as she might, perhaps, be of service to her, and Kitty with little reserve told her the narrative of her life as it has here been related. After the lady had chid her for her imprudence, she said her father was still more to blame than her; first, for bringing her up in such an extravagant manner, without having any fortune to give her, and for having been so ridiculously fond of her, as to have refused her the adopting her of her own. This was the lady who had taken a fancy to Kitty in her tender years.

After saying this, she told her if she would give up all thoughts of the captain, and resolve upon a virtuous life, in despite of conjurers prophecies, she would support her as her companion, which she had so long before proposed doing.

Kitty fell upon her knees, and, with a heart of deep contrition, solemnly protested she never more would think of man, but devote her whole life to please her patroness, who had so generously saved a wretch from certain perdition.

In this agreeable situation our heroine remained for some months, always accompanying the lady, who called Kitty her niece; notwithstanding all the artifices and cabals of the servants, whose jealousy made them invent the greatest falsities against her, in hopes to supplant her in their lady's favour.

Her constant employment was to read to the lady both night and morning books of piety and devotion; to accompany her to church, and overlook the servants.

Don Allenzo, nephew to the lady, visited in the family, and had for some time taken notice of Kitty in a more than common manner. She was strictly upon her guard how she made any return of his attention and politeness; but as he took frequent opportunities, when his aunt was out of the way, to converse with Kitty, she found herself a good deal embarrassed how to behave to him.

He told her one day, that he had acquainted himself with all her misfortunes, and sympathized with her in the most minute part of her distress; that could he but command her attention for a few minutes, to inform her of his unhappy situation, and flatter himself she had but the most slender feeling upon the occasion, he should not only think she sufficiently requited his humanity, but the very cause of his grief would be removed.

So genteel and insinuating a declaration of his passion necessarily forced from Kitty some kind of reply. "I am sorry, Sir," said she, "that my distress should ever give you any uneasiness; but I am still more chagrined that you should have any upon your own account."

"My lovely girl," replied he, "I know not whether I can properly call it upon my own account or yours.—You are still the cause of my sufferings.—I love, I adore you.—You must have perceived my frequent attentions to you alone, whilst absent from every thing else—how improperly I have answered to the most trifling questions when you were present—how eagerly I have sought opportunities to open all my soul to you, and reveal the source of my distraction. I have now done it; and out of charity, if not gratitude, do not tyrannize over a heart where you reign with such despotic sway."

The words forced involuntary tears from Kitty, who saw the precipice she stood over. After she had somewhat recovered herself, she begged him not to persevere in her undoing; that if his aunt had any intelligence of his pretended passion, which the ill-natured servants would take all imaginable care to acquaint her with, she would no more look upon her; and therefore beseeched him never to think more of her again.

This was but adding fuel to his flame; he told her he could provide for her as well, and more agreeably than his aunt did, and that her displeasure would be a plausible reason for his making some provision for her.

Chapter XVII
The discovery of Kitty's intrigue by her patroness; is dismissed [from] her house and taken into keeping by Don Allenzo, who is immoderately fond of her; but this soon changes into the utmost coldness, and he abruptly leaves her.

The news of this young cavalier's frequent visits to Kitty, when alone, was presently spread in the house, and the lady's maid, who was so jealous of her, took the first opportunity of acquainting her mistress therewith. She at first believed it was the effect of envy; but being informed an appointment had been made for that afternoon, the lady told Kitty she was going to a relation of hers, and she need not accompany her. The lovers were greatly pleased with this news, and were very punctual to their rendezvous. The lady returned to her closet unexpectedly, and found her nephew upon his knees at Kitty's feet.

Her rage was so great, that it stopt the utterance of all words. She hastily retired, and Kitty received the following note from her the next morning:

"Is this the return, ungrateful wretch! For all my generosity and benevolence?—To carry on an intrigue with my nephew under my very nose, is not to be borne, and I desire you will immediately provide for yourself elsewhere."

A flood of tears gushed upon the paper at Kitty's reading this sentence of exile.—She knew it was in vain to expostulate with her benefactress, whose decrees were irrevocable; she therefore packed up her baggage and set out.

She took a lodging not far from the market of Hay,[1] where her lover soon waited upon her, and made such protestations of sincerity, that the regard she

---

1 Haymarket, an area known for its theater and for prostitutes.

had for him, (which was not small) added to her present indigent circumstances, soon prevailed upon her to accept the tender of his love upon his own terms.

He made her an allowance of five guineas a week, and purchased her besides all the cloaths and trinkets she had occasion for. Never was man more fond of woman the first three months;—all was festivity, joy, and mirth. He escorted her to every public place, and though she still went by the name of her first lover, the world was credulous enough to believe the ceremony had actually been performed between Don Allenzo and Kitty.

She imagined his love, at first so fervent, would never subside, and therefore did not cast a thought towards any future support. At length his visits grew less frequent; he seldom passed an evening with her, and she soon after received the following letter:

Madam,

There is nothing so agreeable as an ancient friendship, and nothing so frightful as a stale passion. Do not imagine there is any kind of merit in being faithful; constancy is the most detrimental thing in the world to the reputation of a beauty. Beside, who can determine upon your honesty? your attachment to me may have all been imaginary.

What difference there is between a glowing and a declining passion! In the first, every hour glides upon the wings of love, and every day brings fresh pleasure as it increases one's flame. In the last, moments appear days, and the slothful index of time does but point out the diminution of one's love.

Therefore I am resolved no longer to repeat my visits, which being burthensome to myself, must be disagreeable to you.

Allenzo

Kitty read this epistle over and over, thinking at first she misunderstood its meaning; but the oftener she read it, the more she was convinced of the rectitude of her first judgment. Though she was not so much shocked at its contents, as the alarming situation she saw herself in, she could not help upbraiding perfidious man with his treachery and deceit.

After she had fully commented upon Allenzo's unkindness, she began to seriously consider the most probable means of supporting herself. The indulgence of two lovers had greatly effaced her former virtuous sentiments, and she began to view prostitution through a more favourable glass than she had formerly seen it. Allenzo's reasoning had a great weight with her, and she thought there was some foundation in "constancy being the most detrimental thing in the world to the reputation of a beauty."

Buoyed up with these salutary notions, she found herself not at all averse to receive the caresses of any man who should properly recompence her; and it was not long before she came to a firm resolution of disposing of her favours to the best bidder. She had, however, the modesty still left, not to put this project in execution at the house where she had passed for Allenzo's wife, but quitted her lodging with all the decent appearance of a married woman.

Chapter XVIII
Some account of Kitty's various conquests, with an entertaining adventure at a bagnio, and a curious matrimonial dialogue, which may be read with some advantage by every inconstant couple.

Kitty's figure and appearance, her youth and novelty, we may easily imagine soon attracted a variety of lovers, when they might be indulged upon their own terms. Though she had an entire disgust to such promiscuous gratification, as she reaped the harvest in a time of great scarcity, she was easily allured by the sweets to swallow the bitter draught.

In her troop of gallants she could muster from sixteen to sixty, bachelors, married men, and widowers; from these she could not fail collecting an easy competence, and living in such a manner as she would chuse, the indulgence of her lovers only excepted.

She was walking in the place of public resort (nearly resembling our park) one evening, with her companion, (who served her also in the capacity of a servant) when a middle-aged gentleman gave her the wink to retire, and he followed her. They soon agreed upon the tavern they should sup at, and afterwards the bagnio they should adjourn to for the rest of the night.

Scarce had they made one sacrifice to the Paphian goddess,[1] before the whole house was alarmed with the cry of "Fire! Fire!" Kitty would have been the foremost to have made her escape, if her gallant had not persuaded her to lay quiet till he went and enquired the cause; however, she listened at the door, and still heard the name of that element uttered with great vociferousness. At length candles being brought, and all the male nocturnal lodgers of the house being assembled, they enquired where the fire was. "In my throat by G—d," answered a drunken rake who lay sprawling upon the stairs, "and if you don't give me some liquor to quench it, I shall burn the house."

After laughing at this inebriate conceit, they procured the rioter some liquor, and he was pacified. Every one then returned as he thought to his respective bed, but the door of Kitty's chamber joining with the next, and her lover seeing another man enter it, thought the adjacent one must be his. The mistake was not immediately discovered, but Kitty readily imagined there was a considerable difference in her lover since his return, which, added to the frequent repetition of "my dear Mrs. S—, I never was so happy in my life before," induced her to believe she was not the imagined object of his

---

1 Aphrodite, goddess of love.

embrace. However, as she conceived her lover might from the first have taken her for some other woman, in quality of whom he might better recompence her than as herself, she deferred coming to any eclaircissement upon this head.

When Aurora had just began to appear, she was awakened by a very clamorous chattering in the next room. "I'll lay no longer with such a drousy bedfellow. I might as well have staid at home with my old impotent husband. Do you think you shall have five pistols for this? No! I warrant I can get better men and cheaper." These words were uttered by a female in the utmost rage, whilst hitherto her companion kept time to her discord by snoring, and Morpheus had still sealed the eyes of Kitty's lover: but ere this energetic declamation was finished by the neighbouring female, half awake he took Kitty in his arms, desiring her to appease her wrath, for that she should soon have no reason to complain.

These unintelligible words were scarce uttered, before the clamorous lady scream'd out, and cried, "I am undone! I am ruined! My husband!" Kitty's lover jumped out of bed and flew to the door, where he met the drowsy amoroso of the adjacent chamber.—They remained motionless for some time, staring at each other with their eyes fixed, without either having the faculty of speech. Kitty, who could not comprehend the meaning of this disorder, got up, and perceived the cull she had supped with at the tavern the other side of the threshold. Her curiosity now led her to enquire how he came to depute another to supply his place, and the *party-quare*[1] being convened, the enigma was unravelled.

Mr. S— (Kitty's first lover) had had an intrigue with his own wife the latter part of the night, without knowing it; and her stallion had been caressing Kitty through mistake for his mistress, in every sense of the word.

The married pair were each of them ashamed to look one another in the face, and the stallion, thinking he made but an awkward figure naked before his lady's husband, sneaked off during their confusion. Kitty took the hint from him, and retired to her room, and the loving couple had now an opportunity of comparing notes.

"Very fine indeed, madam," said the husband in first breaking silence, "so this is the way you serve me in my absence."

"Sir," replied the lady, "I think you have no reason to upbraid me, when it is plain you are as guilty as I am."

H. "Yes, madam, but I think there is some allowance to be made for the difference of our sex, and your ill treatment of me."

W. "And I think Sir, there is a great allowance to be made for the difference of our age and your inability."

H. "How, madam, the difference of our age and my inability!—there are

1 Strange party.

but five years difference, and I am younger for a man than you are for a woman;—and as to ability I can procure a sufficient witness in the next room to prove I am as able as any man."

W. "Perhaps you may, Sir, with the woman that you like, but I never found you so."

H. "The defect, then, madam, is on your side.—If you have not charms to excite desire, can you blame me for not being fond?"

Here the waiter coming in the discourse was interrupted, which would otherwise, in all probability, have ended in an open declaration of war; but the gentleman recollecting he had not satisfied Kitty, he came into her apartment, and presented her with a couple of pistoles, when she prevailed upon him to forgive his wife, as he was as culpable as her. The good-natured man was easily persuaded to this, and the fond couple went home together without any kind of seeming dissatisfaction.

Chapter XIX
Kitty's present notions of the men; her disposition for dress, and the causes of her poverty.—Her apprehensions of a certain fashionable disorder.—Miss Tonzeno's sentiments upon the risks of women of gallantry.—Which is to be preferred by prudent women.—Kitty's fear of the loss of her beauty.—Her great ill fortune in having ten ideal gonorrheas;—the roguery of her surgeon set in a strong light by a gentleman of the faculty, who becomes acquainted with her;—the nature of his fee, &c.

In the course of Kitty's business she was spectator and auditor of many such scenes as that represented in the last chapter, which appears surprising to those only who are unacquainted with the variegated prostitution of both sexes. Our heroine had never entertained any very favourable opinion of either the merits or probity of the male sex in general; but this acquaintance with their whoredom gave her a thorough disgust to the indulgence of their passions and appetites.

Though Kitty earned her five or six guineas a week very easily and amorously, yet her natural penchant for dress and appearance, left her but seldom a guinea in her pocket, and her watch and trinkets were often at a relation's for the produce of current cash. So that we need not be surprized to find her poverty kept pace with her prostitution, and that a succession of lovers furnished her only with the mere means of living.

Our heroine had from her first entrance upon the stage of gallantry, been very apprehensive of what she had so frequently heard in her chaster days called under the name of the bad distemper. When at the boarding-school, Miss Tonzeno, that libidinous tutress, had inculcated into Kitty, and the rest of her pupils, that there was nothing to fear in the converse with men, but pregnancy and the bad distemper. That variegated indulgence would prevent the first, and promote the latter; and as this was more easily concealed from the world than a prominent ventre,[1] and consequential to more diversified indulgence, it was to be preferred by all prudent women, who had their character at heart.

Notwithstanding these sagacious notions, Kitty was not without great apprehensions that her unbounded career must terminate at this point.—Her fears did not arise from a too sollicitous regard for her constitution, reflecting on the solitude of confinement, or the disgust of nauseating medicines; but from an opinion that her nose would be in danger, as she had often heard that feature made its downfall upon these occasions.—It was therefore the terror of having her pretty face spoiled, that gave such great uneasiness to Kitty: nor can we think this unnatural, when we have been told by an eminent writer, that "the last sigh of a fine woman, is not so much for the loss of life, as the loss of her beauty."[2]

Kitty's nose was ever foremost in her head; after passing a night with a new lover, the first thing she did was feeling if this feature was as firm as when she went to bed the preceding evening, and looking the glass to see if it remained in the same place; after this operation her mind was pretty easy, till she had occasion to make use of a necessary utensil; when her imagination was so fruitfully venereal, that it instantly infected the genital parts.

Upon these occasions she never failed applying to an *eminent* surgeon, who told her it was well she took it in time; it might have been worse; but that he hoped he should soon master it, with the help of proper remedies, if she would take care and live soberly and regularly, which he most certainly did, for the reasonable sum of five pistoles.

Kitty was so unfortunate as to have no less than ten of these inveterate ideal gonorrhoeas in about six months; for the cure of which she always applied to the same surgeon, who very honestly administered to her the usual cathartic medicines; which, after having purged her head of the infection, left her body precisely in the same situation it was before, but her purse much lighter, which was one great cause of her finances being in so bad a situation.

At the time she was imaginarily ill of the eleventh infection, a gentleman of the faculty became acquainted with her; and testifying a desire of being still more intimate, she frankly told him her situation. But he distrusting it to be a finesse of her, to avoid his embraces, begged of her to let him examine, and he would give her his best advice. Upon inspection he found the parts somewhat excoriated by too severe an application to business, but that she was perfectly clear of infection. This confirmed him in his opinion that she wanted to impose upon him; which she discovering, acquainted him with her sur-

1 Belly or womb.
2 Richard Steele in *The Spectator* Vol. 1, no. 33, Satuday, April 7, 1711. Steele cites (Charles de Marguetel de Saint-Denis de) Saint-Évremond as his source. This sentiment appears in Saint-Évremond, *Works*, 1714, i, 160. Donald F. Bond, editor, *The Spectator* 5 vols. (Oxford: Clarendon Press, 1965), 1: 138, n. 2.

geon's name, whom she assured him had already cured her of several claps, which were not indeed so inveterate as the present, but which proved him to be a man of great honor and skill in his business.

The physician could not refrain from laughing at this information, telling her if she never were more infected than at present, she had been greatly imposed upon, which he very certainly believed; but that on the contrary if she had been really injured, the surgeon she applied to would never have perfected her cure, as it would have prevented her propagating the disorder, the most advantageous source of all his gains, that the surgeons began already to complain of the honest practice of some physicians, who had probity enough to dispatch their patients out of hand, and not undo one day what they had done the day before, in saying, "the medicines had already gained the superiority over the disorder; and if the women of the town were ever radically cured, the malady would very soon be extirpated, and then adieu to their chariots, and even their flowing periwigs, for that anatomy and phlebotomy would never restore their constitution, if the want of the pox threw it into such a galloping consumption. But for my part," continued the physician, "I think these only are their provinces, and if they cannot thrive with broken limbs, they should break the whole ones—let the physician prescribe, the apothecary prepare, and the surgeon execute.

This son of Hippocrates having so thoroughly convinced Kitty of her sanity, and the roguery of her surgeon, she readily gave him his fee in the currency of love; and resolved for the future to be less timorous, and better acquainted with the nature and symptoms of the disorder, which she had so often had in her head, when she fancied it in the other extremity.

Volume II

Chapter I
Kitty's application to physical studies, and her great desire of practicing her skill. Becomes acquainted with a little Jew. Some anecdotes of his gallantry. Is enamoured with Kitty. He becomes her patient. She exercises her medicinal knowledge upon him. He is given over, and she resolves to confine herself to the theory of physic only.

The recompence she made her physical lover for his instruction was not thrown away. From this time she consulted the best authors upon the subject of this disorder, and soon became so great an adept, that she eagerly wished for an opportunity of fairly practicing her skill, and would not have been sorry to be really ill, in order to have had an opportunity of exercising her medicinal knowledge.

At this juncture she became acquainted with a certain little man, whom the general opinion of Madrid pronounced a Jew: though one of the most diminutive men nature ever produced not deformed. He was a very great intriguer;

but his amours were like himself, trifling and uncommon. In the zenith of his glory, for he was now reduced, he had dared to pay his addresses to some of the finest women in the kingdom; and though so small himself, he was a great admirer of tall females. Signora G——, the singer, had been his predominant flame; he had presented her with an elegant sideboard of plate, got off her benefit tickets at an extravagant price, and even went to Holland to pass some time, in order to forget her. He was thus desperately in love with her, for no other reason as can be discovered, but because she was a tall woman. He never had attempted to even kiss her lips, because he was so short as not to be able to reach without being elevated, and she would not have her chairs dirtied; he accordingly made her a present of a handsome tabouret,[1] with a view of making use of it upon such occasions; but unfortunately the first time he got upon it to embrace her, signora was out of temper; she pulled him down, and having laid him across her knee, gave him a handsome whipping.—This was such a memento to him, that he never afterwards attempted so great an indecency.

Such was his extravagant passion for tall women; when being one night at a public ball, and running with some haste across the room, he trod in Lady Peeporo's train, and was tript up. "Bless the child," she cried, and in taking him up, said, "My dear, I hope you have not hurt yourself." This so irritated the self-sufficient enamorato, that he publickly declared that night, he did not think her ladyship so handsome as people cried her up, for that she was too tall, and thereby awkward. This declaration he did not dare recant by his attachment, for fear of falling once more into the hands of a tall woman; and henceforward he thought a woman five feet two inches of a tolerable height.

To this reason alone we can ascribe him condescension of protesting himself desperately in love with Kitty; for he still retained his former majestic personage—three feet and an inch! However, so it was—and a more constant dangler was never seen within the gates of Madrid.

Kitty was not unacquainted with his history or disposition, and therefore knew when he was once attached to a woman, she might use him at discretion. So insignificant a figure protesting his love, naturally excited contempt; and Kitty's physical disposition surmounting all her other passions, she resolved to convert her little lover into her patient. She accordingly told him, if he had a mind to prove the sincerity of his declaration, he would not refuse to undergo a little corporeal mortification, which would give her the highest opinion of his regard for her.

He naturally inquired what was the operation, swearing that if it was at the price of one of his (little) limbs, he would satisfy her no bodily pain, however exquisite, could be equal to his mental anxiety. She told him in a few words, that if he would get a gonorrhœa, (a real, not a fictitious one) and let her cure him, which she flattered herself she could do as well as any surgeon

---

1 "A low seat or stool, without back or arms, for one person: so called originally from its shape." [OED]

in town, being deficient in nothing but a little practice, he alone should be the happy man, and reign monarch of her bed.

He made no reply, but taking his hat, immediately visited a public stew, (in a street not unlike our Drury-lane) where having as he thought sufficiently wallowed in filth and disease, he returned to display the trophies of his conquest: but at the end of the three days the case being dubious, he repaired to his former rendezvous, and there soon remained no doubt of his being very decently clapped.

Kitty's heart was greatly elated at having this opportunity of practising her medicinal skill,—and she for the first time embraced him in wishing him joy upon his lucky acquisition. Upon examination, the inflammation being found very great, she prepared and gave him the necessary fomentations; and having physicked and purged him till the poor devil was scarce visible, she thought she had near perfected her cure,—when certain symptoms appeared, which baffled all art. Her lover was soon brought to such a pass, that she began to be apprehensive for his life; and her fears upon this head at length induced her to call in the aid of her physical acquaintance, who told her, that she had treated her friend in such a manner, that nothing but a miracle could save his life, as his disorder had got to such a height, as not to be cured without salivation;[1] and as the present emaciated state of his body rendered that operation most imminently dangerous. However, after the faculty had absolutely given him over, and his death was every moment expected, he recovered, to the no small satisfaction of Kitty, or her physical friend.

This medicinal experiment, which had like to have proved so fatal to her little lover, deterred Kitty from ever thinking any more of turning practitioner; and henceforward she contented herself with the theory, without wishing to be disordered for the sake of experiment.

Chapter II
The flame of Kitty's little love is extinguished, and he repeats no more his visits. Becomes acquainted with a citizen, who makes her a handsome allowance. Her uneasiness at the absence of her real lover Don Cupidino. Her soliloquies, with their effect, and an uncommon epistle from her keeper.

Notwithstanding the ardour of her little lover's flame, she quenched it by those medicines which were in vain administered for his malady. He never

1 "[A] *Salivation may alike be raised by rubbing with mercurial Ointment, fumigating with Cinnabar, or taking mercurial Preparations* inwardly, which new Method of cleansing the Body was unknown to Physicians in former Times, though now the most certain Remedy for the *Venereal Diseases,* and by some Physicians applied in curing several other Diseases; I wish I could say, with equal Success." John Astruc, *A Treatise of Venereal Diseases, in Nine Books* (London: Printed for W. Innys and J. Richardson, C. David, J. Clarke, R. Manby, and H.S. Cox, 1754), xii.

paid her a single visit after his recovery, but was sincerely thankful for having escaped so well out of her hands, after being conducted by her to the very threshold of the mansion of death.

The time she had lost in physical researches was now to be made up, and she applied herself closer to business than ever. In the course of trade she became acquainted with a city shopkeeper, who agreed to allow her a handsome maintenance, to the amount of ten pistoles a week.

He never passed but one night in the week with her, which was from the Saturday to the Sunday, when his family thought he went out of town. He was by this oeconomy of love lavishly fond of her at the end of two months, (a double honey moon!) which he testified by frequent presents of every sort; so that Kitty might have thought herself tolerably easy in her circumstances, if in her hours of retirement she could have effaced from her memory the image of her dear Don Cupidino; but he ever presented himself to her view, and for successive hours would she trace him in her imagination through his military conduct. "Now" (would she cry aloud) "is he leading up his company and attacking the enemy. See how they fly before his victorious band!—Ah! Do they rally?—beware of that ambush, dear Cupidino.—Ill-fated shot, thus cruelly to tear my lovely hero from me.—Is the wound mortal? No! Ye Gods, he lives, and we shall still be happy!"

These frantic soliloquies, which she frequently indulged herself in, often attracted a group of listeners to her chamber door, and her landlady, her husband, and all their lodgers pronounced her out of her senses.

"Poor young woman!" they would cry, "you find she has been crossed in love, and that has turned her brain—she should have some advice—her friends should be acquainted with her disorder, it will grow upon her if not taken in time, and it will be dangerous to meet her about the house."

The first time her landlady had an opportunity, she acquainted Kitty's city friend with the observations that had been made upon his imagined wife, telling him she was afraid his lady was not quite so well in her sense as she could wish, for very frequently when she was alone, she would call out upon some person, and talk of killing, shooting, and fighting; that she had cautioned her maid to take care and put the knives out of her mistress's way; but that she had great apprehensions she would commit some desperate act with her scissors.

Her lover was greatly surprised at this information, as he had never perceived any thing irregular in her behaviour, and as he could not discover any reason for so young a woman, whom he affluently supported being under any mental affliction. The landlady, however, prevailed upon him to hearken a little before he went into her apartment, as she did not doubt but that he would soon be convinced of the truth of what she said; but having waited half an hour in expectation of her mad fit coming upon her, he could no longer refrain from visiting her, being fully persuaded that what the hostess had told him was an imposition.

Kitty met him with her accustomed chearfulness, and the landlady's remarks upon her behaviour afforded them food for conversation and mirth the greatest part of the evening; but the next time her lover came, unfortunately the street door was left open, and she not being advertised of his visit, was actually in one of her deepest soliloquies when he came to her chamber door. He stopt short upon hearing her cry out in the most theatrical tone, "See how he bleeds!" He at first imagined some rival had intruded upon her presence, and in her defence she had wounded him; but when he heard her continue, "Ah! wretches!—miscreants!—cowards!—dastardly Gauls! Do you croud your legions thus to mangle one dying man, who living defied you all!" he began to recollect what the landlady had told him, and descended to enquire whether Kitty was now in one of her frantic moods, or whether she had actually some persons with her whom she was thus upbraiding?

A congress being accordingly assembled at her door, her madness was unanimously ratified; and her city friend departed thoroughly contented that she had not yet bit him. As soon as he returned home, he wrote her the following letter:

Madam,

I am extremely afflicted with your situation, notwithstanding you disowned to me the last time I had the pleasure of your company that you were out of your senses. I have this day been myself convinced of it; you cannot therefore be surprised that prudence should dissuade me from repeating my visits to you, as perhaps in one of your extravagant fits you might communicate your disorder.

I have desired a mad doctor to wait upon you, in order to prescribe for you the proper remedies in your case, and shall take care you shall not want till you are perfectly recovered.

I am,

dear madam,

(much chagrined at your misfortunes)
Your most obedient servant

Chapter III

Kitty is visited by a mad doctor.—His opinion of her sanity, which is afterwards changed by the expostulation of her landlady. Is forced to a madhouse, with some account of the unwarrantable practices of their keepers, exemplified in the affecting stories of a much injured husband, and abused brother; with the recovery of her liberty.

Scarce had she received this uncommon epistle, the contents of which she had some difficulty to understand, before the famous mad doctor attended her; informing her that Mr.— her city friend, had desired him to wait upon her to give his advice.

He had before he came up stairs enquired of the people of the house concerning her behaviour; when they unanimously informed him, that she had been raving all day 'till just then. He accordingly entered her chamber thoroughly convinced of her being non compos;[1] but what his surprise at finding her answers so reasonable, pertinent, and sensible; he at first attributed it to one of her lucid intervals; but endeavouring to discover from what source her disorder sprung, he touched upon the usual topics that occasioned madness: adversity, disappointments, application to study, poetry, and at last on love. He discovered no discomposure in her countenance in conversing upon these different subjects, which she discussed with great judiciousness and prudence.

His opinion was now entirely alerted concerning her being disordered; but Kitty's landlady waiting for his coming down, asked him when he took her to a madhouse. He answered, he could not see any cause for her being sent there, as she appeared to him as much in her senses as himself. "Bless me," returned the old lady, "in her senses! I am sure then you know nothing of your profession, for never was there a woman or man more mad in any Bedlam;—and I am sure she shall not sleep another night in my house, do what you will; for if you won't take her away, I must." This assertion, with the corroborating opinion of all the lodgers, once more staggered the doctor's judgment, and self-interest now suggesting the advantage he should reap from her being kept at his madhouse, a coach was presently called, and she was forced into it.

Kitty was greatly terrified at this compulsory journey, as she could not imagine any means of relieving herself. All the people to whom she addressed herself, telling her tale, made no other reply than, "It is a thousand pities! Poor young woman! She is very pretty." This ill-timed compassion provoked her more than the insult, and made her resolve to extort no further pity at the price of her story.

The doctor and she soon arrived at a private madhouse, a few miles from the capital; where he desired her to make herself easy, as no ill treatment should be offered her, and if at the end of a week she testified no symptoms of the disorder, she should have her full liberty. Though she did not entirely credit this, as she found she was to have the freedom of the whole house, she imagined she might find some opportunity of escaping, and this thought alone solaced her under her disagreeable confinement.

She had soon an opportunity of acquainting herself with the number of prisoners confined within these lunatic walls; and as most of them had the same liberty of patrolling the house as herself, she presently made some kind of acquaintance with them.

The person she first met after the doctor left her, thus addressed her: "I perceived, madam, you are sent here with as little reason and justice as

---

1 Not of sound mind.

myself, who never gave the least tokens of madness since my childhood, but what the inhumanity of thus confining me has extorted from me. I am, madam, indebted to my wife for this favour. I married her through mere fondness, without any fortune, though mine was very considerable, and settled seven hundred pistoles a year upon her; but this was not sufficient either to promote her love, or excite her gratitude. I returned one day hastily home, and found her in the embraces of a young cavalier of noble family. I had so much command over myself, as not to destroy either of them, and in return, I was the next day kidnapped and brought to this place, under pretence of my being out of my senses, where I have now remained upwards of eleven months, without being permitted to have any correspondence with my relations, whom I suppose fancied me dead, as a person in pretty near the same situation as myself since immured within these walls assures me that a few days after I disappeared, there was a grand funeral procession upon the occasion of my supposed death; that my wife took widow's weeds, and with the artifice annexed to her sex, appeared inconsolable; that she had made me bequeath her my whole fortune, and that her lover whom I found in the act of adultery, was her constant visitor, and it was then expected he would marry her in a few days."

This narrative of female perfidy greatly shocked Kitty's tender nature, who though she had through necessity submitted to prostitution, had never yet injured any man, either in his fortune or constitution; but she was soon diverted from reflecting upon the treachery of her sex, by the address of a young gentleman, who condoled with her upon her arrival in that disagreeable mansion, with so little reason believed the dwelling of madness.

Kitty's curiosity naturally induced her to enquire into the cause of his detention. He told her, "it was through the villainy of a younger brother, who not content to wait till his death, had usurped his patrimony, and got him confined as a lunatic." Nor was there any reason to believe his brain turned, either from his conversation or behaviour, so that she readily concluded these places were ill-named inquisitions, bastilles, or any the most illegal prisons, rather than madhouses.[1]

This time of Kitty's probation now elapsed, and as she had been particularly careful to avoid her soliloquies, which she found had been the cause of suspecting the soundness of her intellects; and the doctor not being bribed to detain her, he readily acknowledged he could see no cause for her further confinement, but restored her liberty.

---

1 The corruption of these institutions comes up elsewhere in the period as well. See, for example, Eliza Haywood, *The Distress'd Orphan, Or, Love in a Mad-House* (London: J. Roberts, 1726).

Chapter IV
Kitty's return to her lodging; her landlady's behaviour thereupon. Her resolves
at taking another. Frequents public places more than before, and attracts the
attention of the libertine cavaliers of Madrid, with its effects. Kitty's refinement of
prostitution. Don Harrisino's proposal; and her manner of rejecting it, with the
disagreeable consequences of a retaliation.

Our heroine returned to her lodging, to the great suprize of her landlady
and her lodgers, who thought she had made her escape without the knowledge
of the doctor, and were therefore upon the point of re-conveying her to the
madhouse; but Kitty producing a certificate from him of the sanity of her mind,
and threatening to prosecute them for their former outrage, they readily let
her take away her cloaths and moveables, without any further annoyance.

At her entrance into her new lodging, she made a firm resolution not to
indulge herself in any reveries upon her absent lover, which had already cost
her a week's liberty. In order to avoid this she lived a less recluse life than during her intimacy with her city lover, being constantly at the public walks at
noon, and at the theatre at night; by this means she was taken notice of by
most of the young rakes about the capital, who began to distinguish her from
the herd of women of pleasure. There were few jolly parties at a tavern at
which Kitty did not assist; and as she was always properly recompensed for her
company, and retired with a lover for the remainder of the evening, these
associations could not fail turning out greatly to her pecuniary advantage,
and she found she got more money than she could well dispose of.

Don Harrisino, who had so early endeavoured to be factor of her charms,
thought now he could not be looked upon as a forestaller, in disposing of a
commodity which had already been in so many hands.[1]

This worthy gentleman, so famous for the art of pimping, has a catalogue
of all the names of such women as dispose of their favours at fixed prices, who
are ready at his call, to be brought out to such customers as use his female
magazine. Kitty, notwithstanding her unlimited acquaintance with men, was
not arrived at that pitch of prostitution to be registered in his list. In all her
amours there was something of the modest woman retained.—Her purchased indulgence always carried with it an air of intrigue.—She was to be
partly forced to consent to what she was paid for.—There was some kind of
ceremony, and even decency to be used, in proposing to her the practice of
what she professed. Her natural delicacy and good sense gave a refinement
to the greatest carnalities, and most libidinous dissipations.

Such a woman could not fail being shocked at the thought of being
brought out to hire as a horse by the common groom of the stable,—or drove

---

1   "Commodity," in addition to its more common meaning, was also a slang term at the
    time for female genitalia.

off the stand when called, as the first coach, by the smack of the driver's whip. This was debasing human nature too much for Kitty, who thought the most indecent action might be glossed over by the manner of performing it,—and that there was something more disgusting in the parade of prostitution, than in the most lascivious, but secret indulgence.

Don Harrisino, who was unacquainted with her refined sentiments, proposed to enroll her upon his list, saying it would be very advantageous for her, as he would always give her the preference, whenever a new face was called for.

This proposal so greatly irritated Kitty, that she could not avoid bursting into the following declamation.—"Thou monster of human nature, without parallel in infamy, is it not enough that thou practised thine every art to betray me in my most tender years, into the arms of your letcherous employer; that false pretences, protestations, and promises, were on every side echoed in my ears, to allure me to perdition, when by a miracle I escaped thy snares? Wilt thou still endeavour to intail more infamy upon me than my unfortunate lot confers, by making me the common convenience of every abandoned profligate, at whose command and thy nod I am to be brought forth, as at a public market for sale? Thou mayst think me so abandoned as to accept of this proposal, but I despise it as much as I do thyself, and all thy infamous, villainous, treacherous arts!"

Don Harrisino, whose ears had not been accustomed to so much truth, and who did not expect it from the mouth of a woman of her stamp, sneaked off before this harangue was well finished, muttering to himself, "she was a d—nd fool to be so squeamish, when he had made her such a good offer."

This rupture between our heroine and this noted pimp was not unattended with some disagreeable consequences to Kitty. As he had the ear of all the debauchees who frequented a noted tavern near the playhouse, they seldom commenced any acquaintance with a woman, without first asking his opinion of her. Whenever Kitty's name was called in question upon these occasions, he retaliated her reproaches, by saying, "she was a most extravagant girl, who could never be satisfied 'till she had ruined a man;—that he had made her such offers from Sir Thomas such a one, as no other woman in her situation could refuse; but forsooth she would listen to nothing less than a settlement of five hundred pistoles a year,—and that between friends, it was at the same time a matter of great debate whether she was well or no, for that to his certain knowledge she had been with captain such a one, who since proved so excessively out of order, that he was down in a sal."[1]

These insinuations of Don Harrisino had their desired effect, and it was presently propagated throughout Madrid what a mercenary disposition Kitty had, and how dangerous it was for any man to have an intrigue with her.

---

1 Short for "salivation." See note 1, page 114.

Chapter V

The discontinuance of Kitty's success in intrigue, which she ascribes to her dress,
but finds its alteration have no effect. She resolves upon changing her way of life.
—Is persuaded to try her genius upon the stage.—Applies herself to the study
of dramatic poetry.—The difficulties of procuring an audience with the
manager of one of these theatres.

Kitty perceived that her former lovers began to cool, and they were not
replaced by such a numerous succession as lately supplicated her favours.
She examined her glass, and finding no alteration in her face, readily concluded it must be owing to her dress, which she imagined was not so attracting as it had before been. She accordingly purchased some very gay and costly dresses, with which she appeared in every public place; and though she
was always the most conspicuous figure in the place, she was always the least
taken notice of.

This was a mortifying trial to Kitty, which made her resolve upon changing
her way of life, and having been some time acquainted with Miss Loretto, one
of the actresses at the theatre, who had often commended her voice, delivery,
and action, in declaring she would make a great figure upon the stage, Kitty
began to turn her thoughts seriously that way.

She accordingly frequented the theatre still more than ever, and took particular notice of the manner, action, and emphasis used by the most celebrated performers, in those parts they most shone in. As soon as ever she returned
to her lodging, she repeated the same passages over, in endeavouring to imitate as far as she was able, what she had just been seeing represented.

Her whole study was now confined to plays, and for near two months she
scarce ever discoursed with a man except in her parts. Her toilet, instead of
being covered as usual with patches, washes, pomatum, eaus de luce,[1] and all
the retinue of a lady's dress, was now entirely hid with dramatic pieces. Poets
alone found admittance into her bed-chamber, and instead of their studying
her charms for the subject of their verse,—their beauties were the sole objects
of her attention, which she assiduously endeavoured to represent.

Had she still remained in her former lodging, where they were so easily
convinced of her madness by her soliloquies, they would certainly have
been still more confirmed in their opinion, by her midnight repetitions of
dramatic speeches; and perhaps they would, out of mere charity, have re-
conveyed her to the doctor's house, notwithstanding her threats and his
certificate.

---

1   Pomatum is pomade, "a scented ointment (in which apples are said to have been orig-
    inally an ingredient) for application to the skin; now used esp. for the skin of the
    head and for dressing the hair." [OED] "Eau de luce": "a medicinal preparation of
    alcohol, ammonia, and oil of amber, used in India as an antidote to snake-bites, and
    in England sometimes as smelling salts." [OED]

When she imagined she had sufficiently applied herself to the study of acting, having the approbation of her acquaintance, Miss Loretto, in most of the parts she rehearsed, she thought she might venture to offer herself to the manager of one of the theatres.

She accordingly attended at his house for a whole week together, without being once able to gain admittance. This induced her to believe she had forgot to give the porter his expected fee, and the next morning she made him a handsome compliment, which extracted from him an enquiry into what her business was. She though this was rather an impertinent question from a porter. However, she ingenuously answered him; when he told her he believed it would be fruitless to attempt being engaged that season, for that to his certain knowledge above a dozen actresses had been rejected, on account of there being already above the usual number employed. But that however, if she would return the Thursday morning following, which was the day he gave audience to those who offered themselves for performers, he would get her admitted to his presence.

She was not a little mortified at this intelligence, after having been so assiduous in arriving at what she thought such a pitch of perfection in acting.— Having lost many opportunities of getting money in her former employ, and nearly exhausted the little she had saved thereby, she had almost firmly resolved to give up any further thoughts of appearing upon the stage, after meeting with such difficulties in even arriving at the presence of the manager, before she could be examined concerning her real merit; adding to this, the little hopes there were of her being engaged, when so many had already been rejected; she was coming to this notable conclusion, that she must even wh—e on, in spite of her aversion to prostitution, and her attachment to the stage, when Miss Loretto entered, and enquired the cause of her being so serious.

Kitty told her how unsuccessful she had been in her different attempts to arrive at the presence of the manager, and the unpromising intelligence she had at length received from his porter. "O lord," replied Miss Loretto, "this is nothing at all, in comparison to the obstacles I had to surmount.—I was two years before I could gain an audience of the manager, and was at the end of that time rejected, as being absolutely unfit for the stage, having neither voice, gesture, action, or pronunciation,—and yet you see I have turned out a tolerable good actress, and get my four pistoles a week, besides my benefit, without being beholden to any man for it."

The first part of this remonstrance was not a little disgusting to Kitty, whose patience was already entirely exhausted; yet the sweets of four pistoles a week and a benefit, without being necessitated to prostitution, were so alluring, that she was persuaded to attend his mightiness the manager the ensuing Thursday.

Chapter VI

*Kitty perseveres in her theatrical study. Has an interview with the manager of
one of the theatres. His uncommon manner of address, and her mistake thereupon.
The dialogue that ensued, and her application to the manager of the other theatre.
His behaviour, and curious remarks upon her person.—He rectifies her faults in
speaking, and acquaints her with his great abilities as an actor, which character
however he declines. Observations upon her action, and a standard for the
same recommended.—He gives her the freedom of the house.*

Notwithstanding the repeated disappointments our heroine had met with
in endeavouring to obtain an audience of the manager, and the little hopes
of succeeding, she continued applying herself with her usual assiduity to the
study of those characters she thought he might demand a specimen of, and
when the day came, she could rehearse upwards of twenty capital parts without omitting a sentence.

The porter being again properly noticed, and a similar attention paid to a
valet, who conducted her to the apartment where Mr. Manager[1] received
audience, she was introduced to him.

After he had pulled up his breeches, and given two shrugs with his shoulders as an apology for a bow—he began.—"A—A—your servant, madam.—"

Kitty would have broke silence before, but she was apprehensive she had
disturbed him from a natural vocation,—and she was therefore going to
retire,—but recollecting she had heard that this was his usual way, she
addressed him as follows:

"Having entertained, Sir, a long while a great desire to appear upon the
stage, I have for some time past applied myself very assiduously to the study
of dramatic poetry, and have rehearsed frequently by myself those parts which
I thought best suited me; and I now come, Sir, to offer you my service."

"A—A—Madam," he replied, "I am greatly obliged to you for the honour
you intend me, I must own you are a very agreeable figure, and don't doubt
you would appear with great success in most capital parts,—but—A—A—, I
am very sorry that my company is quite compleat at present, and that I've no
occasion for any additional performers;—but if you apply to the other manager, as his company is very deficient, I make no doubt but he will engage
you.—If not, perhaps next season I may want an additional performer, and
should be glad to hear from you."

Kitty judging there was no reply to be made, dropt a curtesy and retired.
She immediately repaired to the manager of the other theatre's house,[2]

---

1 David Garrick, or James Lacy, both managers of the Drury Lane Theater at this time
   (since 1747). Garrick usually hired the actors, but the narrative does not connect this
   figure to Garrick when the actor-manager is discussed at Kitty's next audition.
2 John Rich, the manager of the Covent Garden Theater from 1732 to 1761.

where she did not find so much difficulty to gain admittance, but was presently conducted to his presence.

He was seated in his elbow chair by the fire, with one leg up against the chimney piece reading the play bills over his chocolate. He scarce perceived her at her first entrance, and after he noticed her, he still remained in the same posture, without giving any hints that seating herself would be agreeable to him. "What," said he, "I suppose you want to turn actor?—Why your figure (taking up his spying glass), ay, your figure,—but there is worser.—Not a bad face, (rising attentively with his glass)—but fair women seldom succeed.—I see you have very light hair, and not much expression.—Do you mouth well?—Miss Nossero had brought it entirely into vogue from the tall Irishman.—But how are your legs?—Ay, not amiss;—but you turn your toes out too much,—it has a very bad effect upon the stage,—it has too much the look of a dancer;—they have left it quite off."

Kitty having not yet said a syllable, but continued displaying the different parts of her body he took notice of, she thought it was now time to make some apology for her intrusion;—but just as she was going to begin, he bid her rehearse one of her best speeches, which she accordingly did; whilst he interrupted her in the middle of every line, telling her she laid the emphasis quite wrong,—for that it should be spoke in the manner he repeated. Kitty submitted, though she was convinced he pronounced half the words improperly.

When she had finished her speech, he told her she had not a bad voice, but that he must be her tuteror for a good while, before he could bring her any thing; "for,"said he, "you must know if I had a mind to act, I should beat them all, ay, the little man[1] and all; only I don't chuse to disgrace myself so much.— Indeed doing harlequin is nothing, any gentleman may perform that part, because there is no speaking in it, and of course he does not come under the denomination of an actor,—but if I had a mind to exult myself, the little manager would soon find I could bring houses enough, for there is no manner of comparison between his acting and mine.—No, none in the least, as my prompter, and scene shifters, and even the candle-snuffers can inform you; to shew you I am not prejudiced in my opinion. But," (continued he), "as I was saying, you have not a bad voice, and your figure is tolerable, but that action will never do,—its quite aukward;—your left hand should always remain in the same posture, and your right arm should do all the work. For instance now, when harlequin draws out his sword, he draws it with his right hand,— when he takes off his hat, it is with his right hand,—when he gives the signal of it's being him to Columbine, when in disguise, it is the right hand that is put up to his breast.—In short, the left hand is never used except in a jump, or some feat of great activity."

---

1   David Garrick, who was relatively short. He was also a brilliant actor as well as manager. Rich excelled in pantomime.

She agreed entirely to what he said, though she could not discover any reason for harlequin's tricks being the standard of action in tragedy. He was greatly pleased with her approbation, and though he had a very indifferent opinion of her as an actress, he was not without some penchant for her as a woman.

He told her she wanted experience, that she must come to the house, and see a sufficient number of representations, in order to improve her judgment, and correct her vicious action; and that he would give orders for her admittance.

Chapter VII

Our heroine's satisfaction at the manager's privilege.—Her constant use of it, and acquaintance with the players and dancers. Gains an insight into their conduct and dispositions,—reconciles her former profession with that of an actress.—Accepts the proposal of Don Livinio, with the advantages she proposes to herself therefrom. Don Harrisino's new endeavours to hurt her retorted. Her introduction to Don Bassono.— Some account of his travels,—the favourable hint he gives Kitty, which she endeavours to improve, and produces a rupture between Lavinio and her.

It might be imagined that Kitty was by this time pretty nearly surfeited of managers, their conduct, and judgment; and therefore declined all further thoughts of the stage. But the boon which was granted her by the last, she thought more than compensated all her application and disappointments. The freedom of the house was what she often had wished for, not only because she would thereby save a considerable sum in the season, which she spent in plays, but as she would also have an opportunity of going behind the scenes, and being initiated into the whole arcana of theatrical representations.

This privilege was not neglected by Kitty, who seldom missed a night being at the play, and generally behind the scenes. She soon became acquainted with most of the actresses and dancers, who looked upon her as one in training to compose their fraternity. She presently discovered by their conversation, that very few of their sallaries supported them in their manner of living, and that their principal design in coming upon the stage, was not so much for obtaining the income they were paid, as in hopes of getting into keeping.

The greatest part of them were already upon this honourable footing, and those whose successes had not been equal, made a virtue of necessity; their want of charms compelled them to chastity, and they railed at those they envied, because they were more fortunate in a face, and its consequence, a lover.

This discovery was a further consolation to Kitty, who was glad to find that in pursuing her theatrical plan, there was no necessity of giving up her gallant one; and this induced her upon the first favourable overture to accept of a lover.

The gallant Don Livinio, that great admirer of theatrical exhibitions, and dramatic critic, addressed her upon the score of a keeper.—Kitty had a double view in accepting his proposal; the allowance was handsome, and her present indigence readily approved it. His interest with the manager, and his real judgment in acting, were secondary incentives.

Harrisino was greatly chagrined at hearing of Kitty's success, and took some pains still to prevent her reaping the fruits of it. He found an opportunity of having an interview with Don Livinio, when he told him he thought it was his duty to acquaint him with what he knew concerning the girl he proposed taking into keeping, and then repeated the old chime upon her extravagance, and the doubtful state of her health. Livinio told him her acceptance of the proposal he had made her, cleared her from the first imputation, and his cohabitation with her for upwards of three weeks, without having any symptoms of infection, greatly invalidated the latter. That he was very much obliged to Mr. Harrisino for the regard he paid to his purse and constitution, but that if ever it came to his ears, that he had from that time made free with Kitty's name, he might depend upon it his carcase would suffer for it. Harrisino took the hint, and remained tacit from that time forward.

Kitty might now be said to be tolerably easy in her situation and circumstances, and as her gallant's taste and hers entirely coincided, there was a great likelyhood of their intimacy being of long continuance; but unexpected circumstances frequently dissolve the most seeming unalienable friendship. Don Bassono, who had just returned from the tour of Europe, and had sucked in all the virtù of all the connoisseurs, came to visit Kitty's lover, and stayed to dinner.

He gave them an account of his travels; that he had been to Rome to tune his violoncello with that of the famous signor de Remargo; that unfortunately as he was re-passing the Alps one of his strings broke, and he was obliged to return, at the most imminent danger of his life, by reason of the difficulty of turning about at that narrow pass;—that the chaise afterwards broke down, and he was obliged to carry that unwieldy instrument upon his back upwards of thirty leagues, before he could get another carriage;—that he had bought up all the music in Italy, and was upon the point of bringing over a new set of singers, to perform, under his direction, an opera, which he himself had composed. That there was but one part he could not fill, and he would give five hundred pistoles to any woman who had such a voice and figure as Kitty, to perform it.

The hint was not unattended to by our heroine, who, after his departure, acquainted herself with his history; and finding he was a rich man, who threw away upwards of twenty thousand pistoles a year upon women and music, half the opera singers being supported by him, she readily concluded he was a man entirely for her purpose.

He was a few nights afterwards behind the scenes at the play, and entered into a long conversation with Kitty, who gave him to understand she was very ready to accept his proposal, if he was certain the piece would be represented. Don Livinio unfortunately overheard this, as well as her complaisant reply to some tender things which the virtuoso said to her; and upon her return home, she found the following billet left for her upon her dressing table.

Madam,

Your intrigue with Don Bassono I am no stranger to; nor shall I deny that he has it in his power to make you more advantageous offers than I possibly can; but as I cannot reconcile to myself the participation of a woman's favours with any man, I beg you will consider this as your *lettre de congé*,[1] and depart hence as soon as it is convenient, with what belongs to you, that I may have an apartment for one more faithful to me and my bed,

I am, &c.

Livinio

Kitty was greatly surprised at the perusal of this letter; and would have readily answered it, but knowing the difficulty of dissuading Livinio from his opinion, she declined it, imagining as he said that Don Bassono was every way a more advantageous party, and concluding from what the latter had told her that night, she might easily obtain a lucrative settlement from him.

Chapter VIII

Kitty's great expectations from Don Bassono's proposals. Her letter of invitation to him, and his answer, with the cause of his noncompliance, in which a virtuoso and admirer of music are strongly delineated. Her disgust thereupon. The manager's coolness, which she attributes to a wrong cause, wherein she is rectified, and her reflections thereupon. The manner of her having an interview with her father and mother.

In consequence of this billet from Livinio, she left his house the next morning, and took lodgings not far from the theatre. Fully buoyed up with Don Bassono's proposals, she constantly attended every night behind the scenes at the theatre, in hopes of having another conference with him; but a whole week being elapsed without her seeing him, and her finances beginning to be upon the decline, she wrote the following letter.

Sir,

Don Livinio having discovered our growing intimacy, which though so lately budding, I hoped would ere now have been in blossom, he has discarded me his favour, and I am at present under no restraint; therefore I should be glad of having the pleasure of your company when it is agreeable.

I am,

Dear Sir,

Your very humble servant.

Kitty F—r

---

1 Letter of leave, or in this case dismissal.

Don Bassono, who lived upon harmony, had been all the morning extremely busied in getting every thing ready for his new opera, when he received a letter from one of the eunuchs he had engaged to perform in it, acquainting him with an accident that had happened to him, whereby he had sprained his ancle, and his journey was retarded. Bassono did not hesitate a moment what was to be done, but resolved immediately to set out and meet him with his own physician and surgeon, for better advice, in order to facilitate the cure of this singer's disorder. He therefore wrote Kitty the following answer in the greatest haste, being to depart that very night for France.

Dear Madam,

The most unfortunate of all accidents has happened to one of the most enchanting creatures in the world. Signor Lomelli, in traveling through Languedoc, has had the misfortune to sprain his ancle, therefore I cannot defer a moment flying to his relief with all the assistance I can give him.

I doubt not but you will be as sensibly touched as myself with this great disaster, that threatens the life of the only being on earth that can solace me with that divine harmony, which flows only from his tongue.—If he should die, I shall not survive him.

This you must needs think a sufficient apology for my not accepting at present your invitation, but wishing you health and happiness till my return.

I am,

dear Madam,

at present in the utmost consternation,

Yours,

Bassono

Upon the receipt of this letter she readily concluded she had nothing to hope for from that quarter, as he might make a tour to Italy, before he came back to replace his lame singer, or perform his opera in France, for fear of injuring the health of Signor Lomelli by travelling. She was so thoroughly disgusted with virtuoso's, that she would not knowingly have been the mistress of one, to have been in as much esteem with him, as Don Bassono held his violoncello.

Kitty's finances were in a bad condition, though she had resolution to withstand the temptations of prostitution; notwithstanding all hopes of coming upon the stage with success were now at an end.—The manager had forgot her as a candidate performer,—even his amorous inclination for her, which had induced him to give her the freedom of the house, no longer remained. When she curtsied to him behind the scenes, he scarce noticed her. This behaviour she attributed to the influence Don Lavino had over him, whom she imagined had represented her to the manager as the most profligate of her sex; but she was informed by those best acquainted with the theatre, that the manager's conduct to her was no way extraordinary, and that without Don Livinio's ill representation, every woman in the house had been treated by him in the same manner.

This convinced Kitty of her mistake, but did not serve her for an index to point out what road she had to take. A girl of her sense and reflexion, who had still the dear image of one man deeply at heart, could not fail considering her past conduct in all its most ridiculous lights. The folly of leaving her father, her absurd reliance upon conjurer's predictions, her abandoned amorous indulgence, and even her love for Don Cupidino, did not escape the censure of her more serious moments. She was ere now thoroughly convinced of virtue being its own reward, and would gladly have been reinstated behind her own counter in the milliner's shop, but the difficulty lay in being reconciled to her father, and regaining the good opinion of the world.

An unexpected accident gave her a conference with both her father and mother, which the most premeditated scheme could not have produced. At an actor's benefit she sat next to them in the gallery, before she perceived who were her neighbours; and they did not discover, till a considerable time after, that they were in their daughter's vicinity.

Chapter IX

An unexpected interview between Kitty and her father at the play, with the tender sympathetic scene which ensued between them.—His affectionate speech to her.—She returns with him home,—relates her adventures; —their great effect upon John.— Kitty reforms;—some emotions that arise upon reading books of gallantry.—John recovers his constitution, &c.

The play which was represented was the story of *The Fair Penitent*,[1] with which Kitty was so greatly affected, that she never once, during the three first acts, turned her head, or took her eyes from the actors, except to discharge that moisture, which the over workings of nature produced.

Honest John, who was no great admirer of Melpomene,[2] and had had a very compleat nap before the curtain drew up, fairly slept through the three first acts. Whether the affecting catastrophe which now ensued roused him from his lethargy, or the reflexions he made upon the similarity of his daughter's distress with the heroine of the piece, we will not determine, but he was not only awake, but so deeply touched that his eyes gave testimony of the sensibility of his heart. Just as he had been giving way to the force of representa-

---

1   By Nicholas Rowe (1703). In this play, Calista succumbs to an affair with Lothario, who seduces her in part to exact revenge on her family for refusing him her hand in marriage. She eventually repents and kills herself. The relationship between Calista and her father is particularly dramatic: both are headstrong but appear to reconcile at the end.

2   The muse of tragedy.

tion, he perceived Kitty in the same tender situation as himself. And now for the first time their moistened eyes met; which were presently overflowed by a more feeling and sympathetic cause than the play.

Such a scene, had the audience known the source, would have drawn their attention from the stage, to the father and his daughter, who were representing nature and her powers. Every thing was expressed without any thing being uttered, and the most elaborate advocacy for Kitty's conduct, could not have so thoroughly cleared her in John's opinion, as this unexpected, silent, communicative, weeping dialogue.

He could scarce remain till the end of the play, before he retired, having beckoned Kitty to follow him, and they were no sooner out of the gallery, than he took her into his arms, crying, "My dear Kitty, how could you leave me all this while, without letting me know of your welfare?—I have enquired every where about you, and have heard such various reports, that I have been almost afraid to make further search, lest I should have found you in such a situation as would have shocked nature, and that feeling I have for you.—But why do I upbraid you, after you have convinced me this night that all your faults have not been the effect of choice, but of cruel necessity, after having made one false step?—Let that no longer terrify you, for I am yet your father, and your friend, or anything you can think still more dear!"

Kitty was greatly moved at this affectionate harangue of her father, but was unable to answer with anything but tears. In this situation he conducted her to his house, where he soon reconciled her with his wife. She related to them her adventures since she had left them, to which honest John listened with the greatest attention, and in every moving part torrents of tears gushed from him. When she came to her resolution of drowning herself, and her lucky meeting with her patroness, he could contain no longer, but bellowing cried,—"and could you, Kitty, have been so cruel as to have put an end to your own life and mine, for I should never have survived the news of your death!"

She was sensibly touched at his affliction, upon hearing her relate her misfortunes, and was thoroughly convinced that his love for her was still as great as ever. This induced her to resolve upon reclaiming, and cast aside all thoughts of man, except in an honourable way, which, however, she greatly feared her character was too irretrievably lost to expect.

Kitty had ere now discharged her lodging, and withdrawn all her cloaths and moveables to her father's, where she entirely fixed her abode; and for some time lived the most recluse life imaginable.—Her whole occupation was confined to working and reading. In a few weeks she perused all the novels and romances of a compleat circulating library.

The gallantry and intrigue of these pieces, for which Kitty had, notwithstanding her father's partial opinion of her, still a great hankering after, reanimated her gay desires. When she read of such a conquest, or such a love scene, she imagined her recluse life the utmost pitch of folly, and looking in the glass, perceived such charms as might captivate the first grandee of Spain. When she laid down her book, and re-applied herself to work, she could then reflect with more rationality upon launching out again into an abandoned life, and these cooler moments ratified her former good opinion of her present chaste plan.

Honest John, who from the time that Kitty had so abruptly quitted him in pursuit of the conjurer's predicted paradise, fell away, and was reduced almost to an anatomy, recovered so well in a short time after his daughter's return, that his neighbours all congratulated him upon the recovery of his health. These compliments he always answered, in acquainting them with the cause of the amendment of his constitution, which he assured them was entirely at his daughter's disposal, and that as long as she remained good, he was proof against all disorders, and even doctors themselves; but that if ever she took to her evil courses again, he believed he should die of grief and the physician, who would in vain endeavour to prescribe for a distempered mind.

Buxom Kate, our heroine's mother, who had taken such pains and run such risks to prevent Kitty being spoilt in her infant years, had not felt any of those parental anxieties upon her sally from virtue, which John was so susceptible of. She had a secret pleasure in finding her prognostication come true, and had therefore no great satisfaction in her daughter's reformation.

Chapter X
Kitty's unsettled disposition. The unjust conduct of the Spanish peace-officers exemplified in the annoyance of Kitty, and her detention at a watch house. Their fleecing behaviour at that place; with an uncommon scene between an old bawd and a nymph, who reciprocally charge each other.

The ballance of chastity and ambition was still poising in Kitty's mind, and each by turns gaining the ascendant, when an uncommon accident happened to her, which served to prove that the innocent are frequently punished for the guilty.

She had been visiting a relation, who lived the other side of the capital, to that of her abode, and it was near ten in the evening before she returned. She had perceived a cavalier for some time follow her, and take every opportunity the lamps afforded to peep under her hat: but as she had no intention of favouring his suit, she suspected no harm from his attending her; so that he followed her from the beginning to almost the middle of one of the capital streets of Madrid (no unlike our Strand), without her taking any seeming notice of him, or chiding him for his impertinence.

As she passed on she saw numbers of the most abandoned prostitutes lying in wait for and attacking every man, or even boy, that passed; and some were committing such indecencies in the public street, as shocked Kitty's not overstrained modesty. She was lamenting to herself that the good order and police of the capital were not more attended to by the peace-officers, than to allow such violations of modesty.

Just as she was making these moral reflections, she was accosted by an officer of the night (nearly resembling our constable) who told her she must go along with him to the watch-house, for that such doings were not allowed in the streets of Madrid. She replied, she was quite of his opinion, but was greatly surprised that he should mistake so grossly the objects of the disorder; that those women (pointing cross the way) should certainly be secured for their behaviour; but for her part, she could see no reason for his molesting her, who had neither offended decency or modesty, but was going straight home to her father's.

This remonstrance was of no avail, he telling her that such examples as her were more dangerous than what those poor wretches practiced, and it was necessary to strike at the root of evil. In so saying, he called the watch, who presently surrounded her, whilst she was endeavouring to espy her gallant who had accompanied her so far, and to whom alone she could attribute this violence; but he had sneaked off as soon as the peace officer approached, so that she was conducted without any more ceremony to the watch-house.

Kitty, whose spirits were not the most easily dejected, was nevertheless somewhat terrified at this outrage, and gave vent to her grief in a flood of tears. The constable perceiving this, told her she had better have something to comfort her, and without waiting for an answer, sent for a bottle of wine. She began to entertain some opinion of this officer's compassion, and readily accepted a glass he offered her; but was soon convinced that she was to be treated at her own expence; for the man who brought it, waited till she paid him: the beadle and his wife, with two other constables, besides her conductor, soon emptied the bottle, and another was as readily called for.

Kitty had not recovered herself from her fright, but finding this would turn out a very expensive affair, if they went on at this rate, she interposed, saying she could drink no more wine, and therefore would not pay for any; but the constable replied, "It was sent for now, and she must have it." In her present situation, she thought it was most prudent to comply, and again discharged the wine.

She had now plucked up spirits sufficient to enquire whether she could not get a porter to go to her father's, to acquaint him with the accident that had happened. It was by this time past twelve, and they pretended they could get nobody to go, 'till such time as the men came off the watch. This intelligence chagrined her, not so much on account of her detention, as that her absence from home would greatly grieve her father.

Whilst she was lamenting her fate, to be thus innocently confined, whilst the real objects of correction were permitted to exercise their infamies in public, there was a knocking at the watch door, which at first elated her heart, in hopes that by some accident her misfortune had gained her father's ears, and that he had come to her relief; but her joy was soon dissipated upon opening the door, when her ears were saluted with a volley of oaths from an elderly lady, whom she afterwards found supported the honourable character of a bawd. She did not come unattended; one of her nymphs, whom she had charged with the watch for detaining her property by force, had in turn charged her for breaking the peace, and forcing into her apartment contrary to her will.

After some female declamation, vulgarly called scolding, the damsel told her tale. "I got a good cull, who gave me ten pistoles without staying all night, and after he was gone, that b—h my landlady would know how much I got, and having told her, she insisted upon having all but a pistole, which she said was more than I deserved. Upon this I locked myself into my room, and swore she should not have a piastre.[1] She then got a man to break open my door, and they were upon the point of taking away all my money, when I called the watch, and she charged me, and I charged her,—and I warrant you I will have justice tomorrow.

The pious old lady now took up the cudgels, and swore it was all a lie, for that she only wanted what she owed her for board and lodging, which came to above ten pistoles; but that she was generous enough not to insist upon it all, after her good success, notwithstanding it would have been less than her due.

The merits of this cause being thus apparently stated, the constable told them they had better have a bottle and make it up, for that it would only turn out to both their disadvantage to go before the judge (or justice) in the morning. The young lady readily agreed to have not only one bottle, but half a dozen; swearing lustily, however, she would not let that old b—h cheat her in the manner she had done.

Kitty was not displeased at her generosity, for no other reason but because she imagined it saved her pocket, as in all likelihood if this last affair had not happened, they would with little ceremony have drawn upon her for more wine. As it was, the constable, the beadle, his wife, the bawd and the whore all got drunk, and fell fast asleep by five in the morning. Kitty might easily have made her escape now, but as she knew they could alledge nothing against her, and as she must have disturbed the house, and exposed herself in the neighbourhood by returning at that time in the morning, she did not profit of the opportunity, but remained till they waked, in order to be conduced to the justice.

---

1   A Spanish coin.

Chapter XI

*A Sequel to the night scene.—The prisoners are conducted to justice,—
the examination of the old bawd and her lodger.—An equitable determination,
—and a further discovery, which sets it in a stronger light. Kitty's release.—
Her acquaintance with a gay lady, and its unexpected consequence.*

Aurora had now appeared for some time; the watch were returning to
deposit their lanthorns and staves, and the inebriate prisoners and guests
began to yawn from repose. It was still too early to appear before the justice,
and the generous nymph, who so bountifully supplied them with wine, procured them coffee and tea for breakfast; which Kitty finding herself much disposed for after her night's fatigue, she was easily prevailed upon to partake
of.

Kitty had received several hints the former part of the evening, that by
properly tipping the officer she might obtain her liberty, but as she had no
more money about her than would have paid for a third bottle of wine, she
was obliged to decline making such an offer, though she would gladly have
proposed it, could she have hoped for success. The constable now took her
on one side and told her in plain terms, that it was a pity so pretty a girl as she
should go to prison, for want of a trifle to give the officers of the night, and
that out of compassion he would accept of as much as she had about her, let
it be ever so little. She was greatly irritated at this intimation, after having
been detained all night. This, added to her conscious innocence, made her
reply that she would not give the smallest sum in the world, for having been
wrongfully confined all night,—and that she was certain the justice would not
connive at such iniquitous practices. The constable muttered a reply, to the
tune of her being a d—mn'd foolish b—h, for refusing so good an offer, and
that she would presently repent it.

The officers of the night began now to make the necessary preparations for
conducting their prisoners to the magistrate; and a coach being called, Kitty
and the two other ladies got in with Mr. Constable, after he had taken care to
see all the reckoning cleared, which reduced the successful enamorata's stock
to nine pistoles.

Being arrived at the justice's, they remained some time in an ante-chamber,
before they could gain admittance to his worship's presence, he being not yet
risen. At length they received notice to appear before him, when the elderly
lady, being a housekeeper, was first examined.

"Well, madam," said he, "what have you to alledge against that young
woman?"

Bawd. "An't please your worship's goodness, she is a very naughty girl, and
won't pay me my rent."

J. "And was that the only reason for your charging her with the watch?"

Bawd. "No, an't please your excellence's worship, she locked herself into her room, and swore she would not let me have a piastre, though she got a great deal of money from a worthy gentleman, who was not with her above an hour."

J. "Good woman, I'd have you be more circumspect in your answers, and not lay yourself so open; for by your replies one might imagine, without knowing otherways, that you kept a house of ill fame.

Bawd. "Bless your worship's sweet eyes, you know otherways.—I've been often enough before you for warrants for my lodgers, who have been sometimes, as one may say, naughty women, and bred riots.—But I,—ay, I say it that should not say it, I've lived in this parish, with as good a reputation as ever, these twenty years, and paid scot and lot—your worship knows I have."

J. "Ay—ay,—enough of that.—But have you any thing else to alledge against your lodger?"

Bawd. "No an't please your worship."

J. "Why, then let's hear what she has to say for herself.—Why here—you jade you, do you hear what your landlady lays to your charge,—that you owe her money and won't pay her,—and that you had a very good cull last night?"

Wh—e. "It's true, an't please your honour's worship,—but she would not give me time.—

J. "Time you jade,—why you ought to have given her all the money immediately, and left it to her discretion.—How do you think, you baggage, she can pay house rent, and taxes, and hush money and all, without such brimstones as you make their payments regularly?—I'll teach you to whore, if this is the case,—aye, that I will.—Here write her mittimus,[1] and send her to prison immediately."

Whilst the justice's clerk was writing her mittimus, the gentleman came in who had been the cull of the preceding evening, in order to make deposition of having had his pocket picked of his watch, whilst his breeches lay upon a chair, and that there was nobody in the room, beside his enamourata, but the old bawd; who now fell upon her knees and blubbering protested her innocence; but the justice tipping her the wink, she returned the gentleman his watch, with which he retired very contentedly, and the young woman was committed.

Kitty was a good deal terrified at this distribution of justice, when the guilty escaped with impunity, whilst the innocent suffered; apprehending she herself might accompany the young gentlewoman to beat hemp.[2] But these apprehensions soon subsided, when her father appeared, with neighbouring housekeepers, to vouch for her character, and she was immediately set at liberty, and retuned home.

---

1   The warrant to send her to prison.
2   The justice system commonly punished "disorderly women" by sending them to Bridewell Prison, where they had to beat hemp.

This adventure was the talk of some days in Kitty's neighbourhood, and the less good-natured of the female part were censorious enough to give out that she had not only taken to her former courses, but that she had actually turned street-walker, and was detected by the watch in the very act of picking up. However, her relations and acquaintance still entertained a more favourable opinion, and they demonstrated no signs of coolness towards her upon account of this accident. Her passion for dress still operated, and as she chose to have cloaths made in the most genteel taste, she of course employed those mantua-makers who worked for the gayest of her sex. She accidentally fell into company one day with a lady at one of her faiseurs de robes,[1] whose figure, appearance, and sense, she was much taken with, and an acquaintance was soon commenced between them, which produced quite different effects to what Kitty at first imagined.

This lady had at this time an independent affluence, which she had acquired by intrigue; and Kitty's virtue, which was none of the most rigid, (notwithstanding her late chaste resolution) was easily warped by this successful example of incontinence; and she was persuaded to once more quit her father's house, in pursuit of riches and pleasure.

Chapter XII
Miss S——'s prudent advice to Kitty. Her story. The unnatural perfidy of her mother, who is meritoriously rewarded. Her prostitution, and experience, with her artful way of avoiding disorders, and accumulating money sufficient to purchase an annuity. Her present plan.

The lady who had this influence over Kitty went by the name of Miss S——, who greatly improved the experience she had already gained in the profession.

"My dear," said she to Kitty one day, "I perceive you are very young, and though you may have seen a good deal of life for your age, it is impossible you can have made so many necessary remarks, and formed such essential plans, as one of riper years, more experience, and greater opportunities. You have entered upon a scene of life, which, perhaps, of all others, is the most difficult to perform with success.—Nothing but consummate prudence, and the greatest fortitude, can prevent your being ruined in the very first act of this difficult piece. It's true, you have beauty, learning, and other accomplishments of a gentlewoman, but these will be of no signification to you, without your making use of them in exhausting the whole cunning of your sex. The men's passions, follies, and caprices are to be studied. These are their leading strings, and these you must be mistress of. For one man that has nothing but his carnalities, fifty have their vanity to indulge. Blind them with an opin-

---

1 Dressmakers.

ion of your choiceness, and it is sufficient that they have the honour to be seen in public with you, to make you the most extravagant presents. Had you indulged them with the enjoyment of your person upon the first interview, they would have made you a trifling acknowledgment, and never thought of you afterwards. A woman who makes herself cheap, loses by receiving; your importance and difficulty of access, will decide your value; and when you have got what sum you please, it is still at your option to gratify their desires.— Whilst a good-natured girl rots in an hospital, the jilt rides in her coach. The first rule of action is to declare perpetual war against the whole sex; love no man, but fleece and gilt them all as much and as often as you can."

Kitty was easily convinced of the rectitude of these notions, and was firmly resolved to guide her future conduct by them. But as she was inclined to believe that Miss S— must have had more than common reason to be so callous to, and inveterate against the men, she begged of her to inform her what first gave rise to these rigid notions, and she was so complaisant as to answer as follows.

"My dear, it is not suprising you should desire to know from what source my misanthropy first sprung; but what appears to you the effect of revenge, is nothing more than the dictates of self-love and female prudence. If either sex were to decide my hatred in proportion of their ill usage, it would be my own that I should most detest; for not only to a woman, but even to my own mother am I indebted for being a prostitute. My father, who was an officer in the army, dying when I was young, my mother had nothing but a small pension to support me and two other sisters. As we grew up we were taught the use of our needle; but my sisters were more assiduous at work than myself, and at that time I did not reflect upon the reason of their having no other provision, but what they earned by their fingers, whilst no such sentiment was ever enforced to me; but when I advanced towards riper years, I found there was a great disparity in our persons; one of my sisters being crooked, and the other much pitted with the small pox; so that I was the beauty of the family: for that reason my mother was the most indulgent to me. I was not to work at candle-light, for fear of spoiling my eyes and making them look red, whilst my sisters never quitted their needle till midnight. This great partiality easily prevailed upon me to believe I was my mother's darling, and that she had my happiness more at heart than that of my sisters.

"In my fourteenth year, at a time her house, which she let out in lodgings, was empty, and her landlord was extreamely pressing for a year and a half's rent, which had been some time due, for which he threatened a seizure; my mother took an opportunity to tell me I had made my fortune, if I acted with prudence, and as she dictated; for that Mr.— (the landlord) had actually asked me of her in marriage. I was greatly delighted with the thoughts of being a gentlewoman, and agreed to be entirely ruled by her in my conduct.

"He accordingly drank tea with us two or three times a week; and he was frequently left alone with me to say soft things.—The day of sacrifice now approached;—my sisters were sent upon a long errand, and my suitor came at the usual hour. My mother had pre-informed me that he was come to examine and see if I had no natural hidden defects, for that we were to be married the next morning.

"I strenuously opposed submitting to such an examination before marriage; but my mother told me it was always customary, and that if I did not agree to it, no man would have me. I could not imagine my mother would deceive me in so nice a point, and she promised to wait in the next room to come in upon the least alarm, in case he because rude, or attempted my virtue. I was accordingly in my bedchamber, without any stays, ready for my inspector, who was very punctual to his time. He embraced me, and told me he supposed I was acquainted with the subject of his visit;—a blush was my only answer. Then, without any more ceremony, he disposed me in such a posture as to reveal all my charms, which he kissed with the utmost rapture.— Though alarmed at this, I remained quiet till I saw him upon the point of possessing me. I then screamed out, and my mother came, but instead of assisting me, to disengaged myself from my ravisher, she told me to be quiet, and the gentleman would not hurt me.

"I now submitted, for I found the monster who bore me—can I call her mother?—not unwilling to assist by force in the rape. After I had been repeatedly sacrificed to the brutal lust of her landlord, she told me I had by my prudent condescension saved her from gaol; for upon that condition he had given up all his rent. So blind frequently is guilt, as not to see the very mark it aims at.—She took no receipt for my virginity (instead of the rent) and her goods were the next day seized, notwithstanding my prostitution.

The monster told her story, but it excited detestation instead of pity.—She died soon after in a gaol, eat up with vermin and remorse, and I was left to the wide world for a support. Necessity soon prompted me to sell that which my mother had already disposed of. Small were the returns of this commerce;—I frequently bilked through a false modesty of not insisting upon my reward before enjoyment,—and a city buck at length possessed me, without making me any other present than a severe gonorrhœa.

"Experience is most frequently worth its purchase; and this calamity taught me prudence. From this time I always insisted upon my fee beforehand; and where I had any suspicion of my man's health, I, with a feigned conscientiousness, told him I myself was injured. If he still persevered, I was certain he was disordered, and peremptorily refused him if he declined. He was generally satisfied with my generous information, and gave me a further reward for my honesty. By these and such like arts, five years public prostitution were attended with no further ill consequence to my health, and I saved as much money as purchased me an easy annuity.

"I am no longer common.—I am above the necessities of life.—I despise the men, who, to a woman that has seen so much of them as I have, are compleatly disgusting. Their money has always charms, and the best way to get this is to flatter them with your love, and the expectation of gratification.— Favours are no longer such after they are conferred."

Chapter XIII
A new plan of operations, with its success. Don Roderigo becomes enamoured with her.—The difficulty he has to get introduced.—His generosity, and Kitty's first éclat. Her acquaintance with the Duke d'Amelo, and his great fondness of her. She now shines in the predicted sphere. Her reflections thereupon, and her grateful and beneficent conduct.

This conversation with Miss S— was immediately followed by an entire revolution in Kitty's former plan of operations: she was no longer to be visited by a diversity of lovers, upon the smallest, or no introduction. Some ceremony was requisite to arrive even at her presence;—and the woman of pleasure was entirely veiled in the girl of fashion.

The gay, the amorous Don Roderigo, was greatly smitten with her charms.— He followed her in public, protesting in her hearing, she was the most angelic woman eyes e'er beheld; ogled her without being seen, and wrote to her, without being answered. He found these means would not serve for an introduction, and at length discovered a person who was acquainted with her.

Kitty immediately began to perform the part she had been so lately rehearsing, but he anticipated her in every passage.—Did she hint she wanted a sum of money? it was immediately doubled and presented to her. Did she give the least token of desiring a footman? an equipage was provided her.

We now see our heroine rolling her in chariot, with her original lover's cypher upon it,—living in affluence, and dressing extravagantly gay. The eyes of all Madrid were presently upon her;—the men found out charms she never possessed, and the women endeavoured to annihilate those she was mistress of.

Though Don Rodrigo's heart had received a great impression from Kitty, enjoyment, that infallible cure for love, soon effaced it. Prudence readily pleaded for a more oeconomical mistress, and a run of ill luck at play rendered it absolutely necessary.

Kitty had already been taken notice of by some of the first nobility in Madrid.—Her youth and beauty, with an uncommon ease in her deportment, rendered the pretty girl a great toast. When Don Roderigo told her of his ill success, and the necessity of retrenching his expences; she advised him to do it by all means. He was at first much surprised at her approving his turning her off; but she acquainted him that the Duke d'Amelo, whom he had introduced to her, had made her such proposals, as nothing but a resolution of being constant to her present benefactor, had prevented her accepting.

A few days proved the reality of her assertion. This young nobleman, who was just come of age, was so extremely fond of her that he past a whole week without once quitting her company. At the end of that time he took her a new house, and compleatly furnished it for her: the waiting job which Don Roderigo had hired for her was paid off and a coach was purchased in its stead, the duke presenting her at the same time with a set of his best coach-horses.— Her servants were increased to seven, for the support of whom and herself she had a very generous allowance.

In this elevated sphere Kitty frequently reflected upon the variety of fortune she had already passed through, though but in her eighteenth year—by which accidents she had arose to grandeur, which excited the envy of her whole sex;—and the surprising prediction of the conjurer, which was already so nearly fulfilled. She sincerely forgave him the liberties he took in inspecting her mole, and would not have been sorry if he had went still lower in his examination, to have foretold the events of her whole life.

Nor did she thus exalted forget the ties of kindred; her father's circumstances were at this period in no prosperous way, and his wife Kate had but an indifferent state of health: she not only constantly furnished them with provisions from her butcher, poulterer, &c., but also sent them frequent supplies of cash. This enabled John to live at his ease, and do little work, so that he had now time enough to enjoy his bottle and his friend, and animadvert upon Kitty's dutiful conduct. Kitty had two sisters and a brother much younger than herself, and having received a good education, to which she greatly attributed her success in life, she resolved they should not be behind hand with her in mental accomplishments. Accordingly, as her father could not afford to give them such an education as she proposed, she purchased them some genteel cloathing; sent her sisters to a boarding school, and her brother to an academy.

Her benefactions and generosity were not confined to her own family alone; many of her playfellows, when a child, partook of them; some she got well married to the men they liked, and set them up in trade; which with her recommendation almost ensured them future success; others she employed for herself and her family, and some were taken as upper servants in her house.

These acts of benificence indicated a good heart, and that though her ambition and vanity, nurtured in the soil of parental indulgence, had prompted her to a vicious course of life, she had not divested herself of all mortal virtue.

Chapter XIV

Don Gomez's passion,—proposes a party.—his ill success, notwithstanding his experience and knowledge of the same.—Declines the match. Proposes an advantageous revenue for Kitty from the Faro club and succeeds. The decline of the Duke d'Amelo's passion. Kitty's regular siege upon Count Peeporo's desires, and carries them by surprise.

Her lover was not content to enjoy his mistress in private, without the testimonies of his friends and acquaintance[s], to whom he frequently gave dinners and entertainments at Kitty's house. Among these was the rich Don Gomez, whose age and gouty decrepidness, prevented any suspicion of his amorous intentions. When the duke went to the play or a concert, he would frequently leave Don Gomez to amuse Kitty at a party of piquet.[1]

Gomez's age and infirmity were not sufficient barriers to incontinence, excited by youth and beauty. He would frequently lay down his cards, to contemplate Kitty's charms, protesting he wished himself five and twenty for her sake. "Ay, my dear," would he say, "at that age I should have been a match for you, at a more agreeable game than we are now playing.—I was always famous for holding great cards, as the duchess of —, lady —, and several women still living can testify.—Nay, I don't think I've so entirely forgot the game, but what I should make a tolerable figure yet, with a good partner."

Kitty seemed quite ignorant of the signification of what he said, and it was not till he had explained his meaning, by that intelligible definer of all things, a round sum, that she made him any answer. A pair of diamond ear-rings and two hundred pounds in cash, had eloquence to plead his cause to a miracle.

When the party was made, in the absence of the duke, Kitty found she run very little risk of being a loser by him, for though he still retained the theory of the game he had proposed, he had entirely forgot the practice. He imagined his hand would come in by frequent essays, and Kitty's presents were as often repeated; but after various and ineffectual attempts, he gave up the match, as he stood no chance with her.

However, he did not discontinue his visits, as the sight of Kitty and her company were still agreeable to him; and though he was loth to part with his own money for any future infructuous attempts, he told Kitty if it would be agreeable to her, he would propose to several members of the Faro club, whom he had heard profess a great regard for her, to make her an allowance out of their winnings, which if agreed to, would be very advantageous, and would soon enable her to purchase an annuity for her life. Kitty gratefully thanked him for his kind intentions to her, and told him she should be greatly obliged to him for his kind offices in the affair, if he thought it would not give offence to the Duke d'Amelo her keeper. Don Gomez replied, that as his grace was also one of the members of that club, he would mention the thing first to him, and if it met with his approbation, as doubtless it would, their example would be a further promotion of the scheme.

The Faro club was a society held at this time in Madrid, at a noted chocolate house; the principal members were some of the first nobility of Spain, who met to amuse themselves at Faro,[2] when a thousand or two of pistoles were generally lost at a time.

The proposal was no sooner made to the duke but he readily consented

---

1 A popular card game.
2 A popular card game.

to it, and mentioned it that very night to some of the members of the club, whom he thought would the most readily come into it. Five of the members agreed immediately to the proposal: these were Don Gomez, the Duke d'Amelo, Don Roderigo, the Count de Peeporo and chevalier de Cumaro.

These gentlemen entered into an agreement to allow Kitty five per cent out of all their winnings; and as one or other of them never retired without winning a hundred pistoles, this settlement was upon an average worth five pistoles a day.

It may at first appear surprizing that the Duke d'Amelo should relish a subscription of this nature for the support of his mistress; but it was a politic scheme in him, to withdraw himself from her, as he had just found his appetite began to pall, and that he had not resolution enough to break with her all at once.

Whether he gained any intelligence of the intimacy between Don Gomez and Kitty, or he suspected it by the proposal made by him in her favour, we cannot certainly determine; but the duke, it is plain, now thought the agreed stipend of five per cent was a sufficient quota for his pretensions, as he henceforward made her no presents, but what arose from his winnings.

Though five and thirty pistoles a week may be thought a very sufficient income for Kitty, who might not only have lived affluently upon it, but saved a competence for life; yet she thought of singularizing one of her subscribers, as soon as she found his grace had put himself upon half pay.

Don Rodrigo's circumstances she thought she was acquainted with; beside, as he had already been intimate with her, (and a woman very seldom makes a conquest twice of the same man) she dismissed all thoughts of enlisting him into her private service. Don Gomez had by this time been convinced that he was too much an invalid for the commanding officer, and the Chevalier de Cumera had as yet given no great testimony of the power of her charms. So that the Count de Peeporo appeared to her the most likely of the five to succeed with, especially as he had lately had a rupture with his lady, whom the world gave out had been intimate with another nobleman.

She accordingly laid the plan of a regular siege upon the count's desires.— She ogled, sighed, and breathed nought but love in his presence.—The covert way of his passion was already gained.—She disclosed her neck, with her pouting orbs, seemingly by accident,—and mounted the glacis of his lust. She let drop her garter, he insisted upon putting it on.—The fortress was surprized, and the garrison surrendered at discretion.

The spoils of this conquest were three hundred pistoles in notes, which she found in a gold snuff-box, ornamented with the count's picture; besides a continued contribution of twenty pistoles a week.

Chapter XV

The artful part Kitty plays to get five hundred pistoles from the Count de Peeporo, and receives a thousand. The misunderstanding that ensued between them concerning a riding dress similar to Lady Peeporo's. My lord submits.—The encounter between Lady Peeporo and Kitty on horseback, with its consequences.

Miss S—'s good advice to Kitty, though she had hitherto so little occasion to use it, was not thrown away upon her. The Duke d'Amelo's abrupt coldness, after he had been such an earnest sollicitor for her gaming settlement, when she was upon the very point of making the greatest advantage of his acquaintance, added to her former instruction, the maxim of "taking time by the fore-lock."

She was now resolved no longer to defer putting her tutoress's rules in execution, and having formed the plan of obtaining a considerable sum from the duke, just as he broke with her, she imagined it would still succeed with the count, whom she thought she had sufficiently rivetted, not to be startled at the demand of a sum of money.

She put on a look of great sorrow the next time she saw him, and her repeated sighs convinced him something more than usual affected her.—He earnestly entreated her to inform him of the cause of her grief, for that if it was in his power, she should be immediately relieved. She still refused divulging the secret, 'till she had made him as melancholy in earnest as she appeared to be.

She then said, "My lord, the great and tender regard I have for you, is the only reason that prevents my acquainting you with the subject of my sorrow; but as you seem to participate as thoroughly of my anguish, though unacquainted with the cause, I shall not think I transgress upon the moderation I prescribed myself, in acquainting you with it."

"Do, my angel," said he, "let me know, and if possible I will relieve both your and my own distress."

"My lord," she replied, "it is upon the single condition that you will not attempt to relieve me, that I shall acquaint you with it, as perhaps it would not only be greatly inconvenient, but also detrimental to your welfare, to assist me with so great a sum."

"If money is all," resumed he, "I believe I can soon make you easy, for I was so fortunate as to win a thousand pistoles last night, for which I have brought you my accustomed quota."

She was not at all displeased at this information, and though she told him five hundred pistoles was the sum she was likely to be troubled for, he sent her the next day the whole thousand he had won.

So generous a lover could not avoid forcing from Kitty grateful returns of respect and complaisance; but as her vanity and capriciousness increased with her grandeur and retinue, she could not brook the smallest denial of indulgence from her admirer. A trifling circumstance in itself, but which Kitty made a point of, had near terminated their intimacy.

The countess of Peeporo, who never wore any cloaths or ornaments in common with the other ladies of Spain, having made a particular agreement with all those she employed to make her things in a quite new taste had at this time a riding dress so extremely remarkable and uncommon, that it was noticed and fruitlessly endeavoured to be imitated by many ladies of Madrid. It had not escaped Kitty's observation, and she was firmly resolved to use every art to have one exactly similar. She had already been to every habit-maker's in or near the metropolis, to enquire if they could make one like it, according to the description; but they frankly acknowledged they could not; and as a last resort she desired the count to order one for her, at the same habit-maker's his lady's had been made at; but he expressed himself, saying, that would not only discover their intrigue, but must certainly occasion much uneasiness in his family.

Kitty was greatly piqued at this denial, and in her heat could not refrain throwing out some aspersions against the Countess de Peeporo's character and conduct, and concluded with saying, she could see no reason for his having any terms to keep with a woman, who had treated him in such a manner.

The count could not still be prevailed upon to agree to her proposal, which enraged her so much, that she declared she never would see him again. In saying this she flew out of the room, and was not visible to him for three days, notwithstanding he constantly repeated his visits twice a day.

At the end of this time, his passion got the better of his prudence, and he sent Kitty a letter, in which he informed her, he had himself been that morning at his lady's habit-maker, and given the necessary orders for making Kitty a riding dress exactly like hers. The habit maker waited upon Kitty accordingly, and my lord and she were reconciled.

The first time Kitty had this new habit on, she took an airing on horseback, in a place near the capital, not unlike Hyde-park, where she had scarce rode once round, before the Countess de Peeporo appeared, dressed exactly like our heroine. As soon as the countess perceived Kitty, she made a full stop with her horse to examine, and Kitty equally stopt to view the countess. A staring match accordingly ensued, which lasted near a quarter of an hour; and even in retiring, their eyes were fixed upon one another behind, as long as they remained in view.

My lady was no sooner got home, than she sent for her habit-maker, to enquire how he had dared make a riding dress like hers for any other person; he excused himself in saying it was by the Count de Peeporo's order, with which she was satisfied from him; but the rupture that ensued between the married pair was not so easily reconciled.—Separate beds took place for two months, nor would they then have been reduced to one, if the Count de Peeporo had not discontinued his visits to Kitty.

Chapter XVI

The intimacy between Kitty and the Count de Peeporo discontinued, with the reason. Don Cupidino returns, and the renewal of their fondness. Don Camelio's attachment and generosity. Kitty's transcendant grandeur, excited the envy of her whole sex. Some groundless stories propagated concerning Kitty set in their true light.

Pretty near the same cause produced the different revolutions of Kitty's lovers; her great demands, and their exhausted stock of fondness. The count de Peeporo, whose estate was not the most affluent for a nobleman, was not a little incumbered by the frequent and extravagant presents he had made Kitty; and though the premium of 5 per cent upon his winnings, which he paid her, may at first appear nothing out of his own pocket, when it is considered a man as frequently loses as wins at play; this in fact was as certain a diminution of his property, as paying the sum abstracted from gaming. In the same light may we look upon the thousand pistoles he presented her with in her pretended distress. So that the Count de Peeporo had in fact been one of her principal benefactors, and she was therefore in the same proportion in a drawback upon his income.

These considerations, added to the satiety of enjoyment, and my lady's resolution of not admitting him to her bed, as long as he visited Kitty, at length induced him to discontinue the intimacy between them; and Kitty was once more to be disposed of to the best bidder in the auction of love.

It was at this time Don Cupidino, her original flame, returned from abroad: he had no occasion to enquire after Kitty, for the first equipage he met after he entered Madrid was hers. Not suspecting any acquaintance in the coach, he did not turn his eyes that way, but hers were full upon him as he passed, and she ordered her coach to stop. Her footman told him his lady desired to speak with him. What was his surprize at seeing Kitty so magnificent, is more easily imagined than expressed. He got in, and after an inundation of amorous protestations on both sides, she acquainted him with all that had happened since his departure.

She now no longer thought of disposing of herself but to her dear Don Cupidino, who was equally happy and content in the embraces of so fine a woman he esteemed.

Their constancy was, however, of no very long duration, for Don Cupidino being again obliged to join his regiment, and Kitty having smitten the rich don Camelio. He wrote to her, and enclosed two bankers draughts for fifty pistoles each, which gave her a very good opinion of his generosity; a visit on his part early ensued, and a repeated present procured the desired favour.

Don Camelio was the richest of all her lovers, under grandees, and she took care frequently to fathom the depth of his purse. In a few weeks she got from him fifteen hundred pistoles, besides a new green-varnished vis-a-vis,[1] accordingly to the last high taste, still retaining Don Cupido's cypher.

---

1   "A light carriage for two persons sitting face to face." [OED]

Her equipage was one of the most brilliant in Madrid; her house as elegantly furnished as any in that metropolis, her table as sumptuous, and her face as pretty as any woman's need to be.

It became a matter of debate about this time whether or no she painted, and many wagers ensued thereupon in the Faro Club. Lord Peeporo won a thousand pistoles by wagering she did not use white; and Don Roderigo won the Duke d'Amelo's set of bays, by saying she did not enamel.

It is not surprising to think she was now as much the envy of the women, as she was the admiration of the men; the first could find nothing in her, the others thought Kitty centered the charms of the whole sex. The women invented fifty false reports concerning her, to make her character more odious than that of a woman of pleasure need to be. They exhausted their imaginations to render her vanity insupportable, her pride insatiable and her avarice without bounds.

The whole calumny of the sex was now exhausted upon poor Kitty; their tea-table talk was entirely concerning her, and the female visitor who could not bring in a fresh story about her, was scarcely welcome. To these sources may we attribute the reports now current to her disadvantage. The following is in every one's mouth though their falsity is notorious:

"That a certain young nobleman of the house of Castile was introduced to her, and after very little ceremony passed a night with her, and presented fifty pistoles in the morning. That he repeated his visit a few evenings after, and having no more money about him than twenty pistoles, he desired her to accept of them, which she did; but gave orders to deny her for the future to him, as she imagined he would the next time present her with twenty piastres."

The other is, "that the Count de Slendero was so extreamly enamoured with her, and not having sufficient cash by him to make her a suitable present, gave her all his lady's jewels, to the amount of near four thousand pistoles, which Kitty accepted, and appeared in them the same week at the play, sitting in the very box, and upon the same seat, as the Countess de Slendero, who having scarce a diamond about her, and knowing her jewels again, was so extreamly disconcerted as to be obliged to leave the place before the representation was half over."

These stories are mentioned here, only to demonstrate to what a pitch of envy she must have wrought her whole sex, by having supplanted them in toasting, adulation, and splendor.

Chapter XVII

Her adventure with Count Demargo, with his satisfactory manner of making love. The effect of her vanity manifested in an extraordinary sumptuous sedan chair. The accident with Miss S——. The transports of the sex thereupon. The candidates for a successor. Their hopes frustrated.

Notwithstanding these reports were vague and without foundation, the effects of spleen, malice, and envy; yet this phænomenon of female gallantry had many real adventures, which were not less extraordinary or entertaining.

The Count de Demargo, whose marriage, though of some years standing, remained still unconsummated, imagined he saw in Kitty an object that could create powers to enjoy what his desires in vain attempted. He accordingly got introduced to her, and would at first have opened his mind upon the score of his visit; but he found there was some ceremony requisite by way of pre-lude.—He submitted to the custom she imposed, and then declared himself.

"My lord," returned Kitty, "I am extreamly surprised that so fine a lady as your wife should not be able to gratify all your desires, and that you should be thus necessitated to apply to me for relief."

"My dear girl," replied the count, "you quite mistake the thing.—I own my wife is handsome, and that some men might be happy enough with her; but as I married her for the sake of family connexions, I never could yet prevail upon myself to enjoy her."

"Extraordinary cause of disgust indeed, my lord," said Kitty, "because she has great alliances, you are surfeited before possessing her."

The count made no reply to this, but presented her with a very handsome diamond ring, which prevented any farther remonstrances on her part, though she still entertained a very shrewd suspicion of his inability. However, she informed him she was engaged all that week with Don Camelio, but the beginning of the ensuing she would be at his service.

The count was a little chagrined at this retardment, which he attributed to not having made her a present equal to what she might have expected; and he therefore furnished himself with a very handsome gold snuff-box, by the time of the appointment, in which he put a note for two hundred pistoles.

The appointed day being come, he waited upon her, and presented her with the box and its contents, with which she seemed thoroughly satisfied.— He passed the evening with her, and left her as much a maid as he found her;—but he was contented, and protested he had never been so happy in all his life. He repeated his visits every other day for a month; when he made her presents equally valuable to the first; and she made him the same satisfactory returns.

From these impotent letchers it was Kitty gleaned such immense sums; so that with very little wear and tear she earned more money than any other woman of the same profession ever did before.

At this time a lady of the first fashion, worthy of all elogiums, had a sedan chair made in a peculiar manner, and particularly ornamented with enam-elled flowers. Kitty saw it, and she resolved immediately to have the like. The chairmaker had heard some reports to her disadvantage, concerning her pleading her non-age against the payment for superfluities; and when she asked him the price the lady had paid for hers, he told her fifty pistoles more than he had actually received, in hopes of deterring her from having the like made; but she was greatly surprised at the cheapness, and ordered one immediately, which was accordingly made; which she soon appeared in, to the further mortification of all the women of fashion.

An accident that happened to Kitty at this juncture, gratified the spleen and envy of the whole sex for some hours. She was riding out as usual with Miss S—, and having made the tour of the upper park, adjacent to the metropolis, she descended into the lower; when a file of soldiers, who had been relieving the guard, turning abruptly upon her, frightened her horse, which ran away with her. That of Miss S— followed the example of Kitty's pyebald, and they were both thrown from their seats. A group of cavaliers presently surrounded to assist them, and Kitty's first fright being over, from a fit of crying, she changed into one of laughing; though she still remained in the posture the accident had thrown her, whereby the spectators had a favourable opportunity of viewing those charms, which decency dictates should be hidden.

Being risen from the ground, she found she had a great pain in her hip; and her fine chair being at hand, she immediately got into it, and was conveyed home. The report was immediately spread over the whole metropolis of what had happened to Kitty; and every one rumoured it, as their fancy or inclination suggested. According to some, she had broke her thigh, others said her leg, and very few let her off for less than a dislocated hip.

What was the joy of the whole sex upon this agreeable news, can better be imagined than expressed. Suffice it to say, all female hearts were so elated, that every one studied her glass an hour longer that day, as a candidate successor.—Signora B—, and Madam R—, the two competitor dancers, were that night at the opera, in the opposite boxes, as the two first champions upon the list.—They had already disputed the prize for some time; when alas! how mortifying! Kitty herself appeared as beauteous and gay as ever. The competitors declined the election, and no more votes were canvassed.

Chapter XVIII
The effects of Kitty's accident in the city of Madrid. An uncommon advertisement upon the occasion, with her friends remarks. Two congratulatory letters from two celebrated courtezans.

The affair presently made a great noise throughout Madrid, and the streets and lanes re-echoed with Miss Kitty F—r's downfall.—Songs, lampoons, and epigrams flew about on every side, and prints of the scene were publickly exhibited. The song of "Kitty Fell" was now in every one's mouth; and parties and cabals were actually formed, some for the ridicule, others for the vindication of Miss Kitty's conduct. Every coffee-house was become a public oratory, where the merits and demerits of the cause were stated and opposed. Female tongues were not silent upon the occasion,—and the ghosts of envy still hovered round Kitty's phaetonic car; whilst public advertisements appeared to apologize for our heroine.—A very remarkable one, to which she subscribed her own name, was in substance as follows:

To her immortality is a blemish intailed upon women, and however *indiscreet* their conduct, they should be *secure* from *censure*; for the *more ridiculous* their *behaviour*, the more *indulgent* should be the *voice* of *fame*, which should doubly, nay trembly, re-echo their *success* to the most distant corners of the universe. Though malice may shoot against them all their stings, *and even the snakes* of envy be let loose, *true* and *impartial honour* will ever be their *champion* and *protector*. It is that *jurisdiction* which is to secure Miss Kitty against all the attacks of *puny scribblers* and *pocky malevolence.*— She has been *disabused* in public papers, *apposed* in print-shops, and, to *blow* up the *hole*, some mean, ignorant, *venereal* wretches, would dispose *of her in public*, by DARING TO PRETEND TO DARE, (*though they have not yet dared or pretended any thing*) about her Memoirs.—In order to prevent the expected success of their *daring pretences*, she hereby publickly declares, that there cannot be the slightest foundation for publishing her Memoirs, which have been kept so extreamly *secret*, that even she herself is unacquainted with them.

This advertisement did not fail making as much noise as her late accident, and even her greatest advocates could not avoid owning it extreamly ambiguous, if at all intelligible; that she had much better have been silent upon the occasion, as she hereby exposed herself more, than she had yet been either in the public papers, or in the print shops; and that common sense (of which she was not deficient) might have dictated to her, that she should have been tacit upon the score of the veracity of her biographer, at least till such time as her Memoirs appeared since the world would not be convinced of her sincerity, in disowning their truth, even afterwards, when she had so firmly resolved upon discrediting them beforehand.

She received two congratulatory letters, upon her late accident being attended with no ill consequences, by the late tyrants of mankind, whose throne Kitty had not only successfully usurped, but to which she had annexed considerable provinces. The epistle from Fanny ——,[1] was pretty nearly to the following purport.

Madam,
The accident, which has lately happened to you, has made so much noise throughout Madrid, that it could not fail coming to my knowledge. Although I have more reason than any other of my sex to be piqued at your

---

1 Fanny Murray.

success, as you have supplanted me upon the polite theatre of gallantry; yet I have long since looked upon intrigue, and all its attendant circumstances, in their true light, and have retired from every thing that had even the appearance of criminality, to live soberly and virtuously the remainder of my days. I therefore envy no woman her success,—but pity her folly, if she does not in time, during her halcyon days, make such a provision, as may ensure her from all the necessities and calamities of past vice and folly.

I sincerely congratulate you upon the accident being attended with no fatal consequences; and hope it may induce you to reflect upon the transitory reign of beauty and success.—Had it been attended with a broken limb, or even a less calamitous incident, your triumph would have been at an end. Fame says you gain more money than any woman that ever trod in the same path, the famous Constantia Phillipa[1] not excepted; but that you are so extreamly poor, through imprudence, that you have scarce ever money sufficient to satisfy your domestic calls.—In such a situation, how great would have been your fall! Unfit for your calling, the men would no longer have signalized you,—and your own sex's envy would have been converted not into pity but contempt. Your ambition and misery would have kept equal pace, and prevented your attempting earning your bread.—Your friends and relations, unable to support you, could not have been induced to sacrifice their all to your vanity!

This is not the idle phantom of a distempered brain, but a real picture after nature, which experience has convinced me is neither outrée'd or overcoloured.[2] Take then this advice, from one who can have no other interest in counselling but your welfare. You have still an opportunity of making a handsome provision for yourself.—*Act prudently for a while, reform, and live virtuous.*

You cannot upbraid me with giving advice I cannot follow; for without ever being so advantageously situated as you are at present, and after being further plunged in vice and debauchery than ever you were, I saw my condition through the medium of reason,—long sought for an opportunity of penitence—and embraced the first that presented itself. I am,
    Madam,
        Your sincere well-wisher and very humble servant,
            Fanny M—.

---

1 Teresia Constantia Phillips, a well known elite courtesan. See her *Apology for the Conduct of Mrs. Teresia Constantia Phillips* (1748-9) and also Kathleen Wilson's excellent account of her career in *The Island Race: Englishness, Empire and Gender in the Eighteenth Century* (New York: Routledge, 2003), chapter 4.
2 That is, Murray insists that she is not exaggerating.

The other letter Kitty received upon this occasion was conceived in the following terms.

Dear Miss,

I am extreamly glad to hear that you are so well recovered from the accident which happened to you the other day; and that you are, as the French say, *quitte pour la peur.*[1]

But did you really shew higher than your garter, Kitty? One would not have minded it, had it been to genteel people; but to make such a discovery to the canaille[2] is what must give you great uneasiness. I really feel for you upon the occasion,—but never mind it,—remember what Queen Anne said upon the balcony.[3]

You may, perhaps, imagine I am envious of your success, and would insinuate those charms were displayed, that were really hidden; but far be any such scandal from me— though you have rivalled me in my old lover,—but the settlement remains,—and that is all I care for. I am told you know your trade, and practice it as well as I ever did; and that you think with Hudibras,[4]

—The worth of every thing
Is just as much as it will bring;

After we have fleeced our culls of all we can, we leave the mere *caput mortuum*[5] as a monument of its own folly.

I have heard of your tricks, and have heartily laughed to think how well you play my game.—Take care of your cards now you have so good a hand;—but in case of a revoke, it is but cutting-in with a player, as my predecessor and I have done.—It is the fashion, and I am sure you will not be out of it, except it is to be particular, as you are in every thing else.

I am,

Dear Kitty,

In great hast going to P—'s benefit,

Yours obsequiously,

Lucy —.[6]

---

1   Gotten off with merely a fright.
2   "A contemptuous name given to the populace; the 'vile herd', vile populace; the rabble, the mob." [OED]
3   Reference unlocated.
4   Eponymous hero of Samuel Butler's poem *Hudibras* (1678), an approximation of part 2, canto 1, 465-466: "For what is *Worth* in any thing,/ But so much *Money* as 'twill bring?" From *Hudibras*, ed. A.R. Waller (Cambridge University Press, 1905), accessed through *Literature Online.*
5   Death's head.
6   Lucy Cooper. This narrative is followed by two satirical poems, "The Stream of Kitty" and "A Song occasioned by a late Event (To the Tune of Kitty Fell)."

CHAPTER THREE

From *The Histories of Some of the Penitents in the Magdalen-House as Supposed to be Related by Themselves*

ANONYMOUS

Unlike the other prostitutes represented in this volume, Emily Markland is a fictional character—although one, as her author insists, whose story represents a plausible case of a penitent. The Histories of Some of the Penitents in the Magdalen-House, *in which this narrative appears, was first published in 1759 as part of a new reform movement that emerged in the middle of the century. It tells four different stories of women who significantly benefited from the Magdalen Hospital, a private charity where repentant prostitutes could find support and undergo training for work in industry or service. Some reformers even believed that penitent prostitutes could reintegrate themselves into society as wives and mothers.* The Histories, *along with other sentimental narratives and reformist pamphlets, encouraged support for and contributions to this extraordinarily popular yet nevertheless controversial charity. The establishment of the Magdalen Hospital marks a significant change in attitudes toward prostitution, suggesting that the public view prostitutes as objects of charity rather than as social menaces. Supporters of the Magdalen Hospital promoted sympathy for prostitutes as a mark of virtue, while detractors satirized the project as a retirement home for aging whores. Wouldn't such an institution, they asked, only encourage prostitution by making it less dangerous? Certainly hostility toward prostitutes did not disappear and libertine versions of the prostitute's life remained part of British culture; nevertheless, novelists, pamphleteers, and reformers urged the public to replace moral judgment with compassion. In the context of the sentimental version of the prostitute's predicament, however,* The Histories *also stands out for its full confidence in prostitution as a reversible condition and the relative absence of the heavy condescension that often characterizes reformist writing. Emily is even permitted to express sexual desire for her original seducer without alienating the sympathies of the virtuous reader.[1] The narratives in* The Histories *represent prostitution as a desperate and sometimes even laudable strategy for survival and the preservation of her children that does not destroy a woman's character or lead inevitably to a pitiful death.*

---

1   I owe this point to Katherine Binhammer, "Epistemology of Seduction: Women, Knowledge and Seduction Narratives in Britain 1740-1800" (unpublished manuscript), chapter 2.

★ ★ ★

The Histories of Some of the Penitents in the Magdalen-House, as Supposed to be related by Themselves

Chapter 1

Let my tears thank you; for I cannot speak:
And if I could, ———
Words were not made to vent such thoughts as mine.
Dryden[1]

The pleasure everyone finds in talking of themselves, may serve to convince us, that so many persons as seek refuge in the Magdalen-House from guilt and infamy, cannot forbear giving some account to each other of their past actions, especially as they will contain much variety and adventure. That they must thereby call to remembrance all their distresses, is no reason against it; for we daily see people more inclined to dwell on the relation of their misfortunes, than on the happier events of their lives. Whether it proceeds from the satisfaction they receive in reflecting that the storm is over, or from the desire of being pitied, which seems implanted in our natures, He only, who knows all the springs of the human mind, can tell. That these penitents must by this means publish their own infamy, is as small an impediment; for that is sufficiently known by their being there; and their hearers have none of that obdurate virtue, which makes people not know how to pity weakness they never felt: All are in much the same state, tho' brought to it by different steps.

We have had examples of females, whose frailty has not been accompanied with half the extenuating circumstances that these persons can allege, yet have blazoned forth their crimes to a world, part of which, innocent of the life, must blame; and still a greater part, who have been more private, tho' not more virtuous, will certainly censure loudly, when they see

———Each fair advance,
The luscious heroine of her own romance.[2]

---

1 From John Dryden, *Don Sebastian, King of Portugal* (1690), Act 4, scene 1. Jenny Bachelor and Megan Hiatt have found that most of the epigraphs in *The Histories* come from Edward Bysshe, *The Art of English Poetry*, the eighth edition (1737). See their introduction to *The Histories of Some of the Penitents in the Magdalen-House, as Supposed to be related Themselves* (London: Pickering and Chatto, 2007).
2 Richard Graves, "The Heroines: or, Modern Memoirs" first printed in the *London Magazine*, for March 1751 (20): 134-35. My thanks to Jenny Batchelor and Megan Hiatt for sharing their identification of this quotation.

But in the society which I am speaking of, the case is different; Each looks on the other with an eye of pity: Equal distress, and equal relief, begets a sort of mutual affection; while their hearts overflow with gratitude to their noble benefactors, (noble, if not by blood or descent, intrinsically so from the generous benevolence of their worthy hearts) they rejoice not only in their own deliverance, but in that of all they behold; and, sufficiently humbled by former misery, they relate with compunction, from hearts overcharged with the remembrance of past wretchedness, and the comforts of present ease; not with vanity, like those I have mentioned, who exult more in their number of conquests, than blush at having themselves been so often conquered; and are more vain of their beauty, than ashamed of their vice.

When but a small numbers had flown for refuge to this blessed asylum, they were one evening sitting together, after the work of the day was past, when one of them turning towards the youngest in company, who had long sat silent, observed that tears trickled gently down her cheeks. This young woman was not twenty years old; her person was extremely elegant, her hands and arms finely turned, her neck white as alabaster, and exquisitely formed. Her face expressed all the humble modesty of a Madona, with a countenance languishingly sweet. The young woman who observed her, asked, what sorrow could reach her in that comfortable retreat? "For here," continued she, "what can we grieve for, except it be our sins? And such grief is accompanied with consolation, as it brings with it a hope of pardon, and a satisfaction in thinking we are come to a necessary sense of our own guilt, the first step to repentance."

"You mistake the cause of my emotions," replied the young woman: "Mine were not tears of sorrow, but of joy and gratitude. When I beheld with what content, and innocence, that necessary ingredient to content, we sat here surrounded with all the comforts of this life, and all the assistances requisite to bring us to the blessings of the next, and compared it with the wretchedness from whence I was redeemed by it; my heart overflowed with gratitude to our excellent benefactors, who, like our blessed Lord, come as physicians to the sick, and call sinners, not the righteous, to repentance; who offer rest and refreshment to all those that are heavy laden with their miseries. From these worthy instruments of divine mercy, my grateful thoughts rose to Him who is the Author of all goodness, and consequently inspired them with this charitable intention; till, oppressed with my own sensations, they found some vent in tears, and wore the appearance of sorrow."

"The liveliness of you gratitude," replied the other, "reproaches me for want of sensibility, who ought to feel so much more, and yet appear less affected. But my heart is for ever full, and how should it be otherwise? For I have suffered some years more of wretchedness than you can have done, who I imagine have scarcely seen your twentieth year."

"You are right as to my age," answered the young woman, "but I am old in misery. Were I to measure my years by the pangs I have felt, my life would appear of an antediluvian length."

"Your misfortunes must have begun early indeed," said a third, "and seem peculiarly affecting; they excite the curiosity of those who have enough to employ their thoughts at home, without concerning themselves about others; for idleness of mind is generally the parent of curiosity; but for all this, I confess myself curious."

Many others expressed the same curiosity, the young woman told them she would not refuse to gratify them: If any thing she could say would withdraw their thoughts from themselves, it might be some relief, as we seldom feel other people's misfortunes so severely as our own.

Accordingly she proceeded, as the next chapter will show.

Chapter 2

How happy is the harmless country maid!
Who, rich by nature, scorns superfluous aid:
Whose modest cloaths no wanton eyes invite,
But, like her soul, preserve the native white:
Whose little store her well-taught mind does please;
Not pinch'd with want, nor clogg'd with wanton ease:
Who, free from storms, which on the great ones fall,
Makes but few wishes, and enjoys them all.
                    ROSCOMMON.[1]

My father was a clergyman in the West of England. He served two curacies and one living;[2] all which together did not bring him in £100 per annum; but entirely engrossed his time, as he endeavoured to do his duty in each parish, to the utmost of his power, and obliged him to be at the expence of keeping a horse. This, with the continual repairs necessary to his parsonage house, which was much decayed, and the ill state of health wherewith my mother was afflicted for many years, made his income but barely sufficient for himself and his family, tho' it was not large; for of many children my mother bore him, one elder sister and myself only lived to grow up.

When I was near fourteen years old, my mother died, which occasioned my sister's return home. She had spent three years with an aunt, who was a milaner[3] in a large town in that county; but, by the loss of my mother, became nec-

---

1 Wentworth Dillon, Earl of Roscommon (1633-85). From "Part of the Fifth Scene of the Second Act in Guarini's *Pastor Fido*," Roscommon's translation of a fragment of Giovanni Battista Guarini's 1590 pastoral tragicomedy.
2 A holding of land granted by the Church [OED].
3 A milliner. Originally "a seller of fancy wares, accessories, and articles of (female) apparel, esp. such as were originally made in Milan." [OED].

essary to take care of my father's family, whose health declined so fast, that nursing him was her chief employ.

In a little more than a year, we lost my father; a great misfortune to us both, but particularly to me, who was thus left to my own guidance and support, when I was but fifteen. My appearance indeed was womanly; I had been bred up in religious principles, but at that age they could not be deeply grounded, nor so fixed as to stand against the temptations of the world, into which I was now thrown.

My father's effects, when sold and all accounts settled, yielded us but a few pounds. My aunt was dead, and we had no near relation who could assist us; but a Lady in the neighbourhood, who had always professed a great regard to my father, called upon us, when the first agonies of our grief were so far over, as to enable us to perceive the forlornness of our situation.

My sister applied to this Lady for her protection for me, for whom she was most uneasy; being, as she said, able to provide her own support; but my youth and person, which perhaps she beheld with partial eyes, filled her with apprehensions for me.

The Lady assured us she would do her utmost to serve me; that if she had no sons, or I was less handsome, she would receive me into her house; but that was now impossible: however, she would enquire among all her friends, if she could find any thing proper for me, and hoped to succeed before we were obliged to quit the house.

This Lady was as good as her word; and not being so much afraid for other people's sons as for her own, she prevailed with a Lady of her acquaintance, who lived in the next county, to receive me as her woman. She had suffered me to assist in the dressing of her daughters several times, that I might be qualified for my place; and at the time appointed, gave me a letter of recommendation, to secure me still a better reception.

To take leave of my sister, was like losing my only parent; for such she was to me, tho' not above five years older than myself: I think I could not have felt much deeper affliction for her death, our separation appearing to us not much less grievous. I was frighted at the thought of going amongst entire strangers, and into a new employ; and my sister's apprehensions were such as were but too well verified in the sequel. She spent the last day we were together in warning me against the temptations which would perhaps fall in my way; of which I remember the following words were part, for they made a strong impression, tho' to little purpose; and the misfortunes into which I fell from disregarding them, fixed them stronger in my mind.

"My dear Emily," she said, "I cannot fear for your honesty or sincerity, tho' I have said so much on those subjects. Your nature is superior to any offences of this kind; but my apprehensions are numerous in another respect. I would not attempt to tell you, you are not handsome; our own eyes in such particulars give us sufficient evidence, and we seldom doubt their truth; besides, the less persuaded you are of this, the more you will be pleased with those who tell it you, which all will be ready to do. Such a person as yours, in your situation, will attract many admirers; for while the one charms, the other will excite hopes; which I would flatter myself will be disappointed; but I confess my apprehensions arise as much from the tenderness of your heart, as from the snares that will be laid in your way. If that does not betray you, all the rest may be easily baffled: but what can I say that will steel your heart with indifference! Alas! It is above my power: He only who made it can correct it. To him, my dearest Emily, you must apply; and bear constantly in mind, that your present and eternal happiness depend on the proper regulation of your affections."

Advice to this purpose she repeated the whole day, with many tears, and anxious prayers for my preservation.

The next morning parted us, never to meet again with so much satisfaction, melancholy as that last interview appeared to us.

One day's journey brought me to the house of Lady Markland, my new mistress. I was immediately introduced into the parlour, where she then was sitting with Sir George Markland her husband, their son Mr. Markland, a young gentleman about twenty-five years old, and another Lady and Gentleman who were then with them on a visit. My confusion was so great, I was scarcely able to answer the questions she put to me, or even to deliver the letter with which I was charged.

While her Ladyship was perusing the epistle, my distress increased; for the rest of the company fixed their eyes so entirely upon me, that I could find no place for my own, and began to think the questions which had before distressed me, were a great relief, in having taken my attention. I have reason to believe the Lady took compassion on me; for she called me to her, asked me how I had performed my journey, and such sort of questions as seemed to have no other intention but to encourage me; then, turning to Lady Markland, said, "I perceive, Madam, you are not of a jealous disposition."

"No indeed," replied her Ladyship, "but if I was, it would be no reason why I should be plagued with an ugly face about me; for Sir George must see handsome ones abroad, if I suffered none but Hottentots at home."[1]

This short dialogue increased my confusion; and no words ever sounded more acceptable than the orders Lady Markland gave to the servant who introduced me, to shew me to her house-keeper.

This house-keeper was one who had lived a great many years in the family, and, as I afterwards found, was held in great estimation. She understood all

1 Lady Markland's racist comment refers to "one of the two sub-races of the Khoisanid race (the other being the Sanids or Bushmen), characterized by short stature, yellow- brown skin colour, and tightly curled hair. They are of mixed Bushman-Hamite descent with some Bantu admixture, and are now found principally in South-West Africa" [OED].

the necessary parts of a house-keeper's office, and none better than flattery; which, perhaps, gave a great charm to her other qualifications, for she was not without defects. Tho' she was an useful director in the kitchen, and an assiduous watch over the other servants, yet her first attachment was to her own interest, of which she was never neglectful. She was no bigot to truth; and in her Lady's absence, made herself amends for the flattery she thought proper to bestow on her before her face; falling as much short of what she deserved at one time, as she went beyond it at another. Nor did she excel more in chastity than in other virtues; for she had for some years been suspected of an intrigue with Sir George's valet-de-chambre; but being both thought excellent servants, it was winked at, tho' all the family were certain that it was well known to their master and lady. Indeed, being often present when they conversed freely, I found they made a jest of it, not from disbelief, but from thinking it of no consequence.

This greatly shocked me at first; and the familiarities between these two lovers, who were my only companions at meals and on evenings, were very distressing; however, as they gave me reason to think my absence would not be disagreeable, I sat with them as little as I could.

Chapter 3

Love gives esteem, and then he gives desert;
He either finds equality, or makes it:
Like death, he knows no difference in degrees,
But plains and levels all.

DRYDEN[1]

My Lady was very good-natured and indulgent to all her servants, and to me among the rest; tho' I had no hopes of becoming a favourite, when I saw, by her house-keeper's practice, how much she loved flattery. She would often say, when I omitted an opportunity of imitating her, that I was dull; and sometimes, that she fancied I could think nothing commendable in any one by myself; but all this without any bitterness.

I seldom saw Sir George, but in his Lady's presence; he would often talk to me and compliment me, called me Lady Markland's Venus; and when I entered the room, would cry, "Here comes your goddess, my dear;" but all with so much mirth, and so little design, that in time I learnt not to mind it, and answered to the name of Venus as readily as to that of Emily.

---

1 An approximation of lines from John Dryden, *Marriage à la Mode (1673)*, Act III, scene i. (1673). The lines are spoken by Leonides: "Love either finds equality or makes it./ Like death, he knows no difference in degrees/ But planes and levels all." *The Broadview Anthology of Restoration and Eighteenth-Century Drama*, general editor J. Douglas Canfield (Peterborough, ON: Broadview Press, 2002), 352.

Mr. Markland was much less free, but more attentive; he treated me with such respect, that his mother would sometimes tell him, she believed he thought I was a goddess in reality. He would answer, that a fine woman was a better thing; that no situation in life should make a man fail in politeness to one of the other sex; and that really there was a modesty in my appearance, which was truly respectable. These sort of compliments he would make me before his parents; and often gave the conversation such a turn, as afforded him opportunities of applying others to me by his eyes, which were unobserved by every one else. He found excuses to come into the house-keeper's room, where he would rally her and her lover on their mutual passion, taking occasion from it to vent some libertine sentiments, wherein they were sure to second him; and sometimes to behave with a tenderness and gallantry to me, which I ought with shame to say, rather alarmed than offended me; so little was I the better for my sister's good advice.

I wrote her an account of all the family into which I had entered; but at first, for fear of increasing her apprehensions, and afterwards from the conscious weakness of my own heart, did not tell her how very amiable Mr. Markland was, both in person and manner; in both of which he has seldom been equalled; nor of his addresses to me. But I communicated to her one circumstance, which surprized me; That were it not that they sometimes attended the parish church on Sundays, I should not know whether the family I lived in was Jew, Mahometan, or Christian; for there was never any sign of worship among them. I never heard the name of a Superior Being uttered, but as a word of course, or by way of strengthening an assertion. While the Gentleman and Lady I mentioned remained there, cards employed the Sundays as regularly as the other days; and when they failed to do so after their departure, it was for want of a party.

I was much surprized at a manner of life, which I thought could be found only amongst the reprobate; whereas Sir George and my Lady appeared universally respected; she behaved with good humour to her servants; and he with humanity to his tenants; that is, he did not require more of them than they could possibly pay, and chose rather to turn them out of their farms, than support them in gaol.[1] In short, they committed no vices, and had constitutional good-nature; their characters might be well drawn by negatives; but as for positive virtues, they thought them unnecessary; they would declare they never did any harm, and did all the good they could: A strong assertion, and difficult to be made good by the best people: For as every action is an example to somebody, and has numerous consequences, many that the actor esteems innocent, will prove pernicious. Thus Sir George and my Lady, by winking at the intrigues of their servants, and speaking lightly of religion and virtue, banished both from their family, and became not only answerable for

---

1 Jail.

their own faults, but for those which their examples encouraged in their domestics.

My sister was as much vexed with the account I sent her of the family, as I was surprized at what I related. She wrote me word she wished me in a worse place, if I had but a better example. She had been taken into a milaner's shop in the town, where her aunt had lived, and where her conduct had recommended her.

I had not been above a month at Sir George's, before Mr. Markland began to make real love to me; he took every opportunity of finding me alone, which my practice of avoiding the house-keeper's room rendered more easy. I was sensible of a new-born partiality for this gentleman; and not having forgot what my sister had said to me, resolved to endure more of the house-keeper's company, that I might be less alone. This did not make much alteration; for Mr. Markland was too quick-sighted not to know that interest had its due weight with the house-keeper. He began therefore by making her presents, which his behaviour to me explained the reason of; and she, willing to deserve his bounty, multiplied opportunities for his coming into her room, and was continually in his absence telling me of his passion for me, of my good fortune, and how much it might turn out to my advantage, without my understanding in what manner she meant. I could comprehend no other method of being benefitted by his love, than marriage; every thing else to me appeared attended with guilt and ruin.

I was now much at a loss how to avoid Mr. Markland; and what was worse, my heart was ready to furnish me with excuses for not doing it. My religious principles grew weaker every day; piety was treated as enthusiasm, strictness of manners as folly; for "our Maker was merciful, and designed to make us happy; which we could be only by following our pleasures: that our tastes and passions were given us as benefits, that we might receive happiness from gratifying them."

My Lady having found me several times reading in a religious book, at last snatched it out of my hand; and throwing it down, said, "The girl would turn her head: She never knew a puritanical servant, who did not turn out a whore or a thief; and that she wanted not to have her jewels stolen to feed methodist parsons; or her cloaths pawned to furnish out their weekly contributions." As I had never seen her so angry, I began to think there must be some crime in religion, which I did not know, to make it appear so offensive.

The house-keeper one day caught me at prayers. This was told in the house-keeper's room, as a most ridiculous circumstance. Much laughter ensued. She asked me, if I was praying for a husband. Mr. Markland called me his fair saint; told me, I mistook the matter; for I was made not to pray, but to be prayed to.

To find religion both the object of serious censure and of ridicule, made me think there was something very uncommon in it; and that in having it, I was certainly guilty of a great peculiarity. My religion was rather founded on habit than reason. I had been told *what* I should do; but my father's continual occupation abroad had prevented his teaching me *why* I was to do so. Thus I was unprovided with reasons for my practice; and Mr. Markland, whose understanding furnished him almost at one view with all that could be said on every subject, was diligent in removing what he called the prejudices of education.

Every frailty that had been committed by any person who professed some regard for religion, if it had come to their knowledge, was repeated by them with triumph: But I was not weak enough to think this availed them much; for I had never been taught to believe that any common degree of piety would always conquer natural disposition, or be a certain defence against the temptations of the world; nor that the most religious were infallible. While they were mortal, they must be frail; and none pay so great a compliment to religion, as those who imagine every one who professes it must or should be a saint: But often wide is the profession from the practice!

In this manner we went on for near half a year that we continued in the country. Mr. Markland grew more assiduous and more open in his courtship, and I listened to it every day with more pleasure, and fewer fears. Nor did my companions suffer his cause to lose in his absence; they continually contrived to leave us alone together; when he would lavish all the vows and oaths that ever lover broke, with such tender importunity, that I sometimes wondered how, with a heart so filled with frailty, I had resisted. But principle still got the better of my passion, tho' it was risen to the utmost excess of tenderness.

Mr. Markland was too well acquainted with the human passions, and I too little with the arts of concealment, for him to remain ignorant of the state of my heart: And had he not perceived it, his faithful assistants would have informed him of it; for they would in their discourse wind me in such a manner, that sometimes my blushes, and often my tears, explained it more fully than words could have done. On the knowledge of my weakness, Mr. Markland built his hopes of success. He often wondered at my resistance, but for ever expected it to fail. I sometimes had nothing but tears to answer to his tenderest professions. I wept for shame at listening to them, and for grief at thinking it necessary to reject them.

Chapter 4

"Where more is meant than meets the ear."[1]
MILTON

When we were in London, Mr. Markland had still more opportunities of seeing me. Sir George and my Lady were always abroad, or engaged in company. They seldom enquired after their son, thinking it the duty of polite parents to suffer him to take his own way; or if they happened to ask any ques-

---

1 John Milton, *Il Penseroso* (1745), line 120.

tions, the servants knew what to answer. Thus almost all his time was passed with me. While I was busy in attending my Lady at her toilette, he made his necessary visits, that the rest of the day might be his own.

I confess I was not always desirous of avoiding him; but if I had, I could not easily have contrived it, for every servant was bought to his interest. I desired the house-maid, who had leisure in the afternoons, to come and work with me, thinking thereby either to prevent his coming, or at least to put some restraint on his addresses. But he no sooner entered, than she retired; and I found, upon questioning her, that every servant had felt his bounty, either to procure their secrecy or assistance.

Sensible of my own weakness, and how far every one was combined for my destruction, I had still virtue enough left to wish that I could find some refuge against myself; but could see none, unless I could obtain it of my Lady. Filled with this thought, I determined to apply to her for advice and assistance, acknowledging my own excess of passion, and giving her as little reason as possible to be angry with her son.

I waited with impatience for a summons to attend my Lady at her toilette, and took no small pains to keep up my resolution; which perhaps I had never been able to form, had not Mr. Markland been obliged that morning to go abroad with his father.

The time at length came; but, to my great disappointment, I was followed in by a country neighbour of her Ladyship's, who immediately desired to speak with her alone.

I was accordingly dismissed, and not recalled till the arrival of more company; upon whose appearance the first Lady took her leave. My purpose was equally disappointed; four visitors had taken the place of one.

One of the Ladies observed that she who was gone away looked very melancholy. "Had you been mistress to the king, or his prime minister," added she, "I should have thought you had just refused a petition."

"The most ridiculous woman," said my Lady, "surely that ever was born! What do you think is the subject of her affliction?" Here her Ladyship laughed so violently, that she could not immediately answer their enquiry; tho' they all expressed great curiosity to know what it was.

"Would you believe," continued Lady Markland, "that all the excess of grief you see painted on the poor woman's countenance, proceeds from having discovered that her son, a young man of about three-and-twenty, keeps a mistress; and she came to communicate her sorrows to me, hoping that from my friendship she should receive some compassion?" Here they all joined in such peals of laughter, as Comus's crew can scarcely equal.[1]

"And pray," asked one of the Ladies, "what consolation did your Ladyship

---

1 A reference to the raucous attendants of Comus in John Milton's *A Maske; or, Comus* (1637).

give her?" "Consolation!" replied my Lady; "I asked the woman if she expected her son to be a Joseph?[1] That no man of spirit was without intrigues: It was a male privilege."

Is this the person, said I to myself, to whom I meant to apply for refuge against her son's gallantry, and my own passion!

"A male privilege, indeed!" answered one of the Ladies. "We may see the men not only made laws, but customs. They have carved themselves out pretty lives. They the primrose path of dalliance tread, while they would confine us to the thorny way."

"Do not be so severe upon them," said another. "You forget, that if none of our sex were in the path, it would not appear so flowery: They cannot exclude us."

"That," interrupted my Lady, "is an advantage to women of an inferior rank; but people of fashion cannot well make use of it. If Spencer's Sir Calidore had but been a real character, and the blatant beast, Slander, in fact killed, the case might have been different."[2]

"If it is not killed," interrupted another Lady, "it has barked so long, that no-body regards it; for really women are now under almost as few restraints as the men. But, pray, what is the woman this *unfortunate* Lady's son has pitched upon? Perhaps somebody very expensive; and that may have its inconveniencies."

"No," replied Lady Markland; "the young man has been humble enough; he has contented himself with one of *Mamma's* maids."

Here again the Ladies were highly entertained: But one of them observed, that she thought the lowness of his taste might be mortifying to an affectionate parent: There was a want of spirit and proper pride in it.

In this manner the conversation was kept up, till two gentlemen arrived. My office being ended, I withdrew.

I heard with surprize so many women of character, who were so much my superiors in age and experience, and consequently I thought in wisdom, treat that as a privilege, which I had looked upon as the greatest misfortune that could befal me; and against which I wanted a defence, that I might better rely upon than my own resolution. What Mr. Markland had said to me on that subject, had less power over my judgment, than my affection gave him over my heart. His arguments came from a suspected quarter; his interest was visible, and therefore they had less weight; but when Ladies, who had no such inducements, confirmed his doctrine, how could I avoid suspecting myself of those ill-grounded prejudices of which he so often accused me! My heart took advantage of this opportunity; and, with the assistance of such strong authorities, silenced my reason and my principles.

---

1 The Biblical figure who resisted the advances of Potiphar's wife.
2 The lady refers to figures from Edmund Spenser's *The Fairie Queen* (1590). Sir Calidore is the champion of courtesy in this work.

Full of these thoughts, I retired to my chamber, where I found Mr. Markland waiting for me. He received me with a transport beyond what so short a separation could make me expect. The joy so visible in his countenance, communicated itself to my heart; and I, who two hours before wanted to find a means of avoiding him forever, was charmed at seeing him again. He told me that, no longer able to live without me, he had left his father at a chocolate-house,[1] and returned home with the utmost impatience. Fatal impatience!

Chapter 5

The friends thou hast, and their adoption try'd,
Grapple them to thy soul with hooks of steel.
            SHAKESP.[2]

We had now been in London above four months. I had continued corresponding with my sister; tho' not daring to communicate the thoughts that were uppermost in my mind, my style grew so constrained, and my letters so short, that she took notice of it; and, more grieved than offended, expressed fears for my health, attributing to some defect in that, the alteration in my manner; for it wore the appearance of melancholy. But if shame for the weakness I felt in my heart made writing to her so difficult to me, it is not strange, if, when guilt took its place, I was no longer able to write at all. I feared her advice, which was now the severest reproach to me; looked on myself as unworthy to address her; so much did I reverence a conduct, which I had not been able to imitate. From this time my correspondence with her ceased. As it had slackened so much before, she did not immediately observe it; but when a letter of hers had remained above a month unanswered, I received another from her, filled with the kindest anxiety and most alarming apprehensions.

They did not now appear without foundation, for my health was impaired: I grew pale and thin; my chearfulness was changed into tears and self-reproaches: For the little colour I retained, I was obliged to my blushes, which every eye that gazed on me raised in my cheeks.

My Lady and Sir George observed the change, and very obligingly enquired into the nature of my complaints. I could by no means answer them with sincerity; but invented such disorders, as I thought they could not easily disprove.

The kind letter I have mentioned receiving from my sister, having remained unanswered, was followed by another, which informed me that she was soon coming to town; that the milaner with whom she was, had a daughter now grown capable of managing the business; and therefore she had got from her a recommendation to one of the same trade in London; and as soon

---

1   A chocolate-house was similar to a coffee house.
2   William Shakespeare, *Hamlet*, 1.3. 62-63.

as the terms were settled, she should come there with great satisfaction, as it would bring her near me.

This news filled me with distress. How could I, who was not able to take courage to write to her, bear her sight, who would so circumstantially examine me about every particular of my situation and conduct; and whose eyes would no less exactly observe my person, which I had reason to believe would soon appear as visibly altered as my face?

I could not conceal my uneasiness from Mr. Markland, who was both the cause and the consolation of all my sufferings. He told me, it only confirmed him in a purpose which he intended to propose to me; which was, to place me in a house, where I might live free from the continual apprehensions I now was in, and enjoy the ease and affluence I so well deserved; that it was but reasonable, that she who possessed his whole heart, should at least share his fortune. To see me so settled would render him very happy, as he could then enjoy my conversation without restraint and interruption; and he flattered himself, that he should see less melancholy mixed with my tenderness, which was now an abatement to his felicity. He added, that he had considered of the impossibility of my attending his mother into the country; since a few months must affect my shape so as to render it apparent to her; and therefore he had intended to desire me to find some excuse for giving her notice that I should leave her, before the true cause could be perceived: and he was glad, that while he was gratifying himself in withdrawing from a state of servitude the woman, who in all eyes but those of the priests, must be looked upon as his wife (for as such he should ever esteem me in the tenderest sense), he should remove me from a sister, whose prejudices might be the occasion of much trouble to me.

This proposal was indeed a great relief to my spirits: I longed to be removed from the eyes I feared; but could find no excuse for leaving my Lady. However, as the best I could invent, I took the first opportunity of informing her, that a relation in the country, whom I durst not disoblige, insisted on my coming to live with her.

Lady Markland suspected the truth of what I said; and told me, she wished it was not another kind of invitation that carried me away. "But, girl," added she, "depend upon this: All your beauty will not keep one lover, tho' it may gain you a thousand. After a short possession, a woman not half so handsome will appear preferable, and you will be left on the common."

Tho' I had no reason to suppose her Ladyship inspired with any spirit but that of experience, I could not help being shocked at so dreadful a prophecy. Scarcely capable of answering her, and utterly unable to insist on the lye I had made, I with much difficulty, and with tears starting from my eyes, said, I hoped my behaviour had not given her Ladyship grounds for such a suspicion.

"No, no," replied my Lady: "I have no fault to find with your conduct. You seem mighty sober and modest; but I never in my life knew a very demure girl come to any good."

I was glad to come off with so general a reflection; for I was not without apprehensions from what she had said, that she suspected part of the truth. As for the fears she had excited, as soon as I told them to Mr. Markland, he dispelled them all, by the kindest assurances of constancy and unalterable love: Professions, which, contrary to all experience, will, I fancy, be believed, while love and folly exist.

Lady Markland having soon another servant recommended to her, I obtained liberty to depart before my sister came to town, and was guided by Mr. Markland's servant to my new house, which was very pretty, and furnished in the neatest manner imaginable, tho' not expensively. Mr. Markland was there to receive me, and was delighted with seeing me so well pleased with it, and with perceiving it was so much beyond my expectation; for Vanity had not yet found its way into my heart; Love too entirely filled it all.

I was desirous of putting my lover to as little expence as possible, therefore took but one servant; and endeavoured, by the regularity of my *ménage*,[1] to persuade the neighbourhood, that I was his wife, but obliged to conceal that circumstance during Sir George's life.

This opinion Mr. Markland gave all the colour to that he conveniently could; and indeed might safely do so; for whatever comfort my inexperience might draw from it, thinking I thereby avoided slander, he must well know that such indulgences to women in my situation are so common, that they find credit with none but the very lowest people; and that, instead of making a mistress pass for a wife, they often occasion one who is really a wife, to be taken for a mistress.

Sir George and Lady Markland did not stay long in town after I left them. Their son excused himself from going into the country with them, and by various pretences prolonged his stay.

He was now always with me, and always equally a lover. His tenderness continued unabated; tho' my frequent indispositions cast a languor over my countenance, and deadened my complexion. Whenever I was tolerably well, he carried me to some of the places of public diversion most frequented during the summer season. They were entirely new to me. His conversation would have rendered any place pleasing. It is not strange then that I was delighted with places so calculated to entertain. He thought the satisfaction I shewed in them a sufficient reward for the trouble of attending me; for he had been so long accustomed to them, that they had in great measure lost their charms to him.

Mr. Markland was extremely pleased at seeing me attract the notice of the company; and would, with particular satisfaction, make me observe the admiration that was paid; which was entirely overlooked by me, so wholly was my attention fixed on him. At first I was pleased with being admired, as I thought

---

1 Household.

the approbation of others might recommend me the more to him; but at last I liked it for its own sake. Vanity, which had so long lurked unseen in my heart, began to grow perceptible; and the pleasure of being admired, made the greatest charm of a public place.

Mr. Markland was sometimes obliged to go down to his father for about a week; but short retirement urges sweet return. He always left me with regret, and returned with impatience. These little absences were great afflictions to me; from having been so long habituated to his company, I knew not how to live a day without him; a week was an age; and I became almost as insensible as a statue, till again cheared by his presence. I every moment regretted the loss of him; and sometimes, I confess, lamented that I was deprived of admiration; for when he was away, I never went abroad, unless some family business carried me: So that I not only lost the pleasure of my heart, but the delight of my vanity.

Towards the end of autumn, during one of these short excursions, I walked out to make some small purchases. In my way, I went thro' a street which I had not been in before; and going by a milaner's shop, I stepped in for some little thing I wanted; when the first person who offered to serve me, proved to be my sister. We were both so affected, that we became motionless for some time. My sister recovering herself the soonest, ran to me to embrace me; when casting down her eyes, she perceived the alteration in my shape; and instead of coming up to me, sunk down into a chair, where a flood of tears relieved her.

I stood in no less want of relief, but could find none. I was almost suffocated with the struggle in my breast, between the various passions that affected me. My sister, seeing the condition I was in, cried out, "Oh! My poor Emily!" And leading me into a parlour behind the shop, called for some hartshorn;[1] and when she had brought me to myself, "Oh! My dear child," said she, "what can I say to you! How can I bear to see you in the condition you appear in! And yet, how dare I say what I would, when I fear that even the sight of me may have done your constitution irreparable mischief! I would not increase the shock I have given you; and yet can I, with any degree of propriety, see you again? The account I received at Lady Markland's door, when I went with the most tender and anxious impatience to enquire after you, is but too well confirmed. O thou fallen Angel! How can my fond heart support the sight of thee, thus involved both in present and future misery!"

I could answer only with my tears. I threw myself on my knees, and catching hold of hers, my streaming eyes begged for pardon, but my words could find no utterance, till at last I got power enough just to say, "Forgive me, my dearest sister! My parent, best of friends, forgive me!"

---

1   "The aqueous solution of ammonia (whether obtained from harts' horns or otherwise)" [OED]. Used in a similar way to smelling salts, which derive from hartshorn.

"My dear sister," said she, "ask not forgiveness of me: Ask it of Him whom you have most offended, and who not only can pardon the past, but preserve you from all future crimes."

My sister thus continued her exhortations for some time, till she asked me if I would quit the way of life wherein I was engaged, and never see the man who led me into a state of ruin and destruction; promising, that if I consented to this, she would take all possible care of me, and provide me with every convenience: For tho' she was then going to be married to a young man, who was a very advantageous match for her, and whom she sincerely loved; yet if he, disapproving of her conduct in this particular, should attempt to restrain it, she would for ever forego all her expectations, and should think herself greatly rewarded by saving me from eternal ruin.

What could I say, when I could not resolve to accept of so kind, so generous an offer! I begged her not to oppress me with her goodness: That I was not deserving of her care; and would never suffer her affection for me to prevent her happy establishment: Wished heaven might shower down all its blessings on her; but that as for myself, the die was cast; I was too far engaged to retreat. She again pressed her offer: I told her, "I could not deprive the child I went with of a parent; nor was it possible for me to forsake a man whose whole happiness was centered in me, and who deserved every thing from me, having no aim but to promote my felicity.'

When my sister found me unalterable in this respect, "Then," said she, "my dear Emily, I will not urge what I might properly say, because I fear to hurt your health: I will not now endeavour at what I see your passion would render ineffectual to any purpose, but that of making you uneasy, when ease of mind will be most necessary to your recovery: I can only pray that your life may be spared till you are fitter for another world; and that He who alone can turn the heart, will take compassion on yours: But it is impossible for me to see you any more; it would only be increasing my wretchedness and creating yours. The thought of the situation you are in will embitter my most prosperous days; but it is my duty not to suffer it to disgrace them."

I cried out, in agony which no words can express, "My dearest sister, do not despise me, do not hate me: Your hatred or your contempt would break my heart."

"No, my dearest Emily," replied my sister; "be assured I can never hate or despise you: I shall pity, grieve, and pray for you; but, with all your faults, must love you; love you with a tenderness none but a parent can know; for such I have always felt myself for you: And whenever you will love yourself as truly as I love you, shall with joy receive you, forget the past, hope for the future, endeavour to relieve your griefs, and confirm your happiness."

With many tears and embraces, we took leave of each other. A chair was called; for I was not able to walk; my body felt so strongly the effects of the agitation of my mind.

I never was so sensible of the sacrifice I had made Mr. Markland, as when I returned home, and reflected how true, how amiable a friend I had given up for him. When I considered my sister's whole conduct, how little did I appear in my own eyes! I do not know how I could have supported the view of my own meanness, had not Mr. Markland arrived in town, and restored me to my vanity; for nothing but vanity could preserve me from my own contempt; for I think I may properly give that name to an opinion that exceeds what we deserve.

A young woman called at my door, to inquire after my health, for two or three days successively, after this interview with my sister, who I judged was sent by her, in kind anxiety, lest the greater flutter of my spirits should have impaired my constitution. After that, I heard nothing of her; nor durst I make any inquiries at that time.

Chapter 6

The world's a scene of changes; and to be
Constant, in nature were inconstancy:
For 'twere to break the laws herself has made:
Our substances themselves do fleet and fade:
The most fix'd being still does move and fly,
Swift as the wings of time 'tis measur'd by.
T'imagine then that love should never cease;
Love, which is but the ornament of these;
Were quite as senseless, as to wonder why
Beauty and colour stay not when we die.
          COWLEY[1]

No change happened in my way of life, till I was brought to bed of a very fine boy: Nor did this make any alteration, but my temporary illness, and the addition of this lovely child to our family; which was an increase of happiness. Our fondness for it was equal; and instead of our affection's being lessened, by having a third to share it with us, each seemed to look on the other's being parent to this little darling, as a new merit, which caused, if possible, an increase of fondness.

The winter altered, not lessened, our attendance on public amusements; but we were obliged to go in a more private manner, as there was a greater chance of meeting with some of Mr. Markland's graver acquaintance. This caution, if I had not been lost to shame, must have shocked me; but the violence of my passion, the extreme tenderness of Mr. Markland's behaviour, and the care he took to furnish me with books, that should in his absence

---

1 Abraham Cowley, from "Inconstancy" (1647).

keep alive my infatuation, made me regardless of every thing else; and no one was ever disposed to say more cordially from her heart,

Fame, Wealth, and Honour, what are you to Love![1]

A second year passed away in this madness of the mind; but at the beginning of the third, I thought I discovered an alteration in Mr. Markland: He endeavoured to appear the same; but the tenderness of his behaviour, instead of being the free emanation of his heart, seemed forced and constrained. The impediments to his coming to me were multiplied: One would have thought that people were now making themselves reparation for having lost so much of his company, and were determined to engross him entirely. Even his child grew less dear to him, tho' every day more engaging.

At first I endured this change in silence, and in tears I may add; for weeping was now my principal employ in his absence; and I believe nothing could have prevented its being constantly so, but the fear of rendering myself odious in the eyes of him, to whom it was too grievous to be looked upon even with indifference. At last, I gently hinted my apprehensions; but I found I gave offence, because I saw too clearly; and to avoid any thing that might make me lose the little of his company which I now enjoyed, I determined hereafter to bear all in silence. But it is not in the power of language to describe the anguish of my heart, nor the difficulty I found in concealing it.

In this wretched state I continued for three months; a state which seldom changes for a better, unless when it creates indifference in us, which, to some women, is almost as difficult as to conquer that of their lovers; and to add to my misfortunes, I was one of those, who, obstinately fond, can

Doubt, yet doat; despair, yet fondly love.[2]

Cruel as I thought my situation, yet I found there was a state of distraction beyond it; for into such I was thrown by a letter brought me from Mr. Markland, wherein he acquainted me, that he was then at his first stage towards Harwich, where he was going, in order to embark for a foreign port, having accepted an employment under one of our ambassadors.

The distress of my mind was now beyond what any one can comprehend, who has not sacrificed all she did or ought to hold dear, to one man, whose tenderness seemed for some time to recompense her for all she had relinquished, whose love constituted all her happiness, and who at last, by the most cruel inconstancy, threw her from the airy height of bliss to which he had exalted her, into the lowest abyss of misery.

Before the receipt of this cruel letter, I thought my grief could not admit of increase: To lose Mr. Markland's affection, appeared to me the heaviest

---

1   From Alexander Pope, "Eloisa to Abelard" (1717).
2   *Othello* III.iii., 170. The Pelican Shakespeare has ""Who dotes, yet doubts—suspects, yet strongly loves!" Alfred Harbage, general editor, *William Shakespeare: The Complete Works* (New York: The Viking Press, 1969), 1038.

misfortune: I did not then understand how soon a woman, who cannot possess a man's esteem, loses all his regard when he ceases to love her. But to be left with such indifference! A child abandoned without one parting kiss! was a shock too great for my constitution to bear. My weak understanding was so shaken, that for two days I was quite out of my senses: To this a fever succeeded, which was violent, but not tedious.

As soon as my shattered brain grew a little composed, anxiety for my child made me desirous to preserve a life which seemed to promise me nothing but misery: But what would I not have undergone, rather than leave that dear babe friendless and defenceless, in a world which now was very low in my estimation! For it is the way of us all, if one person uses us ungratefully, to quarrel with the whole human race: Never sensible of universal faults, till we suffer by those of some individual.

Care for my child rendered me obedient to all the orders of my physician, who told me, I must not hope for recovery, without I could compose my mind to some degree of resignation. This argument made me use every means to change the natural current of my thoughts.

My little boy, as the only object now of my affections, (and the only inducement for my endeavouring to raise myself out of that state of despair) I would have always with me; but how often did that increase my grief, by reminding me of his father! If he smiled on me, I thought I saw his father's sweetness, which had charmed my soul: An endearing action brought to my remembrance his father's tenderness: If he was diverting, I said to myself, "How would these once have delighted his father!" If he looked pale, how would this air of sickness have alarmed his father's fondness!

In spite of grief, my fever left me; and I found it necessary to resolve on some means for my child's and my own support. Mr. Markland had left no provision for us; but, as if he justly thought that after the loss of his affection every thing else was insignificant, he was as regardless of lesser particulars for me, as he might imagine I should be for myself.

While Mr. Markland loved, he was generous; and as I was a good oeconomist, I had near a hundred pounds by me; and having some cloaths, which were better than would be required in the way of life into which I intended to enter, I converted them into money; and turned the parlour, with little expence or alteration, into a haberdasher's shop, laying out all my money in stock. I sent my landlord warning that I would quit his house after the necessary notice, intending to take myself a cheaper habitation.

The execution of this purpose was of service to me: It employed my attention, and gave me a subject to think of; which, tho' productive of no pleasure, yet gave me no pain. I had not ease of mind sufficient to be anxious about my success; every thing appeared too trifling to move me much. As for my child, I wept over him, instead of rejoicing in him. I had now no affection but what gave me uneasiness: What I fancied was the source of sublime happiness, I found was productive of the greatest misery. But my sorrows were grown quiet; I was composedly wretched.

Chapter 7

I pass'd this very moment by thy doors,
And found them guarded by a troop of villains:
The sons of public rapine were destroying;
They told me, by the sentence of the law,
They had commission to seize all thy fortune.

OTWAY[1]

I did not succeed ill in my business; the humbled air, which grief gave me, I believe softened the rigid virtue of my neighbours; and as I sold rather cheaper than most people in the same way of trade, in order to incite them to deal with me, I seemed well established in about two months after I had furnished my little shop.

But great was my surprize, when one morning two men entered my house, who immediately arrested me, and seized my goods.

I was more amazed at this insolence, than frighted; for I was sure I had incurred no debts, and therefore told them they must have mistaken the house and person. Of which I had no doubt; but greatly was I shocked, when they informed me, that they were employed by my landlord, who had never received any rent from the time Mr. Markland took the house, nor payment for the furniture, with which, being an upholsterer and cabinet-maker, he had furnished him; and that he could easily prove that whatever I had belonged to Mr. Markland.

All the horrors of a prison now presented themselves to my imagination: I easily perceived my stock could not discharge this debt; and with little ceremony was told by these men, that nothing else could save me from a gaol, and that I must go with them. What now to do with my child I knew not: To expose it to the colds and damps of so nauseous a place, shocked my nature: As for myself, had no other depended on me, I should have been less anxious: I had resigned myself to misery, and which way it was brought upon me seemed of little consequence. One relief I immediately felt from this misfortune; the love which I had till now borne to Mr. Markland, whose inconstancy I almost forgive, as a weakness in his nature, was entirely obliterated, by so mean and cruel an action as leaving me exposed to such infinite distress; for he could not but know that his absence would determine the landlord to take care of his own interest: And probably I should not have been left so long in quiet possession of the house, but that he might the more certainly get all I had, when my shop was furnished in the best manner I was able.

---

1 Thomas Otway, *Venice Preserved* (1682), 1.1.232-36.

I now despised the man I could not hate, and no longer felt the pangs of slighted love; but the terrors of my approaching fate took their place: I was weeping over my child, who, frighted at my agonies, was more clamorous in his grief, hung round my neck, and screamed, he knew not why, only he perceived the men were the cause of my affliction: And as they, provoked at the noise he made, began to swear at him, he grew more terrified; and with the assistance of the lamentations my maid uttered, who thought the degree of grief was to be measured by clamour, the uproar was great enough to bring in an old Lady, who came to hire a house at the next door to me.

She had been to see it the day before, and had taken notice of my child, with whom I was standing at the door, and asked me some questions about the neighbourhood, more, in appearance, for the sake of conversation than curiosity.

This Lady, as I said, was attracted by the clamour she heard in my house, and came in to ask the cause of it.

The bailiffs were the most able to speak, and gave her a surly answer; but one which was so much to the purpose, that in a few words they made her comprehend the whole matter.

She came up to me, and enquired if the balance against me was great. I told her I could not tell how that might be, as I knew not what difference would be made in the valuation of the goods, when they came to be appraised, from what they had been sold at; but that it ought not to be considerable, for the damage was small, they having been always used and kept with great care: That except this difference, the balance on either side could be but trifling, for my stock would answer the rent; but that to one who had nothing, a debt of thirty pounds was as bad as one of three hundred, and must render me equally insolvent.

She then asked the men what they designed should become of me till the affair was settled: They replied, I must either go home with them, or to gaol.

"Have you nobody," said she to me, "to be bail for you?" "No one," answered I; for my sister was the only person to whom I could apply, and I would not harbour a thought of making her a greater sufferer by my ill conduct than she already had been, or of running the least hazard of causing any difference between her and her husband; for long before this time I imagined she was married. I was sensible that if she knew my distress, she would be anxious to relieve it; and as her husband might not chuse to give his money to one so unworthy, disputes and disgust might arise on the subject.

"It is hard," said the old Lady, "you should know nobody who will perform such an act of humanity. Tho' I am not fond of having any thing to do where the law is concerned, yet I cannot withhold my assistance from one who is in so very distressful a situation, and who seems born to suffer from the cruelty of mankind. I will bail this young woman, and will take upon myself the settling her affairs" (turning to the bailiffs).

I was all gratitude: A thousand blessings and a thousand thanks I gave her. But the men were not so ready to accept her offer; they said they must first enquire into her character and substance, and know whether she was responsible.

"If you have any doubts of that kind," said she, "let the goods be appraised directly: The day is long enough for settling the whole affair."

This proposal was agreed to; my landlord was sent for; my stock in trade was valued by the bills of what I had paid for it, and appraisers determined the value of the furniture.

My benefactress had left me before my landlord came; and as evening drew on, I grew under great apprehensions lest prudence should get the better of charity, and prevent her return: But before the whole was entirely settled, she came; the balance was drawn, and I remained debtor but about 20 pounds. She paid the money, and said she would require no consideration of me but a note of hand, in case I ever should be able to pay her; and as I was at a loss where to go that night, offered to carry me home with her.

This additional kindness charmed me: My heart was inexpressibly relieved by such generosity: For the present I forgot the destitute condition I was in: I was delivered from immediate distress, and Mr. Markland's baseness had relieved my heart from the tenderness which till then oppressed it; so that I think, entirely pennyless as I was, these were much the happiest hours I had enjoyed from the time that Mr. Markland's affections began visibly to alter.

My benefactress took me and my little boy into the coach, and we soon arrived at her house. She told me, that as my spirits had undergone a great deal of fatigue, and she was to have some company that evening, it might perhaps be more agreeable to me to retire to my own room; to which she led me, and ordered a servant to see that I had everything I wanted; and then, taking her leave of me, wished me good night; saying she feared she should not be able to get to me again that evening.

I repeated all the acknowledgements my gratitude could suggest, and wished her a rest equally refreshing to the infinite relief she had given to my despairing mind.

Chapter 8

Prospects at distance please, but when they're near,
We find but desart rocks and fleeting air:
From stratagem to stratagem we run;
And he knows most who latest is undone.
GARTH[1]

When I was left alone, and began to reflect on the various events of that day, it seemed a general scene of confusion; they had pass'd in such quick succession, that the recollection made me giddy.

---

1 Sir Samuel Garth, *The Dispensary* (1699), Canto 3.

The variety of thoughts which all these things suggested to my mind, would have engrossed my attention a long time, had not my little boy interrupted me; the bustle of the day had wearied him. I put him to bed, and that being done, I began to observe the furniture of my room.

The furniture was old and tattered, and everything very dirty; but had once been handsome. I was surprized at the condition it was in, as I imagined the mistress of the house to be a woman of fortune, from the generosity she had shewn towards me; and from her age I expected such a degree of oeconomy, as would prevent so much dirt and rags. I wondered, therefore, what could occasion this appearance, and flattered myself I might be of some use in doing my best to repair the destruction, which seemed less owing to the ravages of time than to want of care.

A servant, not much more cleanly than my chamber, came to ask me what I chose for supper: I told her any thing the family had; I begged I might give no additional trouble. "My mistress," said she, "thought you might be tired, and want to go to bed before their supper time, so ordered me to enquire."

"At what time do they sup then?" I asked. "It is quite uncertain," answered the servant; "sometimes it is vastly late, but never before eleven."

I had been used to late hours at Lady Markland's, so was not surprized: I thought I had got again into the house of a fine Lady; but, since that was the case, desired a piece of bread and butter, which would be a sufficient supper for me.

My request was not soon complied with; but as I heard many raps at the door, I easily guessed the servants were either busied by the arrival of so much company, or it had made them forget me. It was near eleven o'clock before anyone appeared again in my apartment, and then the same maid brought me part of a fowl, some punch and wine, telling me, that as she had found the company came earlier than common, she thought she had better stay till she could offer me a more comfortable supper than what I had ordered.

I asked her if they had often so much company; to which she answered in the affirmative; and added, with an air of pride and satisfaction, she did not believe there was a house in town that had more.

I had observed while I lived at Sir George Markland's, that my Lady and many others piqued themselves on having a great concourse of people at their houses, and that, to acquire the more honour, they would often stretch the truth as to the numbers that had been there the night before; but I was diverted to find this pride descend to a servant, who, by her appearance, must be in the very lowest place in the house; and wondered what advantage she could find in her Lady's drums[1] being more frequent or more crouded than other people's.

Being heartily tired, I went to bed as soon as I had supped; but had not

---

1   Drum: "An assembly of fashionable people at a private house, held in the evening: much in vogue during the latter half of the 18th and beginning of the 19th century; a rout." [OED]

been long asleep before I was startled with a variety of noises: some seemed laughing, others scolding, others at romps. I was terrified with the clamour; the first effect of my fear was jumping out of bed and bolting the door, and then I could attend to it with a little more composure, but not without a thousand apprehensions, which, tho' the house grew pretty quiet about four o'clock in the morning, would not suffer me to get any sleep.

I rose early, but found the family were making themselves amends for the time they had stolen from the night, for nobody came into my room till near ten o'clock, nor had I courage to go out of it, to see if any one was up: The same servant whom I had seen the night before, then made her appearance: I asked her if any disaster had happened, which occasioned so much noise at so late an hour? "Nothing particular," she answered. "Is your company always so loud?" said I. "Not always," replied she, "but sometimes still more so." "Indeed!" cried I, "And pray how often may you have company?" "Oh! every night," answered the girl, "whatever house may be empty, ours is always full."

My apprehensions had encreased during this whole dialogue, and now they were almost risen to their greatest height: But to remove all doubt, I asked her, whether their company consisted mostly of gentlemen or ladies?

The girl laughed at the foolishness of my question, and told me they had few Ladies come there; not but a Gentleman might, if he pleased, bring a Lady, and they would be very genteely accommodated; but they seldom chose it, as all her young Ladies were so handsome, it would not be easy to find any equal to them.

I was now indeed past any doubt: Uncertainty, however anxious, would have been a blessing to this certainty: I thought I should have fainted; and indeed I believe nothing could have recalled my senses, which were just fled, but the screams of the servant, who was so used to clamour, that she did not think any moderate noise could be sufficiently expressive of fear, and set up her pipes with such a violence at seeing me sink, pale and breathless, into a chair that stood by me, that she not only called back my departing spirits, but brought two or three of the young *Ladies*, whose beauty she had been boasting, into my room.

As my colour had not returned with my senses, I still looked more like a corpse than one alive. The girl was asked the occasion of this disorder, but could give little account of it: She told them, the young gentlewoman had been asking her questions but the minute before, and she could not imagine what was the matter. My poor little boy, frighted to see his mamma look so pale, ran to me, and, by his tender and amiable caresses, did more to recover me than all the attention of the young *Ladies*, who held salts to my nose, rubbed my temples, and did all they thought requisite for my relief; but their appearances counteracted their care, by terrifying me more than the other could revive me.

Uncomb'd their locks and squalid their attire,
Unlike the trim of love or gay desire.[1]

The dirty rags in which they were cloathed, shewed their wretchedness.
Their face, which in the evening were to shine with borrowed charms, were
now the emblems of decay and fickleness; swoln excess, riotous intemperance, and foul misrule, were imprinted on each countenance.

I do not believe I could have quite recovered myself while they were in my
sight, but, fortunately for me, they were called to breakfast, from which my
indisposition excused me, and I was indulged with a dish of tea in my own
room.

When I was left alone the distraction of my mind found some vent, by tears
and lamentations. I now felt a degree of distress beyond what I had yet expe-
rienced, or ever feared. How severely did I arraign myself of folly, in having
conceived no suspicion of this wretched woman; and quarrelled with my
heart for having seen her action in no such very strange light, as to suppose
it must arise from any thing but generosity. I thought that, in the same situation, I should have done like her, and therefore was grateful, but not surprized: so far was my candour in thus judging of her from administring any
comfort to me, that I wished my temper more suspicious, tho' rendered so by
defects in my own heart, from which it was now free: indeed, in this case, the
most common prudence might have preserved me; but I was rendered so
senseless by the terrors of my situation, that I was blind to every other danger.

I shall not tire you with endeavouring to describe the agitation of my mind,
which was far beyond all power of description; but shall only say, that the
prison I had so much feared, now appeared to me an eligible asylum; and all
my hopes were, that if I was found refractory to the purposes of the person
who had thus bought me of myself, resentment might tempt her to throw me
into the gaol from whence she had so cruelly relieved me.

After breakfast was over, the woman, who the night before I had beheld
with reverence and gratitude as my noble benefactress, came into my room;
and taking hold of my hand with a fawning affectation of kindness, told me,
she was sorry to find I had been so ill; she supposed it was occasioned by what
I had suffered the day before; but she did not doubt but I should soon recover, as my mind would forget all past disasters in her house, which was a temple dedicated to pleasure; and continued in such intelligible terms, that no
further explanation was necessary.

To sit and hear the profession of such abandoned sentiments, was an additional shock: Criminal as I had been, my detestation to this way of life was as

---

1   From John Dryden, "Palamon and Arcite" in *Fables, Ancient and Modern* (1700). (Dry-
    den has the poem's subject in the singular.)

great as if I had been more consistently virtuous. I informed her, that she was disappointed in her views; but offered, if she would forbear all attempts to induce me to comply, that I would with pleasure submit to the lowest offices in her house, or rather what she esteemed the lowest, and perform the part of her menial servant, till she herself should acknowledge that I had amply paid my debt.

She told me that every word I spoke, more fully proved my folly; for I must be extremely silly indeed, to think she would be contented with my saving her three or four pounds a year, when she did not despair of my gaining her as many hundreds, for the first year at least; and after that, by paint and dress, I might make a very attracting figure amongst the rest of her girls.

All that prayers and entreaties could do, I tried without success; and when that failed, I endeavoured to provoke her to send me to prison; but all to no other purpose, than, as she said, to shew my folly, in supposing she had not taught every passion, as well as every principle, to be subservient to her interest.

All I uttered had no other effect than to make her give orders that I should not be suffered to stir out of the house.

While I opposed her, she set me at defiance, and threatened me with immediate revenge; which she was too well able to execute, having every one at her command, and I no one to defend me. I therefore tried to delay what I could not repel; and by promising to endeavour to get the better of my reluctance, prevailed upon her to allow me time to learn to command my behaviour, which, in my present disposition, might disgust those she chose I should please.

Chapter 9

Who can all sense of others ills escape,
Is but a brute at best, in human shape.
TATE[1]

Under this pretence, I obtained liberty to live entirely in my own chamber for a whole month, hoping still that some fortunate accident might relieve me; but all in vain: At the end of that time, she assured me she would be fooled no longer, and made me dress myself with more than usual care, in a gown and ornaments which she provided for me; and told me, that she would absolutely bring a gentleman to see me that evening, whose generosity she so much extolled, that I had some hopes I might find him generous indeed; not in lavishing money on a bawd, but in relieving the distressed. I found I had

1 From Nahum Tate's translation of Juvenal's Fifteenth Satire. This translation first appeared in *The Satires of Decimus Junius Juvenalis: and of Aulus Persius Flaccus* (London, 1693).

been promised to him, which proved that he paid high; but this was but a poor dependence for my expectations.

This wretched woman kept her word with a diabolical exactness. She introduced the gentleman pretty early in the evening, for expectation had made him come sooner than her visitors usually did: She retired. I was sorry to see how much this man was struck with my appearance; it in great degree damped my hopes, but despair encouraged me to proceed, and I began to attack his compassion in the strongest manner I could, by uttering all the sentiments of my soul. I kneeled at his feet, used tears and prayers to soften him, and did my utmost to excite his generosity.

At first he seemed to think all this was mere hypocrisy, with a design to raise the value of his conquest; but he soon found I was perfectly sincere, and with joy I perceived him affected. This animated me still more, and I pursued my intreaties till he granted them, and told me he would desire no more of me than that I would inform him how, in such a disposition, I could come into that house.

I then related to him the whole affair, suppressing only the manner in which I had lived with Mr. Markland, whom I called my husband: not, I think, out of pride: I was too much humbled to attempt to conceal even my crimes; but I feared, if he knew this circumstance, he would have less regard to my petition; and think my having offended with one man, gave every other a right to expect I should be the same to them.

When I had ended my story, the gentleman told me I might judge of his compassion from the mortification he inflicted on himself; for that, tho' he was much attached to the sex in general, and had always been so, he had never seen a woman he thought half so lovely as myself; that she who had the disposing of me was sufficiently sensible of my charms, as appeared by the price she set upon me; which, however, he was much more willing to lose, than to give up his title to me; but to shew me he could be generous to virtue as well as to vice, he would relinquish both, and at my desire, pretend himself better satisfied with my conduct than he had reason to be; for I had begged he would not betray me to the woman, whom I now beheld with as much horror, as I had once done with gratitude.

That he might be the better credited, he sat with me near two hours after he had made me this promise. I wished he would have secured me from persons less generous than himself, by redeeming me from this horrid place, but durst not hint my desire, for fear of offending him; and he stifled my hopes, by observing to me, how impossible it was for me to escape out of it, for that the money which she had laid down for me, would be but a small part of my debt; she would charge so much for my board, and the cloaths I had then on, that would run it up to a much more considerable sum.

After having represented all this to me, and the impossibility of my prevailing with other men as I had done with him, he endeavoured to persuade me to submit patiently to my lot, and not to grant to one less generous, what I denied to him; promising that I should share his bounty, whereas it commonly was dispensed only to the person who claimed the power of selling us.

He bore my refusal of this proposal as generously as he had done the first, and took his leave of me in the politest manner, and, if I may be allowed to form any judgment from his appearance, with real concern for me.

As soon as the gentleman was gone from the house, the old woman, and some of the young ones who were disengaged, came to me, and carried me down into a small room to supper, where none but ourselves were admitted; not so much to indulge me as a reward for my good behaviour, as because I was thought too valuable while new, to be exposed to common eyes.

My odious companions were all in very good humour, and I was so delighted with, and encouraged by, my success, that I had never before appeared so easy. I flattered myself I should continue as fortunate as I began, and the effect this hope had upon me, gave room for a supposition that I was grown better reconciled to my way of life.

I was not to continue long in doubt, whether my arguments would be always equally prevalent; the next day brought fresh occasion for my rhetoric. The appearance of the man was less encouraging; he wanted the politeness of manner and good-natured countenance, which was remarkable in the other; however, I was not turned from my purpose by my fears of failing in it; on the contrary, I was animated by despair more than before by hope, and by my tears and aversion, extinguished all thoughts of pleasure or of love in his rugged breast; but leaving me with curses, he went to the old woman, and bestowing some oaths on her, made her refund the money she had received from him.

This threw her into a violent rage, and not being able to vent it on him, I must necessarily fall the victim. She brought up with her into my room three of her young women, who, angry that I should by my conduct shew a disapprobation of theirs, were fit to assist her in executing her wrath on me; accordingly they fell on me with the utmost fury, and beat me in the most merciless manner, till one of them hit me such a blow on my temples as struck me senseless to the ground.

As murder was a crime which was not professed in this infamous house, they were alarmed lest they had killed me; and fearing the consequences of their rage, put me to bed, and took all possible care to bring me to myself.

As soon as they had done so, I found my person was one general bruise. I was so sore, I knew not how to lie or move; but my greatest pain was in my eye, near which the last blow was given. It was soon so swelled up, I could not see; and as defacing me did not at all answer the wretches' purpose, they omitted no care to remedy the ill they had done, plaistering me up in the manner they thought most likely to hasten my recovery.

I was in hopes they had put out my eye; shocking as the thought was, it appeared in a desirable light to me, as I might reasonably expect from it a total dismission from that house, where I could be of no value when so disfigured. I had suffered too much by my beauty to be anxious for the preservation of it, and one eye might guide me to a more comfortable livelihood, than I was likely to gain in the house where I then was.

These thoughts made me take off the things they applied to my eye whenever I was alone, if possible, to prevent my cure; but, in spite of my endeavours, the swelling abated, and I found my sight had received no hurt; but the blood settling round it, I had such a black eye, as rendered me too rueful a spectacle to be produced.

This accident obliged me to be concealed for above a month; for it was thought imprudent to shew me till I was in full beauty.

This delay was precious, and I would have endured another beating for the like benefit; but they had suffered too severely already for this exertion of their power, therefore they resolved upon a method less detrimental to my person.

Chapter 10

——————Famine is in thy cheeks,
Need and oppression sharing in thy looks,
Contempt and beggary hang on thy back.
OTWAY[1]

As soon as I was thought to look tolerably well, the infernal woman told me that all my resistance would be in vain; that my ingratitude had quite disgusted her, and she was resolved no longer to shew me any indulgence, but would expose me to the addresses of people too low and brutal to regard my tears, till I was broke of my niceness; and would send my child to the officers of the parish where it belonged, for she should no longer gratify me with its company, when I shewed so little consideration for her.

These menaces were dreadful indeed; and to talk of exposing my little darling to the cruelty of parish officers and nurses was too much to bear. Enraged at such a monster, I replied, "The law would grant me some redress against such inhumanity."

"The law! thou idiot," answered she, "Dost thou take lawyers for knights-errant, who have nothing to do but to deliver distressed damsels? Know, that money only can obtain justice; those who cannot buy, must go without it; the redress of the law is out of the reach of poverty; content yourself, there is no

---

1   From Thomas Otway, *The History and Fall of Caius Marius. A Tragedy.* (London, 1680). The 1680 edition has: "Famine is in thy Cheeks, /Need and Oppression starveth in thy Eyes, /Contempt and Beggary hang on thy Back" (Act 5, p. 61).

law for you. But I shall not give myself the trouble of saying any more to you; I give you till tomorrow to chuse; either determine to conquer your squeamishness, or I send your brat away, and deliver you up to the first man who will disregard all your tears and intreaties. Your will shall make no other difference in the case, than in the degree of your lovers, and your brat's fate."

With these words she left me to consider the alternative. The dear babe understood something of being sent from me, and running to me, hung round my neck, crying he would not go away without me, and begging me not to let that woman take him.

Alas! dear Innocent, I did not mean it: I could much sooner have parted with my life. The wretch had now found the means of subduing my resolution. Delicacy, for by that name, not by the sacred one of virtue, I must call my resistance, after a conduct so criminal as mine: Delicacy, I say, gave way to maternal love: Nor could the latter boast any great triumph; for I had no prospect of gaining any advantage by my further perseverance; on the contrary, I was only likely to be exposed to the greater insults.

The declaration of my resolution was received the next day with great satisfaction; I was flattered and caressed, and my child fondled; but I could not be sensible to kind treatment so obtained.

In this detestable house I had remained about a month after this, when the old woman was taken ill of a violent fever, occasioned by having eat and drank immoderately for some nights successively. This illness put a stop to her trade; and three days carried her into a world, where one cannot think of her without horror.

As soon as she was dead, a relation came to look into her effects, who had been ashamed to own any connexion with her infamy, but at her death was willing to receive the profits arising from her crimes.

By this accident we were all set at liberty; what became of the rest I know not; I was too glad to get clear of them all to make any inquiries; but for my own part, my joy at this release was beyond expression.

The best cloaths which were worn by us were sold; but those of less value were given amongst us; and the notes of hand, and such other obligations as had been used as means of getting us into her power, were cancelled, the purpose of them being too well known to her relation.

I was quite destitute of money, for our pockets were searched every morning, so that what presents any gentleman made us were sure to be taken away; therefore I sold the best gown which had fallen to my share, in order to support me till I had found some means of gaining a subsistence.

Sensible that I should find great difficulty in maintaining myself and child, I took the cheapest lodging I could find, only mending it by cleanliness. I then enquired for plain work;[1] but received every where for answer, that they

---

1 Ordinary needlework, as opposed to specialized embroidery.

could not trust their things to a stranger; they were acquainted with people enough who wanted such employment; they need not give it to me they knew nothing of.

This was a melancholy answer. I now thought I would try to get a place;[1] but when I offered myself, one said "I was too handsome," another, "that I appeared too genteel for such a place as I offered for," (not daring to attempt any high one, as having no hopes to get it) and, "there must be something very bad in my conduct, or I could not be reduced to such low services." Those who were not deterred by my appearance, asked, What recommendation I had? Who would give me a character?[2] In this manner I was repulsed from every door, and found that one who can do no work but what great numbers of others do as well, may be reduced to want employment. I now wished I had learnt of my sister a variety of works, some of which might have afforded me a support; for people are less nice[3] in those they employ, for things they cannot easily get done elsewhere.

I was now reduced to manifest danger of starving. I would have attempted the most laborious work, but no one would try me in what I am afraid I should have acquitted myself but ill, tho' I offered my labour at half price; but even my industry was made an argument against me, "I must be very bad to be reduced to that," and they "supposed I intended to steal the other half of my wages."

In this deplorable condition I determined to apply to my sister. I did not now live in actual sin, and therefore could do it with the more courage. By enquiring at the milaner's where I had seen her, I learnt her abode, and thither I went. Variety of misfortunes had altered me extremely. My sister was in her shop, and rejoiced to see me, hoping, by my venturing to her again, that I had reformed my conduct; but my changed countenance shocked her, and rendered her reception of me more melancholy, but not less kind. Before we had had time to interchange many words, her husband came in, who guessing at me by the description she had given him, very abruptly told me "I was not fit company for his wife," and desired I would not frequent his house; for all the ties of kindred were broken by my infamy.

My spirits were lowered by distress, and I may say by hunger, for I had tasted nothing for above twenty-four hours; the cruel reproach, so ill timed, struck me to the heart: I was not able to make any answer; but to avoid encreasing his anger, which seemed falling on his wife for having received me, I withdrew, almost drowned in tears, and scarcely able to support the weight of my afflicted body.

A good woman passed by me as I was dragging myself along, and sobbing

1   That is, a position as a servant in a household.
2   Assurance of her honesty, trustworthiness, etc.
3   Particular.

as if my heart would break, and being moved at my distress, put her hand in her pocket, and pulling out a shilling, asked me "If that would do me any good?"

It is easy to be imagined that I received it with joy and gratitude; in my distressed condition a less sum would have been a great relief. She seemed happy in the good she had done, and said, "She wished she had more for me." I bless'd her for that she had given me, and we parted.

I stopped in my way to buy some food for myself and child with this timely supply, and was there overtaken by a young woman, who told me she belonged to my sister, who having given her a wink after I went out of the shop, she guessed it was designed as a command to find out where I lived, and therefore had followed me.

I soon satisfied her curiosity, and then enquiring into the temper of my brother-in-law, which alarmed me for my sister's happiness; she told me, "she had never seen him so out of humour before. That it was easy to see he was of a very jealous disposition; but her mistress's conduct was so extremely prudent, that he had never had an opportunity of taking offence; and the entire confidence he had in her, and his sincere affection for her, got the better of a warmth natural to him; so that by the excellence of her behaviour, and the sweetness of her disposition, no married peopled lived more happily together; and she attributed his treatment of me to a sort of jealousy, which made him dislike my having any intercourse with his wife, as he imagined me not so prudent."

I could not from my heart blame him, but said, I hoped my future conduct would plead my excuse; and expressed the fears I really felt, lest my going there should occasion any uneasiness between him and my sister, or make her unhappy by awakening her affection for me.

"Oh! Madam," said the young woman, "it would admit of no awakening; for my mistress is continually talking of you, and weeping over your remembrance, whenever my master is not present; for he does not like to hear her mention you. Some time ago she sent me into the street where you did live, to enquire after you, but the account I received was such as increased her affliction."

"What was told you?" said I.

"I do not know how to answer you," replied she, "but I was informed you was gone to a bad house."

"I was indeed," said I; "but not knowingly: However blameable I have been, there I am sure I deserved compassion; and whoever knows all I have suffered, if they are not strangers to pity, will forgive me my faults, in consideration of the punishments they have brought with them."

The good-natured girl could not forbear joining her tears with mine; and perhaps curiosity would have detained her longer, could she have hoped to have learnt any particulars; but she must see I was not in a condition to talk much, and I was in haste to return to my child, and carry him some food; tho' he stood not in the same need as myself, for I had had a little bread left, which I gave him that morning, and that sufficed for a tolerable meal.

Chapter 11

Oh! That I had my innocence again;
My untouch'd honour! but I wish in vain:
The fleece that has been by the dyer stain'd,
Never again its native whiteness gain'd.
                              WALLER[1]

The same young woman came to my lodging the next day: tho' it was a wretched hole, it pleased her by its cleanness. My poor little boy she admired extremely, but I could not help feeling distressed at having reason to be ashamed of a child, of which so many great families would be vain; but his charms could not wipe off the infamy of his birth; an infamy, which, in justice, belongs only to the parents.

As soon as we were seated, she delivered me a letter from my sister, where-in she acquainted me, that she could no longer find any comfort in plenty, since she might not impart it to me. That as all her stock in trade belonged to her husband, she could not, without being guilty of a criminal injustice, attempt to appropriate to herself any thing out of what she sold; and that as her expences had always, by choice, been very small, it was but little she should be able to assist me with at present, as her husband would be watch-ful; but that she hoped in a month or two he might have me less in his thoughts, and then she should find the means of supplying me more suitably to her own inclinations.

This was mixed with expressions infinitely kind, and very valuable, as com-ing from the sincerest of hearts. She had, I found, never been used to ask him for any money; when she bought any thing, the bill was brought him, and he paid it, and would have done so with pleasure, if it had been a much greater sum. If she had any immediate call, she took it out of the produce of the shop, and, in settling the account, told him what it was for. There was such entire harmony between them, that this became her custom, as the easiest way; but now she regretted it extremely, and yet knew not how to break through it.

I saw her difficulty plainly; it was insurmountable, and I had nothing left me but to intreat her to run no hazards for me, for that nothing could rec-

---

1 ·Edmund Waller, *The Maid's Tragedy Alter'd* (London, 1690), prologue.

ompense me for causing the least uneasiness between her and her husband.

She desired me not to write, lest the letter should fall into his hands, and told me she should venture at nothing more than a verbal message, till she had brought him into a better disposition towards me: so in compliance, my answer was only by word of mouth.

Few questions were requisite to inform my sister's messenger of my great poverty, so she staid not long.

From time to time she visited me, bringing such little relief as my sister could secretly bestow, but what scarcely sufficed to pay for my lodging. However, this was a great consolation to me; for, little as the expence might sound, it was a heavy burden on me, who neither had any thing, nor the means of gaining it; and my landlady's provident spirit made her require to have a week's pay in hand, not chusing to give so short a credit. Nor could I blame the woman; for where they are forced to let their rooms to such indigent persons as I was, if they were not to be rigidly exact, they would never receive their rent.

My sister's situation being now added to the other impediments which prevented me from obtaining any support, I was reduced below hope: Willing and able to work, and yet to starve for want of employment, seemed a hard fate, but touched no heart but my own. In this extremity, the humanity shewn me by a stranger in the street, determined me to try if casual charity would afford me any relief; and in the bitterness of my soul, I set out with my child to ask the charitable benefactions of passengers.[1]

But here my success was small: I found that beggars had a society amongst them; that the town was divided into so many shares, and to every one was appointed their particular district, from whence they drove every interloper, by means too formidable for me to contend with, who feared almost equally their oaths and their more forcible methods. Thus I had no places left me, but such as were so little frequented, they were not thought worth their notice. Like the first planters in a colony, they divided amongst themselves all but the barren lands.

Among the few who passed where I durst attempt to beg, I seldom obtained any thing but reproaches for my idleness, in begging at an age when I was so capable of working. It was to no purpose that I told them I desired nothing so much as work, and intreated them to try me, by giving me any employment. They would answer, that they saw I was newly entered upon that trade, and it would be a shame to encourage me in it, as then I should never leave it off.

Sometimes I should be so fortunate as to obtain a few half-pence from peo-

---

1 People passing by.

ple whose compassion got the better of their reason, and who durst not give me an absolute refusal, for fear I was indeed as near starving as I said I was. But these small and uncertain benefactions would not preserve two persons alive, tho' used in the most sparing manner. Sometimes for two or three days I should not procure a farthing.

One time, when I was thus reduced to the last extremity, myself almost starved, and my child in the same condition, and piercing my heart with his cries; as the last effort, I dressed myself neatly, and went out to try if I should have any better success, as a higher degree of beggar; and left my poor boy with an old woman in the same house, who used to take care of him in my absence, tho' she was too poor to relieve his necessities.

I attacked many of my own sex, who told me they never gave to begging gentlewomen: I then addressed myself to the other, and received a refusal from the first; the second told me if I would go with him to the next tavern, I should be satisfied with his generosity.

I answered him, that he mistook my purpose; the smallest alms would content me, but that I could not leave that street. This occasioned some altercation; each kept to their resolution, till at last he produced five shillings to my view to strengthen his arguments. A sum, then, in my estimation, so considerable, at length prevailed.

I returned home to my famished child, as soon as possible, carrying food with me, that I might receive some reward for money so ill gotten; and I confess my recompence was great, in seeing the dear babe, almost at the gates of death, revive as he eat, and the smiles of joy by degrees take place of the anguish which the pains of hunger had imprinted on his lovely face.

I preferred the trade of begging so much to the making a traffic of my person, that I endeavoured by pursuing it to make this little fund hold out; but without success. I was at last attacked by the beadles,[1] who receiving no gratuities from me, declared they would execute the rigors of their office if they saw me there again. Thus the little liberty I before had in this occupation was much restrained, and my gains sunk to almost nothing.

The only consolation I had, was the hope that my sister would be suffered to countenance me so far, that by her recommendation I might obtain some employ; but every time her messenger came, disappointment accompanied her. But still I hoped on, and was often led by it to the utmost extremity of famine, till, no longer able to support it, I resolved to try the means which had once succeeded, when I did not aim at it. How often, shocked at the odiousness of my purpose, have I turned back, determined to suffer myself to die, rather than preserve my life in such a manner! But when I returned home, and saw

---

1   Beadle: "A messenger of justice, a warrant officer; an under-bailiff." [OED]

the distress of my poor child, every other evil appeared light in comparison of his sufferings; and I again fled from the anguish I felt at the sight of him.

I seldom had far to go before I met with some gentleman, who, tho' hardhearted to my distress, would be indulgent to his own vice. I often thought the cleanly simplicity of my dress, (for I had no ornaments) pleased more than the tawdry decorations of the women who generally follow that course; for while a man courts our vice, his reason hates our impudence.

I was sensible that, by entering into a society of prostitutes, I might gain a settled subsistence; but I could not think of engaging in a way of life I detested: I still hoped some means would at last relieve my necessities, and that I should not always be reduced to a prostitution, to which I could not bring myself to consent, till the severe pains of hunger, and the still sharper pangs I endured from those my heart's darling felt, got the better of the little delicacy I still had remaining. There could not be a more sparing manager than I was of what I gained, as, while it lasted, I was freed from a course most odious to me.

Chapter 12

Want is a bitter and hateful good,
Because its virtues are not understood
Prudence at once, and fortitude it gives;
And, if in patience taken, mends our lives,
For ev'n that indigence that brings me low,
Make me myself, and Him above, to know:
A good which none would challenge, few would choose,
A fair possession, which mankind refuse.
                    DRYDEN[1]

In this manner I lived for near three months; the sobriety of my behaviour at home giving no suspicion to the people where I lodged, who were not used to be over-curious in prying into the lives of their lodgers, which perhaps would seldom bear a strict scrutiny. I concealed it equally from my sister; sensible, that if she knew it, the desire of bringing me out of such infamy and suffering would drive her to extremities, to the hazard of all her conjugal hap-

---

1 John Dryden, from "The Wife of Bath's Tale" in *Fables Ancient and Modern* (London, 1700). A few lines are left out in the epigraph. The full text reads:

Want is a bitter, and a hateful Good,/Because its Virtues are not understood:/Yet many Things impossible to Thought/Have been by Need to full Perfection brought:/The daring of the Soul proceeds from thence,/Sharpness of Wit, and active Diligence:/Prudence at once, and Fortitude it gives,/And if in patience taken mends our Lives;/For ev'n that Indigence that brings me low/Makes me my self; and Him above to know./A Good which none would challenge, few would choose,/A fair Possession, which Mankind refuse.

piness. The vexation I had given, and still gave her, was one of my strongest afflictions; therefore I could not, for any consideration, make her a greater sufferer.

One day, when I was reduced so low that I had not sufficient to purchase a supper for myself and child, my landlady came up to my room, and invited us to drink tea and sup with her, it being her birth-day. Never did a royal birth-day give such joy to the vainest lady. I doubt whether the birth of a child ever was more welcome to the person most anxious for an heir, than this good woman's anniversary rejoicing was to me. We readily obeyed her invitation; and I was too well pleased with the entertainment, to criticize the conversation of my company.

A little before supper, a man entered, who said he was just come from the new *Hospital*, so he called it, and that every thing was now completely finished; but he fancied it would be a long time before it was full.

"Do not talk of it," said my virtuous landlady: "I have no patience with the gentlemen who give encouragement to such wicked wretches: Starving is too good for them."

I, who knew so well what starving was, thought this was almost too cruel a sentence for any crime; and begged to know who the wretches were she spoke of.

I was answered with all imaginable plainness; and felt, that coarse as the name was, I had too good a right to it; and therefore was enough concerned in the conversation to enquire what gave my landlady's virtue such offence.

I then first heard of this blessed charity;[1] I made all necessary enquiries about it; and could scarcely contain the joy I felt, at the smallest hopes of being one of the objects that should be relieved by it.

Sorrow had robbed me of many nights rest; joy had a good title to a tribute I had so seldom paid it: I could not shut my eyes that night; and the next morning, as soon as I thought the Secretary's Office would be open, I went thither; not without fears that my child would be a bar to my admission; for I had heard of no provision being made for children.

My good fortune was without allay: I was not only accepted, but was told I might come the day but one after, and my child should be taken care of.

To form an adequate notion of the rapture I felt, a person should have been reduced to the same excess of misery. My soul overflowed with gratitude, and my countenance shone with joy. It is true, I found I must part with my child; but then I could have no doubt but he would be far better taken care of than I could ever expect he should be while he depended on me. For his sake, I could part with him; and should find a constant consolation for the loss of him, in thinking how well he would be educated and provided for.

---

1   The Magdalen charity, an institution set up to help prostitutes reform. This project is discussed in the introduction to this volume.

The satisfaction of my heart was so visible, that at my return home, my land-lady enquired what had made so great an alteration in me, for she had before often taken notice of my melancholy; and used to tell me, she wondered what could make one so young, and so pretty, look so dismal. I once told her very frankly, that being so young and so pretty were the very things that made me so: But this I found was a riddle to her, which I did not chuse to explain; nor did I now think proper to acquaint her with the real reason for the alteration she observed; but informed her, that within two days I was to go to a good place, which I had obtained that morning.

I wrote a letter to my sister, acquainting her where I had applied for an asy-lum, and of the success my application had met with; and added, that I hoped a course of regularity would so far wash out the infamy from my reputation, that her husband might in time suffer me to see her; which would always be neces-sary to my happiness, but could never contribute to it, till she was at liberty to act in that respect according to the dictates of her own heart, without the least chance of giving offence to the man on whom her happiness then depended.

This letter I gave to my landlady, the morning I left the house; desiring her to deliver it to the young woman who used to come from my sister, the next time she called there. And then I delivered my child where I was ordered; which I confess cost me many tears, for the tenderness of the mother got the better of true maternal love, which should have made me rejoice in this separation. That severe pang being over, I came hither, and was received with a degree of human-ity beyond my expectation. I expected relief; but I found from this good matron tenderness and pity, of which I was then the only object; but a very short time increased the society, and rendered her humanity more extensive.

Thus you see, in compliance with your desire, I have exposed all my crimes and follies; and given a strong proof how much evil one bad action draws along with it. Nor was I sensible of my wickedness when I applied to be received into this place: I sought it as a refuge from distress and misery; my heart grieved, but did not repent till I came hither, where I was shewn my sins in their black colours; and, awakened to repentance by a sense of guilt, was taught to apply for pardon to Him who came on earth to save sinners.

The society returned their thanks to Emily, for indulging their curiosity. She told them they could in no way so agreeably acknowledge it, as by following her example: which being readily promised, it was agreed that they should proceed in the order in which they arrived at the House. A good expedient to avoid ceremony. How often have we seen some such method necessary to adjust the ceremonial between people who have no title to place or prece-dency, nor can pretend to claim any so good as a priority of reformation![1]

---

1 The volume continues as more penitents tell their stories.

An Account of the Death of F.S. Who Died April 1763, Aged Twenty-Six Years. In a LETTER to a FRIEND.

MARTIN MADAN

Martin Madan, who tells the story below of the penitent prostitute Fanny Sidney, served as the chaplain for the Lock Hospital, which provided care to unfortunates suffering from venereal disease. He would have met many women like Sidney at the Hospital, although the heroine of this narrative might have been fabricated. Madan himself became a high-profile figure in debates over prostitution in the eighteenth century, initially for his position at the Lock Hospital and his popular sermons, but later for the publication of his Thelyphthora *(1780), a treatise that ultimately stretched to three volumes and proposed legalizing polygamy as the solution to Britain's overwhelming prostitution problem. In brief, Madan argued that according to the Bible every act of sexual intercourse constitutes a marriage and that men thus become morally obligated to support for life any women with whom they have sex. Madan sees these relationships as, theologically, marriages. If society followed God's law in this respect, Madan insisted, there would be no more prostitution. Madan's treatise ignited a firestorm of publications, some satiric but others enumerating in great detail Madan's presumed theological errors. The whole incident led to his resignation from his position at the Lock Hospital. His earlier story of Fanny Sidney's suffering and repentance received more positive attention, appearing in many editions on both sides of the Atlantic.* An Account of the Death of F.S. *is perhaps more typical of the sentimental prostitute narrative than* The Histories *in its emphasis on Sidney's moral transgression, but as in* The Histories *the author places prostitution in the context of economic vulnerability.*

An Account of the Death of F.S. Who Died April 1763, aged Twenty-Six Years. In a LETTER to a FRIEND.

Dear Sir,

As you wanted to see an Account of the Person I mentioned to you when we last met set down in Writing, I comply most readily with your Desire, and send it you as follows.

This young Woman was the Daughter of a Gentleman in the Army, had a genteel and liberal Education, but was reduced by various Distresses to great Poverty and Want. One who had known her in her more prosperous Days, took Advantage of her indigent Circumstances, and by many fair Promises, and Acts of pretended Kindness, drew her into a criminal Intimacy with him; she was with Child by him, and for some Time after she was delivered he contributed something toward the Maintenance of the Child; but growing tired of her, he left both Child and Mother without doing any thing farther for them.

F.S. had a Mother with whom she lived, but who could by no means support the Expence now thrown upon her. Various were the Ways by which *F.S.* was endeavouring to maintain herself; having a genteel Person, a good Voice, and a lively Genius, she went upon the Stage at the little Theatre in the *Hay-Market*; after this she strolled with Players about the Country, but meeting with many disagreeable Things in this way of Life she quitted it, and went to work at her Needle: this Expedient too failed her: after which she went upon the Town and turned Prostitute; while she was in the midst of all her Wickedness, she had strong Remonstrances from her Conscience, insomuch as to occasion many Tears to flow from her Eyes; Conviction of Sin pursued her wherever she went: she would walk out into St. *James*'s Park, set herself down upon a Bench, and there weep for a considerable Time together; and when she has had Men come to her Lodgings she has made herself drunk to get rid of the Terrors and Anguish of her Mind; but this would not do; this Sin added to the rest still distressed her more, till she was absolutely driven from her lodgings, resolving to take shelter in the *Magdalen House*; she continued there about three Months, when something happened which occasioned her leaving it. Going from thence she looked back upon her past Life with the utmost Abhorrence, and was resolved rather to perish with Want than to return to it again. She therefore sold the few Things she had, leaving herself but bare Necessaries, and determined to go into some part of the World where she was not known. She went into *Kent*; and it being Hay-time, she hired herself to a Farmer near *Canterbury*, who employed her amongst his Haymakers for Ten-pence a Day. Here she often reflected with Pain and Bitterness of Spirit on her past Life, yet thanking and praising GOD, who had convinced her of the Error of her Way, and by his Providence and Grace had delivered her from it.

She comforted herself that though she fared but meanly and laboured hard, yet she was eating the Bread of honest Industry. When the Hay-harvest was over, she was dismissed [from] the Farmer's Service, and proceeding to *Canterbury*, she got a Place in a Tradesman's House. Here she lived till by excessive hard Work, being of delicate and tender Frame, she caught a violent Cold, which proved the Beginning of her last Illness; for it ended in a Consumption, which in about four Months brought her to the Grave.

When dismissed from her Service she soon consumed the little she had saved in the Necessaries of Life, and was then reduced to Beggary. One Day being at the Cathedral Prayers (which she constantly attended) she was observed to weep very bitterly by one of the Clerymen that attended there; after Service was over he called her to him, and said, "Young Woman, what or who are you?—You seem very sorrowful." Said she, "Sir, I am a poor Girl heavy laden with my Sins, and I desire to lay them at the REDEEMER's Feet"—"You seem very poor," said he. "Indeed, Sir," saith she, "GOD knoweth I am poor in Body and in Soul." He gave her Money, and bid her come to his House every Day for Victuals, this she did for some time, till finding her Disorder increase upon her, she resolved to return to *London*, that she might see her Mother once more before she died. Accordingly she set out, and under every Circumstance of Poverty, Pain, and Sickness, reached *London*, where, by the Assistance of a former Acquaintance of hers, she procured a wretched Lodging at Sixpence a Week; here she lay about a Week destitute of every Help proper for her Case; and thinking herself near her Dissolution she sent for her Mother, who came to her and found her in the Condition above described: The utmost Pity and Compassion seized on the Mother's Heart, which made her instantly forget some Differences which had arisen between them; a Chair[1] being brought she was carried home to her Mother's House, and laid upon a Bed from which she never rose more.

The Interval between her coming to her Mother's House and her Death, was about a Month, during which Time, at her and her Mother's Request, I visited her. I had known her in the former Part of her Life before all her Distresses, and not having seen her for many Years was, as you may easily imagine, under much Concern to find her in so different a Situation from what I had remembered her in former Times; but my Concern was soon abated, and my utmost Wonder excited, by the Testimony she bore to the Power and Love of GOD our Saviour. She acquainted me with several Circumstances of her past Life before recited; adding withal, "Oh, Sir, I abhor myself—I abhor my polluted Body, and my more polluted Soul.—I am the filthiest Wretch upon this Earth—but there is Mercy—that holy and immaculate JESUS knows my

---

1   A "chair" or "sedan chair" was a covered chair supported by poles and carried by two servants.

Sorrows, and sees my deep Misery." Said I, "Do you believe him able to save you?" "Yes," she said, "I believe one Drop of his Blood can quench a thousand flaming Worlds. "You believe he is able, but do you believe he is willing?" "Willing" said she, "he had no Errand upon Earth but to shew his Willingness to seek and save that which was lost; my Faith in Him is like a strong Cable fixed to an immoveable Rock. If the Lord pleases to make me an Example, and therefore continues me here in the violent Pains I feel, ever so long, I am willing, I am ready to suffer it all; but should he please to release me, Death hath lost its Sting, and now Death shall be my Life."

I came again to see her the next Day. I asked her how she did; she said, "My Body is weaker, but my Faith is stronger—I am in Pain all over, my Head, Ears, and Bowels are racked, but had I Strength I could dance—my Heart dances within me." Turning to her Mother she said, "Madam, look on me, I am dying, but see how I am comforted; let me have no Tears I beg: look on me be sure when I die, when you see the last Breath go from me, clap your Hands, and say, GOD bless her, she is gone to Glory." Putting her Hands and Arms out of Bed, which were now reduced to Skin and Bone, she looked upon them with great Earnestness, and at the same time Transport in her Countenance, and said, "This is a delightful Sight, no Beauty can compare with this Anatomy: these old Clothes of mine are worn out, but I shall soon be clothed afresh." One standing by repeated *Job* xix. 26. "Yes," said she, "Worms shall destroy this Body, but no Worm can touch my Soul." One of her old Companions standing by, who hearing she was ill came to visit her, she thus admonished her; "Look on me, I am a young Woman, and am dying; so are you, tho' you think not of it: let me entreat you to avoid the pernicious Ways we have walked in, and may the Goodness of GOD to me prevail on you to turn to Him, and turn no more to Folly." "O," she said, "that all my Sins were written, that all the World might see the Blackness of my Crimes, and detest them—O that the Mercies of CHRIST to my soul were written also, and that that might turn their Hearts—How tenderly has he dealt with me a poor sinful worm!"—One observed she had deep Obligations to Him: "O yes," said she, "I am obliged to Him for sparing me in my Sins, I am obliged to Him for my Distresses, for my Pain, for this Sick-bed, this delightful Sick-bed, no Coach and Six so delightful, I would not change it for all the World; but how above all am I obliged to the blessed LORD, for calling me by his Grace, and delivering my Soul! O my poor weak Body, was my Body as strong as my Faith I should be another *Samson*." Her great Thankfulness to all that came to visit her was also an Indication of her unfeigned Humility, she not only thanking them for their Kindness, but noticing at the same Time how unworthy she was of any Favour at all.

Being a good deal spent with speaking, her Voice failed her, so that she could not be heard at any Distance from the Bed; but I sat close by it, and could hear her in broken Accents say, "O what comfort—what Pleasure in dying—O holy immaculate Lamb of GOD, how is it that thou canst look upon such a sinful Wretch as I am?"

Another Time she said, "Mother, do not be a Coward, do not weep for my Happiness." "How can I give you up?" said her Mother, "my Burden is great." "Do like me," said the dying Penitent, "cast your Burden upon CHRIST, and he will bear it for you."

She said something of Unkindness she had met with in the World, but added, "GOD bless them, I freely forgive them all: I was hungry and they gave me no Meat, thirsty and they gave me no Drink; but the blessed JESUS will not let the poorest meanest Lamb in his Flock want any thing that can do them good." She then broke into singing,

The Lord my pasture shall prepare,
And feed me with a Shepherd's Care;
His Presence shall my Wants supply,
And guard me with a watchful Eye:
My noon-day Walks he shall attend,
And all my midnight hours defend.

And then,

Tho' in the Paths of Death I tread,
With gloomy Horrors overspread,
My stedfast Heart shall fear no Ill,
For thou, O Lord, art with me still:
Thy friendly Crook shall give me Aid,
And guide me thro' the dreadful Shade.[1]

"And so it shall," added she, with an Earnestness and Transport not to be described.—"O that all may avoid my Sins, and follow my strong Faith when they come to die."

"Why," said I, "you turn Preacher, you are preaching JESUS CHRIST to us all." "Preach!" said she, "O that I could preach to all the World, and tell then how gracious the Lord is—preach JESUS CHRIST, what else can I preach? — what else can any one preach who knows him? —JESUS, JESUS, O that Name! that sweet Name is life to my soul: I trust that Name will dwell upon my unworthy Tongue as long as it can move within my Lips." She then again broke forth into singing, and sang,

---

1   From the hymn, "The Lord my Pasture shall prepare," written by Joseph Addison, 1712.

Praise GOD from whom all blessings flow;
Praise Him all Creature here below;
Praise Him above, ye heavenly Host;
Praise FATHER, SON, *and* HOLY GHOST.[1]

Thus did this young Creature lie on her Sick-bed; praising and blessing GOD, and filling all that came to see her with Wonder at the Triumphs of her Faith over the Enemies of her Soul.

Another time I came to see her and she had had a great Conflict with the Enemy, who seemed to have thrust fore at her that she might fall, but she was more than Conqueror. She said to me, "O, Sir, it seemed to me as tho' a Legion of Devils have been ready to seize me, but Glory be to GOD they cannot touch me; no, no, that Cross held up in that right Hand has put them all to Flight, my Sins have been represented to me as black as a Sackcloth of Hair, but the Blood of CHRIST hath washed me whiter than Snow."

From this Time her bodily Strength being almost exhausted, she lay without being able to speak as she had done, but her Countenance spake with most forcible Eloquence the Transports of her Soul; and when the happy Moment of her Dismission came, her Mother was near her, and observing her Lips move, and putting her Ear near to her Mouth, heard her whisper, "Holy, holy, holy Lord GOD of Sabbaoth, into thy hands I commend my Spirit!" She then fetch'd a short Sigh or two, and died without the least Sign of Pain.

I leave this plain Narrative in your hands; you will make, I doubt not, such Observations as are suitable to the Nature of so interesting and delightful a Subject. I am

Yours, &c.

M.M.

---

1 From the hymn, "Awake, My Soul, and with the Sun," by Thomas Ken, 1674.

CHAPTER FIVE

An Authentic Narrative of the Most Remarkable Adventures, and Curious Intrigues, Exhibited in the Life of Miss Fanny Davies, the Celebrated Modern Amazon

ANONYMOUS

The Authentic Narrative of the Most Remarkable Adventures, and Curious Intrigues, Exhibited in the Life of Miss Fanny Davies, the Celebrated Modern Amazon *demonstrates that the sentimental view of prostitution did not entirely displace the libertine or picaresque vision. Fanny Davies's wickedly courageous exploits and varied adventures are reminiscent of Sally Salisbury's career, but unlike the other prostitute-heroines in this volume (although not unlike some historical prostitutes), Davies combined sex work with theft and other illegal activities. Throughout the century, reformers warned against such women, characterizing brothels as academies of crime. George Lillo's influential and popular play* The London Merchant *(1731) features a prostitute who tempts an apprentice first to theft and then to murder in order to fill her own coffers. Fanny Davies, however, is no Millwood: her Amazonian gender performances distinguish her from such seductresses, from fashion plates like Kitty Fisher, and from virtuous sufferers like Fanny Sidney and Emily Markland. In* An Authentic Narrative, *prostitution becomes part of a general rejection of the dominant ideologies of both gender and property. The author, possibly one "Mr. Thompson" (whose name appears on a shorter version of these adventures), explicitly presents the heroine as a lesson in female virtue by negation. Davies's remarkable self-assurance, independence, and resourcefulness, however, cannot help but elicit at least grudging admiration as well.*

An Authentic Narrative of the Most Remarkable Adventures, and Curious Intrigues, Exhibited in the Life of Miss Fanny Davies, the Celebrated Modern Amazon

Chapter I

Introduction.—Fanny's birth.—Breeding.—She is sent to Bridewell.—Kept by Justice R—l—His Worship's covetousness.—Fanny withdraws from his miserable mansion.— Goes to Ranelagh with her mother.—A young noble Lord beholds her charms, solicits her company at his country seat, and requests his steward to lay a plan to obtain his ardent wishes.

Both the natural and the moral world, are happily contrasted, not only designed to bestow the greater variety, but likewise the purer pleasure. The beauties of spring seem never so delightful, as when compared to the blighting blasts of winter. Were summer or autumn perpetual, as feigned of the golden age, the glory of the one, and the ripeness of the other, would be less esteemed.

However hard it is to trace the origin of evil, it is evident that it was introduced to display the greatest good. Without vice, virtue would be a sacred something, but ill understood, and little revered—by mortals.

On a review of the historian's page, we presently discover a blazon of blemishes, as well as beauties, in the characters recorded. The poet's pen, and the painter's pencil, have also most aptly been employed in delineating the striking contrasts, agreeable to nature and observation. They dwell upon the frightful features of vice, to give a lustre to the comely countenance of virtue; they portray the path that leads down to destruction, that the traveller may recede from his pursuit, and point to the precipice, that he may beware in time.

At present we attempt to draw a picture of the human heart, in its depraved state, and display vice in its utmost deformity. The character of our piece is a young woman—and who is so capable of evil, as one of the softer sex, when completely vitiated. It is said that the sweetest wine makes the sourest vinegar. A virtuous woman is certainly the glory of the creation, the best boon bestowed by Heaven on man; a source of hope to her humble suitor, and a crown of happiness to her husband; but when a fair one becomes vicious, and gives a loose to the violence of her passions, she is but too apt to imitate with success, that malignant, infernal fiend, who, by his wiley ways, seduced our general mother to touch the forbidden fruit—

—Whose mortal taste,
Brought death into the world, and all our woe.[1]

---

1 John Milton, *Paradise Lost* (1667), Book 1, lines 2-3.

Frances Davies, the celebrated heroine of our history, was born in South-wark, a borough not the best regulated, though the biggest in Britain. Her father died when she was young, and her mother, who had once been in an eligible line of life, was obligated to take the tour of America soon after.[1] Fanny would have been left to the wide world when six years old, had not a distant relation taken her up, and adopting her into the family, gave her a tolerable education, and put her apprentice to a black milliner, in the same borough.

Fanny, in the earliest stages of life, was initiated into the vulgar mysteries, by constantly attending the pawn-broker's office, and the gin-shop. In this way she acquired much art and cunning, and was even at ten years of age, able to outwit both Mr. *Cent per Cent* and the *Balderdasher*, at the instance of her employer.[2] Let parents in the lower walks of life, from this be duly admonished, and never suffer their children to learn that of which they themselves are ashamed; for in so doing, they not only shew a bad example, but oblige them to run before them in the road to ruin.

So early in life did our heroine assimilate herself to the manners of the young wantons, with which the Borough abounds, and with them frequently paraded the streets at night, and grew acquainted with the little boys who ply at the corners of streets, and lodge in the dirty alleys of infamy. This part, however, she acted with so much address, that she was not even suspected for some time; but on the contrary, always appeared with a peculiar modesty and reserve, which were much favoured by the cast of her countenance, and her simple, but neat attire.

But one evening she was found by Baileys, the street officer, in company with several abandoned boys, who being well-known pickpockets, were secured, and, with Fanny, conducted to the New Bridewell, in St. George's Fields. In this sad situation, she was under the disagreeable necessity of sending for her new mistress, the milliner, who rescued her from captivity, and discovered the general complexion of her character.

She informed her mistress, but in a measure, the cause of her misfortune, and assured her, that when she was first carried before a certain magistrate, she beheld a celebrated vulgar preacher, esteemed a holy man by almost every body, actually playing at cards with his worship.—This atheist deacon, for he never was in priest's orders, has since disgraced his calling; so that the mask having been forced from the face of this hypocrite, we are saved the trouble of removing it.

On her return from prison, she was again taken before the above justice;

---

1   Fanny's mother, in other words, was punished with transportation. Possibly she turned
    to crime after becoming impoverished through the death of Fanny's father.
2   "Cent per cent" means charging interest equal to the principal. Thus Fanny could out-
    wit unscrupulous bargainers and tricksters.

her mistress attending on the occasion, received a most ardent rebuke from the curate, who had again been dipping into the history of the four kings, and met the menaces of his worship; to be executed in case she did not take more care of her apprentice. These threats and admonitions, came but with an ill grace from those gentlemen.

Fanny, before she was fourteen, was a very forward girl in stature, strength, and beauty, and began to attract the notice of young fellows bigger than boys. She still retained a modest deportment. To have looked on her fair face, rosy cheeks, coral lips, black eyes, ivory neck, slender waist, delicate arms, and beautiful hair, which hung down in luxurient tresses, yet decorated with decency, one would not have taken her for any thing less than a master-piece of nature; or a being not much lower than an angel. Her voice was sweet and melodious, but her words were few, and cautiously uttered in company. In a word, Fanny was the fairest of her sex in Southwark; but all was false and hollow. Thus situated, and endowed with every charm that could allure the beholder, was our fair heroine, when her mother returned from the Western world, after having suffered a long exile from her native land, to satisfy the sentence of the merciless stern law. The old gentlewoman, not readily finding honest employment, and but little inclined to live frugally, entered into partnership with a notorious thief-taker,[1] and lived with him as his wife.

By this time the fame of Fanny had reached the ears of a certain libidinous old gentleman, and a justice of the peace, most famous for parsimony. Overtures were made to the mother, through the medium of the runner. An agreement was made. Fanny eloped from her mistress, and lived with that son of *Gripus*,[2] of whom the world has recently heard much. Although his worship was a person worth near £100,000 yet he almost starved himself and the fair one. He fared but little better than the poorest peasant in the country; he denied himself the common necessaries of subsistence. His domestic animals died with hunger, and even the rats were obliged to run from under his inhospitable roof.

During a very hard winter, however, his worship's table was considerably enlarged; but the provision with which it was chiefly replenished, was fraudulently taken from the parish poor. This hopeful magistrate pretended to commiserate the distress of Fanny's mother. He sent for her to his house, and informed her that bread, coals, potatoes, and fish, were to be distributed to little house-keepers, or any person who could obtain tickets for that purpose, from any respectable character.[3] He then proposed to give her such an order

---

1 Someone who turned in thieves for the reward money; a career made famous in the character of Mr. Peachum in John Gay's play *The Beggar's Opera* (1728).
2 That is, a miser.
3 These tickets seem to serve as vouchers for the "character" or reputation of the person in need of charity. The scam in this case seems to be that the magistrate qualifies Fanny's mother for such tickets, and the mother in turn brings some of the acquired food back to the magistrate.

from time to time, providing she would promise to bring the several articles above specified to him, in order that he himself, and her fair amiable daughter, might have a moiety of the donation. The old gentlewoman readily acquiesced in his desire, and so not only fared well herself, but prolonged the stay of Fanny with a fellow who had not tasted a good meal for many days, except at an election, a parish feast, or a quarter sessions.

The severe weather was soon gone, and an unaccountable parsimony again prevailing, our heroine withdrew from the miserable caitive,[1] without receiving his worship's bounty. The mother tried to recover damages, but *Gripus*, though the most impotent wretch in the commission for the county, proved too strong an adversary on the occasion, for law or justice.

Fanny, now happily, as she thought, relieved from such confinement, began to give a greater scope to her love of pleasure, by visiting with her mother, the several places of public entertainment.

At Ranelagh[2] the following summer, a young nobleman, of a large estate, beheld her charms with the most ardent emotion. His lordship soon introduced himself into her dear company, treated her, led her round the circle, walked with her about the gardens, and proposed to take her home to his country seat.

Fanny's modesty on the occasion, was remarkable, and even amazing. She talked steadfastly of *honourable terms*, and solemnly protested that his lordship, with all the arts peculiar to his sex, and within the line of his elevated station, should never prevail upon her constant mind; nor, in the most distant degree, induce her to swerve from the rigid rules of virtue.

His lordship, much chagrined in his mind, endeavoured to maintain his civil deportment, and resolved to persevere in pursuing a conquest, which the more would redound to his satisfaction, by its difficulty of being obtained. He opened his mind to his young steward, who attended him, and who promised his utmost assistance.

Accordingly this pimping parasite watched the motion of Fanny, as she withdrew from the rotunda with her mother, and would have followed them all the way to Southwark, had not my lord's coachman stopped him short at Chelsea, and informed him that he was well acquainted with the old lady, and her fair daughter.

This fellow, named John Mathews, had been a prisoner in the King's Bench, for smuggling. On his emancipation, he resided in Mint-street, and became the president of a club, composed of characters the most heterogeneous that can be imagined. He was an odd character, but his master durst not part with him, for fear of certain discoveries. He often withdrew from his

---

1   Captor.
2   Ranelagh was a popular and fashionable pleasure garden.

occupation, and was never completely joyous, but when mingling with the bawds of the Borough, or at the club which was held monthly, at the sign of the *Justice*, a notified low pot-house[1] in the above street.—All this he told the steward, and added, that Fanny was a member of the society, in which he had the honour to be chairman; and that he had so great an ascendancy over her mother, that he could force her to grant him any favour whatever.

Chapter II

The club of Mint-street described.—Lord——, and his steward disguised, carry away Fanny to a hotel in Covent Garden, and next to the country.—Fanny dresses in men's apparel, and rides out a hunting with her lord.—She hears that her lover is under sentence of death—procures him his pardon.—A serious reflection.

The pandar communicated his intelligence to the youthful lord, whose bosom burned with the keenest desire to obtain the fair Fanny to his arms.— It was resolved that his lordship should attend the next club in disguise, the better to effect his design. The day was at no great distance, yet his lordship thought it an age.

Meanwhile Fanny's first lover, a boy in the Borough, whom she first met in Bridewell, having left off his filching, and taken to the predatory line, was committed to the New Gaol.[2] Of this my lord was informed by Mathews, the coachman, which somewhat assuaged his lordship's deep distress, as he had now little to dread from so *formidable* a rival. Our heroine, however, frequently paid the young fellow a visit in prison, to sooth him amidst his misery. We forbear to mention the name of this unfortunate fellow, as his father lives in reputation, and is deservedly deemed an honest man. Through the kindness of Fanny, and other friends, he lived well in prison; indeed but few of those sons of injustice, who have been such for a long season, are suffered to subsist merely upon the pitiable allowance of one penny-worth of bread in twenty-four hours, as those are obliged to do, who, perhaps, for some little offence, for the first time, have been entered into the volume[3] of a trading justice of the peace, and consigned to the care of a callous keeper.[4]

The club night came.—The president, at the fiat of his noble master, prepared an uncommon entertainment for the company. Hams, buttocks of beef, fowls, and plenty of wine, formed the plentiful repast.—Exactly at eight o'clock the president mounted, and the various members were seated in order.

Homer, in his *Iliad*, has presented a very copious catalogue of the Grecian ships. Virgil has imitated the ancient bard, by enumerating his heroes. Milton

---

1   A notorious tavern.
2   Jail.
3   Account books.
4   That is, the keeper of a prison.

has followed their examples, by introducing the infernal daemons. But it is not our design in this genuine narrative, to give way to levity, else the ludicrous groupe, presented in this motley monthly meeting, would easily supply materials for the purpose.

Suffice it to say, the number was forty-five, besides strangers, gathered from the infamous dark lanes and alleys of Southwark, St. Giles's, Saltpetre Bank, Petticoat Lane, with the refuse of the markets. In this collection appeared swindlers, pimps, pick-pockets, bullies, housebreakers, bawds, whores, and every other species of foes to order, and friends of riot, which the prolific Borough, and the other places, could produce.

Supper was set on the table. The chairman said a short grace. The eager company fell on with quick dispatch, and with ravenous appetites devoured all the viands, before the arrival of the young lord and his trusty steward, who were clad in the rustic garbs of country swains.

The president having given previous notice of the coming of two strangers, they were received with a tumult of applause. The music immediately struck up, the table was withdrawn, and the dancing commenced.

The chairman, whose word was law, and whose decree was ever revered, pointed fair Fanny to the young lord, as a proper partner. She considered him as a plebeian son of the road, and readily gave him her hand. They danced amid the pleased multitude, and then withdrew to a room adjacent. There his lordship well improved his time, and gained Fanny's consent to take a coach. The steward followed, and they set off from the Borough, making the best of their way to a famed hotel in Covent Garden, where my lord and the fair one, spent the rest of the evening in mirth and wantonness.

The next morning his lordship arose before Fanny, retired from the chamber, and returned in a rich dress. She quickly recognized his person, and feigned an air of modesty, which she could but ill support. His lordship pressed her to attend him to his country mansion, and by the address of the steward, who now appeared in a genteel habit, she consented.—Mathews also appeared, mounted the box, and drove them down to the country above an hundred miles.

There a pleasant park presented itself to our fair one. His lordship led her to the myrtle grove, and assured her that she was mistress of the place, and all the delightful landscape.

So said he, and forbore not glance, or toy,
Of amorous intent; well understood
Of *Eve*, whose eye darted contagious fire.
Her hand he seiz'd; and to a shady bank,
Thick over head with verdant roof imbowr'd,
He led her nothing loth: flowers were the couch,
Pansies, and violets, and asphodel,

And hyacinth, earth's freshest softest lap.
There they their fill of love, and love's disport
Took largely; of their mutual guilt the seal,
The solice of their sin: till dewy sleep
Oppress'd them, weary'd with their am'rous play.

MILTON[1]

Fanny resided with his lordship all the summer, and frequently made little excursions into the neighbouring countries. Indeed, my lord was under a kind of necessity to look round about him for company, suitable to his new character, for none of the nobility and gentry, as least the female part of them, would go under his roof. The character of our heroine was soon blazoned abroad, and she could not even ride out on a party of pleasure, without meeting the derision and contempt of even the lowest ladies of those parts.

It was this general scorn, that induced Fanny to change her dress, and make her appearance into a masculine attire. She wore buckskin breeches, with all the habit suitable to a foxhunter; and learning to ride a spirited mare, could, without dread or hesitation, leap over a gate or a hedge.

During this period, she received advice from the metropolis, that her predatory lover was under sentence of death at Kingston.—On this occasion she pressed her paramour to procure a pardon for the young fellow. His lordship, who still loved her to distraction, and could deny nothing that she requested, used his utmost interest in favour of the offender, and was successful enough to save his life, on condition of serving seven years on the River Thames, for the improvement of its navigation.[2]

His lordship was so immoderately fond of Fanny, that he could not refrain from discovering the violence of his passion, in places of public resort. Many of his friends dreaded the consequence, and his relations began to imagine that they were actually joined in the hymenial covenant;[3] but an affair, which had like to have proved of the most serious consequence to his lordship and his family, soon turned the current of his affection from his fair Fanny for ever, to run in a different channel.

And why, O noble youth, wilt thou thus stain an illustrious line of ancestry, by descending to the bought embraces of an artful young harlot? This moment she is meditating thy ruin, and thou, lulled in her lap, like Sampson in the lap of *Delilah*, art totally insensible of her deadly design. Arouse! Be no longer one of the silly-simple sons of sinful pleasures, but act the part of a man endowed with reason.

---

1   *Paradise Lost*, Book 9, lines 1032-45.
2   Assigning hard labor on the Thames to improve navigation became one of several new punishments replacing transportation to America after 1776.
3   Married.

"My son, attend unto my wisdom,[1] and bow thine ear to my understanding.—For the lips of a strange woman, drop as the honey-comb, and her mouth is smoother than oil. But her end is bitter as wormwood, sharp as a two edged sword.—She has cast down many wounded; yea, many strong men have been slain by her. Her house is the way to hell, going down to the chambers of death."

Chapter III

Serious reflections on the insensibility of offenders.—Two thieves admitted into the house by Miss Fanny.—They are detected.—The coachman's confession.—He is sent for a soldier to the Savoy,[2] with the thieves.—Fanny is discarded—returns to London.—His lordship, forsaking his folly, marries a virtuous lady.—Fanny fails, in the Savoy, in her design of releasing her lover.

When we observe the flaming sword of justice waved over the wall, we say, this is the city's sure defence. It is the dread of the stern law, that deters the dark and dangerous villain from executing his dreadful design by day, and obliges him to defer his base purpose, till the curtains of the night are drawn around the peaceable dwellings of those whom he has devoted to destruction.

Had he never seen the deep deeds of darkness, discovered to the blaze of day? Knows he not, that ONE, *to whom the darkness and the day are alike*, with the keenest eye, beholds all his operations, and is privy to all his plots? —Has he not seen his fellows in iniquity detected in the very act, when they thought no mortal was aware, and no GOD nigh? —Has not this assassin himself, more than once, been taken in his craftiness, and confounded suddenly, in a moment, at midnight, when he supposed all were asleep?—Yes, even this man, who was detected with plunder in his hand, dragged to a dungeon, brought to the bar, declared guilty, and condemned to die.—This very ingrate, who was rescued from the ignominious tree, ransomed from destruction, is now mediating mischief against the very noble youth who saved him.

The respite[3] made his escape from the New Gaol, with several others doomed to hard labour on the river, a few evenings before the day destined for their removal to Woolwich. Fanny's original lover, with another convict, equal in the most daring deeds, withdrew from London, to avoid the search of officers, and, by invitation of the fair one, retired to a small town in the vicinity of his lordship's mansion. There they met her private support, and waited to execute a plan which she had concerted.

Our fair one found means to disguise these miscreants in the proper appar-

---

1   Solomon [author's note]. Proverbs, 5, a version of lines 1-5.
2   A military prison.
3   One who has been reprieved.

el of her own sex, and introduced them one evening into the hall, to drink tea with her. My lord happened to be a little way from home, and none but the coachman being in the secret, the other servants took little notice of the strange visitants, when our heroine was showing them the several rooms in the house.

At night the supposed females, pretending to withdraw, walked with Miss round the garden; but instead of going out at the gate leading to the road, they concealed themselves till it was quite dark, and then were let in by Fanny, at the door fronting the shrubbery.

His lordship returned about nine o'clock, and having supped abroad, soon retired to his chamber, without the company of Fanny, who feigned illness. He soon went to bed, and was about to betake himself to rest, when a loud knocking at the outer gate, instantly alarmed him. His lordship getting up, and raising the sash, heard the cry of murder and thieves reverberated about the yard. He dressed himself, but before he could open the chamber door, he saw, by the light of the moon, two female figures, unfolding the doors of a closet in the chamber.

By this time the servants were alarmed, and all the family, excepting Miss Fanny and Mathews, stood on the stairs. Amongst them, my lord observed the master of an inn of the adjacent town, with a flambeaux in his hand, exclaiming, "are you safe my lord?" —They then all ran into the chamber, and there found the two supposed females, whom they secured. On searching them, they found two braces of pistols, some powder and balls, a bunch of pick-lock keys, two small hangers,[1] and a letter, which, on inspection, proved to be the hand writing of the faithless Fanny.

The inn keeper now informed his lordship of the discovery. His wife, he said, had entertained a violent suspicion that her new lodgers were sharpers,[2] from the time they first came to the house; but the recommendation of Miss Fanny, removed every obstacle.—However, that morning she found a letter, which, though enigmatical enough, was yet to be understood to mean a dangerous plot against his lordship.

Here the inn-keeper shewed the letter, which perfectly agreed in the hand writing, with that which they had found on the thieves, whom the landlord now well knew to be his lodgers —It intimated that there was much money, and many notes[3] in the house, and hinted that Matthews, the coachman, was prepared to assist them, both in the execution of the plan, and in carrying them off to London in a post chaise.

Fanny was now accosted in her chamber, and at first seemed greatly alarmed. The coachman was also secured, for he had not power to effect his

---

1 "A kind of short swords, originally hung from the belt." [OED]
2 Swindlers.
3 That is, bank notes.

escape in time; he voluntarily confessed the whole affair, and owned that the thieves were fully intent on murdering his lordship, or all the family, if opposed in their wicked attempt.

To be brief, his lordship, from a principle of humanity to the miscreants, but cruelty to the public, freely forgave Fanny the next morning, made her a present of her favourite mare, and some money, and bade her make the best of her way home, or as far from his presence as she pleased. The king at this time, much wanting men, my lord caused the two thieves to be impressed by the constables, and recommended Mathews also as a fit fellow to serve his Majesty. They were conducted to prison, and soon after to London, and lodged in the Savoy; whilst Fanny, equipping herself in her manly garb, pursued her way to the metropolis also, with greater swiftness than her lover, and favourite friends.

From this moment her lordship resolutely turned his mind to a virtuous course, and soon married an amiable lady, of a good family, fully determined to follow no more the high road to unhappiness, but to walk in that which is pointed out by true wisdom, "Whose ways are ways of pleasantness, and all whose paths are paths of peace."

> Here love his golden shafts employs; here lights
> His constant lamp; and waves his purple wings;
> Reigns here and revels; not in the bought smile
> Of harlots, loveless, joyless, un-endeared.
> Milton[1]

It does not appear that our heroine attempted any robbery on the road, on her return to town, although she was ripe enough, for one of her age, to perform wonders in the way which she afterwards followed. Her cloaths, and other articles of luggage, were sent by the waggon, so that she had made a tolerable harvest of her country jaunt.

It is very far from our design to exaggerate, much less to multiply her crimes. There is no need to add to the number, for during her present confinement in prison, she has boldly boasted of having performed more tricks in the swindling line, than would swell this narrative to a large volume. It is from her own free and voluntary account of them, that we have proceeded thus far; but what follows, has met the concurring testimony of others.

It was soon after her return to the Borough of Southwark, that she received a note from her lover, in the Savoy prison. Thither she immediately went, and found the other miscreant, and the coachman, in the same situation, every day expecting to be removed to Chatham barracks, and from thence to be sent—they knew not where.

---

1   *Paradise Lost*, Book 4, lines 763-66.

Here our heroine formed a scheme to effect the escape of her favourite fellow, by dressing him in men's cloaths; but the project, though well planned, was discovered by the turn-key, who took care to thwart the design, and to prevent a future attempt, loaded the lover with chains, and would not suffer Fanny again to enter within the gates of that gothic edifice.

Chapter IV

Fanny visits her lover at Chatham.—She brings him off from on board the Canada.— *He is retaken.—The various exploits of the fair-one, during the dreadful riot, in 1780.—In Westminster—the Bishop—the chapels.—In London, Newgate—The Borough—Black-friar's Bridge.—Fanny's adventure with a London linen-draper, in Essex.—Reflections, &c.*

Extravagance and dissipation now predominated in the character of our amazon. She was soon reduced to a low situation in life, which cast her upon the town. Whenever she picked up people of a genteel appearance, she failed not to find out the contents of their fobs. She still maintained a decent deportment, and a semblance of modesty seemed congenial to her being. In point of dress, a little difference would have made her quite a quaker. Her beauty was yet daily increasing with her cunning, but the simplicity of her manners could not fail to draw after her a number of admirers.

She visited her lover, and friends in captivity, at Chatham, and there smote the heart of the governor of that garrison. But that Hibernian military genius had already an amiable spouse, and also kept a fair mistress, so that he durst hardly discover his passion to our heroine, excepting when he found her in the old guard, amongst the impressed men.

It was her grand design to have insinuated herself into the captain's good graces, in order to find an opportunity of releasing her lover; but all her schemes and arts proved ineffectual, the first kept fair-one ever found means to frustrate all her hopes, and to keep our heroine from too close a connection with her paramour.

The captives being removed from the Barracks, and put on board the *Canada*, bound for Nova Scotia, Fanny attended them, and found an opportunity, whilst they lay on Chatham river, to convey her lover, dressed in women's cloaths, to the shore, in a boat which she procured for that purpose, and so travelled with him across the country, and reached the Borough, which was the centre of all their wishes, and out of whose boundary they were ever unhappy.

But all the travel and toil of our fair one, proved useless, for the young fellow quickly became a prey to the officers of justice, who found him and Fanny at a house of ill fame in Tooley-street, and lodging them both in the

Compter[1] that night, swore the next day, before a magistrate, to the identity of the young man, in the prospect of a reward; so he was committed to the New Gaol, in order to be tried for being found at large before the expiration of his time.

The next summer the great riot in London commenced. Lord George Gordon assembled a vast multitude of all sorts of people in St. George's Fields, and with them proceeded to Westminster, with a petition to parliament for rescinding the act in favour of Roman Catholics.[2] During the violent commotion in Palace Yard, Fanny, and certain of her fellows at large, employed their time to no small advantage. Lord Mansfield that day was insulted; several other noblemen lost their watches, snuffboxes, and money. The Lord Chancellor's brother, the Bishop of Lincoln, being threatened by the banditti, leaped from his chariot on the opposite side to Fanny, who followed his lordship into the house in which he found an assylum. A committee of thirty was chosen in the mob, to pursue the fugitive prelate, and Fanny, who pretended to be his friend. His lordship slipped off his canonical attire, and put on a suit of crimson and gold, with a bag wig, which he borrowed from the hospitable owner of the retreat; and whilst he ran up to the top, and reached the leads over the House of Lords, in order to descend in a basket, like St. Paul from the wall of Demascus, Fanny packed up the prelatical garb, and cast the bundle from her window, to Patrick Madan, one of her coadjutors.[3]

Fanny proceeded the same evening to the chapel of the Sardinian ambassador, in Lincoln's-inn-fields, and there, amidst the motly mob, whilst the chapel was in flames, employed her hand with great avidity.

Nor did our heroine flinch from a testimony *so glorious* against popery, until the prisoners who were taken at the above chapel, and that of the Bavarian minister, and who were to have been tried in the Court of King's Bench, in Westminster, were liberated from Newgate, with all the rest of the prisoners, for she stood steadfastly upon the spot, till Mr. Akerman's house was demolished, his rich furniture committed to the flames, and all the internal parts of the strong gaol, hitherto deemed invulnerable, laid in ashes.

The next day, June 7, 1780, Fanny found ample employ in her own Borough. Dressed in her masculine habit, our heroine mingled in the innumerable company, and missed no opportunity of fishing successively in the trou-

---

1   A prison.

2   Lord Gordon and his followers objected that parliament had rescinded harsh laws restricting Catholics. Riots that ensued came to be known as "the Gordon riots." Prejudice against Catholics remained strong in the eighteenth century.

3   St. Paul escaped from Damascus when his disciples lowered him over a wall in a basket. Patrick Madan was himself a well-know thief and miscreant. See *Authentic Memoirs of the Life, Numerous Adventures, and Remarkable Escapes, of the Celebrated Patrick Madan* (London, [1782]).

bled water. That day, whilst the desperate miscreants on the Middlesex side, were opening the prisons, freeing the captives, burning the houses of Lang-dale,[1] and drinking his liquors, the zealots of Southwark were not unem-ployed. New Bridewell, their old habitation, met the revenge of the rioters. The King's Bench prison was demolished, and all its inmates quickly emanci-pated. The Marchalsea, another seminary of Southwark for training up swindlers,[2] was saved from the fire, but all the students were set at liberty. The New Gaol likewise was opened, and Fanny's first favourite came forth with an uncounted crowd, rattling their chains in triumph, cheered by the mob, for whose use the hogsheads of [an] entire butt[3] were rolled into the street.

It has been affirmed that Fanny, the same evening, dressed in mens clothes, and wearing a blue cockade[4] in her hat, mounted upon the top of a butt, made a motion for the demolition of the toll-gate at Black-friars bridge. Cer-tain it is, however, that the mob proceeded to that place, and had almost gone farther than the original design, when they were warmly charged by a military party, and many of the ringleaders in the riot fell in the midst of their career.

The soldiers next day having obtained a complete victory over the desper-ate banditti, many of the principal actors were taken, and lodged in those prisons which remained undemolished. Fanny, with many others, withdrew into the country, and remained, performing little exploits, till the law was in a degree satisfied, and many of the rioters had expired on a gibbet.

Fanny now visited Essex in her hunting dress, and became well acquainted with that country, before her return to town. Occasionally she dressed herself like a quaker, and won the heart of a young linen draper of Cheapside, who was down in those parts on business.

She vouchsafed to give this rising genius her company, although he was a married man, but took an opportunity one night, to slip out of bed, equip herself in his clothes, and so, taking his horse from the stable, rode post-haste to the metropolis. The same morning, before the linen draper could reach town, Fanny, changing her apparel, repaired to the shop of the tradesman (for she had taken care to learn where he lived) and there delivered a mes-sage, as from the shop-keeper to his wife, and shewing his gold watch, obtained fifty pounds in cash.

But our amazon did not rest in the completion of such projects, in con-junction with a gang of swindlers, who assisted her in several forgeries, but even went upon the road, and had courage enough to stop waggons, stage

---

1   The Langdales were a prominent Catholic family.
2   That is, another prison.
3   "A cask for wine or ale, of capacity varying from 108 to 140 gallons." [OED]
4   "A ribbon, knot of ribbons, rosette, or the like, worn in the hat as a badge of office or party, or as part of a livery dress." [OED] In 1780, a blue cockade suggested sympathy with Lord Gordon and opposition to Catholic reform. Fanny's gesture thus aligns her with the rioters.

coaches, and passengers. In fine, she soon grew the terror of the whole country around the metropolis, and managed her various maneuvers with so much address, art, and cunning, that she began to imagine herself quite invulnerable to the law, and secure against justice.

Such wretches triumph in their wickedness, and glory in their shame. Early initiated to the mysteries of iniquity, and long trained up in the paths of vice, they become insensible and incorrigible. The frequent awful examples of punishment which they behold, only makes them the more callous and case-hardened. Used long to view vice though a false medium, they imagine that it is even amiable. Thus deceived, through the deceitfulness of sin, they go on, and seldom ever know when to recede; joining hand in hand with one another, in the pursuit of those pernicious courses, which naturally lead to destruction. The numerous escapes which they effect from meeting condign[1] punishment, emboldens them to persevere, and "because sentence is not passed speedily, their hearts are set upon evil."[2]

Chapter V

Comparisons.—The Wife of Ninus, *and Fanny.—Queen Mary.—Mrs. Brownrig.— Peter the Great.—Fanny at Vauxhall, in a man's dress, meets the warm affection of an old citizen's young wife.—Fanny's artifice.—The lady's disappointment.—Fanny robs a gentleman on the road—is taken—committed—cleared.—She is picked up by a farmer.*

Semiramis, the great foundress of Babylon, had she been brought up in the Borough, and received the tuition of Fanny Davies, perhaps would have pursued the same path to glory and fame. Queen Mary, of bloody memory, might have proved no better than Brownrig,[3] if bred in the same low line of life.— Nay, even Alexander the Great himself, as has often been said, would have been but a highwayman, or a house-breaker, if he had been brought up under profligate parents in the metropolis of England.

The love of fame appears principally to have prevailed in the breast of our heroine, for there the love of money had but little residence. But fame, of which she was so fond, was almost confined to but a few, from whom only she

1 "Worthily deserved, merited, fitting, appropriate; adequate." [OED]
2 Eccles. 8:11.
3 In 1767, "Elizabeth Brownrigg, a lower middle-class mistress of pauper and charity apprentices, was tried, convicted, and hung for the murder of a girl belonging to the large and growing population of pauper apprentice children in the mid-eighteenth century." The case became a sensation in the press. Kristina Straub, "The Tortured Apprentice: Sexual Monstrosity and the Suffering of Poor Children in the Brownrigg Murder Case," in Laura J. Rosenthal and Mita Choudhury, eds., *Monstrous Dreams of Reason: Body, Self, and Other in the Enlightenment* (Lewisburgh, PA: Bucknell UP, 2002), 66.

could claim applause, and these were prisoners. Such she ever gloried to support, succour, and inspire with her own spirit.

To effect these purposes, was the main pursuit of her mind, and the chief employ of every day. She even could condescend to roll a barrow along the streets, and substitute the cries of cherries, apples, or hot gingerbread, for the less pleasing strains of *No Popery!*

And did not even Peter the Great, the glory of the Russian empire, also condescend to the lowest employ, for the good of his subjects? Yes, Peter parted with his royal diadem, and deigned, at Deptford, to handle the mechanic's tool, and appearing as a mean common labourer, acquired an art which raised Russia to its present grandeur.

But why did Fanny thus humble herself? —Reader, remember she was not actuated by an honest, industrious spirit. Frugality and felony, are as far removed as the poles of Heaven. It was to pry, with a keen observation, into the areas, to gaze on the shutters and doors, which she deemed vulnerable to her veteran tribe, to mark well the places that she could plunder, without the danger of detection and punishment.—In short, as Satan is said to be never so successful as when he transforms himself into an Angel of light, so our fair one, always appearing modest and unassuming, was the more able to insinuate herself into such situations as would best answer her purpose.

Fanny appeared to no small advantage, even in her masculine mien, for she seemed to be a very smart youth, deemed too young to be bearded.—A lady of London, observing her in this attire, in the garden at Vauxhall, soon showed signs of attachment; but there was an old debilitated husband in the way, and that was an obstacle which she resolved to remove.—Signs of mutual affection were given on both sides.—Matters were quickly matured.—They made an assignation to meet the next day, at a tavern.—They accordingly met, but the good man was *at home*, and the good woman was obliged to make an apology by a trusty chamber maid.

Our supposed youth, learning the cause of the disappointment, sent word to the lady that she might rest assured that the objection would be removed next Wednesday, when she hoped to be favoured with her company, about noon.

Fanny repaired to Guildhall, and took out a summons in the Court of Requests,[1] for a debt charged on the husband. This was done easily enough, and without an oath, requiring only the name of the person summoned. Fanny was obliged, however, to serve it herself, and thus explaining the matter to the lady, obtained her promise to meet at the time appointed.

The old gentleman was surprised at such an unexpected writ, being conscious that he owed no money to the person whose name was inserted. But he was obliged to crawl up to the court on the specified day, and there remain

---

1   A local court set up to deal with small debts.

for two or three hours.—The lady was overjoyed on the occasion, as she was perfectly safe during her proposed pastime with her beloved youth, who had kindled such a violent fire in her breast, that all the water in the Thames hardly could have quenched.

To the tavern, therefore, she quickly went, with a handsome present in her purse, for her paramour, and an old family gold watch by her side.—She met the swain, flew with eager rapture to his arms, drank a chearful glass of wine, and raised higher and higher still, her sanguine expectation of unspeakable delight.

But O! the fickleness of fortune to the fair, as well as the fond wife of the sage apothecary! Alas! Poor old debilitated David, is waiting in vain in the hall, and his wanton wild (we cannot say virtuous) wife, is also to meet a sad disappointment!

The room door is fastened.—A stately bed presents itself.—Courtship is unnecessary on the occasion.—The agreement is already made—The lady sits down on the couch—her brilliant eyes emit wild-fire.—All the cupids play on her countenance. Hah! A pistol! —Yes, madam, your money, or—mercy upon me, sir! Is this the return for my unfeigned affection?—Hesitate not a moment, madam, I am *no man for you.*—Do you suppose that I would make your husband a monster? I will not—*I cannot do it!*

The lady was obliged to surrender her purse to Fanny, with her watch, and what else she chose to demand.—The deceived wanton fell into a swoon, and our fair deceiver of woman, as well as man, embraced the opportunity of retiring from the tavern.

Soon after this, Fanny, mounted on a good gelding, rode to Barnet races, lost her money, robbed a gentleman on her return to town, was pursued, taken, carried before a magistrate, surrounded by a vast crowd of spectators, sent to New Prison, Clerkenwell; obliged to send for her friends. Her sex was discovered. She remained till the sessions, was removed to Newgate, but discharged the last day of the session, by proclamation, as the gentleman, though he preferred an indictment at Hicks's Hall,[1] did not like to prosecute *a poor weak woman*, lest he should meet the contempt of the crowd, and the laugh of the lawyers.

Our fair one now was in a very distressed, deplorable condition, and more ready to beg the aid of her friends in captivity, than able to lend them that aid which she wished. She condescended to walk the Borough High-street with the abandoned girls; her beauty and modest demeanour proving favourable to her calling, as a lady of pleasure.

She did not long remain pennyless; for one evening, as she stood at the gate of the White-Hart inn, an aged rustic rover tapped her on the shoulder, whispering in the country dialect, "My dear, will you drink a glass with me at

---

1   The session house for the justices of the peace of Middlesex.

the Boy's Cock?" Fanny, eying the athletic old farmer, turned round, gave him a smile, and, after drinking a glass of gin at the place proposed, walked with him toward a house much better suited to their purpose, and where they could take their fill of love till the morning.

Chapter VI

The story of the hop-planter.—Fanny discovers his bank notes, and steals them whilst he is asleep.—A riot ensues.—The house shut up, &c.

The fond farmer was a hop-planter, of Sussex, and had just received seven fifty-pound Bank notes of Mr. Dyson, of St. Margaret's Hill, for hops. He had a good wife at home, but she being as old as himself, about three score, he generally, as often as he came to town, indulged a leisure hour or two with any young fair one that pleased his eye.

But before he began his evening ramble, he took the prudent precaution to conceal the notes in the lining of his coat, placing them as near as possible to his *heart*, and sewing up the part that he had ripped open. The little loose money in his breeches pocket, he condemned to be spent and sported away in the manner which he thought would most conduce to his pastime.

Fanny was led by our adventurer, to Tooley-street, when she directed him to a notified[1] house in Walnut-tree Alley, nearly opposite the meeting-house of Mr. Rippon.[2] As our unequal pair entered the house, the congregation were singing psalms; but notes of a nature quite opposite were reverberated within, by the vermin of the stews.

What *Daniel Defoe* says, may very aptly be applied in this place:

Where ever GOD erects a house of pray'r,
The devil's sure to have a temple there;
And 'twill be found, upon examination,
The latter has the largest congregation.[3]

The heart of the rustic almost revolted at the dismal scene in the great room, through which he passed with his fair one, who eagerly urged him on to a back apartment. There they drank and sported, till the farmer had spent all his cash but a few shillings. This he but little minded, as he was confident of the safety of his notes. Fanny, however, often observed him touching his left breast, as if to feel for something that much engrossed his attention.— She had already used every art, felt in every pocket, and discovered no more

---

1 Notorious.
2 John Rippon (1751-1836), pastor of Carter's Lane Baptist Church in London.
3 The opening lines of Daniel Defoe's poem, *The True Born Englishman. A Satire* (1701).

than what she had obtained; but now began to think that she had missed the main mark.

This induced her to procrastinate the farmer's stay in the unhallowed house; and to entertain him, she opened the chamber door, and proposed that they should have a dance in the great room, amidst the groupe of thieves, pickpockets, bawds, and common prostitutes.

Still the rustic shewed a wonderful sympathy for his left side, and Fanny was more and more convinced that there something of value was secreted.

She beckoned to an ugly fellow, who was a penny barber, whom she had kept company with in Bridewell, where he served half his apprenticeship. He was a fellow perfectly inimical to all order, and the staunch friend of riot. He possessed a horrible dark designing visage. The *Death* and *Sin* of Milton, could not be more monsterous. He trailed a wooden leg, for he had morti-fied the original, to keep him from the army, after he had found that the loss of his thumb, which he had cut off before, would not prevent him from going abroad.—One of his eyes was totally darkened, by a blow which he received in the street, from a person whose pocket he had just picked, and who also marked his cheek with a terrible gash. The projection of his gnomon,[1] which had been long on the wane by wenching, was diminished to a quarter of an inch. In brief, his whole aspect was inhuman and frightful.

Fanny whispered something in the ear of this miscreant, which the farmer could not hear, and immediately the dancing began. The rustic enjoyed the scene, called for another bowl, drank freely, fearless of his property, and so indulged a soft repose on an elbow chair.

Surely this was a dangerous situation for a stranger, surrounded with mur-derers, and every specie of villains, which the infamous parts of Southwark could supply! In such a perilous place, how can a man hope? How can he pray for the protection of a kind Providence, previous to his slumber?

Fanny soon discovered the place where the farmer's strength lay, and hav-ing obtained the £350, quickly withdrew, leaving her lover to lament his loss and bewail his folly, as soon as he should awake and miss his notes.

—So rose the Danite strong,
Herculean Samson, from the harlot lap
Of Philistean Delilah; and wak'd
Shorn of his strength.——
                    MILTON[2]

---

1   Literally, a pillar that "serves to indicate the time of day by casting its shadow upon a marked surface, such as a sun-dial." [OED] "Gnomon" refer jokingly to his nose, which has waned by "wenching" because venereal disease has ravaged it.
2   *Paradise Lost*, Book 9, 1059-62.

The moment the farmer was aroused, he felt his side, and found that he had been robbed of his notes. Again he felt, but to no purpose. He cast off his coat, searched all the lining, but all was lost. He ran into the great room in a most violent rage, and for some time acted the part of a man compleatly mad. The thieves and prostitutes rejoiced, and shouted aloud. The landlord demanded his reckoning with an imperious tone. The landlady shut the doors to keep out the mob, many of whom had already broke in.—All this was vociferation, tumult, and wild uproar; so that when Mr. Dyson came to the aid of his friend, the farmer, (for somebody had apprised him of the affair) he imagined at the first that chaos was come again, and all order banished for ever.

—Behold the throne
Of Chaos, and his dark pavilion spread
Wide on the wasteful deep: with him enthron'd,
Sat sable vested night, eldest of things,
The consort of his reign; and by them stood
Orcus, and Hades, and the dreaded name
Of Demogorgon, Rumor next, and Chance,
And Tumult, and Confusion, all embroil'd,
And Discord, with a thousand various mouths.
MILTON[1]

Another hop-merchant of the Borough, led by rumour to the place, with an air of authority, demanded peace; and attempting to break open the door, had a chamber utensil,[2] with its full contents, thrown upon his head from the window above. However, his *pericranium* proved impregnable to the projectile; and if even that piece of a mill-stone, which the old Hebrew gentlewoman cast from an elevated tower, on the head of kind Abimelech,[3] had fallen on the head of the hop-factor, it would have made but little impression. The fellow, by his vociferation, and unmeaning jargon, irritated the mob, who would have proceeded to violence, had not a magistrate, with a number of constables, come to the aid of the landlord, and the besieged banditti.

Fanny was not to be found. Several girls and thieves were taken into custody, examined, and discharged. The rustic advertised his loss in the papers, and the numbers of the notes were specified by Mr. Dyson. But all could not bring them back to the owner, who, the next day, was obliged to return to his

---

1 *Paradise Lost*, Book 2, 959-67.
2 Chamber pot.
3 Abimelech was an aggressive ruler of Israel who had his seventy brothers put to death. A woman, however, fatally injured him when she dropped a millstone on his head when he was attacking the town of Thebez. He asked his armor-bearer to run him through with a sword so he would not have died by a woman's hand. Judges 9:50-57.

farm, to satisfy his wife by all the soothing strains that he was master of, and all the fair promises that he could please her with.

This favour of fortune, raised Fanny almost above mediocrity. Had she employed this so considerable a sum, to advantage, her situation might have proved independent. But there is a worm at the root of every plant which is not reared in the garden of virtue. A curse was entailed on every scheme which she endeavoured to carry into execution, in consequence of this acquisition. Her riches, on the wings of prodigality, soon took their flight. The money, thus gotten by injustice, daily diminished, and within a little month, left not a wreck behind. This was in the autumn of the year 1783. The licence was immediately taken from the house, in which the robbery was perpetrated, and the bullies, swindlers, pimps, and prostitutes, who there carried on their riot, and concerted their deep designs, were obliged to abandon that infernal dwelling, since devoted to destruction. But in that neighbourhood, as well as in many other streets, lanes, and alleys, in Southward, it is always easy for such people to find a welcome reception. Would to Heaven that the magistrates of this place would arouse from their long lethargy, and vigorously exert those powers with which they are invested, in the removal of many more of those infamous haunts.

Fanny frequently applied to a register office for a place, and referring to a swindler for a good character, proved pretty successful, as she never staid long in service, and seldom returned home without a considerable booty. She either caused the house where she lived to be plundered by her partners in guilt, or so managed the matter herself, as to strip the premises of plate, and other valuables, and afterwards elude the law, by every effort of art and cunning, which most depraved mind, aided by the advice of sharpers, could suggest.

Chapter VII

Justice R—l dies.—Fanny is one of the chosen Virgins.—The rich Bachelor's Adventure with the Sorceress and Fanny.—He is stripped naked at Norwood, whilst his house at Camberwell is plundered.—Fanny robs a young gentleman in Essex, lies with him in Southwark, and steals his breeches.—She appears in the character of a horse-dealer in Essex, and robs a grazier of a large sum, in money and notes.—She is taken, committed, tried, sentenced to die—respited for transportation.

In October 1784, Justice R—l, of libidinous and miserable memory, was obliged to leave his gods of gold, and give up his ungodly ghost. He had ordered in his will, that his body should be attended to the church by a number of pure virgins, dressed in unsullied white satin, to strew the way with flowers in the procession. Fanny was fixed upon as one of the *immaculate* maids of Southward, and received the bounty, for she had once been the dear delight of that memorable miser.

Fanny, in her argent robes, appeared by far the fairest, and most modest of all the other virgins. As she dealt her odours around, she captivated the hearts of hundreds, on whom she deigned to look with her bewitching eyes. Such virgins as our heroine, and her fair companions, no doubt might have bent their flowery steps up to the temple, without dreading the dogs of Vulcan![1]

Immediately after this farcical funeral, Fanny was followed home by a rich old bachelor, who, having amassed a large fortune by fraud, had retired to Camberwell, to rest his enfeebled limbs after his fatigues in the wars of Venus, and service of vice. Fanny had left the Mint,[2] and now lodged in a decent lodging on the road to Vauxhall. The chariot of her enamoured admirer, drove up to the door. He called aloud to the fair one, as she looked from the window, and prevailed on her to come down, and favour him with her company in the carriage to Camberwell.

The fair one resumed her usual shyness, and put on her assumed modesty. The debauchee found her invincible to every attack. His latent fire was re-kindled. He offered money, and made many fair promises, but his price proved much too low to accomplish his purpose, and so the treaty was broke off for that evening.

The blighted bachelor applied to an old procuress, an eminent bawd of the Borough, in order to call in her help on the occasion. He dressed the hag in the attire of a gypsie, and desired her to meet him the next morning, near Norwood, where she was to tell the fortune of Fanny, whom he appointed to meet him at that celebrated place of pretended prophecy.

The bawd proved unfaithful to her trust; for she failed not to apprise the fair one of the maneuver intended by her seducer. Fanny concerted measures accordingly; met her lover at the place appointed, got into the chariot, and attended him to the wood.

As they passed on, they met the pretended sorceress. The carriage was instantly stopped, the witch began her conjuration, and gradually drew the enflamed bachelor, with Fanny, into the wood, till they were a considerable way from the road.

Now was the golden opportunity of the doting lover, in the solitary shade. He laid the fair one on a mossy bank, whilst all the joys which he had anticipated, appeared within his immediate reach. The sorceress seemed all the while to sooth the fair one, and by spells and uncouth incantations, urged her to yield.

But just as happiness appeared—just as the bachelor's blood began to

---

1 The dogs of Vulcan could tell the difference between virgins and non-virgins by smell. See *Mythology Made Easy; or, A New History of the Heathen Gods and Goddesses* (London, 1790), 60-62.

2 The Mint traditionally provided refuge for debtors.

boil—in the critical juncture of affairs—in the very paroxism of passion, an athletic arm is projected from the thicket; a pistol is presented to his high heaving breast, by a frightful fellow of the Herculean breed, who, with a voice furious as that of Moloch,[1] demanded his money, or his life!

This unexpected intrusion, quickly marred the play, and closed the scene before the act was finished. A terrible trembling seized the enamoured swain—a sudden shaking among his dry bones commenced.

He was about to feel in his pocket, to satisfy the dread demand, when the son of rapine bade him hold his hand, and immediately strip to the skin. He was obliged to comply, as he had no help within view. The Sorceress and Miss had withdrawn, and his coachman, unconscious of his master's misfortune, was gathering nuts at a great distance from the chariot.

In short, the bachelor was obliged to part with all the clothes which he wore, excepting his stockings and shirt; the robber, who had several accomplices near, packed up the clothes, and after having examined the breeches, and found a very considerable sum, threatened the lover with instant death, if he made the least noise, or attempted to pursue him. He lay still in deep confusion, speechless, and almost quite insensible, till at last his coachman discovered him in that naked posture. At length he put on his servant's great coat, reached the chariot, and was carried home to his house, which, the more to his mortification, he found stripped of all the plate, linen, and every portable article, through the artifice of Fanny and the bawd, who had employed other people of the gang for that purpose, and found means to intice the servant maid to a public house, on the opposite side of Camberwell Green, and there kept her in play till they had carried the plan into execution. The bachelor was too much confounded with shame, to publish his distress, but Fanny, during her confinement, has often made her fellow prisoners pleased with the adventure.

In the bachelor's suit, which was scarlet and gold, our amazon performed several deep and daring exploits in Essex, and at one time robbed a young gentleman of sixty pounds in money, with a gold repeating watch, worth forty or fifty more, which she sold to a Jew in Whitechapel, for ten guineas. He insisted upon having the watch at any rate, and talked highly of the Rotation Office,[2] in case of a refusal. She complied, as he had been a friend before, in taking off some bills and notes, which she could not otherwise dispose of.

---

1   An ancient deity, worshipped in parts of the Middle East, to whom child sacrifices were made. The author, who elsewhere quotes from *Paradise Lost*, may have Moloch's appearance in book 1 of that poem in mind.

2   Before the establishment of a regular police force, the rotation offices assured that citizens could find a magistrate on duty to whom to report a crime. [See <http://www.old-baileyonline.org/>, Project Directors: Tim Hitchcock and Robert Shoemaker]

The following part of this story is most remarkable.—Fanny, in her fine white satin dress, used to stand in the Borough High-street, with one Nancy, the Quaker, a young woman whom she had enticed to her ruin. A few evenings after the above robbery, she saw the identical gentleman passing King's Head Court, and followed him through to Tooley-street. Nancy acted as her maid on the occasion,—Fanny caught hold of the gentleman's arm, asked him to treat her with a glass, and at length persuaded him to accompany her to a noted tavern in the vicinity. The gentleman was perfectly pleased with her modest demeanor, and agreed to sleep with her that night. An elegant supper was prepared. Nancy waited on the couple, and saw them safe into the chamber of love. But after sweet meat, sometimes comes sour sauce. The gentleman in the morning missed his dear delight the moment he awaked, and his breeches in the bargain, which contained about thirty guineas, besides silver. She escaped from the chamber by jumping from the window, in which she was assisted by the fair quaker.

But we hasten to the catastrophe of the piece.—Our amazonian adventurous fair one, with several of her male auxiliaries, penetrated many parts of the country, and especially committed burglaries and highway robberies in Essex. One evening, Fanny being accidentally left alone, dressed in rustic garb, called at the sign of the Three Rabbits, in the road near Stratford and Ilford.

She introduced herself in the character of a horse-dealer, and told the people of the inn that she was going to London, and being rather benighted and unwell, requested that they would accommodate her with a lodging.

This being granted, she dropped into the company of a Mr. Wrigglesworth, a country grazier,[1] whom she, it is said, had in the course of that day, watched with great diligence.

The grazier was familiar, chearful, communicative, and perfectly free in conversation, with our supposed *horse-dealer*. They smoked their pipes over a tankard after supper. The chief topic was trade, taxes, and the ruin of poor old England. However, Fanny knew well how to turn the drift of the conversation. She learned from the grazier's talk, as well as from several circumstances which had before fallen under her observation, that he had been taking a large sum of money. Indeed, so very intimate were the two new companions grown that the farmer even specified the sum which he had in his bag. Her ardent breast now glowed, and anticipation assured her of success.

The strangers parted and retired to different rooms; but not far distant from each other. The grazier was much fatigued,—said a short prayer,—perhaps none at all—fell asleep, and snored in concert with the people of the inn.

---

1 Someone who grazes or feeds cattle for the market.

Dreadless of the least danger, the farmer desposited his breeches under his pillow. But, as the malign enemy of man, like a hungry hound, prowls about for his prey, without deviating from his design till he has gained his object, so Fanny rested not, till she had carried her resolves into effect.

She anxiously and warily watched, till all was safe. The doors of both chambers were but on the latch; she gained, therefore, an easy access to that of the grazier. She entered the room, approached his couch with a pistol in her hand. She gained the pillow, and dexterously drew the breeches from under his head.

The daring invader, having secured the contents in a canvas bag, hasted away from the house, and reached the metropolis before morning.

On inspection, the bag was found to contain the articles following: one hundred and fifty guineas, a bill of exchange for four hundred pounds, bank notes to the amount of seven hundred pounds; total one thousand two hundred and fifty two pounds ten shillings. The bank notes to Fanny were as good as cash as she was so intimate with swindlers, that even the bill of exchange might have been turned into money, had she consulted her friends in that iniquitous line.

Exulting in the greatness of her booty, Fanny was even fascinated and off her guard, on viewing the smiles of fortune. She dressed, bought everything that she wanted, drank freely with her companions in prison; and, visiting a female friend in Newgate, made her a present of a guinea, gave her a pair of silver buckles, boasted of her late adventure, and even declared the several circumstances attending the robbery.

The woman, whom she thus intrusted with a secret so momentous, cautioned her against speaking so freely: but as soon as Fanny was gone, informed two of the runners of what she had heard. They were all ears on the occasion. The grazier had by this time advertized his loss, and offered a large reward. They knew the haunts of our heroine, and caught her in bed, at a house in New Court, near St. George's church, with all the property about her, but three hundred and fifty pounds, of which she refused to give any account, and persisted in that resolution to the last.

She was immediately carried over the water, taken before a magistrate, and, after several hearings, committed for trial at the next assizes for the county of Essex.

As Fanny was committed soon after the last summer assize, she was obliged to remain many months in prison previous to her trial. She now threw off the mask of modesty which she had hitherto worn with some dignity, and gave her life in captivity up to intemperance. The cash which she had artfully concealed from the officers, served to keep her during the tedious winter; but she squandered much of it away in riot, both in Newgate, and in Chelmsford Gaol; at the latter of which places, she was pleased to procure three rabbits, which she kept as a memorial of the house where she perpetrated the fact.

Her trial came on before Mr. Justice Ashurst, on March 6th, 1786, when Mr. Wrigglesworth the grazier appeared, swore to the above notes, and the identity of the prisoner's person; as having been in her company at the above inn, on the evening of that night on which he had been robbed.

The people of the inn positively swore to her person also, although she was so disguised at the time in question; and the officers attending to prove, that the notes, and bill of exchange were in her custody when captured, the matter appeared exceeding plain to the jury, who found her *guilty* of the charge laid in the indictment.

The mother of the prisoner appeared in court much inebriated, and all that the rest of her friends urged in her favour, could have but little effect, after such substantial evidence, as was produced.

The judge proceeded to pass *sentence of death* upon the prisoner. His lordship observed, that as she had planned and executed the robbery with so much exactness and dexterity, it probably had not been her first offence. He said he was well assured that it was not, for she had been some time the terror of the country. His lordship earnestly exhorted her to make the best use of that little time which would be allotted her. A pardon was not to be expected, in a case of so heinous a nature; nor should she expect that her sex would protect her from the hand of justice on the occasion. His lordship concluded, by passing the sentence of the law in the usual form, as follows:

"You, Francis Davis, are to be taken back to the place from whence you came, and from thence to the place of execution, there to be hanged by the neck until you are *dead*: And may God Almighty, of his infinite goodness, have mercy upon your soul."

From the manner in which his lordship prefaced the solemn sentence, few people were inclined to believe that she would be rescued from the jaws of death; but though an old offender, she is but young in years, and may reform a bad life abroad, when removed from temptation.

Mercy is the darling attribute of the *great Supreme*, and all the human race perpetually have need for forgiveness. A judge never imitates *Him* so much, as when employed in exercising the same *glorious attribute of Mercy*.

The quality of MERCY is not strain'd,
It droppeth, as the gentle rain from Heav'n,
Upon the place beneath. It twice is bless'd;
It blesseth him that gives, and him that takes,
'Tis mightiest in the mightiest, it becomes
The throned monarch better than his crown;
His scepter shews the force of temporal pow'r,
The attribute to awe and majesty,
Wherein doth sit the dread and fear of Kings;

But mercy is above the scepter's sway,
It is enthroned in the hearts of kings;
It is an attribute of GOD himself;
And earthly pow'r doth then shew likest GOD's.
When mercy seasons justice.——————————

SHAKESPEAR.[1]

---

1   *Merchant of Venice*, IV.i. Another version of this narrative by "Mr. Thompson" ends with much less sympathy: "She heard her sentence pronounced without shewing the least sign of fear, and went out of court with a smile, mixt with remorse and regret for being prevented from doing the like again. Since her condemnation she has lived the same thoughtless creature as before." *The Female Amazon, or, A Genuine Account of the Most Remarkable Adventures and Complicated Intrigues, Displayed in the Life of the Celebrated and Notorious Miss Fanny Davies* ... (London, 1786), 32.

APPENDIX
BIBLIOGRAPHY OF PROSTITUTE NARRATIVES IN THE LONG EIGHTEENTH CENTURY[1]

The Adventures of Melinda; a Lady of Distinction Now Living. Founded on Real, Authentic Facts, and Such Diverting and Suprizing Incidents as Can Scarce Be Parallell'd in History. London: Printed for H. Carpenter, 1749.

Ambross, Miss. *The Life and Memoirs of the Late Miss Ann Catley.* London: Printed for J. Bird, 1798.

Cleland, John, attr. *Genuine Memoirs of the Celebrated Miss Maria Brown. Exhibiting the Life of a Courtezan in the Most Fashionable Scenes of Dissipation. Published by the Author of a W** of P*** (1766). New York: Garland Publishing, Inc., 1975.

The Crafty Whore; or, the Misery and Iniquity of Bawdy-Houses, Laid Open in a Dialogue between Two Subtle Bawds. London: Printed for Henry Marsh, 1668 [1658].

Dodd, William. *The Sisters; or, the History of Lucy and Caroline Sanson, Entrusted to a False Friend.* 2 vols. London: T. Waller, 1754.

——. *The Magdalen; or, History of the First Penitent Received into That Charitable Asylum.* London: Printed for W. Land, 1780?

Dunton, John. *The Night-Walker; or, Evening Rambles in Search after Lewd Women* (1696). Edited by Randolph Trumbach. Facsimile. New York: Garland, 1985.

The Effigies, Parentage, Education, Like, Merry-Pranks and Conversation of the Celebrated Mrs.Sally Salisbury. Corbhill: J. Wilson, 1722-23.

Faulkner, Miss. *The Genuine Memoirs of Miss Faulkner; Otherwise Mrs. D**L**N; of, Countess of H***X, in Expectancy. Containing, the Amours and Intrigues of Several Persons of High Distinction, and Remarkable Characters: With Some Curious Political Anecdotes, Never before Published.* London: Printed for William Bingley, 1770.

Garfield, John. *The Wandering Whore, Numbers 1-5.* Published by the Rota at the University of Exeter, 1977. Facsimile, 1977.

A Fortnight's Ramble through London. London, 1792.

Geniune and Impartial Memoirs of Elizabeth Canning, Containing a Complete History of That Unfortunate Girl, from Her Birth to the Present Time, and Particularly Every Remarkable Occurence from the Day of Her Absence, January 1, 1753, to

---

1   In compiling this bibliography, I have left off familiar novels, such as John Cleland's *Memoirs of a Woman of Pleasure* and Daniel Defoe's *Roxana*. The extent to which eighteenth-century novels rely on such narratives is already well known.

the Day of Her Receiving Sentence, May 30, 1754. London: Printed for G. Woodfall, 1754.

The Genuine History of Mrs. Sarah Prydden, Usually Called Sally Salisbury ... London: Printed for Andrew Moor, 1723.

*Genuine Memoirs of the Late Celebrated Jane D****S [Douglas].* London, 1761.

Hanger, George. *Life, Adventures, and Opinions of Col.George Hanger.* London, 1801.

Harris's List of Covent Garden Ladies (1788). Edited by Randolph Trumbach. Facsimile. New York: Garland, 1986.

Haywood, Eliza. *Anti-Pamela; or, Feign'd Innocence Detected* (1742). Facsimile ed. New York and London: Garland Publishing, Inc., 1975.

The History of Emma, or the Victim of Depravity; ... To Which Is Added the Life of the Abandoned Kitty Clark. London: Printed by S. Fisher, 1800.

The History of the Human Heart: or, The Adventures of a Young Gentleman. London: Printed for J. Freeman, 1749.

*The History of Intriguing, from Its Original, to the Present Time*s. London: Printed for T. Boreman, 1735.

The Humours of Fleet-Street and the Strand; Being the Lives and Adventures of the Most Noted Ladies of Pleasure; Whether in the Rank of Kept-Mistresses, or the More Humble Station of Ladies of the Town. By an Old Sportsman. London: Printed for Anthony Wright, 1749.

The Jew Decoy'd; or, The Progress of a Harlot. London: Printed for E. Rayner, 1733.

Johnson, Captain. *The History of the Life and Intrigues of That Celebrated Courtezan, and Posture-Mistress, Eliz.Mann, alias Boyle, alias Sample, Commonly Call'd, the Royal Soveraign.* London: Printed for A. Moore, 1724.

Kelly, Hugh. *Memoirs of a Magdalen* (1767). Facsimile. New York: Garland, 1974.

King, Richard. *The Frauds of London Detected.* London: Printed for Alex. Hogg [1780?].

Knipe, Charles. *A City Ramble: Or, the Humours of the Compter.* London: Printed for E. Curll and J. Pemberton, 1715.

Laura; or, the Fall of Innocence: A Poem. London: Printed for E. Macklew, 1787.

Leeson, Margaret. *The Memoirs of Mrs. Leeson, Madam, 1727-1797.* Edited by Mary Lyons. Dublin: Lilliput Press, 1995.

Legg, Thomas. *Low-Life: Or One Half of the World, Know Not How the Other Half Live.* Third edition. London: Printed for the Author, 1764.

The Life, Amours, and Secret History of Fracelia, Late D ... ss of P ... h, Favourite Mistress to King Charles II. London: Printed for A. Amey, 1734.

The Life and Actions of That Notorious Bawd Susan Wells. London: F. Clifton, 1753.

The Life and Adventures of a Reformed Magdalen in a Series of Letters to Mrs.

B***, of Northampton. Written by Herself. 2 vols. London: Printed for W. Griffin, 1763.

The Life and Character of Moll King, Late Mistress of King's Coffee-House in Covent-Garden. London: Printed for W. Price, 1747.

The Life and Intrigues of the Late Celebrated Mrs. Mary Parrimore, The Tall Milliner of 'Change Alley. London: A. Moore, 1729.

The Life and Opinions of Miss Sukey Shandy (1760). Facsimile. New York: Garland, 1974.

The Life of Lavinia Beswick, Alias Fenton, Alias Polly Peachum: Containing Her Birth and Education. London: Printed for A. Moore, 1728.

The London-Bawd: with Her Character and Life. Fourth edition (1711). Edited by Randolph Trumbach. Facsimile. New York: Garland, 1985.

Look E're You Leap: Or, a History of the Lives and Intrigues of Lewd Women: with The Arraignment of Their Several Vices. London: Printed for Edw. Midwinter, [1720?].

Love upon Tick; or, Implicit Gallantry. London: Printed for J. Billingsley, W. Meadows, T. Worral, and J. Stagg, 1724.

Memoirs of a Demi-Rep of Fashion; or, the Private History of Miss Amelia Gunnersbury. 2 vols. Dublin, 1776.

Memoirs of the Life of Eleanor Gwinn, a Celebrated Courtezan, in the Reign of King Charles II and Mistress to That Monarch. London: F. Stamper, 1752.

Memoirs of the Shakespear's-Head. 2 vols. London, 1760.

The Midnight Rambler: Or, New Nocturnal Spy, for the Present Year. London: Printed for J. Cooke, [1772?].

Mill, Humphrey. *A Night's Search, Discovering the Nature and Condition of All Sorts of Night-Walkers with their Associates ... Digested into a Poeme by Humphrey Mill.* London: Printed for Richard Bishop, 1640.

Montgomery, Miss Betty. *A Funeral Oration in Honour of Miss Jeany Muir, a Celebrated Lady of Pleasure.* Amsterdam, n.d.

Mother Needham's Lamentations; in an Epistle to a Certain Nobleman. London: Printed for A. Smith, 1731.

Noctural Revels; or, the History of King's-Place and Other Modern Nunneries. 2 vols. London: Printed for M. Goadby, 1779.

Oldys, Alexander. *The London Jilt; or, The Politick Whore Shewing the Artifices and Stratagems which the Ladies of Pleasure Make Use of for the Intreaguing and Decoying Men.* Parts 1 and 2. London: Printed for Hen. Rhodes, 1683.

Phillips [Muilman], Teresia Constantia. *An Apology for the Conduct of Mrs. Teresia Constantia Phillips.* 3 vols. London: Printed for the Author, 1748-49.

———. *A Letter Humbly Addressed to the Right Honourable the Earl of Chesterfield.* London: Printed for the Author, 1750.

Phillips, Phebe or Maria Maitland. *The Woman of the Town; or, Authentic Mem-*

oirs of Phebe Phillips; Otherwise Maria Maitland; Well Known in the Vicinity of Covent Garden. Written by Herself. London: Printed for Ann Lemoine, 1799.

Pilkington, Laetitia. *Memoirs of Laetitia Pilkington.* Edited by A.C. Elias. 2 vols. Athens: U of Georgia P, 1997.

The Practical Part of Love. London, 1660.

Pratt, Samuel Jackson. *Life of a Lady of the Town, Who Afterwards Became a Penitent in the Magdalen House. In Beautiful Poetry. With the History of Ann & Mary Woodfield.* Portsea: James Williams, 1801.

The Ramble; or, A View of Several Amorous and Diverting Intrigues Lately Pass'd between Some Ladies of Drury. London: Printed for J. Bodle, [1730?].

The Secret History of Betty Ireland. London: Published by S. Lee, [1750?].

The Secret History of Meadilla. London, 1733.

Sheldon, Ann. *Authentic and Interesting Memoirs of Miss Ann Sheldon (now Mrs. Archer).* 4 vols. London: Printed for the Authoress, 1790.

A Spy on Mother Midnight; or, The Templar Metamorphos'd. Being a Lying-in Conversation. With a Curious Adventure. In a Letter from a young Gentleman In the Country, to his Friend in Town. London: E. Penn, 1748.

Straus, Ralph, ed. *Tricks of the Town: Being Reprints of Three Eighteenth Century Tracts.* New York: Robert M. McBride & Company, 1928.

The Suicide Prostitute: A Poem. Cambridge: Printed by Mary Watson, 1805.

Tanner, Anodyne. *The Life of the Late Celebrated Mrs. Elizabeth Wisebourn.* London: Printed for A. Moore, 1721.

The Temple of Prostitution: A Poem. Dedicated to the Greatest *** in Her Majesty's Dominions. Written by a Woman of Fashion. London, 1779.

The Temple of Venus. London: Printed for C. Moran, 1763.

[Thompson, Edward]. *The Courtesan. By the Author of the Meretriciad.* Third edition. London: J. Harrison, 1765.

———. *The Demi-Rep. By the Author of the Meretriciad.* Second edition. London: Printed for C. Moran, 1756.

———. *The Meretriciad. Second edition; Revised, and Corrected, with Large Additions.* [London]: Printed for the Author, 1761.

Tom King's; or, the Paphian Grove. With the Various Humours of Covent Garden, the Theatre, the Gaming Table, &C. Second edition. London, 1738.

The Uncommon Adventures of Miss Kitty Fisher. London: Printed for Thomas Bailey, 1759.

The Velvet Coffee-Woman: Or, the Life, Gallantries and Amours of the Late Famous Mrs. Anne Rochford. Westminster: Printed for Simon Green, 1728.

The Vices of the Cities of London and Westminster. Dublin: Printed for G. Faulkner and R. James, 1751.

A View of London and Westminster; Or, the Town Spy. In Two Parts. London, 1725.

Ward, Edward. *The City Madam, and the Country Maid; Or, Opposite Characters of a Virtuous Housewifely Damsel, and a Mechanick's Town-Bred Daughter*. London, 1702.

———. *The Insinuating Bawd: And the Repenting Harlot. Written by a Whore at Tunbridge, and Dedicated to a Bawd at the Bath*. London, 1700.

———. *Rambling Rakes: Or, London Libertines*. London: J. How, 1700.

Watson, Sophia. *Memoirs of the Seraglio of the Bashaw of Merryland. By a Discarded Sultana*. London: Printed for S. Bladon, 1768.

The Whole Life and Character of Jane Shore. London: Printed by J. Read, 1713(?).

The Whore's Rhetorick, Calculated to the Meridian of London; and Conformed to the Rules of Art: in Two Dialogues. London: Printed for George Shell, 1683.

Wynne, John Huddleston. *The Prostitute, a Poem*. London: Printed for J. Wheble, 1771.